Novels, Novelists, and Readers

SUNY Series in the Sociology of Culture

Charles R. Simpson, Editor

Novels, Novelists, and Readers

Toward a Phenomenological Sociology of Literature

Mary F. Rogers

State University of New York Press

Parts of Chapter 8 are reprinted by permission of the publisher from *Current Perspectives in Social Theory: A Research Annual*, vol. 6. (Greenwich: JAI Press, © 1985 by JAI Press. All rights reserved.)

Published by
State University of New York Press, Albany

© 1991 State University of New York

For information, address State University of New York
Press, State University Plaza, Albany, N.Y., 12246

Production by M. R. Mulholland
Marketing by Dana E. Yanulavich

Library of Congress Cataloging-in-Publication Data

Rogers, Mary F. (Mary Frances), 1944–
    Novels, novelists, and readers: toward a phenomenological
sociology of literature / Mary F. Rogers.
        p. cm.— (SUNY series in the sociology of culture)
    Includes bibliographical references and index.
    ISBN 0–7914–0602–4 (alk. paper). —ISBN 0–7914–0603–2 (pbk.:
alk. paper)
    1. English fiction—History and criticism—Theory, etc.
    2. American fiction—History and criticism—Theory, etc.
    3. Literature and society—Great Britain. 4. Literature and
society—United States. 5. Books and reading—Sociological aspects.
    6. Authorship—Sociological aspects. 7. Authors and readers—United
States. 8. Authors and readers—Great Britain. I. Title.
    II. Series.
PR826.R64 1991
823.009—dc20   90-9890
                                                                            CIP

10 9 8 7 6 5 4 3 2 1

for Maurice Natanson

❦ Contents

Preface 1

1. The World of Literature 5

2. Self-experiences and Novel Making 21

3. Novel Making and the World of Everyday Life 35

4. Novels and Everyday Life 51

5. The Uses of Privacy 71

6. Readers' Self-experiences 91

7. Novel Making, Novel Reading, and Literary Interaction 107

8. Literary Socialization 129

9. The Business of Literature 153

10. The Art of Social Worlds and the Science of Social Worlds 175

11. The Fictive 203

    Appendix: Additional Novels in the Sample 213

    Notes 217

    Bibliography 261

    Proper Name Index 311

    Subject Index 321

🍒 Preface

toward *or* towards *prep. 1:* in the direction of   *2a:* along a course leading to... *5a:* in the way of help or assistance in....

Webster's Seventh New Collegiate Dictionary

This work demands its subtitle with a vengeance. I offer as
much a scholarly sketchbook as a social-scientific monograph, as
much an exploration of possibilities as a report of findings.

The notions of social action and, to a lesser extent, social structure
provide the mortar for this sociological foray into that part of the literary world involving novels, novelists, and readers. My foremost interests are the human experiences portrayed in novels and how such fictionalized experiences relate to those of flesh-and-blood beings lodged
in sociohistorical worlds; the experiences of imaginative writers
engaged in novel making as well as in family making, meal making,
and other commonplaces of everyday life; and the experiences of readers constituting novels as cultural documents as well as artifacts of
pleasure. All these experiences take shape within and give further
shape to historically specific social structures. Although writing and
reading novels appear to be private ventures (and are often treated as
such), they in fact institutionalize distinct forms of social action—
forms giving way to the world we know as literary.

Of necessity, social action comprises individuals' experiences of
other individuals' appearances and activities, and it anticipates others'
reactions. Social action involves some measure of mutuality or, as Max
Weber put it, "mutual orientation." It is undertaken with some awareness of Other, whether a concrete individual or a social aggregate, a
positive or negative reference group, a contemporary or predecessor
or successor. The patterns social action exhibits over time constitute
social structure. Less directly but no less surely than social action,
social structure grows out of the experiences of concrete human beings
constituting distinctive worlds. To grasp social action and social structure means, at root, to unravel the fabric of people's experiences. I aim
to do that here, tending most carefully to people's literary experiences
while keeping in view how those experiences interweave themselves

with other experiences, particularly those of everyday life.

In the end, social action in its literary forms will become less mysterious, and the concept of social action will become more amenable to theoretical illumination. Since literary experiences center on expression and communication, baring those experiences means baring the essential core of social action—an expressive "I" or "we" communicating to a "you," a "him" or "her," a "them." Social action is, at least implicitly and partially, a discursive activity linking insistently first-person narrators across diverse roles and situations. Studying the pre-eminently expressive, communicative world of literature thus opens big windows on social action as society making while disclosing the distinctive social actions novel making comprises.

Here I can achieve no more than a survey of the major research sites inviting sociologists' attention. Each of the following chapters broadly delineates one such site, theoretical or empirical. The theoretical coherence of those sites is most obvious from the vantage point of Wendy Griswold's cultural-diamond model presented in *Renaissance Revivals*. The cultural diamond comprises four points—the cultural object itself (such as the British-American novel), its creator, its audience, and its social context (or its social world). Griswold says cultural analyses demand attention to all six relationships among those four points. The research sites I explore concern those relationships.

Before turning to the four points of the cultural diamond, I look at the cultural world wherein novels yield meaning and pleasure. Chapter 1 thus looks at the literary world. Chapter 2 focuses on the experiences of those cultural creators engaged in novel making, while Chapter 3 links them to the social world of everyday life. Chapter 4, which shifts our focus to the cultural object, examines the novel in relation to everyday life. In Chapter 5, the audience centers our attention—that audience of "common readers" whose literacy secures their access to modernity and whose experiences of novels infiltrate their commonsense experiences of selfhood, interpersonal bonds, and social worlds. Chapter 6 focuses on readers' experiences with literary texts as cultural objects. The interaction between cultural creators and audiences focuses Chapter 7, which applies Erving Goffman's principles to the novelist-reader bond. In Chapter 8 the connections between the novel's cultural context and its thematic concerns get attention. "Literary socialization" anchors that effort to take into account all four points of the cultural diamond. Chapter 9 focuses on those commercial and closely related institutions central to the social context of both the novel and its creators.

Chapter 10 somewhat enlarges the cultural-diamond model by

treating the cultural object and its creators not in a social but in a cultural context. Every institutionalized type of cultural object occupies a more or less clear position within an array of cultural objects. Illuminating the cultural space an object occupies enlarges our understanding not only of that object but also of other objects in the array. My concern with the cultural promise of sociology leads me to treat it as a cultural as well as a scientific undertaking. By examining sociological texts as cultural objects alongside those cultural objects called novels, Chapter 10 aims at enhancing our insights into both types of objects. At the same time that chapter brings to the fore an aspect of the cultural diamond heretofore left implicit.

Chapter 11 synthesizes the principles set forth in preceding chapters. It brings the "fictive" to the narrative surface as a notion capable of disclosing cultural coherence amidst a massive proliferation of cultural artifacts. Attention to the fictive also discloses the essential connections among the worlds of literature, everyday life, and science, thereby showing what fundamentally holds our multiple worlds of experience together—what, in other terms, allows us to experience selfsameness amidst the diverse and competing demands of our multiple realities.

The trail of my indebtedness is wide and long. It begins perhaps with Sisters Adele and Clementine, who taught me to read, spell, and write, and then winds its way through a host of dedicated educators. Always in the forefront were my parents Don and Gen Rogers, who encouraged my progress and applauded the most modest of my successes.

To The University of West Florida, I am indebted for the sabbatical leave allowing me to complete the first draft of the manuscript. I am similarly indebted to the National Endowment for the Humanities for support that let me study British economic and literary history with Professor Wilfred Stone and eleven other colleagues in an NEH Summer Seminar at Stanford University. Yet no formal organization can match the gifts of those individuals who make one's work an emblem of community. More than a few such individuals will find their high spirits and wise counsel expressed here. Among them are Paula Brush who took endless notes, tracked down bibliographic fugitives, and held out encouragement and good thoughts as constant offerings; Steven Curry who injected awe into my literary interests; Bill Dailey who lent graphics assistance; Arthur H. Doerr whose capacious intellect and indefatigable magnanimity are constant reminders of why we learn and why we teach; Wendy Griswold and other reviewers of this work whose critical nurturing of the text provided precious insights; Brooks and Dorothy Juhlin who gave me shelter during my final forays in the library; and Madison Morrison who keeps on believing I have a voice worth sounding even when I doubt its capacity for utterance.

I also thank Aaron Randall, another believer whose own intellectual energy and unrelenting good will are constant sources of inspiration. My thanks also go out to Neil Riordan for his unabating encouragement and to Stephen Turner for his steady support. My husband Don Eisman has been a fierce critic and exemplary helpmate. He has taken notes, foraged in libraries, proofread, edited, debated, and complimented with singular devotion. I also owe a great deal to Charlie Mae Steen whose typewriter first transformed a beast into a beauty. More recently, Connie Works's competence, stamina, and good cheer have made multiple revisions a pleasant chore. At SUNY Press, Rosalie Robertson has been a first-rate colleague and critic.

Finally, a few words must weave a fitting testament to the person paramount in my awareness during this project. Maurice Natanson soars above the bureaucratic shibboleths and shallow pretensions commonly infiltrating academic communities and often fueling academic careers. He has shown me that intellectual honesty, compassionate involvements, and an unabating respect for language ensure a trying but meaningful life of the mind. His splendid wit, his thoroughgoing gentleness, his undue modesty, and his tireless quest to encounter the human in its full wonder stand countless others in good stead. To him I owe my hopes for a journey of discovery that enlarges my sympathies while expressing the humanity of those whose voices speak between the lines and beyond the pages only superficially belonging to me.

1

🍃 The World of Literature

We must take ourselves seriously, all of them.

Robert C. Elliott, *The Literary Persona*

"Why are we reading," asks Annie Dillard, "if not in hope of beauty laid bare, life heightened and its deepest mysteries probed? Why are we reading, if not in hope that the writer will magnify and dramatize our days. . . ."[1] Dillard's questions smell of a musty age when meanings felt less fragile, authority was less uncertain, and everyday life was empty of electronic signals. Clearly, Dillard is no poststructuralist. Insistent on meaning and beauty, she is aesthetic kin to George Santayana: "Things are interesting because we care about them, and important because we need them."[2] Literature stands among those things.

Today the charge of sentimentalism often attaches to such stances. Contemporary thinkers commonly eschew meaning in favor of structure, stories in favor of texts, and lived experiences in favor of linguistic codes. Flesh-and-blood people are of less concern than linguistic functionaries "defined solely by [their] place in the text." The "entropy of language," not its shared continuities, commands attention. Out of such preoccupations emerges the author as an "anachronistic personage," as musty as Dillard's questions seem among language-game thinkers.[3] Such poststructuralist stances remain ascendant, making balderdash of modern aesthetics and relegating thinkers like Dillard and Santayana to the dustbins of modern culture. I might also seem a purveyor of "discarded orthodoxies"—ideas considered "retrograde and insupportable" among many literary critics today.[4] The very idea of *a world* of literature flies in the face of poststructuralist thought. 'World' implies an irreducible unity of some sort, not a multiplicity of elusive meanings. It posits order, however complex and dynamic; shared realities, however unique individuals' experiences of them; and the possibility of transcending one's biographical situation, however fleeting the opportunity.

In music, architecture, painting, choreography, film, and literary criticism, understanding poststructuralism is essential to understanding post–World War II developments. My purposes lie elsewhere. I want to grasp the experiences of those who read and write British-American novels. To begin grasping those experiences requires respect for readers and writers standing some distance from the literary vanguard. It requires recognizing readers and writers as individuals with everyday lives comprising nonliterary obligations and pleasures; accepting individuals' need for beauty; allowing for the transcendental and respecting idealism without enshrining either as an obvious, easily won good. My purposes require an aesthetics shaped by modern advances like democracy, mass literacy, and the slow spread of human rights. To grasp the experiences of the so-called common reader and the popular novelist (whether critically acclaimed or not) means to back away from poststructuralism without denying its critical centrality to contemporary thought. The finest of sociological traditions mandate something other than a poststructuralist stance anyway. As I have implied elsewhere,[5] poststructuralism is anti-sociological to the extent that its field of vision excludes the historical, sociocultural worlds wherein language can work at all. Although poststructuralist thought is useful for many analytical projects and will, at times, contribute to the methodological pluralism holding this project together, my undertaking requires focusing on the meaningful worlds human beings constitute for themselves.

Human beings live in multiple worlds, each comprising meaning-compatible experiences. People build up various worlds by endowing their experiences with meaning and finding that those experiences fall into subjectively distinct clusters. Among the worlds human beings thus constitute is the world of literature comprising meaningful experiences of fiction, poetry, and drama. In turn, every such experience—whether of writing, reading, criticizing, editing, or publishing—helps to constitute the literary world. Like most worlds, this one produces more than a few artifacts. Yet artifacts illuminate a world only insofar as they express the experiences of those constituting that world.

A world thus concerns what and how people experience. In Georg Simmel's terms, a world is a form whereby "the contents of life are structured, treated, and experienced" distinctively.[6] As Alfred Schutz later showed, each world demands a specific cognitive style; that is, a distinctive sociality, tension of consciousness, suspension of doubts, time-perspective, and forms of self-experience and spontaneity. Describing the world of literature means grappling with its cognitive style. First, though, it means describing the world of everyday life, the "paramount reality" serving as the experiential touchstone of all other worlds.

The world of everyday life comprises experiences like brushing one's teeth, preparing a meal, talking on the telephone, and putting gas in one's car. Getting things done predominates. Projects and problems are "just there," taken for granted as "givens" demanding attention. The cognitive style specific to everyday life entails a sociality oriented to the "common intersubjective world of communication and social action"; its tension of consciousness is that of wide-awake, "full attention to life"; it suspends doubts about the reality of whatever currently concerns the individual; its time is the "standard time" of clocks, calendars, and schedules where "*durée* and cosmic time" intersect; it involves experiencing "the working self as the total self." In everyday life, spontaneity takes its forms in and through work; that is, in and through "action in the outer world, based upon a project and characterized by the intention to bring about the projected state of affairs by bodily movements."[7]

The world of everyday life leaves no room for imaginative writers and their readers any more than it leaves room for participating in religious ceremonies, athletic contests, or theatrical performances. Like the worlds of religion, sports, and the theater, the world of literature displaces its participants from everyday life. Yet no world stands wholly apart from that of everyday life. All human experiencing presupposes the commonsense world where people "know" that they can communicate with one another, that standpoints are interchangeable for all practical purposes, that *the* world is reliably, unquestionably "there." Even though everyday reality informs all experiencing, individuals may give an accent of reality to any world; that is, they may temporarily set aside the familiar reality of the commonsense world in favor of experiences mandating a different cognitive style. They may temporarily abandon their "working" selves for religious, athletic, playgoing, or literary selves. Temporarily displaced from attention are the practicalities of getting on in the world. Yet these "other" realities they temporarily favor are, relative to the paramount reality of everyday life, "quasi-realities."[8] Though experienced as real, their weight is less massive than that of commonsense givens. Reality in its most assuring and taken-for-granted forms lies in the mundane world of practical affairs. Nevertheless, as Simmel observed, human existence is structured as "a sum of worlds, each of which comprehends . . . existential content in a distinctive form or a form that represents a totality."[9] Distinctive cognitive styles thus weave together people's lives, but only the one demanded by everyday life involves feeling fully at home in solid, familiar realities essentially inaccessible to doubt. Not surprisingly, phenomenologists label that cognitive style the "natural attitude."

The Writer's World of Literature

People sharing a world typically take its principal features and apparent purposes for granted, continuously constituting their common world without consciously intending it. As sociologists following Peter L. Berger and Thomas Luckmann put it, human beings socially construct their realities. I prefer the term "constitute" if only because the metaphor "construct" connotes a master plan, a careful effort, and a self-sustaining outcome uncharacteristic of social structures. Central to Husserl's phenomenology, "constitution" concerns how people continuously engage in world making and self making. The concept thus necessitates a focus on human action. Inherently expressive and commonly communicative, human action is unrelentingly constitutive. Only in the world of literature, however, do expression and communication become ends in themselves. Thus, the world of literature simultaneously illuminates the nature of human action, the roots of human worlds, and the interplay of selves in the making.

Human expression is primordial and pervasive. Whenever they act, people inescapably imply something about who they are. Expression is "the passage from interiority to exteriority" through words, gestures, glances, dress, or another medium.[10] Expression is thus the individual's social-psychological fingerprints. Among its forms, the verbal predominates.

People rely heavily on language to constitute their worlds. When they speak and write, they express selves appropriate to their worlds and communicate perceptions sustaining the taken-for-granted stuff of those worlds. Among human worlds, though, only the world of literature makes verbal expression a paramount project. In pursuit of expression writers cultivate the imagination, consciousness exploring possibilities rather than analyzing actualities. At root, a poem, novel, or play expresses its creator's experiences of his or her imagination. That same work may also express its creator's real-life experiences. In *The Mill on the Floss,* for example, George Eliot refashioned some of her childhood experiences, as did Charles Dickens in *David Copperfield;* Henry Miller's early novels refract his years as a young bohemian; Thomas Wolfe wrote novels about his experiences writing and publishing novels. Yet their pasts provide only some of the experiences captured in novelists' texts. Above all, novelists tell stories as they give expression to their imaginative experiences. A story emerges when consciousness turns toward the possible and molds its multiplicities into some meaningful shape. Possibility allows for growing up as Maggie Tulliver or David Copperfield, but storytellers obscure the boundary between the possible and the actual. The events in most stories might *actually* have happened or could *possibly* happen. Playing with possible actualities and actual possibilities makes up part of the tension of consciousness writers experience, tension that derives from expressing oneself as an explorer of the conceivable.

Although a story does express an imaginative self, writers' imaginative experiences need not get communicated to readers. Most readers pick up a novel to read a story, not to acquaint themselves with another person's imagination as such. Besides, what novels communicate derives not only from authors' imaginative experiences but also from their responses to narrative conventions, editors' suggestions, friends' feedback, and so forth. Thus, a finished story comprises writers' virtual translations of their imaginative experiences. To that extent novels only refract writers' imaginations much as people's biographies only refract their past experiences.

In a sense every individual narrates a life story as pliable as perception and as malleable as memory. When they write, novelists pursue that commonplace activity with heightened awareness and intensified imagination. As storytellers pursuing a project all human beings face in one way or other, they show us something of ourselves as well as themselves in and through their texts. Unlike people in everyday life, however, imaginative writers exemplify expression, as the idea of art for art's sake implies. Yet such writers do aim to communicate. As Maurice Merleau-Ponty puts it, "The will to speak is one and the same as the will to be understood."[11] Again, writers exhibit a fundamental kinship with people in everyday life. Their essential pursuits differ more in degree than in kind from those central to the commonsense world. Their stance toward language is illustrative.

In most worlds people take language for granted, but writers reject that unawareness. The best of them regard words as "the wildest, freest, most irresponsible, most unteachable of all things."[12] Such writers probe the essential connections between the structures of verbal expression and the structures of experience. Artistically approached, language becomes an object of reflective consciousness—a mystery, a provocation, a limitation, a liberation. Creative writers dismiss the technological language of preachers, politicians, businesspeople, and scientists. Their language of the imagination, lacking reliable reference to actual people and situations, exposes the constitutive character of all language by revealing the profusion of possible relations between the activities of human consciousness and the shapes of human worlds.

Strange as such uses of language may seem in other worlds, the world of literature builds up around such meaning-compatible ends. Displaced is the "working self" of everyday life. In its stead stands an imaginative self plying the language capable of shaping a configuration of conceivable people and events into a story. Left behind, then, is "action in the outer world." The imaginative self gives full attention not to the exigencies of everyday life but to an inner world of language-dependent characters and events built out of imagining and remembering. Thus, the actual "intersubjective world of communication and social action" moves to the margins of consciousness. The imagining self has no capacity for worrying about next month's bills, rejoicing in a child's first steps, or planning the syllabus of Creative Writing 301. Such activities catapult the writer back into the world of everyday life.

The sociality of this world is mostly indirect and implicit. The commonsense social world where people greet, flatter, advise, and chat with one another gets subordinated to an imagined world where those sorts of face-to-face interactions routinely occur but only through the musings of the writer's consciousness. In the writer's world "standard time" shares the same fate as the mundane social world. Clocks become bothersome reminders of that "other" world one must reenter on time for a dental appointment or dinner. No longer does the individual suspend doubts about workaday realities either. The creative writer often entertains the very doubts commonsense individuals suspend, as possibilities unthinkable in everyday life yield themselves to the scrutiny of an imagination testing the limits of the conceivable.

The self-experiences of such individuals are thus distinctive, as the next chapter shows. So, too, are their prevalent forms of spontaneity. In the writer's region of the literary world, spontaneity takes shape not from working, as in everyday life, but from whatever activities sustain the imagination. Thus, writers' "eccentricities" are often a measure of the forms their spontaneity can fruitfully take, for example, Ernest Hemingway's habit of standing while writing or Lawrence Durrell's of writing in a windowless room.

The Reader's World of Literature

Historically, literature has often instructed its readers, often through religious works such as *A Pilgrim's Progress*. Less obvious examples include travel novels that introduced readers to new lands and strange lifestyles or Victorian novels that informed their readers about technical developments. *Tess of the D'Urbervilles,* for instance, acquainted many with the turnip-slicing machine and bright-red thrasher. Until the late nineteenth century, novelists were often willing authorities on such matters.[13] Contemporary novelists continue that tradition by portraying war, prison life, mental breakdowns, and other experiences foreign to most readers. Writers like Irving Wallace inform millions about such things as the Nobel Prizes (*The Prize*) and biblical archaeology (*The Word*). Experimental and avant-garde writers, insistent that literature illustrates human fictions in general, modernize the age-old notion that literature reveals truth. "In a paradoxical and fugitive way, mimetic theory remains alive."[14]

Yet didacticism remains incidental to strong literature. Our best novelists rarely say how to live or what to believe. The modern novel presupposes that human beings must choose among the options they perceive; that they are agents in as well as objects of their societies; that social structures take shape from debates and decisions as well as the resources of environments, the weight of history, and the thrust of technology. Resting on such presuppositions, novels inescapably say something about human freedom.

Literature can thus enliven a sense of possibilities or curtail a sense of inevitability. Reading fiction means transcending the limits of one's biographical situation. At least temporarily, readers extend their realities when they step into an imaginative text. There they find a safe vehicle for exploring unfamiliar territory as well as plowing up the possibilities beneath their familiar tracks. Literature lets readers romp in the fringes of their consciousness by experiencing worlds whose only limits are the possible and the conceivable. Surveying the unfamiliar and the unknown, literature can put readers in imaginative touch with their most distant predecessors, their socially and geographically distant contemporaries, and their imaginable successors; for example, John Fowles's *The French Lieutenant's Woman,* Tom Wolfe's *The Bonfire of the Vanities,* and Aldous Huxley's *Brave New World.* Paradoxically, literature thus intensifies the hearty accent of reality given to the world of everyday life. By offering forms for exploring the horizon of unfamiliarity (and "unreality") bordering the commonsense world, literature makes individuals' everyday realities seem more solid.

Besides unveiling possibilities and securing realities, literature also heightens self-awareness. Modern literature makes the self its first priority, its standard for evaluating culture.[15] At least surreptitiously, literature underscores each person's need for expression and recognition. At the same time it lets readers experience and express intense emotions unashamedly, granting temporary release from the emotional limits of everyday life. Sometimes it "makes us realize for the first time how we feel . . . ," opening us "to the dark side of our deepest ambivalence toward violence, sex, parents, mates, children, selves, toward the daylight deities we are proud to boast we honor alone."[16]

Literature also offers its devotees intense experiences of beauty—not "mere prettiness but something possessed of the power to rend one's heart."[17] For readers, literature is a pleasure-filled, though sometimes demanding, respite from everyday life. The poignant, the lyrical, the awesome, the wondrous, the beautiful—these are the fine threads of literature. Consider daylight, for instance:

> The sun was rising. Very slowly, it came up over the horizon shaking out light.

> The clouds themselves are moving to reveal enormous cavities of sky. They peel the morning like a fruit.

> The sky was blue and serene, as though it had never known a tear.

> In the evenings she liked to look seaward and see that perfectly round sphere sinking to meet that perfectly straight line.

> That enormous smoldering sun lay on the horizon like a dissolving orange suffused with blood.[18]

No less than writers, readers of literature exhibit a distinctive cognitive style. Enjoying literature displaces the working self and action in the outer world; attention shifts from the actual to the imaginary; workaday matters become unwelcome intrusions. For a while, sociality is indirect and implicit, though sometimes experienced more intensely than in everyday life; temporarily, an imaginary world governs time-consciousness. Doubts necessarily suspended in everyday life may find safe harbor in the text, and experiences unavailable in one's biographical situation become imaginatively accessible.

To deny people's need for that luxuriantly imaginative world is to deny them their full humanity. The values, the human voices, the tragedies and comedies and romances of the literary world address individuals' needs as surely as those same human realities in their nonartistic forms do. In both cases needs may remain frustrated, appear impossible to satisfy, or find brief fulfillment only to cry out again for satisfaction. Yet human beings persist, as it seems they must, in their quests for meaning and values, for connections with the Other, and for their very own stories comprising unpredictable amalgams of tears, laughters, and something felt to be love. We are only beginning to appreciate art as "a self-renewing, life-restoring force" capable in the extreme of literally saving lives.[19] In times of great or small need, literature (and the other arts) is responsive with a generosity of spirit sometimes hard to find among the breathing beings in one's world.

At the cultural level, literature serves collective needs often unrecognized and, therefore, unexpressed in any straightforward way. Indirectly, often unintentionally, imaginative writers shape our cultural iconography, planting in the social stock of knowledge such figures as Frankenstein and Dracula, Jekyll/Hyde, Huck Finn, Hester Prynne, Stephen Daedalus, Gatsby, Kunta Kinte, and Garp. Whatever our secular mythologies, literature is certain to have shaped them. It is more than a precious part of our cultural capital, to use Simmel's metaphor; literature vivifies our cultural inheritance.

The Sociology of Literature

Even though literary critics congregate in schools with different frames of reference, the critical pluralism of Wayne C. Booth makes more sense.[20] So does Lionel Trilling's insistence that "criticism may use any instrument upon a work of art to find its meanings."[21] Despite their open-ended stances Booth and Trilling, like most critics, do subscribe to some version of the autonomy of literature. Literary critics largely agree

> that a poem or novel has properties distinctive to itself; that such a work must be perceived, analyzed, and judged with categories distinctive to its kind; that it is an imaginative verbal composition, which cannot be reduced to other kinds of communication since it involves a use of language different from the ways language may be used in exposition, argument, or exhortation. . . . Difficulties arise when we try to discover the relations between this literary work and the external world of familiar experience.[22]

The sociology of literature confronts precisely those difficulties.

Historically, sociologists of literature have favored social realities as a starting point and then examined how literature distorts or reflects those realities. They often reduced literature to a cultural data base used to illustrate what they claimed they already knew or to show how literary works refract the social worlds of their authors. The former purposes were (and remain) mostly pedagogical, best illustrated by Lewis Coser's *Sociology Through Literature.* The latter purposes mostly move sociologists of culture. An impressive work in that vein is Elizabeth Long's *The American Dream and the American Novel,* which traces shifting models of success in post–World War II works. Both sets of purposes are worthy, but neither approaches literature as a full-fledged world or a social institution *sui generis.* In the aggregate, literature has usually gotten second-class treatment in the hands of sociologists—treatment different from that accorded to religion, law, science, and other worlds where print and codification are central. As a result, the sociology of literature has estranged literary critics and stymied its own development.

Somewhere between the exclusionary posture of some literary critics and the reductive approaches of some sociologists lies a sociology capable of illuminating literature as a social world. Such a sociology would refuse, as some literary critics do, to treat literary works as "complex but essentially self-contained forms, cut off from the untidiness and discontinuities of the world outside."[23] Its principal focus would be the varieties of language, form, and social action that make literature a world whose participants exhibit distinctive cognitive styles.

Such a sociology of literature is already emerging. During the 1980s the sociology of culture began moving toward the forefront of American sociology. Its proponents—sociologists like Wendy Griswold and Gaye Tuchman—often approach literature as a world rather than a refractory institution. Renewed concern with rhetoric, exemplified in the work of Richard Harvey Brown, invites attention to the cognitive styles necessitated by different sorts of narratives. Ethnomethodologists continue to feed awareness of how widely commonsense reasoning serves as a resource; not only school counselors and jurors but also sociologists and coroners—and, one supposes, novelists—use it. Feminist scholarship encourages the emergence of a more ambitious sociology of literature, too. Evelyn Fox Keller's findings about the infiltration of gender stereotypes into the natural sciences is but one example of work stimulating attention to the cultural boundaries dividing fact from fiction and science from art. All these developments concern language, narrative forms, and the constitution of culture. The times, it seems, are favorable for a seriously interdisciplinary, conspicuously creative sociology of literature.

Yet some scholars may deem literature relatively undeserving of attention in the face of staggering social injustices. That concern with beauty can take no moral precedence over concern with human indignities goes without saying. What needs reiterating, however, is that literature lives on human expression and communication. Only in the literary world does the expressive, communicative nature of human beings expose itself more or less purely. If one wants to understand human expression and communication, one can find no more promising place.

Expression and communication are the human activities that provide for social action, at least in Max Weber's sense, and thus for social structure and culture. Moreover, these activities are as central to individuality as the body itself: Each human being has an utterly unique voice. These, then, are the activities ultimately at issue when we brand a state of affairs a social problem. The human rights of the poor, women and minorities, lesbians and gay men, children, the handicapped, prisoners, and everyone else fundamentally revolve around the right to express one's self and to have one's voice effectively heard and taken into account. Put differently, in one form or another silencing lies at the root of oppressing.

Does it not behoove us to make every effort to understand human expression and communication—to expose their roots so as to better understand social structure, culture, social problems, and social change? All these standing concerns of sociologists presuppose social action, and no action is fully social unless it expresses something about its agent and communicates something to one or more human beings. Sociologists needing to understand expression and communication will experience beauty and wonder as they study literature in order to satisfy that need. At the same time they will find inexhaustible grounds for illuminating the human capacity to constitute complex, shared worlds.

Clearly, a sociology of literature cannot embrace all literary forms at the outset. Theodor Adorno rightly insists it must treat poetry;[24] it must also consider plays and short stories. As the sociology of literature takes fresh shape, however, its most fruitful focus is the novel, in part because sociologists of literature already concentrate on that genre. Most of all, though, the novel offers the optimal starting point because of its generic characteristics.

The novel offers a unique "summary and paradigm of our cultural life." It shows "the look and feel of things, how things are done and what things are worth and what they cost and what the odds are."[25] The novel portrays complex worlds not unlike those ethnographic sociologists study. Both novelists and social scientists use narrative forms to tap "a culture's hum and buzz of implication."[26] Both reject appearances as reliable indicators of character, motives, experiences, or even reality. The modern novel shows how people constitute their realities together and how experiences shift with expectations, situations, and vocabularies. Characteristically, then, the novel not only creates but also depicts illusions.[27] Similarly, sociology is a debunking, skeptical discipline that insists things are not what they seem. Like the literary imagination, the sociological one reveals "the extent of human variety and the value of this variety."[28] The connections between individual and group, self and culture, and biography and history concern both novelists and social scientists. Those commonalities make the novel the best point of departure for a sociology of literature focused on the fundamentals of human action—expression and communication.

On Method and Meaning

Working with literary data taxes the sociological imagination. Reducing those data to numbers destroys their distinctive character; treating them like ethnographic or conversational data carries the same risk. Literary data rest on distinctive uses of language and constitute aesthetic wholes, imposing on sociologists the clumsiness of quotation marks, the weight of huge volume, and the insufficiency of sampling (among other things).

The problem of quotation marks is largely aesthetic, a punctuational testament to the recalcitrance of literary data. One cannot paraphrase novelists' most valuable achievements the way survey researchers summarize their subjects' opinions. Paradoxically, working with literary data imposes severe aesthetic problems. Perhaps the aesthetic satisfactions of the data themselves soften the blunt blows of quotation marks, ellipses, and other punctuational paraphernalia.

The volume of data necessary to support generalizations about literature pits evidence against aesthetics. Literary critics decide that battle in favor of aesthetics, for the most part favoring depth over breadth by focusing on one novelist or a handful of novels. Although it does provide keen insights into specific novelists, novels, or literary periods, literary critics' usual method refuses to yield the sorts of evidence deemed necessary for sociological generalizations. Yet the wide-ranging data necessary for generalizing leave the sociologist overwhelmed by sheer volume. One way out is a variety of what André de Muralt calls "Husserlian exemplarism." As I use it, that method entails examining a broad range of literary data and then illustrating that range with instances exemplifying the many cases at hand. That approach does deflate the evidential force commonly supposed to underlie sociological explanation, but its breadth offsets that deflation, much as the tradition of ideal-type analysis in the social sciences does.

The sociologist of literature nevertheless faces the methodological problem of sampling. Routinely, it would seem, random sampling of some population of literary works represents a cultural travesty. Literary data have an irreplaceable character seldom found among other data that interest sociologists. Here random sampling eventuates in the very biases such sampling was meant to short-circuit. If one draws a large enough random sample in order to survey a population on some issue, for example, Jane Doe's absence from the sample means that some socially equivalent respondent will offer responses comparable to those she would have provided. Yet no other novelist offers data equivalent to those offered by a Virginia Woolf, a William Faulkner, or a Toni Morrison. Sampling literary works requires sketching broad boundaries and insistently including all the widely read and/or critically acclaimed writers whose work gives those boundaries literary and cultural meaning.

In the end, sociologists of literature face exhilarating methodological challenges that fuel the imagination, revitalizing one's sense of possibilities while tempering the dreariness of mere probabilities. At the same time, such challenges demand interdisciplinary responses that are philosophically self-conscious and sociologically open-ended; hence, phenomenology and grounded theory.

Phenomenology insists on philosophical self-consciousness devoted to "things themselves" as presented to consciousness. Phenomenological method requires acutely reflective attention to one's own consciousness—both its noetic activities such as perceiving, judging, and remembering and its noematic objects such as *Beloved*-as appreciated, narrator-as-inferred, and reading-as-remembered. Phenomenological findings show that consciousness offers our sole access to "reality," that consciousness is constitutive of taken-for-granted "realities," that what-is-*taken*-as-real readily undergoes experiential translation into what-*is*-real. Phenomenologically guided, self-consciousness entails world-consciousness; that is, consciousness of language as a social repository of types, of history as a continuous influence on social structure, of culture as a collectively constituted achievement, of individuals' biographies as dramas played out on a panoramic stage where countless characters dance and cry and grow old together. Preoccupied with the amplitude of human experiencing and the achievements of human consciousness, phenomenology offers the most fruitful grounds for my project. Phenomenologists investigate intersubjectivity, meaning, typification, the self, and the worlds that individuals constitute together out of shared projects, similar plans, and common sense. Phenomenology discloses what taken for grantedness hides and what taking for granted entails.

A sociological approach particularly compatible with phenomenology is what Barney Glaser and Anselm S. Strauss call "grounded theory" (most recently delineated in the latter's *Qualitative Analysis for Social Scientists*). Rudimentary as it is, grounded theory is nonetheless systematic. In Strauss's terms, it grants no "license to run wild." Grounded theory revolves around progressive interpretations that require revisiting one's data until one nearly sickens of them. (Implicitly, then, it urges the selection of research problems one genuinely cares about.) One's interpretations self-consciously evolve; one's conclusions take shape as "provisional suggestions."

Grounded theory entails *theoretical sampling* governed not by probabilistic models but by one's evolving theoretical stance based on interpretations and reinterpretations of the data constituted out of sampling. The goal is *theoretical saturation*—arrival at the point where neither further data nor further analyses elicit additional insights of any theoretical import. In practical terms, that goal is unattainable in an undertaking like this. Nevertheless, it can serve as a reference point capable of signaling semi-closure.

"Experiential data" play a central role in grounded theory. These derive from the researcher's nontechnical experiences rooted beyond the world of science, outside the role of scientist. In a project like *Novels, Novelists, and Readers* such data comprise memories of the summer reading clubs at the Alton public library during the 1950s, my experiences first reading *Pride and Prejudice* in high school, the "Tom Wolfe phase" my friend Helen and I shared after reading *Mau-Mauing the Flak Catchers*, or the emotionally exhausting, aesthetically overpowering wonder of reading *Beloved*. Traditionally, scientists have denied the play of such experiences beneath the surface of their work. Grounded theory releases them from that denial. It warrants the self-conscious, disciplined (and satisfying) use of such experiences in one's work—a use as unavoidable as it is deniable among scientists in any event.

Finally, grounded theory is "conceptually dense." It gives way to many concepts, some old and some not, that assert themselves as the researcher keeps reencountering the data at hand. Here, concepts like world, debunking, tension of consciousness, system of relevances, literary canon, expressive language, strategic interaction, genre, culture, and mediating institution kept demanding attention. I repeatedly gave it to them while foreshortening any temptation to pretend I could do more than enrich their meaning. To be literally definitive here would be to miss my own points. Besides, as Raymond Boudon observes in *The Crisis in Sociology*, the most successful sociological concepts are often the most "polysemic." Conceptual density —minus any conceptual proliferation serving no theoretical end— would seem theoretically advantageous at all junctures in the scholarly enterprise. In exploratory works it is essential.

My progression is thus bound by what I take phenomenology and grounded theory to demand. I know no better way to rouse my imagination and discipline my energies in the face of a world that incessantly claims my attention. Differently put, I subordinate broadly Marxian stances centered on reflection models of literature, the artworlds perspective of Howard S. Becker, the production-of-culture framework of Richard Peterson, and related stances to phenomenological findings and grounded-theory guidelines in order to find my way to insights that extant perspectives tend to foreshorten.

2

❦ Self-experiences and Novel Making

> This Saturday evening belonged to me and my work, and I had spent the greater part of the day preparing myself for it. Toward eight o'clock I got my supper out of the cool neighboring room, a jar of yogurt and a banana, then seated myself with my little desk lamp and picked up my pen.
>
> Hermann Hesse, *My Belief*

William Makepeace Thackeray's *The History of Pendennis: His Fortunes and Misfortunes; His Friends and His Greatest Enemy* portrays writers' self-experiences. Its narrator says Pen "wrote for his own pleasure," but Pen says poets feel so keenly that they *must* express themselves.[1] Such writers need solitude and associates who accommodate their special needs. Since they experience "paroxysms of frenzy" and "enthusiasm of temperament" (p. 71), writers commonly develop eccentricities. Pen, for example, "could not compose without his cigar, and quoted the late lamented Lord Byron's lines in favor of the custom of smoking" (p. 172). Pen's roommate Warrington knows Pen feels "authorized to be flighty" (p. 332). Like the narrator, he rejects such self-indulgence. Warrington says some writers merely relieve themselves, bemoan their lot in life, or bolster their self-esteem. Many are mere hacks.

Pen and Warrington carry on a running debate about hacks and the literary marketplace. Warrington says writers "cry out that they suffer more than any other mortals; and when they have experienced feelings enough they note them down in a book and take the book to market" (p. 413). Pen argues that if writers aim to express their talents rather than acquire money, their commercial involvements need not jeopardize their integrity. Pen fails to see that his dubious talents leave him woefully vulnerable to publishers' whims. As the narrator points out, "When a gentlemen is cudgeling his brain to find any rhyme for sorrow, besides borrow and to-morrow [*sic*], his woes are nearer at an end than he thinks for" (p. 134).

Pendennis portrays the literary division of labor conditioning writers' identities. By the time Thackeray was writing the novel, Paternoster Row was already institutionalized as "the famous haunt of the Muses and their masters" (p. 319). Publishers with little literary judgment had begun hiring readers like Mr. Hack to compensate for their literary deficiencies (p. 318)! Such publishers marketed and profited from the fashionable writers of the day. County newspapers had Poet's Corners for aspiring amateurs (pp. 56–57), and the Sunday papers reviewed recent books (p. 409). Literature had become lucrative. Portraying the self-experiences shaped by such forces, *Pendennis* explores the "contrast between practice and poetry, between grand versified aspirations and everyday life" (p. 240).

The Novelist's Vocation

Between the lines of *Pendennis*, one finds a literary exposition of Max Weber's principles about vocation. In "Politics as a Vocation" and "Science as a Vocation,"[2] Weber observed that the individual with a vocation makes its activities her or "his life, in an internal sense" (p. 84). A vocation evokes "passionate devotion to a 'cause,' to the god or demon who is its overlord" (p. 115). Devotion "*solely* to the work at hand" is the *sine qua non* of a fulfilled vocation. Such inner devotion can "lift the scientist to the height and dignity of the subject he pretends to serve. And in this, it is not different with the artist" (p. 137). Having a vocation thus means that a single role centers one's identity across the "various life-spheres" (p. 123), or worlds, one experiences.

The person with a literary calling cannot, then, slough off the sense of self-as-writer. Such an individual *must* write; he or she lives for writing. Yet in an "internal sense, every sincere [person] who lives for a cause also lives off this cause," whether by virtue of the self-aggrandizement it allows or the inner satisfactions it offers (p. 84). The distinction between "living for" and "living off" a cause thus boils down in practical terms to whether the individual depends on that cause as a source of income (living off) or not (living for). Together with the external or material conditions of a vocation, this distinction will concern us later. The immediate task is to see that some novelists respond to the dictates of a vocation and others do not, thus providing for two distinct configurations of self-experiences among them.

The journals, notebooks, and letters of some novelists show that the world of literature does issue callings to live for imaginative struggles with the wondrous, the ineffable, and the ordinary. Fairly often, the calling to write fiction emerges early in people's lives—

early enough to go unquestioned and to exert considerable force. The adolescent Eudora Welty knew she "wanted to be a writer."[3] Many others lodge that knowledge in their earlier years. Susan Sontag reports, "I have been writing since I was seven years old"; Bernard Malamud, that "At eight or nine, I was writing little stories in school and feeling the glow"; Katherine Anne Porter, that she "started writing when she was six or seven"; Lawrence Durrell, that "since the age of eight, I have been madly scribbling"; John Gardner, that "I started writing stories when I was five or so...."[4] Nadine Gordimer remembers having been a published writer "when [she] was twenty-one or twenty-two"; by the time she was twenty-three, Joyce Carol Oates "had already written [her] first two books...."[5]

Whence come such early promptings? Only a detailed study of writers' childhoods will provide a sure-footed answer, but voracious reading is common enough in writers' recollections to pinpoint it as an enabling circumstance of their early years. Surely children are radically vulnerable to capture by fictional texts. Gore Vidal, who started trying to write novels at the age of seven or eight, learned to read when he was only five. By the age of six, he "was reading tales from Livy." Growing up, Vidal "was constantly reading to [his] blind grandfather Senate Gore," and he started five novels between the ages of fourteen and nineteen. The fifth became his first book.[6] The connections between his boyhood reading and writing seem analytically unavoidable. In fact, such connections are not rare.

Gordimer describes herself at twelve or thirteen as "living in books." She insists, "You're never going to write if you don't read!"[7] Vonnegut, Porter, and Gardner each recall many books in their childhood homes.[8] Gardner offers a detailed scenario: His mother, the teacher, and father, the farmer, were "great reciters of literature." Besides the Bible, they enjoyed Shakespeare and the classics, and they put their children "to bed with a recital of poetry." Gardner's father wrote sermons and stories he would "compose in his head" while working, and his mother often read to his father while he milked the cows. The orality of his boyhood experiences of literature is "one of the reasons I write the way I do," says Gardner.[9] Like these others, Ralph Ellison flatly states, "I became interested in writing through incessant reading."[10]

Whatever the other conditions conducive to an early sense of literary vocation, one might suppose that they are—like reading—fundamentally social. The voices, the stories, the characters young readers enjoy are no simple figments of the imagination isolated from the real, throbbing world. The stuff of fiction is so vividly real to serious young readers that it can land them in the most alluring of places. We should expect no less than that the seeds of a vocation might be found on the pages of such readers' books, especially when the young person inhabits a relatively privileged environment. The social-class environments comfortable enough to provide homes stocked with books also tend to be those that look kindly on a child sitting quietly with a book rather than roughnecking in the yard. Even in these classes, however, female readers probably find more favor on average than their male counterparts inasmuch as the passivity of reading is more compatible with femininity than masculinity.

Whether it comes early or late in a person's life, the calling to write demands a poignant faith. Lacking the emblems of a distinct calling, the individual must above all think of himself or herself as a novelist. Without that belief, the person "simply can't do it."[11] Armed with it, individuals devoted to imaginative writing must nevertheless wrestle with the "catastrophe of vocation"[12] that entails securing solitude, risking madness, and sustaining suffering. The catastrophic dimension of the literary vocation guarantees self-experiences different from those of writers lacking vocations.

The notions of self and survival loom large when novelists say why they write. Truman Capote thinks "the toughest thing in the world is to survive decades of creative work, working creatively and consistently, trying to do what you want to do. . . . "[13] D. H. Lawrence said he "must write to live," and William Carlos Williams wrote to keep himself as he wanted to be. Sylvia Plath felt "literally sick" without it.[14] As Ernest Hemingway puts it, "Once writing has become your major vice and greatest pleasure, only death can stop it."[15] Vidal, who tried "kicking the habit" of creative writing, found he "simply could not *not* write." He concludes that "you can't make yourself do anything else but that."[16] Oates reports that "sometimes the prospect of writing leaves me virtually faint with longing; a yearning, a desire so palpable it's almost physical. . . . "[17] Such yearning may reflect the single-mindedness vocations dictate. Describing "congenital novelists," Aldous Huxley notes that fiction "is an absorbing thing which fills up [the] mind and takes all [one's] time and energy. . . . "[18] Such a state of affairs rarely breeds sustainable exhilaration. Porter reports, "I did not choose this vocation, and if I had any say in the matter, I would not have chosen it . . . yet for this vocation, I was and am willing to live and die, and I consider very few other things of the slightest importance."[19]

Voices like these bear witness to need, not preference. Subjectively felt, a calling imposes necessities where other people experience choices. No one can say how commonplace such experiences are among the most widely read and the most highly acclaimed British and American novelists, nor can one draw a reliable line between novelists' private self-experiences and their public self-dramatizations. A random sample of such writers is beyond reach, and no one can say what biases infiltrate their published journals and letters. Here I try, then, not to sample novelists systematically enough to support statistical generalizations but thoroughly enough to capture the variability across their experiences. While this approach erodes some of the stereotypes romanticizing writers' experiences, the patterns at hand remain elusive to some extent. The sheer prolificacy of a George Sand or a Joyce Carol Oates does, however, suggest that more than the drive for money, fame, and security is at work. The measures writers take to secure good, if not ideal, working conditions suggest the same conclusion.

Imaginative writing often requires arranging one's life around solitude. Writers "escape from the traffic's roar," sometimes going for weeks without knowing "whether the sun [shines] upon the earth and whether the stars above still move on. . . . "[20] They sometimes work "hour after hour, day after day, away from the world, and to the exclusion of all that makes life really lovable and gentle. . . . "[21] Over time, few writers sustain such exclusion. Gardner says, for instance, "Since I have a family of whom I am very fond and a teaching job with students of whom I am very fond, and we have friends who visit us, I often don't get much writing time in."[22]

Writing fiction reverses the ratio of social to solitary moments characteristic of everyday life. One frequent outcome is a sense of isolation or disconnection. Porter, for example, "never belonged to any group or huddle of any kind," and Henry Miller was a self-reported "lone wolf."[23] Sometimes a writer's distaste for the baggage of belonging leads to expatriation, as with Henry James and Stephen Crane. Terry Eagleton claims the great English writers of the twentieth century are mostly exiles, emigrés, or outsiders.[24]

Yet escape from interruptions, release from everyday obligations, a sense of isolation, or expatriation are hardly constants among people living to write. John Barth says he needs connections with "the rest of the world," and George Eliot, Katherine Mansfield, and Colette "all needed to be closely and happily in touch with life in order to do their best work; they could not live alone. . . . "[25] Anthony Trollope's extensive travels as a civil servant never kept him from writing, and George Sand never let far-flung, intense involvements deter her from writing. As Ellen Moers observes of Sand, "throughout all her years of passions, pleasures, politics, and domestic responsibilities, she went on producing at the rate of at least two long novels a year, and hundreds upon hundreds of pages of other kinds of writing."[26]

Nonetheless, the vocation to write does demand the displacement of everyday life. Solitude is its most frequent accompaniment. Solitude devoted to novel making may heighten one's chances of madness or, at least, manic-depressive illness, as the research of psychiatrist Kay Redfield Jamison[27] suggests. More reliably, it increases one's prospects for anguish, self-doubt, and related sorts of suffering. The mysteries writers probe and the faculties they exercise put them in greater psychological danger than their creative counterparts in fields like the sciences. Moreover, Jamison's research suggests that many artists (literary and otherwise) "believing that the source of their cycles of euphoria and despair is the same wellspring from which their creativity emerges . . . commonly refuse treatment or discontinue drug therapy."[28]

Even those who reject the stereotype of the mad artist recognize the mental-health hazards of imaginative writing. E. M. Forster claims the artist drops "a bucket into his subconscious and draws up something which is *normally* beyond his reach."[29] Charlotte Brontë says the writer's gift is "something that, at times, strangely wills and works for itself," as with Henry Miller's "dictation" where "Someone takes over and you just copy out what's being said."[30]

For many, Virginia Woolf with her "moments of vision" is exemplary in that respect. Woolf had what she herself called an irrational notion that

> we are sealed vessels afloat on what it is convenient to call reality; and at some moments, the sealing matter cracks, in floods reality: that is, these scenes—for why do they survive undamaged year after year unless they are made of something comparatively permanent? Is this liability to scenes the origin of my writing impulse?[31]

While writing, Woolf sometimes experienced events "as if [she] were there." Sometimes, too, she experienced a "rapture" revolving around the idea that "we—I mean all human beings—are connected; . . . that the whole world is a work of art; that we are part of the work of art."[32] Outside the literary world Woolf's experiences seem "abnormal." She was aware of that circumstance. She says that after writing *To the Lighthouse,*

> I ceased to be obsessed by my mother. I no longer hear her voice; I do not see her.

> I suppose that I did for myself what psychoanalysts do for their patients. I expressed some very long felt and deeply felt emotion. And in expressing it I explained it and then laid it to rest.[33]

Woolf's experiences imply that imaginative writing may prevent as well as stimulate madness. Yet her own mental breakdowns suggest writing's ultimate impotence in the face of a fractured sense of reality, especially when one's culture renders illness a *desideratum* at some level. All things considered, Victorian culture made invalidism and illness tantamount to normative among middle-class women by supporting the perception that those atrophied states of being somehow sustained women's moral superiority. Woolf herself was Victorian enough to associate illness "with a retreat into oneself and . . . creative power."[34] Perhaps at some level she also sensed, like Doris Lessing, that "madness can be a form of rebellion."[35]

Among contemporary writers reporting experiences like Woolf's are Joyce Carol Oates and William Goyen. Oates describes her writing "as an active pursuit of 'hauntedness'" that carries her "sometimes to the point of distraction or obsession."[36] She sometimes writes "to relieve [her] mind of things that haunt it, not to create literature that will live." Oates says she does not "make up" stories; she records or remembers them, often without the sense of being "any particular person, with a particular ego." Her characters "dictate themselves" to her like figures from a dream. Oates reports, "I can see them at times very clearly, and indeed I 'am' them—my personality merges with theirs."[37] Such experiences can leave Oates feeling an "acute homesickness" after completing a novel. She sometime experiences "melancholy," for example, at the thought "of Bellefleur—the landscape, the castle, the people whom I came to love in odd surprising ways."[38] Even when she is with other people, Oates sometimes undergoes a "waking sleep" she can hardly control. Although she regards herself as conventional, she finds it difficult "to keep herself going as. . . a professor of English, a wife, a woman, with certain friends, certain duties. It is sometimes such a duty to remain sane and accountable."[39]

Goyen says that his *Ghost and Flesh* "made me quite mad. . . . It comes in a loss of reality. If we say madness, that sounds funny. But let's say an other-worldness. It has to do with identity. I go through phases of not knowing my own history. It's amnesiac, almost." Goyen generalizes, "It's enraging to work in words sometimes; no wonder writers are often nervous and crazy. . . . " Like Oates, Goyen cannot readily abandon the fictional worlds he fashions. He says that "the characters in my first novel haunt me to this day. Actually *haunt* me. They stay with me. . . . They not only enter my [inner] life, but I begin to see them in life [the world], here, there." Like many of his cultural colleagues, Goyen nevertheless says he "can't imagine *not* writing."[40]

Woolf's, Oates's, and Goyen's experiences are not uncommon

among imaginative writers. The critic Frank Kermode concludes, "There is nothing inauthentic about the anxiety and suffering they describe. To survive is their preoccupation."[41] In part, the psychological hazards of imaginative writing derive from its generous allowance for self-expression. Gail Godwin finds herself wondering whether she has "the courage to write. I do everything to put it off. I am afraid to get close to it—afraid of what I might say."[42] Godwin alludes to the self exposed in the course of imaginative writing. Heavily dependent on the wiles of their own imaginations—bound more by the possible than by the actual—writers would seem subjectively prone, if not objectively doomed, to experience their triumphs and their failures as telltale measures of the self. To a large extent, every vocation levies that psychological toll, but the literary vocation requires its followers to make their way without a wardrobe of systematic empirical data or even a closetful of methodical procedures. On average, their journeys would seem more maddening than those of journalists, scientists, and others whose writing is also essential to fulfilling their vocations.

Ironically, the psychological hazards of imaginative writing also derive in part from the subjective, periodic abandonment of one's biographical self. Gordimer says that "the solitude of writing is . . . quite frightening" and that "you always feel that that demon is waiting behind the back of your brain." Those observations resonate with her observations about "projecting into other people" while writing: One is no longer oneself at the subjective level.[43] Oates cites its impersonal character as a paradox of imaginative writing. Because its "unconscious, hence unwilled," dimension is sizable, such writing can dissolve one's sense of self.[44] We instinctively incline toward thinking of fantasizing as a relatively unadulterated experience of the free, unique self, but writers' fantasies differ from those momentarily catapulting individuals out of the everyday world. The latter fantasies are "by definition . . . sufficient and compensating," whereas the former are incomplete until "transmit[ted] to somebody else." The fruition of such fantasies often demands "sink[ing] way down to a level of hopelessness and desperation . . ."[45] where one's biographical self may lose its force in the imagination's struggle to complete its work. Thus, Plath could say she felt "not-herself" when not writing, and George Eliot could say she felt "not herself" when writing.[46] The one is alluding to the fulfillment of one's self in writing—expressing one's own self in and through creative acts; the other, to the projection of one's self into characters—abandoning one's own self in and through imaginative acts.

In any event, suffering does seem fairly common among novelists pursuing vocations. They recognize the irony of Whitman's "I loaf and invite my soul." Woolf says that "the novelist's task lays . . . a load upon every nerve, muscle, and fibre." Tolstoy says, "One ought only to write when one leaves a piece of one's flesh in the ink-pot each time one dips one's pen." Dostoevsky, who found writing "real hard labor," became physically ill when he wrote. Dickens took "extraordinary night walks—as much as twenty-five miles at a steady four miles an hour—which could serve either to summon up fictional fantasies or put them to rest." O. Henry "had to be watched and guarded and *made* to write. . . . It was an agony for him to write at all."[47] Yet a few novelists—Ernest Hemingway, Kurt Vonnegut and Lawrence Durrell, for example—find writing pleasurable.[48]

Frequent suffering, the risk of madness, and extensive solitude put writers at a remove from everyday life. The commonsense world simplifies the complexities they want to untangle; its discourse provides no channels for their visions; the flux of practical affairs impedes their ability to concentrate. Pursuing a literary vocation requires, in Woolf's words, "a room of one's own." Yet writers dislodged from the world of everyday life nevertheless illuminate its experiential grounds through imaginative expression and communication.

The Novelist's Career

Among living authors, Janet Dailey is the fifth best-selling in the world. Her first novel, published in 1976, was a major success followed by six more novels that year and thereafter many more. Available in seventeen languages, her sales exceed 90 million copies in ninety countries. A high school graduate, Dailey was the first American to join Harlequin's 140 British novelists. At home in Branson, Missouri, Dailey usually writes a quota of pages each day. Writing twenty pages a day, she finishes a Silhouette romance in nine days; at fifteen pages a day, she completes a work for Pocket Book in thirty to forty-five days. Uninterested in writing "the great American novel," Dailey now produces television movies with her husband, having personally financed their first movie for a million dollars.[49]

Frank Yerby, an expatriate living in Madrid for more than twenty-five years, is also a best-selling writer. The author of twenty-nine historical romances, beginning with *The Foxes of Harrow* in 1946, Yerby writes novels with "roguish heroes, libidinous heroines, and subplots lovingly embellished with derring-do and duplicity, miscegenation and mayhem, sex and sadism." Says Yerby: "I've written some very bad books." Yet 55 million copies have sold in seventeen languages. Yerby earned a master's degree in English from Fisk University. He abandoned doctor-

al studies at The University of Chicago to teach at Southern black colleges. In 1944, *Harper's* published "Health Card," a short story with
racial themes that won the O. Henry Prize. Yerby then turned his sights
to the best-seller lists; *The Foxes of Harrow* resulted. Yerby no longer
treats racial matters; he considers such themes "artistic dead ends."[50]

Ken Follett has written three best-selling novels. *The Eye of the
Needle, Triple,* and *The Key to Rebecca* won him international fame, a
Rolls Royce, and homes in New York, England, and France. *The Eye of
the Needle,* published in 1979, won the Edgar, the annual Mystery
Writers of America award. Before that novel, Follett wrote ten others
using a pseudonym. Success has changed not only his lifestyle but
also his work habits. Once he wrote three or four novels a year; he
now writes only one. Follett's first successful novel became a film
starring Donald Sutherland and Kate Nelligan. Follett says he had
Nelligan in mind when he developed "her" character in the novel.
His next goal is a screenplay. In fact, the film sale of *The Key to Rebecca*
was contingent on his writing the script. Follett attended journalism
school and worked as a reporter, feature writer, and managing editor
for a British publisher before becoming a novelist.[51]

Dick Francis hit the best-seller lists with *Twice Shy.* Since he
retired as a champion steeplechase jockey in 1957, Francis has written
a mystery novel every year. Francis turned to writing novels at the
suggestion of his wife.[52] Dean R. Koontz says Francis writes "finely
crafted mysteries." He criticizes Francis's first publishing company
for billing him as a mystery writer, which held Francis's sales down.
For Follett, Koontz has little praise. He says publishers buy his
"weakly plotted novels" because his name sells books.[53]

Koontz has published more than two dozen novels, beginning
with science fiction novels written pseudonymously. He has also written two books for aspiring fiction writers. *Writing Popular Fiction,*
published in 1972, tells "how to build successful careers as a category
[or genre] novelist"; that is, how to write novels publishers can
pigeonhole for the public.[54] Nine years later, in *How to Write Best-Selling Fiction* Koontz advises avoiding genre writing and concentrating
on "mainstream fiction," works transcending popular categories
"even while borrowing from them."[55]

Koontz's books stand among many successors to Sir Walter
Besant's *The Pen and the Book* (1899), perhaps the first modern handbook for aspiring writers.[56] Such books address a more diverse audience than textbooks on composition or creative writing. Their authors
are little known in academic and literary circles, though they usually
publish a lot of fiction. Such works disclose the self-experiences of fic-

tion writers who get little academic attention.[57] Since their notebooks, diaries, and letters appear less often than those of writers studied in classrooms, their handbooks offer windows on their worlds.

Although writers with clear-cut vocations differ in their needs for solitude, their vulnerability to madness, and their degree of suffering, novelists as a group differ more widely. Their experiences, not sales or reputations or categories, further our understanding of their identities and motives. Later the content, not the popularity, of novels will further expose differences among writers. Thereby "popular" and "mass" literature take on experiential (as opposed to critical) import, clarifying the connections between the worlds of literature and everyday life. A first step is to see what authors of writing handbooks say about fiction writers.

Like most how-to books, those for aspiring writers offer contradictory messages: No one can teach you to write, but this book will help you; writers need little education, but they are as professional as physicians and lawyers; "hacks" are bad, but you can turn out five books a year as a "commercial writer." Thus, some authors imply ambivalent identities or identity conflicts. Whether those implications reliably report their experiences or reflect a characteristic of how-to manuals is unclear. Nevertheless their possible identity problems are sufficient to set these writers apart from novelists whose firmer identities are likely to disallow writing books for would-be writers. Thus, the data initially point toward profound differences in how writers experience their role, what goals they pursue, and—more inferentially—the identities they carve out on those bases.

Ken Purdy says becoming a writer is fairly easy. One reads, writes, studies, and then declares oneself a writer, resolving to write eight hours a day.[58] Marian Gavin claims writing requires only "respect for your craft and a few tools exactly as you want them, when you want them."[59] Erskine Caldwell says,

> Any person with the ability to spell reasonably well, with a way of knowing the differences between infinity and infinitive, with a rampant reach for paper and typewriter, with a proclivity for communication, with a surmise of what can be made interesting for information or entertainment, and with all the verve and fervor that a politician can generate—well, a happy combination of these things will give the [aspiring writer] a fair start.[60]

Successful writers are neither intellectuals nor literati. As Tom Clancy recently put it, "Literature means a hundred years after you're dead they make kids read you in high school. I'm in the entertainment business, like John D. MacDonald, Jack Higgins, and Freddie Forsyth. Our mission is to take people away from . . . their drudgery. That's a good enough purpose for any man."[61] Disdain for "highfalutin' literary guff" comes through in many manuals for would-be writers.[62] Alan Devoe denigrates the "little magazines," and Koontz criticizes authors like Barth who "write *at* and *down* to the masses."[63] Such stances imply identities where "literature," "imagination," "vocation," and "artist" are peripheral notions. In their stead stand notions such as "bestsellers," "schedule," and "career." These writers contrast themselves with the literary crowd by stressing the craft, not the art, of writing. Often "professional writer" conveys that emphasis.

According to the Burnetts, professional writers regard writing as a job, spend at least two thirds of their time on it, and no longer write "mostly for secret pleasures." White says, "The author should be a genuine craftsman who will not permit a manuscript to leave his shop until it is as perfect as it is humanly possible for him to make it." Yet he also says, "Every commercial writer considers his work a business rather than an art."[64] Thus, some professional writers are self-identified "novel manufacturers," most assuredly "*not* in literature."[65] They "ply two trades—producing manuscripts and selling them."[66]

Even though commercial success may involve "huckster[ing] . . . with shameless abandon,"[67] some professional writers are proud of their prolificacy. Barbara Cartland, for example, says she "brought out a mass of books in 1961. I was now writing five books a year. . . . " Since 1976, Cartland has claimed the world's record for the most books published annually. Her average is twenty-three. Early in 1988, she was working on her 461st novel, billing herself "the bestselling author in the world."[68] Similarly, during his first six years as a full-time writer Koontz wrote twenty-two science fiction novels and even more short stories as well as Gothic romances and pornography "on the side"; he could write a romance in a week. His work hardly required him "to commit [his] heart and soul." Today, Koontz is a "humble storyteller" whose novels are "carefully crafted" now that he no longer writes for "quick money."[69] He landed on *The New York Times* bestsellers list late in the 1980s.

Like many others, Koontz cites examples indicating that some people turn out publishable manuscripts at a furious pace and yet claim the status of craftsperson.[70] Others write for series like the "Nick Carter" novels released monthly under that name.[71] Ayn Rand makes the point Koontz keeps dodging: "When we go below the top level of popular fiction, . . . literary principles are barely applicable."[72] Imitation supersedes creation; characters become stock figures. Writers producing such fiction are neither artists nor craftspersons but hacks who exacerbate the challenge of making "professional writer" a comfortable identity. Not surprisingly, then, many popular writers fear "merely giving an imitation of what they hope to become."[73] These writers, who refuse to keep duplicating their first successes, find it hard to name themselves. They want a more fitting term than artist, but "creator is pretentious and . . . craftsman is not enough."[74] Securing their identities is, then, a standing challenge for those self-consciously working within a shifting structure of readers' demands and publishers' contracts while taking seriously the literary character of their work.

Writers whose identities revolve around "professional writer" or "commercal writer" say little about the need for solitude or vulnerability to madness. Suffering does get attention, usually in terms of hard work and discipline. Most stress the need to follow a rigid schedule regardless of mood or circumstances.[75] Revising also smacks of suffering, and most writers emphasize its necessity. Yet Asimov reports minimal rewriting; L'Amour, no rewriting.[76] Woodford claims "Only hack writers need to rewrite," and he discounts suffering as something only "hopeless tyroes" experience.[77]

Whether the short shrift these writers give solitude, madness, and suffering reflects their marketing savvy or their actual experiences is hard to say. Supposing their advice to aspiring writers more or less reflects their experiences, we confront a sharp contrast with the experiences sketched earlier in the chapter. Apparently, selves get implicated in writing in different ways.

The wordsmiths committed to novel making tend to identify themselves in fundamentally different ways. "Artist" is central to the self-identifications of some and peripheral to or absent from those of others. The former grouping lays greater claim to a vocation and suffering; its members live for the experience of writing, even though some also live off writing in Weber's sense. The latter grouping lays greater claim to a profession and hard work; its members live off writing even though some also live for the experiences it comprises. Needless to say, these ideal types represent only crude reference points on a continuum treating one aspect of novelists' cognitive styles.

Even at this early juncture, though, questions implied in Weber's and Thackeray's considerations fly to the surface. How do the novelists leaning toward one or the other of these reference points differ in their class backgrounds and current class positions? How might their public identities relate to their self-experiences? How much do their readerships overlap? Might that overlap reflect how some novelists move toward one and then another of the poles identified here?

Many additional questions suggest themselves. The one with the most consequential ramifications, both theoretically and culturally, concerns the meaning of "artist." To what extent do novelists' artistic claims or disclaimers reflect their positions in the literary marketplace as well as widespread cultural understandings about the nature of art? Independently of the form and content of his novels, for instance, can Tom Clancy credibly lay claim to an artistic identity after signing a four-million dollar contract with the Putnam Publishing Group for his fifth novel? Isn't art supposed to pay off less spectacularly? Isn't it unappealing to a mass audience? Doesn't filthy lucre contaminate the artist? Given the cultural notions such questions imply, Clancy could scarcely lay credible claim to being an artist. Never mind that his young years involved the same voracious reading common in the lives of "artistic" novelists and that "he continues to read widely." Never mind that his life story, like many of theirs, includes a young boy dreaming of writing and never shaking off the dream. Never mind that as a young husband and father, "still secretly dreaming his dream," he took to writing "whenever he could make time." Never mind that he "has a genius for big, compelling plots, a passion for research, a natural narrative gift, a solid prose style. . . . " This millionaire-writer can claim more credibly that "what happened to [him] was pure dumb luck"[78] than he can claim the identity of artist in societies like ours.

Imagine one of Clancy's female counterparts who meets our culture's norms of feminine attractiveness. Her claims to an artistic identity would likely be even more ineffectual. "Artist" is no narrowly aesthetic label. It reverberates with class, gender, and other associations that open up questions about elitism, classism, sexism, the literary canon, and other matters of no small importance in pluralistic societies. The next two chapters broach those questions. Chapter Three looks (among other things) at how gender conditions opportunities for the form of social action called novel making and, less directly, conditions the content of the novels women and men can readily write. Chapter Four touches more broadly on such matters by interweaving them around the notion of the literary canon.

❧ Novel Making and the World of Everyday Life

Life as we live it from day to day conceals the imagination as social form.

Wallace Stevens, *The Necessary Angel*

In *A Room of One's Own*, Virginia Woolf insists on writers' special needs—needs dictating a distinctive displacement from everyday life. Like her related argument in *Three Guineas,*[1] Woolf's position is persuasive. Nonetheless, arguments like hers obfuscate the full range of lifestyles imaginative writers carve out for themselves. The imagination thrives under diverse conditions, with notions like "artistic temperament" and "creative personality" perhaps serving more as justifications than reliable profiles of writers' needs. Jane Austen led a quiet, stable life, for example; Anthony Trollope wrote under conditions Woolf would have decried as impossible.

Determining whether Austen or Trollope is an exception to some sound rule necessitates looking at biographical data. Those data expose the connections between novel making and everyday life along two axes. Biographical data offer preliminary glimpses into how novelists' everyday lives affect their opportunities to write effectively; the same data also allow for exploring how novelists' experiences in everyday life affect the experiences portrayed in their novels. Biographical data are thus capable of suggesting how novelists' social worlds affect them both practically and aesthetically.

Styles of Everyday Life

The world of everyday life comprises sex roles that mold people's self-images and social identities. Family, education, and occupation also tailor people's experiences of everyday life, making those institutions meaningful reference points for looking at participation in the commonsense world. Broadly, people participate in typical or atypical ways. *Typical participation* includes actions deemed proper, acceptable, or normal for individuals of a given sex and social class in their societies during their lifetimes; *atypical participation* includes actions that routinely or at least frequently deviate from those expectations. Writers participate in everyday life both typically and atypically.

Most novelists, like most intellectuals, never find their Bloomsbury. That "carefully exclusive group" consisted of gifted eccentrics, misfits, and nonconformists.[2] Lytton Strachey was open about his homosexuality; Leonard Woolf was a socialist when it was less than chic; Vanessa Bell and Duncan Grant pursued antitraditional art; all Bloomsbury opposed World War I, albeit passively at times. Bloomsbury epitomizes a community of intellectually lively, politically conscious, and artistically innovative individuals pursuing vocations. It has virtually no duplicate in our cultural history, though, and Gertrude Stein's and Ernest Hemingway's Paris years are nearly as atypical. More common are conventional lifestyles adding up to ordinary, though not average, sorts of lives.

Sex roles, marriage, and family are good starting points for illustrating novelists' diverse lifestyles. Although gender spans a multitude of culturally specific attitudes and activities, the kind of marriage a man makes remains a principal index of his masculinity. The dominated or subordinate husband is, at root, *the* emasculated man regardless of the size of his biceps or the toughness of his vocabulary. Similarly, marriage and motherhood confirm femininity; the single, childless woman remains a sex-role enigma.

Male novelists may lean more toward a traditional sex role than their female counterparts, since such masculinity offers them a measure of domination sufficient to secure solitude and relegate everyday chores to their partners. Yet men who want to write full time are, at least early in their careers, hard put to fulfill the breadwinning responsibilities of traditional men. Such men may hold full-time jobs and write novels during their hours off the job, their sex roles excusing them from intense involvement with their wives and children. Those who seek full-time writing and traditional masculinity can also forego marriage until material circumstances allow for a traditional marriage without jeopardizing their writing. Male novelists have chosen from all of these options. Of particular interest are those who were thirty or older before marrying such as Conrad, Dos Passos, Ellison, Hardy, Hawthorne, Malamud, Twain, and Updike.[3]

Female novelists following the cultural mandate to marry and bear children sacrifice the conditions most favorable for writing.

Michele Murray observes,

How much energy and emotion go to tiny, fleeting facts of daily
life! How easy to sink beneath the weight of newspapers, laun-
dry, report cards, supermarkets, and all the rest.

I have accomplished nothing of what I intended. . . . The children
do not make up for that. They have their own destinies and I
have just a succession of days.

Besides the frustration of recurrent household chores, Murray
grappled with guilt over "how satisfactory a mother" she was
because of her "necessary hours at the typewriter."[4] Janet Burroway
reports similar experiences: the "life clock" of everyday life tugging at
her, the clock of its own every novel has, and her own psychological
clock measuring her "state of readiness." Burroway, who found those
clocks resisting synchronization, felt blessed when her children were
old enough to let her work any time, day or night. Before that, Burroway sometimes seized work time "with great violence."[5] Nadine
Gordimer also reports that when her children were young, she
secured her solitude "by being rather ruthless."
    Yet Gordimer nevertheless admits to having "put the person I
was in love with far ahead of my work."[6] As Doris Lessing observes,
"The number of women prepared to stand up for what they really
think, feel, experience with a man they are in love with is still small."[7]
In societies like ours, then, women working for pay outside the home
routinely leave that work for their "second shift" at home.[8] Women
whose gainful employment is home-based are likely to find their
"first shift" (paid work) often subordinated to the demands of that
second shift (unpaid domestic labor and child tending). Rebecca West
found that "traditional female things" and "family duties" kept her
from writing better and writing more.[9] Katherine Anne Porter
observes that females are "brought up with the notion of . . . giving
service to anyone who demands it." "I suppose," says Porter, "that's
why it has taken me twenty years to write this novel; it's been inter-
rupted by just anyone who could jimmy his way into my life." She
concludes, "I work when I'm *let*"[10] (emphasis added).
    By now, patterns along these lines have gained recognition in
the worlds of social science and feminist politics but have little affect-
ed public policy making and private home making. Less discussed is
the possibility that some creative women find relative advantages in
the typicalities of females' domestic situations. Joyce Carol Oates asks

whether the routines of housework are "numbing, or oddly comforting"; whether "the cyclical nature of domestic employment" might not address one's contemplative needs; whether "the sense that one has a place, a role . . . not to be challenged" might not also be advantageous.[11] Gordimer finds "the ordinary things of life" necessary to her well-being: "The ordinary action of taking a dress down to the dry cleaner's or spraying some plants infected with greenfly is a very sane and good thing to do. It brings one back, so to speak."[12]

Surely we now reject the historical mandate to lump all women into one psychologically undifferentiated mass. It may well be that some of them find the rhythms of family life compatible with those of writing. Alice Walker, for one, sees raising her daughter as "much more delightful and less distracting" than what many writers face.[13] Yet Walker's stance is comparative, not absolute. Perhaps, like Anne Tyler, she recognizes that "infinitely adapting" is "the way to slip gracefully through a choppy life of writing novels, plastering the dining room ceiling, and presiding at slumber parties."[14] Such women's experiences show how potent a vocation is—powerful enough in the long run to overcome demanding circumstances inimical to unfettered artistic activity.

In the end, the matters at hand concern how much choice and flexibility wives' and mothers' everyday circumstances usually allow them. Marriage, motherhood, and homemaking typically land women in a day-to-day situation where their places of work (both domestic and literary) and leisure merge; where their workdays have no reliable quitting time; where genuine vacations are rare; where their availability to family members, particularly young children, is taken for granted; where their emotional needs tend to come last.[15] As a result, some women probably abandon their vocations to the stuff of demanding everyday lives. Others may pursue more manageable genres than the novel. As Toni Cade Bambara found, "The short story is a piece of work. The novel is a way of life." Porter wrote each of her short stories in one sitting, for example, while Oates observes that "the act of writing even a short novel is an act of faith sustained through many months."[16]

On average, the differences between male and female novelists' domestic lives mean men's novel making enjoys greater cultural legitimacy, even when it engenders neglecting one's spouse and children. As Tom Clancy puts it, "Your spouse and children need not get in its way. . . . "[17] In practice, the family remains institutionalized along patriarchal lines lending legitimacy to such neglect independently of the value put on men's income-earning or culture-making activities.

Moreover, Gordimer's observation about the therapeutic payoffs of chasing "ordinary things" needs a big caveat before it rings true in practical terms. Doing mundane chores is, I suppose, beneficial for nearly everyone whose work catapults them out of the everyday world. Mowing the lawn or making a stew can reinstate one's familiar everyday realities. Yet what might be therapeutic when one seeks the reassurances of commonsense realities might be maddening when one is in the throes of writing and wants to remain so. Control matters. Gordimer herself says as much when she credits her husband with knowing when "isn't the time to ask" about mundane matters.[18] Even when their domestic situations are favorable for some wives' and mothers' writing, they seem less favorable than husbands' and fathers' situations on average. Wives and mothers (like Gordimer and Woolf) whose situations depart from domestic typicalities are likelier than their male counterparts to experience gratitude; they are also likelier to make a point of the advantage their domestic situations give them. Female novelists routinely struggle to establish and then feel grateful for domestic circumstances male novelists commonly take for granted.

Like their male counterparts, though, females can choose lifestyles that deviate from the cultural mandates anchoring femininity. Their most obvious option is to ignore the marital mandate and follow in the footsteps of Austen, Alcott, Ferber, and Welty. Another option is to forego motherhood, as did Mansfield, Rawlings, Rhys, Wharton, and Woolf. Other women are born or married to wealth that provides for servants; for example, Mary Roberts Rinehart, Edith Wharton, and Virginia Woolf. Yet those women sometimes experience ambivalence unlikely to infect the experiences of their male counterparts. Woolf is a case in point. With an inheritance large enough to provide a comfortable income, she was able "to hire the help that allowed her to devote the day to writing." But Woolf "could not justify the system that was liberating her"; her experiences conjoined "a need for reform and a sense of impotence."[19]

Like their male counterparts, female novelists also have the option of establishing themselves as writers, at least socially and psychologically, before marrying. Eliot, McCullers, Murdoch, and Porter pursued that course. Again, Woolf's case is illustrative. She "agreed to marry Leonard in part because he firmly supported her sense of vocation." The Woolfs' marriage was not without its strains, to say the least. It lasted, however, in large measure because of "his fundamental respect for her work and her gratitude for his support."[20] Women may also wait to write until the empty-nest stage of their family lives or until they are widows, as Kate Chopin did. Finally, some female writers pursue less obvious options; for example, Margaret Drabble lives apart from her husband Michael Holroyd, at least during the work week.[21]

Novelists' marriages and family lives run the gamut from stable conventionality to unstable unconventionality. Many remain married to their first spouses; for example, Auchincloss, Barthelme, Cheever, Fleming, Grey, Hawkes, Hawthorne, and Heller. Also included are Kipling, Malamud, Melville, Nabokov, Norris, Percy, Styron, and West. Yet others married three or more times, including Bellow, Boyle, Durrell, Hemingway, Kerouac, Mailer, McCarthy, O'Hara, Sinclair, and Steinbeck. For many, marriage brings chronic conflict—overt between the Fitzgeralds, the Lawrences, and the various Hemingways; covert between Sylvia Plath and Ted Hughes. Harmonious or not, the marital arrangements between novelists and their spouses vary enormously. One sometimes finds marriages where the nonwriting spouse slavishly serves his or her novelist-spouse. Jessie Conrad, Charlotte Shaw, and John Middleton Murry illustrate such commitment, as does Leonard Woolf whose support of Virginia's vocation "included reading and commenting on all her works, acting as her literary agent, and making sure that her regular writing time was free from trivial interruptions and distractions."[22] Some novelists' marriages allow for extramarital affairs or intense cross-sex friendships: Thackeray and his friend Jane Brookfield, Dickens and his mistress Ellen Ternan, Arnold Bennet and his mistress Dorothy Cheston, the mother of his only child. Lawrence Sterne was notorious for his philandering. According to Jeffrey Meyers, John Middleton Murry "was the most serious threat to the D. H. Lawrences' marriage—both in 1916 when Lawrence was attracted to him and in 1923 when Frieda was."[23]

Homosexuality is hardly unknown among novelists, for example, Butler, Capote, Cather, Forster, Gide, Mansfield, Wilde. Lesbians' and gay men's intimacies mirror all the glories and pains of the marital institution. Alice B. Toklas and Gertrude Stein are illustrative. Less widely known is Ida Baker who "worshipped Katherine [Mansfield], quite literally devoted her life to her and was at once lover, friend, nurse, slave, and scapegoat."[24] In both American and British society, pervasive homophobia exacts its longstanding toll regardless of the positive or negative character of any specific same-sex relationship. As Gore Vidal observes, "fag bashing" is "going on all the time. They never let up."[25] Like gay men and lesbians, straight women incur greater penalties than straight men for defying the norms of heterosexual, double-standards sexuality. Rebecca West, who bore her and H. G. Wells's son Anthony West in 1914, says "people disapproved of H. G.

so much less than they did of me, and they were very horrible to me, and it was very hard."[26] Even when less severe norms are at work or fame chastens people's scorn, women incur greater costs than men do. The dramatic variability in writers' domestic arrangements and sexual lives demonstrates that novel making dictates no specific paths along these lines. Moreover, there appears to be no reliable crossover between these aspects of novelists' everyday lives and the experiences portrayed in their novels. That circumstance is unsurprising, given that domesticity is widely available for observations about how widely its shape and feel vary.

Novelists' educational attainments are no less variable than their domestic lives. Some dropped out of high school or ended their schooling with a high school diploma; for example, Baldwin, Capote, Hammett, Hemingway, Howells, Nin, Twain, and Wright. Many got university training or baccalaureate degrees; for example, Cather, Clancy, Dos Passos, Dreiser, Ellison, Fleming, Gissing, Hardy, Hawkes, Hawthorne, and Huxley. Also included are Kerouac, Koestler, McCarthy, Nabokov, Norris, Pynchon, Rawlings, Salinger, Steinbeck, Styron, Tarkington, Wells, Vonnegut, and West. Other novelists pursued graduate or professional education: Bellow and Vonnegut in anthropology; William Burroughs, Joyce, and Stein in medicine; Murdoch in philosophy. At Oxford University, Heller was a Fulbright Scholar; Morley and Warren, Rhodes Scholars. Mailer studied for a year at the Sorbonne; Updike at the Ruskin School of Drawing and Fine Arts, Oxford; Welty at the Columbia University School of Advertising. Many novelists hold master's degrees, including Amis, Barth, Buck, Forster, Heller, Malamud, O'Connor, Roth, Sayers, Sterne, Warren, Wilder, and Wolfe. Jerzy Kosinski has master's degrees in history and in political science. Other novelists hold nondoctoral professional degrees. Alger got his divinity degree at Harvard Divinity School; besides earning his master's degree, Sterne was ordained a deacon. Auchincloss graduated from law school, as did Galsworthy, Stribling, and Wister. Arthur Conan Doyle earned an M.D. degree, as did Maugham, Percy, and Smollett. Zane Grey received his D.D.S. from the University of Pennsylvania. The Ph.D. itself is no rarity among novelists. Both John Gardner and Bobbie Ann Mason hold theirs in literature.[27]

Whatever their educational backgrounds, few writers find their work financially rewarding from the outset, so most fledgling novelists must pursue other work or cope with poverty. Many, particularly before high-stakes publishing, continue that course throughout their lives. Yet full-time writing itself often entails activities like interviews, television appearances, lectures, and autographing sessions that make for good business as much as fulfill responsibilities to the reading public. Full-time novelists often differ less dramatically from their employed counterparts than might be supposed. Among novelists, the occupational diversity is stunning. Nin was an artist's and fashion model; Sherwood Anderson worked at various factory jobs; Barthelme was a museum director; Edgar Rice Burroughs owned a stationery store, worked as a railroad policeman, managed an office, and then moved into publishing and journalism. Erskine Caldwell worked as a poolroom attendant, gun runner, hack driver, sodajerk, waiter, cook, bodyguard, stagehand, lecture-tour manager, store clerk, professional football player, script writer, war correspondent, newspaper reporter, and editor. William Burroughs worked as a bartender and as a private detective; Hammett, as a detective for the Pinkerton Agency, a clerk, a stevedore, and an advertising manager. Steinbeck worked as a painter, chemist, caretaker of an estate, and foreign correspondent. Besides his years as a river pilot, Mark Twain worked as a printer's apprentice and as a goldminer. For a while Wells worked as an apprentice draper; also as an apprentice chemist. Yerby was a laboratory technician at Ford Motor Company and a magnaflux inspector for an aircraft company. Durrell played jazz piano, raced cars, and sold real estate; he also held British government positions in Cyprus, Cairo, and Alexandria. Clancy was an insurance agent, and Ellison worked as a dental assistant, receptionist, jazz trumpeter, and photographer.[28]

Although he had no university training, Erle Stanley Gardner studied law under various California lawyers, passed the state bar examination, and practiced law there. Hardy was an architect; Hawthorne, a surveyor. Kerouac was a railroad brakeman; also, a fire lookout for the U.S. Agricultural Service. Lawrence worked for a manufacturer of surgical appliances. Besides working in Malaysia as an education officer for the British government, Burgess composed music. For a while Faulkner was Oxford's general repairperson; he also gave golf lessons. In Pascagoula, he did some rum-running and put in time on the shrimp trawlers.[29] Before his first novel was published when he was 45, Fleming had worked as a banker, stock broker, and journalist. West managed a hotel. Alcott worked as a seamstress; also, as a nurse. Like the Brontës and Lawrence, she also taught school. Other teaching novelists include Cather, Joyce, Melville, and Wilder.

Many novelists have been professors: Barth, Bellow, Malamud, Roth, McCarthy, Hawkes, Morris, Warren, and Nabokov. Amis, Buck, Ellison, Forster, Heller, Murdoch, Porter, Singer, Stafford, and Wilder have also taught, at least for short periods, in colleges and universities. Similarly, professional writing attracts novelists in large numbers. Defoe and Thackeray were journalists for a time, as were Alger, Bennet, Boyle, both Burroughs, Dreiser, Ferber, Gissing, Howells, Koestler, Mailer, Marquand, Mason, Norris, O'Hara, Porter, Rawlings, Steinbeck, and Twain. Shaw did music, art, and drama criticism for the *Saturday Review;* Agee was a respected film critic; McCarthy, a drama critic. At one time Cozzens was an associate editor at *Fortune;* Heller, a promotion manager at *McCall's;* Mailer, a co-founding editor of the *Village Voice* and a columnist for *Esquire.* Pynchon was an editorial writer for Boeing Aircraft Corporation; Sayers, a copywriter for an advertising agency; Vonnegut, a public relations specialist for General Electric. From the 1930s, script writing also attracted novelists. Faulkner spent over four years as a Hollywood screenwriter. The studios pursued him after he sold *Sanctuary* for film production. Similarly, the purchase of *Miss Lonelyhearts* generated interest in West. Agee, Fitzgerald, and Huxley worked as screenwriters; so did Capote, Dos Passos, Hilton, Mailer, Erskine Caldwell, Anthony Powell, and John O'Hara.

Their involvements in various forms of paid work do bear connections with novelists' fictions, though no specific form of employment is apparently conducive to their writing. Obvious positions include Hammett's detective work, Durrell's foreign-service services in "exotic" countries, and Erle Stanley Gardner's experiences with law. Also fairly obvious are those professor-novelists who write "college novels" from a faculty member's point of view or who people their fictions with academic intellectuals, for example, Barth and Bellow. In parallel fashion Gardner's professorship in medieval and Renaissance English literature makes a work like *Grendl* profoundly accessible to his imagination.

Less obvious is the impact of writers' diverse jobs on the scope and tone of their novels. Work that is tedious, sweaty, disreputable, or dead-end is capable of extending not only novelists' knowledge but also their sympathies. Woolf, for one, sensed that. Early on, she "specialized in the art of noticing." She also read incessantly and enjoyed the benefit of living among creative, intellectual individuals capable of enlarging her insights. Yet Woolf felt trapped within the comfortable confines of her social class. "She envied writers who had somehow managed to get beyond the limits of their situation" as well as "writers who had managed to rise in the world (like Dickens or Lawrence) and were not required to sink to expand the range of their sympathies." Nonetheless, Woolf turned that limitation to good purpose by making "the image of one's class as a prison . . . one of the central metaphors of her work."[30] Historically, female writers confined to the home or restricted to few types of employment pursued courses parallel to Woolf's. Here, then, a social form shaping many specifics of people's everyday lives exhibits considerable crossover, both direct and indirect, into novelists' creative work. To the extent that people's schooling governs their access to various types of employment, their education at least indirectly affects novelists' fictions, too.

At this point, my concern lies less with the autobiographical dimension of fiction (see pages 48–49) than with the relationship between the social forms most shaping novelists' everyday lives and the social forms portrayed in their novels. "Autobiographical," a problematic adjective, usually connotes specific situations or events. What I am getting at has less to do with discrete experiences than with how social structure impinges on individuals' streams of experience over time and across situations. Working in positions less prestigious, comfortable, and autonomous—broadly, less middle-class—than those writers typically enjoy provides a taste of social structure zestier than most imaginations could conjure up or, for that matter, what most sociological monographs or mass-media productions cook up. Such experiences enlarge the worlds one can portray realistically and sympathetically, even if no specifics of those experiences show up in the novel.

Needless to say, one can argue that breadth of experience generally empowers imaginative writers. An Emily Dickinson or a Jane Austen shows the hazards of pushing that generalization too far, however. In the final analysis my contentions concern scope and tone, not power as such. Imaginative writers whose everyday lives remain confined to a picket-fenced yard on the social landscape most assuredly can write powerful fictions. Yet the span of their fictional social structures and the range of social types portrayed effectively tend to exhibit relative narrowness. Thus, a broad connection obtains between writers' everyday lives as conditioned by the occupational structure and their fictional worlds as conditioned by their imaginations. Since occupational structures are commonly sex-biased, this connection implies a linkage between the shape of fictions and their author's sex.

In fact, as preceding paragraphs suggest, gender will surface at many junctures of this study. Because it correlates strongly with individuals' occupational opportunities and experiences, their domestic responsibilities and privileges, and their effective freedom of choice and movement, gender is the single most consequential arm of social structure reaching into the lives of writers and prospective writers. Many, perhaps most, sociologists incline toward rejecting that premise, arguing that social class is at least as consequential. That stance ignores the practical connections between gender and social class. Granted, except for their overrepresentation among poor people and their underrepresentation among elite decision makers, women appear to occupy the American class structure in much the same ways men do. That appearance is deceptive, however. Often, a woman's class position involves a profound degree of economic dependence on her husband or, in the higher classes, a practical measure of lifestyle dependence on him. Moreover, if she and her husband are parents, divorce is likely to make her the sole reliable source of financial (as well as physical and emotional) support for their children, thereby cancelling out the apparent equality of the situation where she is as capable of comfortable self-support as he is. Thus, membership in the same social class differs existentially for most women and men, underscoring the singular significance of gender as an emblem of social structure.

In any case, their marriages, educations, and extraliterary work mark novelists as a heterogeneous grouping whose work dictates no specific form of everyday life. Thus far, however, the data fall short of showing typical or atypical lifestyles, since the overall *pattern* of participation makes a novelist's everyday life typical or atypical. I have sampled some of the pertinent diversity in writers' everyday lives, but only biographies reveal full-fledged lifestyles. Such data on lifestyles would yield four types of novelists, considered in cultural terms.

The last chapter laid preliminary grounds for describing the novelist in Simmelian terms, that is, as a social type whose form of life is distinctive and whose relationships bear the practical imprints of that form. As we proceed, the novelist as a social type will assume more definite shape. Yet the novelist is also a cultural type. Making novels, the individual "closes the gap between the self and the object," making it seem as if the imaginative object "were determined only by the nature of the self." Novel making engenders an "emancipation from the stuffy dull pressure of life and the expansion of the self . . . into the objects whose reality would otherwise violate it." Aesthetic projects give "consciousness a free play, a portentous extension of all possibilities without violation or deterioration by reality." Thus does Simmel recognize that "every step toward reality" represents in some sense a deterioration of aesthetic mastery.[31] Intrusions of reality—of the lived experiences in a novelist's past or the existential circumstances of his or her present—shift the novelist's cultural position.

Those intrusions are unavoidable but variable; that is, the imagination *always* reflects the circumstances of its own formation *to some extent*. Like all other activities of consciousness, the imagination takes its nurture and form from what Simmel calls *objective culture*—all the contents "expressed and formed, what exists ideally and what has real force, the complex of which constitutes the cultural capital of an era." Yet individuals experience only part of the objective culture available to them. *Subjective culture* concerns that fraction; it is the "degree, both extensively and intensively, [to which] individuals have a share in the contents of objective culture."[32]

In Simmel's terms, aesthetic mastery means augmenting the objective culture of one's society—that is, contributing to its contents —by imaginatively bursting the boundaries of one's subjective culture. In practical terms, that means transcending one's lifestyle. How so? Beyond childhood learning, individuals acquire subjective culture by reading anything from comics to Shakespeare, attending religious services, going to movies, plays, concerts, and museums, watching television, participating in civic organizations, and so forth. The major determinants of one's participation in such activities are level of schooling and type of occupation, the same factors powerfully conditioning lifestyle. In fact, subjective culture and lifestyle are tightly interwoven. Expecting novelists to transcend the boundaries of their subjective culture thus means expecting that their novels will do more than refract their lifestyles. Literature requires imaginative transformations of what has been or might be experienced as real, and it demands some measure of confrontation with the conceivable if those transformations are to take awesome shape.

It takes no literary critic to know that many novels fail to meet such conditions. Many broadly refract their creators' lifestyles, giving expression to their subjective culture rather than defeating some of its limits. It is empirically indefensible, then, to regard novelists as a single cultural type. They occupy a continuum of cultural types; thus, let us consider the four types of novelists mentioned earlier.

First come writers whose lifestyles and fictions appear to correspond or at least resonate. One might label them *literary chroniclers*, since their novels chronicle the taken-for-granted world they themselves apparently inhabit in their everyday lives. Usually pictured as wealthy and glamorous, Barbara Cartland is one such writer. Her romances resonate with the lifestyle her readers readily infer from bookjacket photographs, gossip columns, and magazine feature stories. Second are novelists who portray worlds stripped of some of their taken for grantedness. Between their lifestyles and their fictions is a gap their imaginations leap. Because they live ordinarily and imagine extraordinarily, these writers might be called *literary artists*. Jane Austen fits in here. Third are novelists whose lifestyles are atypical, suggesting they have grounds for seeing beneath what most people take for granted in their daily lives. Yet these writers fail to communicate such visions in their novels, instead constructing stories about "ordinary" events and people beyond the boundaries of their own lives. Thus, they might be called *literary reporters*. Marjorie Kinnan Rawlings comes to mind here. Last come novelists whose lifestyles are atypical and whose fictions express the debunking stances their lifestyles imply. These novelist are *literary intellectuals;* for example, Gertrude Stein, Virginia Woolf, or Norman Mailer.

Such a typology implies research strategies that remain sociological without losing touch with literature as a world. As the next chapter suggests, adding language to the picture would make the typology sufficient for guiding research into how fiction and fact intersect, how the variety in literature relates to the variety of everyday life, and how the world of literature and the world of everyday life impinge on each other. Such a typology would also further illuminate the vocation and the craft of fiction.

The Literary Imagination and Everyday Life

More than any other artistic or intellectual grouping, novelists disclose the imagination as a social form. Their works often show imaginations at work as characters juggle various possibilities within their socially structured situations. Their thoughts, relationships, projects, and outcomes expose the pleasures and pains anchored in the possible.

Sometimes novels comment less implicitly on the imagination. In *Emma*, the narrator implies the meaning of imagination: "A mind lively and at ease can do with seeing nothing, and can see nothing that does not answer."[33] In *The Abortion*, the narrator implies the imagination's continuous activity by observing that a character's "imagination had just gone into full gallop."[34] In *Henderson the Rain King*, Dahfu the African king sums up what most novels imply: "All human accomplishment has this same origin, identically. Imagination is a force of nature. Is this not enough to make a person full of ecstasy? Imagination, imagination, imagination! It converts to actual. It sustains, it alters, it redeems!"[35]

Novelists' lives themselves show that the imagination is deeply social. Formed out of past experiences and responsive to current circumstances, the imagination negotiates a course that furthers individuality without necessarily jostling social conventions. Novelists' imaginations thrive under social regimes ranging from conventional to bohemian to rebellious. The nurturance of a novelist's imagination ordains no specific lifestyle; and no single lifestyle, in and of itself, feeds or deprives the imagination. The imagination, like the self, takes shape within whatever configuration of social forms impinges on the individual. If novelists' personal histories shape their fictions, their novels refract the imagination describing some of its own social formation. Any autobiographical elements novels contain imply that the imagination is rooted in the factic sphere despite its devotion to the fictive sphere, and novels with autobiographical elements are common.

Earlier, Dickens, Eliot, and Miller received passing attention for their autobiographical novels. More than Dickens's or Miller's novels, Eliot's illustrate the span of convergences "autobiographical" covers with reference to novels. *The Mill on the Floss* portrayed many of her childhood experiences, and "Clerical Scenes" and *Adam Bede* portrayed her experiences clearly enough that some of her family and friends recognized characters in those works. In addition, the plot for *Adam Bede* came from a story she had heard from an aunt.[36] More generally, Eliot left distinct traces of her self in many of her protagonists, mostly as an "exacting and questioning and baffled presence."[37] Her female characters were much like herself.

Many novels are patently autobiographical, at least for informed readers. First novels often tend that way; for example, *The Way of All Flesh* or *Sons and Lovers*.[38] Similarly, *The Secret Agent, Ulysses, Night and Day, Women in Love, A Farewell to Arms,* and *Tender Is the Night* are autobiographical. Each is its writer's "attempt to integrate life and art and to resolve the crucial conflict between domestic and creative fulfillment."[39] Such novels express their creator's commonsense experiences *as well as* their imaginative experiences. *Jane Eyre*, for example, has autobiographical elements but also takes shape around Brontë's inclinations toward the Gothic novel.[40]

George Meredith's *The Ordeal of Richard Feverel* was partly a reaction to his wife's desertion of him and their child.[41] Woolf's relationship with Vita Sackville-West was "the mainspring" of *Orlando,* and Mr. Ramsey in *To the Lighthouse* "is Leslie Stephen [Woolf's father], at one remove."[42] *Ulysses* is strongly autobiographical; Joyce's letters to his wife Nora show "how closely Bloom's experiences with and reveries about Molly are based on [Joyce's] own sexual relationship with Nora."[43] Waugh gave the main character of *Brideshead* his "age, his years at Oxford, and his career there" as well as the same relationship with his family, the same failed marriage, and an artistic career similar to his own.[44] *Peyton Place* is a "fictionalized account of [Metalious's] community" and the high school where her husband taught.[45] Hilton modeled Mr. Chips after his father, a London school-master. In *The Painted Bird*, Kosinski depicts a boy who was mute for three years, about three years less than Kosinski's own mute period. Bellow's Herzog is, like his creator, a Canadian-born professor suffering the collapse of his second marriage.

The weight of autobiographical elements in plot or characterization is often difficult to determine. Sometimes the author's experiences enter in mostly as an insider's viewpoint. Conrad's maritime experiences provide him the viewpoint important to his novels, just as their experiences in Hollywood provided Fitzgerald (*The Last Tycoon*), Mailer (*Deer Park*), and West (*The Day of the Locust*) the insider's viewpoint for their "Hollywood novels."[46] Similarly, Hollywood gave Faulkner the experiences that make *Pylon* and *The Wild Palms* less unlikely for the novelist from Mississippi.[47] More difficult to assess is the insider's viewpoint deriving from experiences as complex as an unhappy marriage. Yet Meyers argues that Conrad's major themes "related to" his miserable marriage; that Fitzgerald's *Save Me the Waltz* and *Tender Is the Night* "refract" his disastrous marriage; that Hemingway's four marriages are "significantly refracted" in his work.[48] Similarly, Defoe's two bankruptcies may underlie his fictional emphasis on economic security.[49] Albert Guerard claims that without their wartime experiences Hawkes and Kosinski "would hardly have written *The Cannibal* and *The Painted Bird*, as Kurt Vonnegut would not (had he not have experienced the Dresden firebombing and its aftermath) have written *Slaughterhouse Five*."[50] Here the autobiographical aspects are dense configurations of intense experiences dovetailing with themes rather than specific incidents or characters.

At some indeterminate point novels cease being autobiographical in any meaningful sense, even though a writer's biography can never stand wholly cut off from the worlds he or she invents. A novelist's experiences of actual individuals and events include more than perceiving, remembering, judging, and doubting. Novelists court their imaginations. They think about their imaginations, remember past imaginative experiences (often in notebooks or diaries), judge the expressions of their imaginations, anticipate imaginative experiences, and so forth. Thereby, they step into the world of literature where expression holds sway, where concern with possibilities moves individuality to its most imaginative forms.

The world of everyday life recedes when individuals seek those meaning-compatible experiences. Although it loses its forceful accent of reality, everyday life nonetheless supplies the most provocative experiences imaginative individuals confront when writing novels.

Inescapably, it challenges novelists—sometimes through their own current preoccupations or distractions, often because of their own past experiences, always as the scaffolding of any imaginable world. Thus, the worlds of literature and of everyday life intersect in myriad ways. The variability of those intersections dramatizes the profundity of the imagination, the diversity of lifestyles among novelists, and the multiple possibilities underlying any actual world of everyday life. Wordsmiths and world makers, novelists are guided by imaginations that originate in the world of everyday life but liberate themselves elsewhere.

❦ Novels and Everyday Life

But if you dremp hit, hit can't be a lie case ain't nobody there to tale hit to you.

William Faulkner, *The Unvanquished*

Among Anthony Trollope's forty-seven novels *The Way We Live Now* is probably his single most widely read.[1] The novel portrays a world of shifting uncertainties spawned by the spirit of commercialism and the ideology of possessive individualism.[2] Its depiction of social change shows how literature subverts reification and thus enlivens culture.

Three types of places predominate in *The Way We Live Now:* the office, the club, and the parlor. The office is a male preserve where Melmotte, the mysterious financier, organizes his avarice, forges documents, and broods over his outcomes. In the Beargarden Club sons of the peerage and gentry share vague misgivings about their futures and less vague ambivalence toward their families. Their gambling at the club makes them mock businesspeople. The parlor belongs to women concerned about their own or their daughters' marriage prospects. Money, gain, and security inform their talk about marriage; the women oversee a virtual marriage market. Like the office and the club, the parlor anchors interactions governed by competition and the desire for gain. The three types of places are analogues of one another.

Trollope's portrayal of the parlor contrasts so sharply with traditional imagery that the women in the novel set its tone. His characterization of the females hinges on how much each of them reifies her social world, her roles, and her identity. Together, Lady Carbury, Hetta Carbury, Georgiana Longstaffe, and Marie Melmotte illustrate how reification stymies people trying to make sense of their lives.

Lady Carbury, the focal character of *The Way We Live Now*, experiences most of her decisions as inescapable offshoots of the maternal role. Lady Carbury also objectifies other people by treating them as mere role players. Hetta her daughter must live with her until she mar-

ries, and Hetta must, of course, marry "to procure a fitting mainte-
nance"³ and advance her family's interests. Lady Carbury objectifies
her son Felix as her most precious status symbol, a "baronet, entitled to
special consideration because of his position and rank,—because also
of his intention to marry the great heiress of the day" (p. 136). She
invokes Felix as an excuse for her mischoices and as an emblem of a
better future. Lady Carbury herself works hard to advance her interests. Her "diligence in making and fostering useful friendships had
been unwearied" (p. 10). She says "pretty things to everybody" and
tolerates mistreatment "if only anything were to be gained by passing
it over" (pp. 92, 243). Despite her utilitarianism Lady Carbury does
finally overcome the stasis of her situation by marrying Mr. Bourne
who undercuts her reifying by loving her for herself.

Hetta Carbury reifies more than her mother. In the roles of daughter and lover she acts strictly along socially prescribed lines. She sub-
mits to her mother out of a sense of duty and enacts her rigid ideas
about romantic love with determined exactitude. Even in her solitary
moments she squelches "inappropriate" feelings (p. 680). Yet Hetta
does eventually "feel herself capable of throwing propriety and delica-
cy to the winds" (p. 727). Such feelings eventuate, however, not because
she curtails her reifying but because her fiercest objectifications conflict:
Hetta the dutiful daughter and Hetta the proper lover collide.

More than either Lady Carbury or Hetta, Georgiana Longstaffe
straddles the traditional and the modern worlds. Although her
awareness of social change weakens her objectifications as reliable
rules of thumb, Georgiana does tailor her expectations of others to the
fit of her family's high social status. Her status concerns blind her to
her options, narrow her interest in society to marriage and money,
and keep her dependent on her parents. Georgiana pursues status so
zealously that she knows no way of life but self-interested exchanges
meant to advance an objectified self.

Marie Melmotte reifies the social world only slightly. Trollope
introduces her as a person "now tempted from time to time to con-
template her own happiness and her own condition" (p. 31). By the
time she rejects the suitor her father favors, Marie senses she must
mastermind her own life (pp. 200, 228). When she finally recognizes
Felix does not love her, Marie does determine to be her own mistress
(p. 670) by embracing the choices available to her. Similarly, Marie
refuses to treat others as mere role players. Regarding the social
world as an aggregate of acting individuals, she rebels against her
father not because he fails in his role but because he fails as a human
being. Although she objectifies herself and Felix as lovers, Marie

largely succeeds as an individual participating in a social world fraught with ambiguity and change.

Trollope's novel shows the destructiveness of reifying the social world and its participants. That Lady Carbury seeks a career in "Literature" is the major irony he constructs in peopling this fictional world with characters distinguished by their propensity to reify the worlds they help to constitute.

Varieties of Fiction: The Portrayal of Worlds

In the world of everyday life reification is common. Reification means experiencing the human-made world as other than a human achievement, as when people experience a class structure or the nuclear family as features of a "natural" world, or the only one possible for human beings.[4] Such individuals experience themselves and others as objects; they lack a sense of agency and an awareness of choices. They fail to feel the human will at work beneath the history and institutions making their world unique. Rather, they experience a deterministic, mechanistic world where people are puppets.

Reification precludes a keen sense of history.[5] The world seems fragmented or atomized; one's own social circles seem disconnected from the larger world of one's contemporaries. People often focus on the quantity rather than the quality of their experiences, tending to analyze rather than synthesize them. Utility and efficiency become paramount concerns.[6] Reification is thus taken for grantedness with a vengeance—an habitual inclination to disattend the culturally arbitrary and humanly constituted nature of the arrangements structuring one's daily life. As I have argued elsewhere,[7] taken for grantedness means prereflectively applying the linguistic types provided by one's culture as if those types represented necessities, not conventions. Taken for grantedness is essential to a familiar world; it is a presupposition of all projects in the commonsense world. Without it, individuals would experience the vertigo of relentless questioning about "reality." Reification is an extreme antidote to such vertigo—an overdose of taken for grantedness, so to speak. It snuffs out the experience of human agency (both one's own and others'), transforming mundane familiarity into a product not of mutual orientations and joint undertakings but of natural forces beyond the reach of human intervention.

By contrast, the novel is a debunking genre. It shows the relativity institutionalized in every world; it illuminates the world-making force of the human will served by language and conditioned by the past; it suspends some of the familiarity informing everyday life; it looks beneath official facades, commonplace ideologies, and stubborn stereotypes. Debunking counteracts reification; it is a defamiliarizing activity. Although novelists may not *aim* to debunk actual worlds by creating fictional ones, their works show people constituting worlds, relationships, and selves. Storytellers expose world making in their world of making believe.

The overwhelming majority of novels debunk some world that could actually exist or that readers take as actually existing in some form. Most often, novelists swim against the tide of reification through characterization, as Trollope's contrasting characterizations of Lady Carbury, Hetta, Georgiana, and Marie illustrate. Frequently, too, novelists' characters or narrators implicitly inveigh against reification:

> As long as we have a man's body, we play our Vanities upon it, surrounding it with humbug and ceremonies, laying it in state, and packing it up in gilt nails and velvet; and we finish our duty by placing over it a stone, written all over with lies.

> I have been looking at the marriage service in the Prayer-book, and it seems to me very humiliating that a giver-away should be required at all. . . . Bless your exalted views of woman, O Churchman!

> The routine of the day seemed a fiction to which he condescended, as if he were playing in private theatricals. The characters were assumed, and not very well done; yet, you must pretend to be in dead earnest, till you actually forgot that you were not.

> There is certain atavistic strain in women—and often in men, too —that makes them admire physical bigness and easy strength.

> Until some gang succeeds in putting the world in a strait jacket, its definition is possibility.[8]

Another debunking device is to imply how people use language to constitute their worlds and selves. The device goes back to Cervantes who had Don Quixote continually chiding Sancho Panza for abusing language. James Joyce and William Faulkner provide further examples. In *A Portrait of the Artist as a Young Man*, Stephen Daedalus often reflects on words as leaky vessels incapable of securing the weight of experience.

> Words which he did not understand he said over and over to himself till he had learned them by heart; and through them he had glimpses of the real world about him.

His own consciousness of language was ebbing from his brain and trickling into the very words themselves which set to band and disband themselves in wayward rhythms....

The language in which we are speaking is his before it is mine. How different are the words HOME, CHRIST, ALE, MASTER, on his lips and on mine! I cannot speak or write these words without unrest of spirit. His language, so familiar and so foreign, will always be for me an acquired speech, I have not made or accepted its words.[9]

Faulkner's novels show that people's words constitute the vital stuff of life, but life eludes language. In *As I Lay Dying*, Addie shapes such understandings for herself.

I knew that that word was like the others; just a shape to fill a lack....

I learned that words are no good; that words don't ever fit even what they are trying to say at.

We had to use one another by words like spiders dangling by their mouths from a beam.

Words go straight up in a thin line, quick and harmless, and how terribly doing goes along the earth, clinging to it, so that after a while the two lines are too far apart for the same person to straddle from one to the other....[10]

The Sound and the Fury offers similar insights.

They all talked at once, their voices insistent and contradicting and impatient, making of unreality a possibility, then a probability, then an incontrovertible fact, as people will when their desires become words.[11]

Although most novelists use debunking devices, some novelists do construct static worlds where people play roles while history sleeps. Such novels usually focus on a relationship or two detached from a complex world and destined for a happy outcome. Mass-marketed romances are particularly likely to reify their characters' worlds. The reader knows little about their problem-ridden lovers; the characters are largely automatons. Yet the small proportion of novels exhibiting reification suggests nothing about what differentiates the thousands of novels that debunk. Do all those novels relate to everyday life in the same ways? When Irving Wallace and Saul Bellow take flight from reification, do they fly at the same altitude? Instinctively, most would say no. In fact, Wallace's and Bellow's novels stand in different relationships to the commonsense world.

My findings about the different relationships between novels and everyday life derive from a sizable sample of novels. After drawing broad boundaries around the world of literature, I set out to read and reread enough novels of different types and periods to test various principles and give them experiential import. Between 1980 and 1983, I used a fairly systematic method of choosing novels representative of diverse critical reactions, appeal to different audiences, and publication dates spanning the past two centuries. That method put 190 novels on my reading list. Later, I added other novels—more recent bestsellers, for instance. These I chose mostly by following my own tastes or responding to reviewers' enthusiasm for particular works, for example, Louise Erdrich's *Love Medicine*, Tom Wolfe's *Bonfire of the Vanities*, or Anne Tyler's *Dinner at the Homesick Restaurant*. Those selections brought my total sample to 339 novels. (In the bibliography an asterisk designates each of those works.)

My more systematic selections rested on lists of bestsellers, Pulitzer Prize winners, and Nobel Prize winners alongside virtually all the nineteenth- and twentieth-century British and American novelists whose works appear in literary anthologies intended for classrooms. I also included a few novelists because of their subcultural appeal; for example, Richard Brautigan.

For sampling best-selling novels, I relied heavily on Alice Payne Hackett's *70 Years of Best Sellers: 1895-1965*. From her lists of the top ten bestsellers in fiction each year during that period, I took the top two plus those from the remaining eight whose author (Frank Norris, for example) or whose title remains well known (*The High and the Mighty*, for example). Given those criteria, my list included 278 novels. From that list, I read 76 novels; I selected 65 randomly. The other eleven represent a 50 percent random sample of those novels that had sold more than four million copies at the time of Hackett's research. For best-selling novels published after the period Hackett covers, my sampling was less systematic. Although I included some bestsellers I had read while doing preliminary research, I mostly used bestsellers lists from *Publishers Weekly* to cover the post-1965 period.

Pulitzer Prizes for specific literary works have been awarded since 1918. By 1980, fifty-two novelists had received the prize. (Some years it went to short story writers.) I took a 20 percent random sample of those novels that had won their authors Pulitzer Prizes prior to 1981, adding 10 novels to my sample. In addition, I sampled the works of Nobel Prize winners. That award recognizes outstanding overall contributions to world literature. First given in 1901, the Nobel Prize went to nine British and American novelists through 1978: Rudyard Kipling, Sinclair Lewis, John Galsworthy, Pearl Buck, William Faulkner, Ernest Hemingway, John Steinbeck, Saul Bellow, and Isaac Bashevis Singer. My sample includes at least one work by each of them. I selected the remaining novels mostly because of the attention scholars of popular culture give them, for example, Janet Dailey's romances.

My aim was to ensure that my final set of novels had no obvious gaps within the temporal and national limits I had set; namely, nineteenth- and twentieth-century British-American works. I aimed for range, not randomness. Thus, the overlap among lists did not trouble me. Nor did the introduction of novels nonrandomly selected. All in all, the sample serves my purposes.

A variety of circumstances accounts for including multiple works by some novelists. Sometimes stature alone justified examining more than one of a novelist's works, for example, George Eliot, Charles Dickens, William Faulkner. In other instances, the novelist had written so many bestselling works that more than one of them was drawn into the random sample of bestsellers, for example, Graham Greene, Irving Wallace. Then, too, some novelists or novels appeared on several of the lists I used. Generally, I included a second or third novel by a given author if my system turned it up.

Contrary to my expectations—and, perhaps, to the common wisdom—the lists overlapped a lot. Some novels awarded Pulitzer Prizes also appeared on Hackett's lists of bestsellers, such as *Arrowsmith, The Bridge of San Luis Rey, The Good Earth, The Store, The Grapes of Wrath, The Caine Mutiny, Advise and Consent, The Reivers.* Moreover, the authors of some of those same novels won the Nobel Prize for Literature, for example, Lewis, Buck, Steinbeck, Faulkner. More generally, the bestsellers lists offer more than a few esteemed names. Stephen Crane, Ellen Glasgow, Joseph Conrad, Willa Cather, and George Santayana wrote best-selling novels, as did D. H. Lawrence, Vladimir Nabokov, Woolf, and Bellow. Thus, bestsellers lists offer considerable cultural range.

The novels in my final sample fell into four broad categories, as we will see in Table 1. The fourfold typology is preliminary. Within each category I suppose, however, that the novels cited do include those capable of specifying the boundaries of each category. Testing that supposition remains a matter for future research. Similarly, most of my classifications rest on careful first readings. How placement might shift with later readings is a matter I will pursue in later research.

Broadly, I have found that how debunking novelists use language typically determines the relationship between their novels and everyday life. Language centers every world. How and why people use it thus differentiates worlds. As written works, novels stand at a remove from everyday life where speech reigns. Yet some novelists extend that distance more than others by making their language decidedly expressive. As "Editor B" puts it in *Giles Goat-Boy,*

> It is everywhere agreed that the best language is that which disappears in the telling, so that nothing stands between the reader and the matter of the book. But this author has maintained . . . that language *is* the matter of his books, as much as anything else, and for that reason ought to be "splendrously musicked out" . . . .[12]

Our strongest novelists override the apparent conflict between language that disappears in the telling and language that aesthetically asserts itself. Nabokov's *Lolita* comes to mind, as does Hawkes's *The Blood Oranges.* Yet novels exuding expressive language and novels largely foregoing such language differ only in degree. Broadly, that difference manifests itself in how novelists describe sensations, how lively and frequent their metaphors are, how much lyricism stamps their narratives, and how much economy they bring to characterization.

Most novels offer a few colorfully described sensations; others offer a rainbow of such descriptions. Consider Faulkner's "salt-colored sky" or Pynchon's "one cigarette, stubbed out before its time in an exasperated fishhook."[13] Welty points to "a color delicate as watermelon juice"; Dos Passos, to a "winking belly-button"; Nabokov, to Lolita's "halter with little to halt."[14] Expressive language is also metaphorical and lyrical. It says some conditions are as "incurable as a planet's orbit" or that something can be "as full as an egg."[15] Some usages defamiliarize the most mundane of experiences: "A museum of moods"; "a broth of a boy"; "bitten-off smile"; "the polite laugher of sixty-four teeth."[16] The expressions are often fuller.

> Monogamy drifted about him—the scent of a hot iron on a shirt collar.

> In the deepening sky where the spearpoint firs scratch the clouds, already a moon like a cast-off paring from the setting sun.

The walls, with their arms around each others' shoulders like a foursome discussing a square secret in inaudible whispers. . . . [17]

Expressive language also tends toward economy. In a sentence or two some novelists conjure up an acute sense of the type of character at hand. They excel at capsule characterization.

Intellectually, I believe in having a good heart, a chirpy penis, a lively intelligence, and the courage to say "shit" in front of a lady.

Major Major's father was . . . a long-limbed farmer, a God-fearing, freedom-loving, law-abiding rugged individualist who held that federal aid to anyone but farmers was creeping socialism. He advocated thrift and hard work and disapproved of loose women who turned him down. His specialty was alfalfa and he made a good thing out of not growing any.

But in her stern code that which thrilled was wicked. She belonged to the tribe of Knitting Women; of the Salem Witch Burners; of all fanatics who count nature as an enemy to be suppressed; and in whose veins the wine of life runs vinegar. [18]

No use of language precludes live metaphors or vividness, and few novels are bereft of expressive language. Occasionally, the first pages of a novel offer metaphorical language, but the remaining pages rely overwhelmingly on communicative language. In *Peyton Place*, for instance, Grace Metalious introduces the village and its environs in metaphorical terms: "The conifers stood like disapproving old men on all the hills"; "the two churches bracketed and held the town like a pair of gigantic book ends. . . . "[19] Thereafter her language becomes one-sidedly communicative.

These principles about portraying worlds and using language allow for saying how novels relate to the world of everyday life. Table 1 summarizes some of my findings, with the remainder presented in the appendix. Although the focus is types of novels, spatial limitations dictate listing authors' names rather than novels' titles in the table. Following some names is a number indicating where more than one of an author's novels is included in the sample. In addition, some novelists' names are followed by a letter in parentheses, referring to the legend where those novelists' works are listed. The novelists involved in these instances are those whose works span two or more of the categories at hand, such as Frank Norris.

TABLE 1

Types of Novels (N=225)

	Reifying	Debunking		
Communicative Language	E. Caldwell Cartland (4) Dailey (2) Grey Holt (2) Loos Rinehart Spillane Werfel Woodford Yerby (2)	Amis (2) Atherton Auchincloss (2) Brookner (2) Cholmondeley Cronin (2) Dunne Ferber (2) Green (3) Greene (2) Hawthorne Hemingway (a) Hersey Howells (2) Jolley	Kennedy Kipling Lee Lurie Malamud (2) Maugham McMillan Metalious Mitchell Norris (2) Oates (b)(2) Pym Rand H. Robbins(2) Sarton (3)	Sayers Sinclair Stribling Susann Thackeray (3) Uris Wallace Waugh Weldon M. West (2) R. West Wilson Wouk
	Formulaic	Bestselling		
	Subcultural	Canonical		
Expressive Language	Burroughs T. Caldwell (c) Cather (d) Dreiser Fern Hemingway (e) Ingalls Kerouac Kingston London Norris (f) Porter Rawlings Salinger Stowe Welty	Austen (4) Barth (4) Bellow (6) Brautigan (2) Burgess (3) Cheever (4) Conrad (2) Dickens (5) Dos Passos (4) Drabble (6) Durrell (4) Eliot (5) Faulkner (6) Forster (4) Hardy (3) Hawkes (2)	Hemingway (g)(2) Irving (3) James (7) Kosinski (2) Lawrence (2) Mailer (3) McCullers (2) Melville (2) Meredith (2) Morris (2) Oates (h) Percy (4) Pynchon (3) Rhys (2) Roth (3) Sontag (2)	Spark (2) Steinbeck (2) Tarkington Trollope (8) Updike (2) Vonnegut (5) N. West (2) Woolf (3)

(a) A Farewell to Arms; (b) Them; Do with Me What You Will; (c) Dear and Glorious Physician; (d) Shadows on the Rock; (e) The Sun Also Rises; (f) McTeague; (g) To Have and Have Not; For Whom the Bell Tolls; (h) Expensive People.

Table 1 underscores that the novel is a debunking genre. Most novelists refuse to mirror reified realities from everyday life. Some show how the world of religion might be constituted; for example, *The Devil's Advocate* and *The Keys of the Kingdom*. Others portray the world of politics (*Advise and Consent, All the King's Men*), literature (*You Can't Go Home Again*), education (*The Prime of Miss Jean Brodie*), or the military (*From Here to Eternity, Catch-22*). Sex roles, family, social class, social mobility, and deviant behavior are novelists' foremost focuses, perhaps because novels typically address our most nagging concerns. Although they usually debunk, novels do take for granted roles, inequality, social change, conflict, and other parts of the social scaffolding. Novels thus presuppose the rudiments of all social worlds as well as the linguistic resources of commonsense actors.

Table 1 also shows that the distribution of novels is less skewed when we consider language. Most novelists do not use literary, or vividly expressive, language. Rather, debunking with nonliterary language is most common. That type of novel, generally including *bestselling* works, stands at an intermediate remove from the world of everyday life. Its language is that of mass journalism and everyday speech sprinkled sporadically with live metaphors and lyricism.

Closest to the world of everyday life are novels that neither debunk nor use expressive language and thus deviate from institutionalized literary expectations. The label *formulaic novels* makes sense here inasmuch as such novels not only follow fairly rigid formulas for plot and character but also rely on commonsense formulas for dealing with social reality. The "natural attitude" pervades these fictions. Formulaic novels are available in supermarkets and other retail businesses also selling current bestsellers; retailers like university bookstores do not sell them at all. Moreover, these novels spawn their own book clubs and newsletters such as *Affaire de Coeur* and *Janet Dailey Newsletter*.

Paradoxically, the kind of novel most closely connected with everyday life is often regarded as the most escapist; for example, Cartland's romances. More often than not, the formulaic novel does produce happy endings for its glamorous heroes and heroines, thus appearing to sidestep the everyday world where such outcomes escape the common reach. Yet formulaic novels leave everyday assumptions and routines undisturbed, often by romanticizing the taken-for-granted realities they reify.[20] Such novels merit critical attention insofar as they help to define the outer boundaries of the literary world and apparently serve some readers in ways other types of novels do not.

Novels with expressive language that do not debunk some world often depict some subcultural grouping.[21] Some regional fiction falls into this category, as do some religious, ethnic, working-class, and feminist novels. The major thrust of these novels is to portray the world of interest, usually in positive terms. Expressive language gives these novels a literary quality formulaic novels lack. Often, however, the language serves primarily to intensify the positive light the novel casts on the world it presents. The best label for these novels is *subcultural* fiction.

The final type of novel both debunks and uses expressive language. These novels, standing at the greatest remove from the world of everyday life, provide for saying what distinguishes the world of literature from every other human world. The term *canonical* is appropriate inasmuch as these novels carry on the tradition of the modern novel, whether one dates it from Cervantes (or earlier) or from Richardson, Fielding, and Smollett. Further, these novels have a place in educational curricula; they are (or stand likely to become) a widely recognized part of our literary heritage; they stimulate interpretation and criticism; their authors receive recognition in such forms as Nobel Prizes, National Book Awards, and the Booker Prize. These are the novels likeliest to get canonized; most of the older ones among them already are.

Novelists who write canonical works most reliably approximate the ideal type called the literary vocation. By definition, their novel making catapults them out of the commonsense world more dramatically than making other kinds of novels. How they use language and how they undercut established forms of taken for grantedness would seem, on average, to presuppose a calling of some sort—a calling, perhaps, to forms of sense making most other people never consciously consider. That calling would seem most powerful among those literary artists disposed toward creating canonical novels. Living more or less typical everyday lives, such individuals stretch language toward its limits while portraying fictional characters constituting their worlds and identities. These novelists' lives and fictions may offer the richest grounds for illuminating literary creativity and exploring how their everyday experiences limit novelists' fictions. At the same time, these are the novelists whose lives and fictions disclose the awesome disjunctions between everyday life and literature that imaginative individuals can shape into coherent forms with lasting appeal.

Novelists who write subcultural or best-selling works may also experience vocations, but the incidence of such experiences would seem on average lower than among those novelists writing canonical works. Nonetheless, those who favor expressive language or adopt debunking stances in their fictions are often, it would seem, the beneficiaries of a literary vocation. Tom Clancy is a case in point, as is Marjorie Kinnan Rawlings. Both appear to have felt the pull of a calling to give fictional form to their dreams and values. With Clancy, the U.S. military is pivotal; with Rawlings, down-home realities in the Florida wilderness. Yet many authors of subcultural or best-selling novels give no evidence of a vocation as such. Rather, their talent for storytelling seems to lead them, albeit circuitously sometimes, into novel making in much the same way that talent of any sort typically shapes individuals' occupational choices. Think here of Dick Francis whose wife suggested novel making to him, apparently because of his gift for storytelling.

Of special interest are those novelists whose works span the canonical and the best-selling realms. Their lives and fictions may particularly interest literary scholars prone to compare novelists' early works with their later works. Most obvious are questions about the sequencing of their moves between the two types of works. Three patterns are possible. In one, the novelist's early works are best-selling fictions, but the later works are canonical; in another, that sequence is reversed; in the final pattern, the novelist's fictions move back and forth between best-selling and canonical over the course of his or her writing life. Economic motives, conscious or not, underlie these patterns. The first pattern may include cases where early commercial success in effect subsidizes later "literary" success, as defined by authorized protectors of the literary canon. The second pattern may include cases where one's "literary" success feeds awareness of opportunities for commercial success leading to greater income, a pattern likeliest among those whose sense of vocation is weak or absent. The third pattern may include cases where a novelist's financial needs vary dramatically during adulthood—due, for instance, to multiple divorces or major health problems—and his or her fictions shift accordingly, though not necessarily consciously. In any event, these "cross-over" novelists may offer insights into the connections between novel making and the economics of everyday life, thus illustrating how thoroughly fictional worlds and biographical situations can get intertwined. Ernest Hemingway is of obvious interest here.

As I have implied, those who write best-selling and subcultural novels are often more career- than vocation-driven. The craft, not the art, of novel making is typically their chief concern. In contrast, those who write formulaic novels practice the craft of fiction in limited ways. Since their work is decidedly repetitious, the meaning of "craft" loses some of its force here. Bound by rigid narrative conventions, for-mulaic novelists are likelier over time to increase the speed rather than the quality of their fiction making. Such novelists work near the boundaries of the world of literature.

The Literary Canon, Cultural Stratification, and Everyday Life

For centuries people of privilege monopolized the world of literature, most obviously when literature disallowed the vernacular. Males from the higher social classes determined which works merited distribution, acclaim, and perpetuation. By and large, *canonical novels that get recognized as such* reflect the cultural authority high-status men carved out for themselves. To that extent the literary canon favors the cultural hegemony of its privileged creators, not the cultural plural-ism of modern society at large.

The history of the modern novel parallels that of modern sci-ence. In both cases, institutionalization entailed masculinization. As Simmel points out, a "naive conflation of male values with values as such" pervades modern cultures. Literary (and other cultural) forms are "male artifacts." Left unmodified by the women who use them, such forms ensure that "a residue of emotion and vitality remains unshaped and unreleased." Yet Simmel supposes "that the novel poses less serious difficulties for female creativity than the other forms of literature" inasmuch as "it has the least rigorous and deter-minate form."[22]

Simmel points to the masculinist values likely to hold sway in the literary world. By and large, the novelistic forms associated with Literature have been more amenable to men's experiences and values than to women's. The fundamentally linear structure of the early modern novel, for instance, better fit middle-class men's highly con-trolled, increasingly compartmentalized lives than women's more permeable, diffuse circumstances. The "Dear Reader" artifices com-mon in the early modern novel often smacked of masculine ways, too. Although they sometimes cast narrators as helpmates of readers, as we will see, such artifices often involved narrators in activities like directing the reader, trying to impose values and meanings, and reminding the reader who the narrative boss is—not the most femi-nine of activities in traditional terms.

Thus, writing women tended to deviate from the novelistic molds their male counterparts shaped to suit (however unconsciously) their own *Weltanschauungen*. By and large, those women followed two pathways. Some continued the tradition of their eighteenth-century sisters whose romances had antedated Richardson by thirty years or so. In Simmel's terms, the literary forms these women favored may have provided aesthetic channels for those feelings and perceptions likely to be left "unshaped and unreleased" by the realistic novel.

Yet what these female romancers were doing dovetailed themat- ically with what most male novelists were doing with the realistic novel. As Joseph Allen Boone notes, the English-language novel grew up alongside the "romantic wedlock ideal, most often weaving its narratives around themes of courtship, seduction, and wedlock. . . . " The rise of the novel involved "the metamorphosis of social conven- tions of love into narrative conventions of form. . . . "[23] To that extent female romancers were exploiting the bare bones of ideas undergird- ing the nineteenth-century novel as a social institution. The flesh they put on those bones, however, had heroinic proportions supposedly capable of addressing the fantasies of bourgeois females and less obviously capable of expressing the frustrations of being female on a sexual battleground shaped by the ideologies of romantic love, virtu- ous womanhood, and tough masculinity. That these romancers exploited ideas about love and heroinism nonetheless put them on the same broad cultural terrain as the realists who scorned their extremely popular fictions.

Yet, as Simmel suggests, that fundamental similarity stood likely to go unnoticed. Siphoned off as "women's fiction," the widely popu- lar romance was simultaneously siphoned off from "serious" litera- ture. At root, "serious" meant "masculine," even though that equiva- lence was as likely to pass unnoticed as the thematic similarity between the works of popular female romancers and those of less widely read, mostly male novelists. As Simmel indicates, "The differ- ential, male moment in ideational images and normative positions . . . disappears much more easily from consciousness than the correspond- ing female moment does." To wit, "the expressions of the male nature are easily transposed for us into the sphere of trans-specific, neutral objectivity and validity (to which the specifically male quality, should it be noticed, is subordinated as an individual and contingent matter)."[24]

Other female novelists adopted a different course of literary-social action. Instead of following distinctively female traditions in prose fic- tion, they wrote countertraditional novels respectful enough of literary- social conventions to be taken more seriously than their more traditional sisters yet undermining those conventions enough to demasculinize the novel to some extent. In these novelists' works a tension between rebel- lious and conciliatory stances is characteristic.[25] Females writing "New

Woman fiction" during the 1880s and 1890s, for instance, "showed their discomfort with realistic modes by mixing forms of allegory, impressionistic monologue, and the political tract. . . . " One recurrent strategy, used during the nineteenth century by Sarah Scott and during the twentieth century by Charlotte Perkins Gilman, was to make the female community "an alternative environment where protagonists learn to sustain themselves through mutual bonds that look beyond men and marriage."[26]

Given the incompatibility between female self-consciousness and literary (actually, canonical) conventions, then, creative women had little alternative but to fashion a distinctive literature. Essentially, they did that by giving birth to heroinism late in the eighteenth and early in the nineteenth centuries. Some, like Ann Radcliffe, favored gothic forms capable of sending "maidens on distant and exciting journeys without offending the proprieties," rendering the gothic novel "a feminine substitute for the picaresque" novel of male writers. For some such writers, "the terrors, the restraints, the dangers of the Gothic novel were not the fantasies but the realities of a woman's life." Others, as we have seen, appeared to curtsy to canonical conventions while undermining them to some extent. As Ellen Moers goes on to point out, for instance, Eliot "hardly wrote a fiction that was not an adultery novel, though tricks of the cautious novelist's trade have tended to obscure this fact"—a literary fact that happens to comprise "a compelling vehicle for heroinism."[27] Along distinctive pathways—"serious" or "popular" in the eyes of watchful critics—women thus carved out a necessarily distinctive place for themselves within the masculinized world of literature. Their own meaning-compatible experiences found no ready place there, so they subverted or even bypassed the respectable conventions of that world in order to make a place. The same points apply to other "minority" literature. Zora Neale Hurston's work comes to mind here as readily as Radclyffe Hall's.

Yet the literary place "minority" writers secured for themselves remains wobbly. Reconsider the lists of canonical novels presented in Table 1 and the appendix. Focus on names like Rita Mae Brown, Elizabeth Gaskell, Nadine Gordimer, Doris Lessing, and Jean Rhys. Then focus on names like John Barth, John Fowles, Ken Kesey, Walker Percy, John Updike, and Robert Penn Warren. Which set of novelists is likelier to appear on literature syllabi in university classrooms? Which is likelier to evoke recognition? Which garners greater intellectual and cultural respect? Which belongs to "special" courses feeding into a women's studies or other "minority" programs? Such queries evoke little hesitancy, even though the works at issue readily occupy the

same cultural category by virtue of respecting the same literary conventions and values. Although female authors may sometimes pay
their respects differently from male authors in order to express what
the realistic novel often stymies, the empirical data support the conclusion of a fundamental kinship among these novelists' works. At the
same time, their differential reception underscores the thoroughly
social constitution of the literary canon.

Such observations suggest that as a social institution helping to
structure the world of literature, the novel has been and probably
remains caught up in questions about gender (as well as race and sexuality). Historically, it has taken shape around conscious and unconscious cultural battles meant to settle the "question" of male superiority once and for all. This seems to have been the case less pointedly in
Britain than in the United States where Puritan individualism and a
wilderness/frontier mythology interplayed with industrialization to
harden the sexes' "proper" spheres. Boone thinks along these general
lines, as do Alfred Habegger, Nina Baym, and other contemporary
critics whose ideas revolve around questions of canon formation.
More generally, however, literary criticism comprises gender and
other cultural struggles as much as the history of the novel does, a circumstance explored in Chapter 9.

Such cultural stratification overrides awareness of the literary
fabric as a single cultural tapestry. That fabric is so sweeping that no
one experiences all of its richness. Rather, each experiences parts of the
whole according to his or her needs and tastes. We readers seek joy
and solace, intellectual stimulation, causes for hope, reasons for being,
and moments of release. Why force these motives into a hierarchy? It
makes more cultural sense to regard each part of the tapestry as serving interests precious to those who return again and again to experience the same parts, small or large, of the literary whole. Moreover,
assessing literary works along whatever lines correspond with readers' reasons for seeking out specific types of works makes the most
humanistic sense. In fact, over the centuries cultural authorities shaping the literary canon have adopted precisely that stance, albeit in nar-
rower form. They canonized what suited their tastes, what addressed
their values, what reflected their interests and commitments.

A more inclusionary stance toward literature also makes intellectual sense. How much understanding and appreciation of literature can its students garner by considering only canonized works?
Even if literary aesthetics remain the paramount concern in literature
curricula—a priority defensible culturally, humanistically, and intellectually—how better to become aesthetically astute and pluralistic

(that is, sophisticated) than by sampling the literary domain comprehensively? Literary studies should, in short, excel among interdisciplinary endeavors meant to illuminate human powers, human needs, and the cultures emanating from and responding to what we universally share in the way of humanity.

More than personal preferences or cultural concerns steer me toward emphasizing the unity of the literary world. At this point a brief look at the romance becomes instructive insofar as it reveals the structural unity obtaining among novels as seemingly different as Harlequin romances and National Book Award winners. Northrop Frye traces the romance back to the Greeks. He finds the romance in the works of William Shakespeare and John Milton, Sir Walter Scott and Jane Austen, George Bernard Shaw and Edgar Allen Poe. Over the centuries and across cultures, the romance makes an insistent appearance in literature. Its structure is vertical, revolving around a demonic and an idyllic world. Descent to the demonic world begins with a "break in consciousness" eventuating in an increasingly confused identity. A "recognition scene" marks the beginning of ascent from that world. As ascent to the idyllic world ensues, identity gets increasingly clarified. Heroines and heroes populate the romance, heroines exhibiting various kinds of manipulation (*froda*) and heroes favoring various kinds of violence (*forza*). The romance portrays the triumph of *froda;* its heroines succeed by achieving "some kind of deliverance" as the story ends.[28]

Studying middle-class women's experiences of formulaic and best-selling romances, Janice A. Radway analyzed the women's favorite fictions. The narrative structure she discovered mirrors Frye's delineation. Radway reports that the romance begins with some destruction of the heroine's identity—she gets uprooted "from a familiar, comfortable realm. . . . " It ends with the restoration of the heroine's identity. Among the works the women disliked—their "garbage-dump romances"—"the degradation, violence, and brutality that the heroine is forced to endure" most offended them. The hero's "unrelieved" masculinity and "extraordinary violence" violate these readers' expectations.[29] That Radway found such striking, consistent differences between the ideal and the garbage-dump romances shows that readers routinely know what they want as they enter the world of literature. More generally, her findings suggest that the narrative structure of the romance allows for quite distinct characterizations, amounts of detail, and—more inferentially—uses of language.

In any case the romance pervades American literature. It dominated nineteenth-century American literature, even though its chief architects in the canonical arena disagreed about its fundamental nature. Interestingly, Michael Davitt Bell argues that the self-conscious, "experimental" (that is, male) romancers of the age—Charles Brockden Brown, Washington Irving, Edgar Allen Poe, Nathanael Hawthorne, Herman Melville—were keenly alienated individuals who chose a "deviant" form so as to "validate, or at least give substance to, their sense of alienation," so as to occupy "a well-defined place" outside the society that seemed to offer them "no secure place."[30] Bell's speculations jibe with those of scholars trying to account for many women's preference for writing romances. Perhaps significantly, though, women's collective, not individual, alienation from society usually monopolizes the explanatory weight in such arguments. In any case, the romance is an American literary tradition stretching from Nathaniel Hawthorne to Ernest Hemingway. Arguing that the best American novels have leaned toward the romance oftener than their European counterparts, Richard Chase notes the effects of Puritanism "with its grand metaphors of election [idyllic world] and damnation [demonic world], its opposition of the kingdom of light and the kingdom of darkness, its eternal and autonomous contraries of good and evil. . . . "[31] Furthermore, the romance centers on individuals *qua* individuals, not as members of a community or society. It suits a culture based on utilitarian as well as expressive individualism.[32]

Thus, readers of American fiction routinely encounter the romance. Yet some readers and critics call their favored romances "novels" and other readers call theirs "romances." More than awareness of literary genres underlies this pattern. "Novel" (masculine, realistic, stimulating) is more respectable than "romance" (feminine, fantastic, escapist). Such literary typifications shape readerly, including critical, responses to a work, while advancing assumptions about its cultural worthiness and the cultural good sense of its readers. All the while, it behooves the humanistic scholar to bear in mind that whether individuals read the romances of Janet Dailey or those of William Faulkner depends largely on what they are *prepared* to find in literature and what they *want* to find there. Thus, readers—not critically acclaimed novels—now invite our attention.

5

♥ The Uses of Privacy

> Not the least eager of the eyes assembled were the eyes of those who could not read. These people, as they listened to the friendly voice that read along—there was always some such ready to help them—stared at the characters which meant so much with a vague awe and respect that would have been half ludicrous, if any aspect of public ignorance could ever be otherwise than threatening and full of evil.
>
> Charles Dickens, *Hard Times*

In *Middlemarch* (1871–72) George Eliot suggests the ill effects of reading only scholarly works and inferior fiction. Dorothea knows "many passages of Pascal's *Pensees*...by heart" and entertains fancies "of sitting up at night to read old theological works."[1] Her ill-fated attraction to Mr. Casaubon begins when the crusty old scholar brings her pamphlets on the early Church. Before long, she is "getting down learned books from the library and reading many things hastily" so as to talk less ignorantly with her suitor (p. 31). Much later, she sadly admits she knows little about music and literature. Still later, Dorothea finds her studies with her husband Casaubon "dreary"; even Pascal fails to soothe her (p. 507). Casaubon himself says his theological scholarship leaves him "little leisure" for reading literature (p. 12). His library is full of "accustomed dullness," and he "dreams footnotes" that "run away with all his brains" (pp. 70, 86).

Although Rosamond does find time "to read the best novels" (p. 177), she dissociates them from "deep" works and is uncertain about the tastefulness of reading works by authors like Lady Blessington (p. 289). Unlike the other major characters, Mary Garth reads avidly and widely. She knows Shakespeare and enjoys biographies as well as novels. Mr. Featherstone, an uncle she tends, scorns her reading, though: "She's got the newspaper to read out loud. That's enough for one day, I should think" (p. 116). Sir James has "no sonnets to write"; he mostly reads technical books on farming (pp. 11, 60). Mr. Lydgate can only hope that his childhood reading "will last [him] all [his] life" (pp. 149, 173, 289). Together, Eliot's characterizations imply that sacrificing literature to scholarship or technical work narrows vision and dulls sensitivities. Mary Garth is Eliot's model reader. Not unexpectedly, Mary is a sensitive and sensible creature.

Alongside her characterizations in terms of reading stands Eliot's subtle critique of mass culture where books serve as mere commodities. Some use their books as displays of "polite literature" (pp. 74–75, 178, 291). Mr. Trumbull says, "I have no less than two hundred volumes in calf, and I flatter myself they are well selected" (p. 335). Like Rosamond, Mr. Trumbull and his ilk concern themselves more with "correct sentiments" than with literature (p. 286). For all practical purposes, they are like the young men who find literature a good "medium for 'paying addresses'" to young women (p. 287). They pride themselves on "literary refinements" exceeding those of the average person (pp. 10, 52, 492).

Eliot portrays a world where some people consider business a "sacred calling" (p. 247), and much that passes for art is scarcely "fit to be seen" (p. 79). *Middlemarch* offers a virtual social psychology of the rise of mass culture. It reminds readers that "the true seeing is within" (p. 203) and that a "text expands for whatever we can put into it" (p. 48). Yet *Middlemarch* involves neither a snobbish criticism of mass culture nor a condescending posture toward "average" people. Its narrator insists that everyone is "imaginative in some form or other," (p. 344) and even semiliterate readers find the world "at least not darker" than it was before their struggle with the printed word (p. 426). *Middlemarch* nonetheless insists that high culture "elevates a nation" (pp. 239, 417) as well as its individuals.

Together, the subthemes of Eliot's masterpiece imply the preciousness of literacy as well as the value of canonical novels. Other novelists champion literacy more than canonical novels as such. In *Bleak House*, for example, when Mr. George asks Grandfather Smallweed how he occupies himself, the invalid replies,

"I watch the fire—and all the boiling and the roasting—"
"When there is any," says Mr. George with great expression.
"Just so. When there is any."
"Don't you read or get read to?"
The old man shakes his head with sharp sly triumph. "No, no. We have never been readers in our family. It don't pay. Stuff. Idleness. Folly. No, no!"

"There's not much to choose between your two states," says the visitor in a key too low for the old man's dull hearing.[2]

Smallweed's denigration of reading reflects his impoverished lifestyle. Lacking literacy, Smallweed occupies a tiny world. When they tacitly instruct readers about what and why to read, canonical novelists usually contrast literacy and orality. As Jack Goody and Ian Watt observe, that contrast operates from *Don Quixote* through *War and Peace* (and beyond). Cervantes's Sancho Panza and Tolstoy's Platon Karataev are both "illiterate; both are rich in proverbial lore; both are untroubled by intellectual consistency; and both represent many of the values . . . characteristic of oral culture."[3] Sancho Panza contrasts with Don Quixote; Platon Karataev, with Pierre Bezuhov. The contrasts many novelists make between the Mary Garths and Mr. Featherstones among the reading public are variants of those contrasts. Readers like Mary Garth feed on the distinctive riches print offers; those like Mr. Featherstone enjoy essentially oral traditions set down in print.

Literacy, Literature, and Liberation

For most moderns, the loss of literacy would mean the loss of their occupations. Also lost would be their capacity to read want ads, to apply for most jobs, and to complete the forms for receiving unemployment compensation and other relief. Gone from their worlds would be books, magazines, newspapers, memoranda, letters, manuals, diaries, billboards, coupons, and all sorts of written agreements. Unassisted, illiterate individuals have no access to these marks of modernity. Taking away individuals' literacy means transforming their worlds as well as their selves.

Written language extends humankind's memory and imagination.[4] It provides people a common ground, even when enormous time or distance separates them. In that respect the printed word embodies culture in historically unprecedented ways.[5] It allows for editing, standardization, and rapid accumulation, multiplying the options for organizing societies and diversifying cultures.[6] The significance of print goes unquestioned.

Even though its causal status is murky, literacy remains a hallmark of advancement, modernity, and liberation. The medieval individual was much more prepared to listen than to read.[7] During Shakespeare's time only one third to one half of London's population was literate.[8] In rural areas literacy was even less common. Today, however, the populations of Western industrialized societies are over 90 percent literate. In those societies literacy snowballed with changes the nineteenth century engendered.

During the first four centuries of printing, books were for religious, scholarly, commercial, and noble sorts of people. Religious controversies stimulated the spread of literacy, and religious interests created schools that furthered literacy.[9] Later, expanding newspaper and book production helped to promote reading. Halfpenny and penny broadsides were available from the sixteenth century onward. The streets were full of various printed documents, but only decreasing printing costs in the nineteenth century gave people of ordinary means access to books.[10] The availability of affordable, efficient lighting, coupled with the shorter working day, also provided opportunities to read.[11] The extension of libraries, the rise of books clubs, the proliferation of cheap editions, compulsory schooling, child labor laws, increases in real wages, and other factors made the printed world less intimidating and more accessible.

In Western societies today reading and writing take precedence over speaking clearly and correctly. Although those skills correlate as bases for social differentiation, literacy is prior. It is normative in contemporary Western societies, serving as a badge of ability and dignity; it is the fundamental asset presupposed in a "credential society."[12] So dignifying and useful is literacy that functionally illiterate individuals often go to great lengths to hide their deficiency.[13]

In general, illiterate individuals want those skills that would put them more in step with their societies. Getting them is no simple matter, however, as recent attacks on illiteracy demonstrate. A National Committee on Reading says a meaningful goal is twelfth-grade literacy for all Americans capable of that achievement.[14] Yet many Americans remain simple illiterates unable to receive and communicate ideas through reading and writing; many more—some 20 to 30 percent[15]—are functional literates able to grasp only the simplest written materials. Many functional literates exhibit the "higher illiteracy" that prevents relating written materials to actual events, that precludes critical and creative reading, that inclines them toward those printed materials duplicating the oral traditions of family and peer group.[16] In our society uncritical illiteracy necessitates literacy training not only in the armed services and prisons but also in business and industry.

Regardless of what and how they read, individuals thereby broaden their knowledge or competence, build up grounds for self-approval, reinforce their beliefs and values, or find respite from tension.[17] In addition, reading sometimes sparks aesthetic experiences.

The effects of reading depend on readers' prior experiences and current purposes. They also depend on what individuals read which, in turn, depends on what is physically, economically, intellectually, and culturally available to them. Then, too, how they read—critically or not, for example—affects readers' outcomes. How they share their reading experiences with others also influences their outcomes.

Reading most liberates when it rouses consciousness rather than reinforces reifications; when it challenges rather than complements prior conditioning; when it advances individuality rather than social conformity; when it offers opportunities for expression rather than occasions for impression.[18] Such reading benefits society by enlivening critical consciousness, stimulating expression, and curtailing the reification that feeds passivity, alienation, and the denial of freedom. Yet much that attracts readers is akin to historical broadsides, chapbooks, and other street literature that "stemmed from traditional culture on which the technique of printing was superimposed. The printed sheets became as much carriers of tradition as the oral transmission from one generation to the next."[19] The fiction attracting many readers duplicates what is interactionally and electronically available to them, drawing them only to the hinterlands of literature.

Determining how many literates fail to reap the full rewards of literacy is no simple matter. In the mid-1940s Henry C. Link and Harry Arthur Hopf divided a national sample of 4,000 adults into *active readers* who read a book within the past month (50 percent), *inactive readers* who read a book within the past year (21 percent), and *nonreaders* who had not read a book within the past year (29 percent). Seventeen percent of the sample, or about 59 percent of the nonreaders, had not read a book within the past five years. The researchers inferred that about one-fifth of the population reads 70 percent of all books read; about half reads 94 percent.[20] William S. Gray and Ruth Munroe's 1930 study of Americans' reading habits looked at all types of reading, finding that Americans were reading an average of more than 90 minutes a day.[21] More recently, Amiel T. Sharon studied Americans' reading using an area-probability sample of 5,067 individuals sixteen years or older. Not surprisingly, the average amount of time spent reading each day is higher than Gray and Munroe found. Sharon reports that the average American reads nearly two hours (106 minutes) on a typical day, with 45 percent reading two hours or more. On average, according to Sharon, Americans spend about 45 minutes a day reading books.[22]

Education predictably affects how much people read. Over 70 percent of those with some college education are active readers; only

10 percent are nonreaders. The respective figures for those with high school or grade school educations are 51 and 25 percent, 25 and 56 percent. People with high school and grade school educations do, though, read more when they belong to higher income groups. Thus, income itself influences reading, though less powerfully than education. Sharon reports that socioeconomics status (SES) correlates strongly with what and how much people read, with high-SES individuals "tend[ing] to read more of all kinds of printed matter." Sharon is one of the few reading researchers who mention occupation, noting that those reading eight or more hours a day (6 percent of the sample) are "probably those whose work involves a lot of reading."[23]

Overall, women are more often active readers than men, about equally often inactive readers, and less often nonreaders.[24] Yet data collected during the Depression show females and males checking out library books at roughly the same rate.[25] In fact, when all types of materials are considered, the data suggest that men do more reading than women.[26] Employment status may have an effect. While full-time work outside the home may reduce a person's likelihood of reading books, it may increase his or her likelihood of reading other (mostly work-related) materials. Overall, it currently appears that their education and employment status exert more influence on the amount people read than their sex does. Sex, as we will see, more affects the content and style of one's reading.

Link and Hopf found that active readers and nonactive readers read different sorts of books. College-educated readers like adventures, mysteries, and romances less than those with high school educations. The latter readers are, in other terms, more inclined toward formulaic fiction. Sharon reports similar findings, as does Waples who found that Westerns are favorites "largely among men of all ages with less than high school education."[27] Similarly, three quarters of Radway's romance-readers had less than a college education; half had only a high school diploma.[28] Active readers are likelier to join book clubs and to read books reviews. They are as likely as others to read magazines and newspapers, listen to the radio, and go to movies, suggesting that book reading supplements rather than supplants other leisure activities. Finally, among respondents who read more now than two years ago, having more time is the most frequent reason (81 percent).[29]

Book readers tend to read more books of fiction than all other types of books combined. Women's reading includes more fiction than men's. In a study of library users, Waples found they borrowed 50 percent more fiction than men; fiction accounted for about two-thirds of the books they borrowed. Data also indicate that women and men prefer different novelists. Waples and his colleagues examined the novels checked out of New York City branch libraries. Circulation data for 1932 showed John Galsworthy was the favorite among women but was "rated" ninth by men. Among the men the favorite was Jack London, whom the women rated between ninth and tenth places. Similarly, the women put Mary Roberts Rinehart in fifth place; the men, in fifteenth place. The men rated P. G. Wodehouse third; the women, twelfth.[30] James D. Hart has also noted sex differences in reading tastes. Interestingly, he associates Jack London—the men's favorite in the New York City study—with the popular "masculine novel," crediting London with giving "great impetus to the so-called red-blooded romance." Earlier, according to Hart, Owen Wister's *Virginian* and John Fox's *Trail of the Lonesome Pine* derived their popularity from a male readership.[31] Paul DiMaggio, Michael Useem, and Paula Brown report similar findings about the visual and performing arts. Their review of 270 audience studies indicates, for instance, that ballet and other dance performances attract the most female-dominated audiences among the performing arts. Moreover, some studies suggest that the specific "content of the performance or exhibit may attract men and women differently."[32]

More recently, Victor Nell cites "wide agreement about what constitutes a good read across language, gender, and career choice differences."[33] In fact, one study of middle- and high-school students revealed "a strong and consistent preference for . . . positive, problem-solution themes among subjects of both sexes and across all [the] grade levels." Yet both girls and boys showed a preference for protagonists of their own sex.[34] This pattern undoubtedly derives from many sources, including the sex-typed marketing of many books. Among those sources, though, empathy—or, more generally, affect—merits attention by virtue of its prospective pedagogical and cultural ramifications. In 1986, two reading researchers reported a strong correspondence "between a reader's empathy for one character or another and his or her interpretation of . . . narrative conflict." Most of the subjects in their study had no trouble grasping plot, but "thematic perception . . . was associated with affective identification with a given character."[35]

Often feminist scholars cite a link between empathy and effective reading. Inclined to emphasize that "the canonical American novel is the 'melodrama of beset manhood,'" they decry the "refusal to recognize women as having stories. . . . " That refusal deprives women of "literary" experiences routinely available to men; namely, "validation of one's reality and reinforcement of one's identity."[36] As Judith Fetterly points out, women reading "men's texts . . . are forced to become characters in those texts."[37] Joseph Allen Boone describes how that circumstance likely affects female and male readers differently. In the seduction novel the reader becomes a virtual voyeur, "yet another of the heroine's victimizers." Boone concludes that "the potential for a kind of ideological abuse of the reader" infiltrates such fictions.[38] Such narratives may stimulate enough revulsion to override some females' empathy for the victim, perhaps curtailing their thematic awareness.

To the extent that females are particularly adept at empathizing with characters and, therefore, at grasping themes, such texts disadvantage them. Preliminary evidence suggests that may indeed be the case. David Bleich reports that "women 'see' feelings" in Hemingway's "Hills Like White Elephants" more quickly than men and that women's retellings of Faulkner's "Barn Burning" involve "a more complex expression of the emotional condition of the boy" in the story than men's do. Women are more prone than men to "construe a general affective logic" for the latter story, even in the face of uncertainty about "what is 'going on.'"[39] In parallel fashion, Elizabeth A. Flynn finds that more than females readers, male readers try to "dominate" the texts they read, tending to "judge characters without empathizing with them . . . or detach themselves from the emotional content of the text."[40] Women and men, it seems, tend not only to choose different texts but also "to read the same texts differently."[41] Sex-role socialization probably promotes such differences in tastes and styles, as do the differences between women's and men's typical social locations.

At this juncture revisiting Radway's romance-readers is instructive. Radway's study details the experiences of middle-class women fiercely committed to formulaic and best-selling romances. Radway herself sees their favorite works as decidedly formulaic so hers is a case study of voracious readers whose appetites run counter to those scholars often associate with "active" (and, on average, "educated") readers. It is also a case study of how reading and affect, including empathy, intermesh for female romance readers. Strong in its own right, Radway's study gains in importance insofar as Victor Nell's more recent findings on "ludic" readers largely dovetail with her findings. Together, the two scholars put us in touch with flesh-and-blood readers.

As we saw, half of Radway's romance readers have only a high school education. They were, on average, 19.9 years old when they first married. Seventy-six percent are currently married, and 70 percent have children under the age of 18. Nearly two-fifths do not work outside the home; 21 percent of the women have only part-time jobs outside the home. It appears that most of the women (roughly three-fifths) are home-centered, largely devoting their energies to family and homemaking. Reading anchors their daily routines; nearly 90 percent "read religiously every day," with 62 per cent reading one to four nonromance books a week.[42] These are the ludic readers Nell describes as "gluttonous"; these are "text gobblers."[43]

What satisfies their hunger is "the verbal working out of a romance, that is . . . the reinterpretation of misunderstood action and . . . declarations of mutual love. . . . " They like the meliorative interaction between heroine and hero, the triumph of communication and mutuality over misunderstanding and separation. They also like "the opportunity to project themselves into the story, to become the heroine. . . . " It also appears that these women enjoy hearing another woman's voice between the lines of the texts they devour. They insist they "can always ferret out romances written by men under female pseudonyms," and Radway gives some credence to their insistence.[44] At root, then, these readers find their most important satisfactions in the positive interaction between heroines and heroes, in a strong identification with the heroine whose experiences vicariously become theirs, and in experiencing another woman's voice. The beliefs these romances validate concern perfectible, long-term relationships between the sexes, the rewards women derive from marriage (and, inferentially, family), the compatibility of independence and creativity with wifehood and motherhood, and the possibility of individuality within the confines of women's traditional roles in patriarchal society. Beliefs in these things get their most meaningful validation from female romancers, not males whose ideas about being female are necessarily second-hand and possibly self-interested.

These readers do not look for lyrical or otherwise strongly expressive language. In fact, Radway observes that the romances they favor often involve a "hybrid opening" (not unlike Metalious's in Peyton Place) where perceivedly literary language is blended with decidedly referential language. Overall, their preferred texts involve the "repetitive use of the same, limited vocabulary"; for example, a small array of adjectives repeatedly drawn on to characterize heroes. Another common feature of these texts is their "careful attention to the style, color, and detail of women's fashions." Such constant elements as these, played out within the rigid structure of the popular romance, allow readers to expend less mental energy and focus on "the more desirable activity of affective reaction. . . . "[45] As Nell has found, "Quite often, readers' judgments of trance potential will override judgments of merit and difficulty."[46] In other terms, ludic readers commonly want their texts to "carry them away" offering "islands of tranquility" that dull consciousness or "involvement with characters and situations" that heighten consciousness.[47] Often, as with Radway's subjects, they want their reading to "raise their spirits."[48] Affect is thus central to ludic reading.

In general, as Nell's studies show, ludic readers believe their reading requires little effort.[49] Radway's readers apparently believe that, too. The romances they choose not only free them to expend more affective than cognitive energy but also facilitate their swift entry into the fictional world whose emotional texture satisfies them. At the same time, the predictable structure and artifices of their texts make it unnecessary for them to concentrate intensely, thus allowing them to enjoy reading even when they are frazzled. Several of Radway's romance readers talked favorably about Jane Austen's novels, for instance, but said they "could read her only if they were not tired, if they were alone, or if they were willing to pay particular attention. . . . "[50] Only those willing to restrict their reading to times when they are alone and alert are likely to read works like Austen's, and most of Radway's subjects are unwilling to put such restrictions on their reading. In fact, among their romances, they distinguish between "quick reads" and "fat books." These readers usually aim to "finish a book" in a single, more or less continuous reading, mostly because their affective satisfactions require arriving at the story's end.[51] Thus, the short, formulaic romances these women favor suit their demanding circumstances. Their romances reliably and efficiently deliver them into the fictional worlds they seek and give them emotional gratification in an amount of time reasonable from the standpoint of a wife/mother/homemaker/(employee) whose energies are widely scattered.

In addition to the thematic and stylistic attractions their romances hold, these women value some time more or less exclusively theirs. Their reading "creates a time or space within which a woman can be . . . preoccupied with her personal needs, desires, and pleasure." Romance reading gives these women experiences of "self-indulgence" and "the opportunity to experience the kind of care and attention they commonly give to others."[52] Their husbands' initial (and commonplace) objections to their reading imply how effectively it serves these purposes.

Yet these women read their romances with a measure of ambivalence. Commonly aware that their reading is "escapist," they also seem aware (though vaguely) that many people regard their romances as "repetitious and formulaic."[53] These women are, for example, "reluctant to admit that the characters appearing in romances are similar";

they "believe the books they read *are* novels"; they insist "the heroines 'are all different.'" (Interestingly, they can and do distinguish among heroines.) These stances are akin to that of a male clerical worker, a ludic reader, who told Nell that "You have to be able to read well in order to enjoy Louis L'Amour. . . ."[54] A distinct defensiveness seems at work—and understandably so. Criticisms of such ludic readers are commonplace, occurring not only in novels like *Middlemarch* but also in everyday life and in the academic world.

More than 50 years ago, Douglas Waples and Ralph W. Tyler stressed that no evidence indicates anyone "benefits from the habit of reading sensational fiction exclusively."[55] During the same period Harold V. Bonny said some people read too much, using their reading "like a sedative, an opiate to keep [them] away from the cruel realities of life."[56] Later, Waples and others claimed that without taking account of "who reads what and why, the notion that reading as such has certain values for every reader is almost pure nonsense."[57] That position is nonsense. The exercise of literacy has intrinsic value. As Holbrook Jackson argues, even when the desire for escape is active, it is no reliable sign of defeat.[58]

Although it may not reliably liberate, reading can consistently revitalize individuals. It may sometimes reinforce false consciousness, but it may also ease the chronic indignity many workers (including homemakers) experience, enliven worthy dreams, and provide respite from fierce demands on one's energies. In any case, reading should be assessed in relation to the benefits of readers' accessible alternatives and the constraints of their situations. For most readers, the likeliest alternative is commercial television. Like the books they read, programs aired commercially are likely to duplicate oral traditions. Unlike books, however, television invites considerable passivity and little imagination. Then, too, reading formulaic work sometimes leads to reading canonical ones. Nineteenth-century ballads and chapbooks, for example, stimulated the desire for books and helped to spread literacy.[59]

One-sided criticisms of ludic readers often illustrate what William Ryan calls "blaming the victim."[60] Typically, the critics are extensively schooled readers whose reading often advances their careers. The targets of their attacks are less educated individuals whose fiction reading is largely recreational and whose practical circumstances often disallow immersion in texts that make heavy demands on their abilities to concentrate. Worse yet, the targets are sometimes readers whose schooling left them ill-equipped for any but formulaic texts. Even though such readers may be reading up to the limits of their current skills, some of their more privileged contemporaries see fit to scorn it.

Critics would do better to slough off the rhetoric of differences that undergirds most victim blaming. When we read fiction for relaxation, not for career advancement or status enhancement, we all seek roughly the same experiences—the pleasures of a good read that catapults us out of our everyday lives. One of my colleagues renewed my awareness of that fundamental similarity ten years ago. A literature professor, he lamented that most of his novel reading was work and that he found woefully little time to read novels "just for enjoyment." When he reads during his leisure, he is like the romance readers Radway studies and like all the rest of us. He wants his beliefs and hopes more or less validated; he wants to identify with the protagonist to an engaging extent; he wants pleasure, not more work; he wants, in the end, to feel good in one way or other. We readers of stories are essentially akin. As Nell puts it, "elite and lowbrow minds share a multitude of drives and gratifications, in literature as in life."[61]

Selves, Relationships, and Worlds

Tied in with the debunking most fiction accomplishes are occasions to constitute meanings that are elusive among modern individuals. More than any body of oral traditions or any other institution reliant on print, the novel probes the meaning of individuality, the challenge of human relationships, and the constitution of human worlds. The novel is also unexcelled for insights into the emotions that express and stymie selves, that bolster and weaken relationships, that pull every world away from the narrowness built into rational models of rational creatures. Thus, the novel readily offers insights that are available but less widely accessible in sociology, anthropology, psychology, history, and investigative journalism. These points seem superfluous yet commonplaces such as "I don't have time to read novels" and "I can't remember when I last read a novel" suggest otherwise.

Novelists show better than any other group how people build up their identities while constituting bonds with other individuals. Selfhood means "a distinct universe walks about under your hat and under mine. . . . "[62] It lands people in the "kingdom of single-mindedness" where "It overflows into everything that belongs to us—and then it flows back again."[63] The self-conscious individual may become a "professional in experience" who "can neither abolish himself as a nuisance nor maintain himself as an institution."[64] In practice, seeking a self means the "robust pursuit of a workable improvisation, uninhibited by consistency" or "an endless struggle to relate mystery and reason."[65]

In a sense full-fledged individuality means "outliving" or "outgrowing oneself."[66] It means to "desire the Other, the Impossible."[67] That desire often kindles experiences of one's environment as "a limit, a barrier, and a perfectly arbitrary one."[68] Thus, some individuals fight against their environments, "avoiding the soul-destroying middle" of staid convention or respectable lifestyles.[69] Whether by passivity and uninvolvement or frenzy and hyperinvolvement, they want "something definite to reject."[70]

Given that "there is only oneself facing forever the problem of one's self discovery," negotiating one's way between self-contemplation and self-fixation is no small feat.[71] Their very nature requires that individuals "sympathetically debunk" themselves.[72] Yet few individuals remember their pasts with "flawless lucidity," since the "retrospective imagination . . . feeds the analytic faculty with boundless alternatives. . . . "[73] Yet the fiercest

mystery lies in the here and now. The mystery is: What is one to do with oneself? As you get older you begin to realize the trick time is playing, and that unless you do something about it, the passage of time is nothing but the encroachment of the horrible banality of the past on the pure future. The past devours the future like a tape recorder, converting pure possibility into banality. The present is the tape head, the mouth of time.[74]

Often, then, the soul sits "unhappily on superstructures of explanation, poor bird, not knowing which way to fly."[75]

Novels offer insights like these in contexts that allow for seeing a character's whole life unfold. Focusing emphatically on the individual, novels dramatize the dialectic between the claims of individuality and the claims of sociality.

The novel portrays individuals at odds with or perplexed by their worlds. How characters deal with their problems exposes how selfhood is intertwined with "minds understudy[ing] each other."[76] The individual normally needs interaction with other people. For human beings, "it is alarming not to be seen."[77] Being seen sometimes involves, though, having to distinguish between things like "being guilty in the sight of God and . . . being publicly harassed by the noisiest manifestation of popular scorn."[78] Sometimes, too, it means being treated as if one "had insisted on being born in opposition to the dictates of reason, religion, and morality. . . . "[79]

Of whatever ilk, social recognition entails expectations. So thor-

ough is that connection that sometimes individuals even "feel obligations toward things [they] like."[80] They can, of course, attenuate their
sense of obligation or even throw off their more perfunctory obligations. As Hesse's Demian puts it, "I live in my dreams—that's what
you sense. Other people live in dreams, too, but not in their own."[81]
Thus, some individuals nurture their selfhood in the fashion of
Stephen Daedalus: "You talk to me of nationality, language, religion. I
shall try to fly by those nets."[82] The sense of powerlessness often
abrades such individualistic enterprises, however. "Perhaps when
people are so desperately impotent, they play that instrument, the
personality, louder and wilder. . . ."[83]

In any case literature illuminates selves as deeply social creatures. Intimate relationships, especially familial and sexual ones, are a
constant interest, if only because individuality and intimacy dovetail
from womb to tomb. In particular, literature dramatizes the subtleties
and shortcomings of communication:

The aims of battle and the fruits of conquest are never the same.

His lovemaking was frenzied dictatorship.

He was an antidote to oppressive secrets; what he offered her
was, in fact, above all things a vast sunny immunity from the
need of having any.

Only connect! That was the whole of her sermon. Only connect
the prose and the passion, and both will be exalted, and human
love will be seen at its height.[84]

Novelists also portray the emotional inhibitions Freud associated with civilization and, at the other end, the emotional license associated with the cult of personality. They indicate, often by showing
individuals undergoing socialization, that

Inhibition doesn't grow on trees, you know—takes patience,
takes concentration, takes a dedicated and self-sacrificing parent
and a hard-working attentive little child to create in only a few
years' time a really constrained and tight-ass human being.[85]

On the other hand, individuals can feel they are "nothing but
sponge[s] sopped full of human emotions."[86] Novelists' economic portrayal of the emotional gamut is one of their grandest strengths. An
individual may, for example, be "empty with happiness," experience

a "brass-band feeling," or feel a "swish of relief."[87] Such economy attests to novelists' artistry, as they silently remind us that "the richest of human experiences is also the most limited in its range of expression."[88] What, for instance, "would be the description of happiness? Nothing, except what prepares and then what destroys it, can be told."[89] Novelists often amplify that message by treating the uneasy relationship between words and emotions.

Many individuals misname their experiences, thus inviting specific emotions, or they misname their emotions, thus setting themselves up for misguided courses of action. Examples abound.

She was not so much shy as distrustful. . . .

Do I really experience this restlessness, this horniness, as an affliction—or as an accomplishment? Both? Could be. Or is it only a means of evasion?

Do you think courage is what it took? It may have been a matter of self-esteem.

To be indulgent to others and severe with oneself was just another trick of pride.

All really selfish people think they're tenderhearted, because they get hurt so often. They mistake the pangs of wounded pride for the real thing.[90]

Such comments illustrate what the narrator says in *The Dead Father:* "You will never guess it in a hundred thousand years some of which I point out have already been used up by you in useless living and breathing but have a go, have a go, do: *What do you really feel?*"[91]

Also frustrating the desire for emotional clarity are the problems of grasping the temporal structure of specific feelings. "The advance of regret," for example, "can be so gradual that it is impossible to say 'Yesterday I was happy, today I am not.'"[92] Sometimes, too, a feeling is "just a ricocheted memory," not a response to current circumstances or imminent events.[93] In other terms, individuals sometimes "backdate a nearer emotion." Sometimes, too, global responses to the human condition assume the guise of other emotions: "In boxing Mr. Maidan's ears Leonora was just striking the face of an intolerable universe."[94] More commonly, emotions originate in expectations. Often "it is the excess above what we expect that makes the force of the blow. . . . " We "die between the too-much and the not-enough. . . . "[95]

Implicated with the problems of recognizing one's emotions is the problem of reconciling one's emotions and judgments. As a genre celebrating the human will, the novel explores the connections between reason and affect. Unlike most scholars, most novelists imply that "hearts may count in Heaven as high as heads."[96] Most also imply that to some extent "true civilization must be based on emotion."[97] Thus, applying reason to human affairs falters to the extent that "our emotional life [has changed] much less" than our technology.[98] Novelists capture such discontinuities with a sweeping scope:

> Feeling without judgment is a washy draught indeed; but judgment untempered by feeling is too bitter and husky a morsel for human deglutition.

> The hopeless easy promiscuity of her sympathies....

> His joy overshot his understanding....

> Man seems formed for action, though the passions are seldom properly managed; they are either so languid as not to serve as a spur, or else so violent as to overleap all bounds....

> He was a just man, and he would apologize for his fault; but he was an austere man, and would take back the value of his apology in additional austerity.[99]

Finally, novelists comment incisively on specific human emotions. Since they focus intently on individuals, their dramatizations typically concern the most private, personally gripping emotions. Love is, perhaps, their most common concern. Like philosophers, theologians, and psychologists—indeed, like most commonsense individuals—novelists stress the necessity of love for human growth and development.

> When you're not at work you should be in love.

> We move from birth to death amid a crowd of others and the name of the parade is love.

> Whatever gains I ever made were always due to love and nothing else.[100]

Yet as early a novelist as Fielding pointed to the indiscriminate usages of "love":

> Love, according to the present universally received sense of that phrase,... is applied indiscriminately to the desirable objects of all

our passions, appetites, and senses, and is understood to be that preference we give to one kind of food rather than to another.[101]

Then, too, a novelist as early as Thackeray noted the pride some individuals take in their inability to love: "It is best to love wisely, no doubt: but to love foolishly is better than not to be able to love at all. Some of us can't: and we are proud of our impotence, too."[102] Thackeray anticipates "independence" or "freedom" as guises for the inability to love. Novelists combat such distortions, defending love as the emotion capable of growing "exactly as big as [one's] soul."[103]

Defining love is virtually impossible, though. Perhaps, it "is how we call our ignorance of what whips us."[104] Love may be

besides desire, . . . confidence, a confident state of mind, a clear and reliable feeling. Your heart is clear, knowing that when it thinks about the person it loves it won't surprise itself by stumbling unaware on some ugly reservation, some knowledge that must be suppressed or excused.[105]

Love involves, then, "the delicate but total acknowledgment of what is."[106]

Yet in cultures like ours, the workings of love get complicated by ideologies of romantic love. For example, we accept as a virtual "law of love that the so-called 'right' person always comes too soon or too late."[107] Given such ideological entanglements, recognizing love becomes all the more challenging, as novelists often remind us:

Love is a wonderfully luxuriant plant, but unclassifiable really, fading as it does into mysticism on the one side and naked cupidity on the other.

She began to love him more and more, not for what he was, but for what she had given up to him.

He wasn't a good lover, of course. He didn't really like women.

How many shades there are between love and indifference, and how little the graduated scale is understood!

You will tell me that you have just learned love; I will tell you that you have just learned hope.

It was part of Gracie's image of herself that she "adored" Matthew.

Half a fellow's pangs at losing a woman result from vanity more
than affection.

Those profoundest of self-delusions . . . come cloaked in the guise
of love. . . . [108]

Novelists also say a lot about the vanities that make appearances unreliable signs of people's feelings and motives. Given the
profundity of the human emotions, what can vanity represent but the
"perfection of a fop"?[109] As a debunking genre, the novel opposes vanity as a pitiable denial of complexity and inconsistency. It bares the
false appearances vanity builds up as a matter of habit. Depicting the
irreducible complexity of individuals, exploring their bonds with one
another, and dramatizing the emotions accomplishes a great deal
more than debunking appearances, however. Those activities also disclose the constitution of human worlds. The novelist may be Austen
portraying village life on the English countryside. Or Dickens portraying the world of schools, the urban working class, or the courts.
Or Woolf portraying the world of everyday life from the vantage
point of a single, acute consciousness. Or Faulkner portraying the
world of the idiot or the world of the rural South. Or Bellow portraying the world of urban intellectuals. No matter what their focuses,
styles, or personal beliefs and values, talented novelists show worlds
being constituted out of the feebleness and strengths of individuals,
out of the bonds they initiate and sustain and destroy together, out of
unpredictable mixes of rationality and affect. Thereby, novelists portray human beings as bundles of possibilities and human worlds as
more or less arbitrary emanations from those possibilities. Thus, they
reveal the roots of social action not only by exemplifying expression
and communication themselves but also by engaging readers in those
social activities.

Writing, Reading, and Social Action

The concept of social action concerns voluntariness, motives,
and influence. What makes the concept fuzzy is that social scientists
commonly ignore its presuppositions. Any theory of social action presupposes principles about expression and communication, but those
matters scarcely get the critical attention necessary for refining the
concept.

Social action is voluntary. The concept presupposes a socialized
individual capable of electing to act in this or that specific way. The

notion further presupposes that choices to act derive from individuals' projections into the future. Seeking some state of affairs, individuals project their desires into the future by phantasizing and then exe-
cuting courses of action as means to their goals.[110] Their in-order-to
motives emanate from more or less coherent systems of relevances,
making their choices more or less rational. Since individuals are inter-
dependent, most of their choices presuppose the ability to influence
those whose assistance is crucial, whose cooperation is helpful, or
whose resistance is fatal to their plans. Only individuals capable of
voluntary undertakings, endowed with motives, and alert to others'
abilities to help or hinder them are capable of social action.

Any activity that is voluntary, motivated, and socially oriented
inescapably expresses something of its originator's self. One cannot
voluntarily act toward or with other individuals without implying
motives or motivated choices. To some extent the individual engaged
in social action expresses at least that facet of his or her self. Yet how
such expression occurs remains defiantly mysterious. From the actor's
side, the pressing matters are achieving control over impressions made
and adapting specific techniques of control to different audiences
without seeming to have abandoned spontaneity or to have engaged
in fabrication. From the audience's side, the pressing questions complement those that concern actors. Audiences need to assess how
much spontaneity typically stamps actors' actions under various conditions and how an actor's techniques vary with roles and situations.

In many respects writing novels exemplifies the expressive control actors are capable of bringing to their performances. Canonical,
best-selling, subcultural, and formulaic novels illustrate how techniques of control vary for different sorts of audiences. Moreover,
imaginative writers deny their audiences the benefits of face-to-face
observations, especially the opportunity to see how painstakingly
writers put together their performances. Novelists have the further
advantage of lining up all their moves without interruption by the
audience. Although they must anticipate and take into account their
audiences' likely responses, novelists need not hold their imaginations back for fear of being ridiculed or scorned. Rather, they need
"simply" to subvert such eventualities by orchestrating the audience's
responses each step of the way through their narratives. Novelists do
express their selves, usually with vivid subtlety. That they do so as
self-conscious, intentional individuals working under nearly ideal
conditions allows them to approach the limits of expression.

How novelists succeed and fail in the realm of expression virtually demonstrates, therefore, the limits human beings face as expressive

creatures. A parallel argument can be advanced concerning communication. Exemplifying expression and communication distinguishes literature as a social world. As an exemplar of those processes, literature conveys at least tacit lessons with moral import, implicitly furthers humanistic values, and proffers practical insights into fundamental human experiences. The more literary a novel is—the more it exemplifies expression and communication—the more it serves moral, humanistic, and practical functions, even though its authors are unlikely to intend those effects. As literary artists and intellectuals know, literature essentially serves those ends. In and of itself, writing novels in a profoundly expressive manner with the aim to communicate effectively is a cultural service to one's contemporaries and successors. Writing anything is usually a form of social action. Imaginative writers take that form of social action to its empirical limits under given cultural and historical conditions.

Reading often involves vicarious social action, as readers take on the role of the author to some extent. In addition, readers often share their experiences with relatives, friends, and colleagues, as Paul DiMaggio indicates.[111] Thus, some of their vicarious social action while reading forms the basis for subsequent instances of overt social action. Most of all, readers vicariously experience social action in connection with characters. In canonical and many best-selling novels, readers "see" individuals pursuing a range of social action wide enough to constitute social relationships and social worlds. Literature exposes social action at its roots. To that extent its cultural position is profound. To that extent, too, novels and other literary works that apply formulas and transmit oral traditions wreak havoc with the liberating capacity "literature" denoted historically and still connotes today.

6

❦ Readers' Self-experiences

> Life being all inclusion and confusion, and art being all discrimination
> and selection, the latter . . . sniffs round the mass as instinctively and
> unerringly as a dog suspicious of a bone.
>
>   Henry James, Preface to *The Spoils of Poynton*

Joyce Carol Oates's *Expensive People* is a puzzle. Cast as a memoir, the novel confuses the reader from its beginning. The narrator's reliability is minimal; his identity, ambiguous; his voice, uncertain. Dickie Everett opens his memoir with "I was a child-murderer." Immediately, he clarifies his declaration ("I don't mean child-murderer,"); then he complicates it ("though that's an idea"). Dickie goes on to announce he is a murderer who happens to be a child or a child who happens to be a murderer. Then he says, "You can take your choice." Before the paragraph ends, Dickie admits he is experiencing a "quiet blubbering hysteria." In the remainder of the short chapter Dickie reminds the reader that a memoir is no fiction and that writing is a sweaty, tense process. He also contradicts himself enough times to establish his unreliability. He offers no details, though, about his victim. Dickie wants the reader's curiosity.

The second chapter, "An Incidental Historical Note," is five paragraphs surveying historical and literary instances where children murdered. What leads Dickie to label these paragraphs "incidental"? Although they appear not to advance the story, they do further acquaint the reader with Dickie, as is appropriate in a memoir. Even more than in the first chapter, Dickie comes across as an emotionally confused child and an intellectually adept adult. Just how old is he? In the first chapter he remarks, "If I told you how old I am you would turn away with a look of revulsion." (At the end of Chapter 11 Dickie provides grounds for inferring he was born in 1949; he is telling his story in 1967, apparently. He finally spills the information about his age in Chapter 22.) This confused eighteen-year-old exhibits detailed knowledge of literature, yet nowhere does he say how or why he acquired that knowledge.

Several other chapters, the only other titled ones in the novel, also do more to expose Dickie than to advance the story. Chapter 8 is "My Earliest Memory." Its second sentence contradicts a footnote in Chapter 3. Chapter 8 ends with a footnote where Dickie says, "Everything I type out turns into a lie simply because it is not the truth." Chapter 23 discusses "How to Write a Memoir Like This." Ironically, this chapter holds Dickie's one major slipup about the nature of his narrative. He continually emphasizes its factual nature, always referring to it as a memoir. Yet the opening paragraph of this chapter considers to whom Dickie would dedicate this *novel*. In Part 2 of the novel, only Chapter 5 has a title, "Reviews of 'Expensive People.'" There Dickie sketches the reviews critics will write of his memoir. The reviews again imply an intellect disproportionate to Dickie's education and interests. At the same time their incorporation leaves Dickie seeming as childish as the first pages of the novel make him out to be.

The titled chapters punctuate a narrative about an only child living in the wastelands of suburbia with upper-middle-class parents whose marriage is itself a wasteland. Elwood Everett is an organization man; Natshya (or Nada) is a novelist. Dickie's narrative describes his anxious participation in the adult world his parents manipulate, his uncomfortable efforts to fulfill their expectations, and the emotional abyss between him and them. At the same time the unfolding narrative tempts the reader to suppose Nada is using Dickie's voice to produce yet another novel. Perhaps the sensitivities expressed in *Expensive People* are hers. Who really authored the memoir? Whose is its controlling voice?

Throughout the narrative a child-adult polarity reigns. Dickie's parents alternate between treating him as a child and as an adult. Wanting to be "Daddy," Elwood addresses Dickie as "buster," "son," or "kid." Yet he sometimes insists that Dickie contribute to adult conversation[1] and treats Dickie as a confidant during the man-to-man times imposed by Nada's temporary absences. His mother seeks in Dickie a live-in companion during the times she lives with her husband. She calls Dickie "friend," "darling," or "honey." Yet she protects him when his dog dies, uses food to manipulate him, and relegates him to the children's section of the library. His parents' circumstances and moods dictate Dickie's status as child or adult. That Elwood and Nada are often at odds means Dickie has to be both simultaneously. In his role as child, Dickie is often "averting [his] eyes and turning away from things [he] was not supposed to see"; in his role as adult, he adopts spying on his parents as his "life's work" (pp. 37, 38).

Yet Dickie is only one of the child-adult characters in the novel. His mother falls into that category, too. Nada is sexually independent of but economically dependent on Elwood. She looks younger than she is and stages her behavior like a rag doll (pp. 6, 11). Her childhood memories are confused, and her adult longings lack a reliable focus. Like Dickie, who cannot establish a consistent identity at home, Nada cannot write her novels there. Her first novel appeared in 1957, her second in 1960; she left Elwood and Dickie in 1955 and again in 1958.

The narrator's belated disclosure that the memoir is about Nada (p. 247) forces the reader to decide whether the narrator represents Dickie's or Nada's point of view. At the same time the reader must decide what the novel is really about. Does it portray the scarred consciousness of a young man psychologically neglected or abused by his parents? Or a psychopathic personality imagining maltreatment from short-sighted but well-meaning parents? Or the merger of a mother's and a son's personalities in the taut world of upper-middle-class suburbia? Or an unfulfilled, talented woman lamenting her misguided decisions and misspent motherhood through her son's voice?

Chapter 14 of Part 2 includes "The Molesters," a short story narrated by a female who was molested by a mysterious man when she was six. The narrator feels nobody cares about her; she hates her mother. The story conveys the trauma, confusion, and loneliness associated with molestation and neglect. Its narrator's point of view is like Dickie's; her childhood memories are confused like Nada's. Dickie says his mother published the story in *The Quarterly Review of Literature*. The story's function in the novel is unclear. On the one hand, it may hold the novel's major irony. Dickie's mother may have acute insights into psychological abuse. On the other hand, the story may hint at who is controlling Dickie's voice. Because the story's and the memoir's narrators speak similarly, the reader might suppose they are creations of the same person. That temptation is all the stronger when the reader considers Dickie has more literary knowledge than is plausible for an eighteen-year-old but no more than is plausible for a novelist who also publishes in literary quarterlies.

Then, too, the novel piques the reader's curiosity about the relationship between Nada Elwood and Joyce Carol Oates. On the novel's copyright page the reader sees that Oates wrote "The Molesters" and published it in *The Quarterly Review of Literature*. When she included the story in *Expensive People*, why did Oates not only retain its original title but also leave intact the name of the publication where it appeared? Did she intend to imply a relationship between herself and Nada beyond that of creator and character? Is she inviting the reader to think about, if not look into, whether other details of Nada's career coincide with those of Oates's? Nada may be a persona of Oates. The solution to the novel's puzzles is scarcely at issue here. Rather, readers who relish the prospect of unraveling such tangles are my central interest. Oates's novel invites a specific sort of reader, as does every novel. Types of readers help to constitute the world of literature just as types of novelists do.

Reading Fiction: Generalists and Specialists

Classical criticism ignores the reader. Reader-response criticism, originating largely with Wolfgang Iser, addresses that gap, as do the works of Roland Barthes, Wayne Booth, John M. Ellis, and Hans Robert Jauss, among others. Some such critics imply that "literature is not in the text but in the reader,"[2] but most refuse to subordinate texts and authors to readers. Rather, they work from an understanding that "We cannot know what a narrative is except in relation to what it does";[3] that is, what readers make of it and take from it. Similarly, reading researchers now favor "a theory of reading that acknowledges the active role of the reader in constructing meanings from texts."[4]

Aiming to give readers their due, scholars confront sociological matters such as interaction, roles, and social action. Unfortunately, though, they find that sociologists say little about reading fiction. Like most literary critics, sociologists favor those aspects of reading "for which we have or can develop clear language," and they disattend "what is more difficult or less interesting to talk about."[5] Although they do command concepts for describing reader-author interaction, sociologists shy away from the phenomenological terrain where reading fiction has its meanings and satisfactions. Happily, a few venturesome souls like Wendy Griswold are changing that pattern, thereby making analytical room for readers as participants in the culture-making enterprise.

The "common reader"

> differs from the critic and the scholar. He is worse educated. . . .
> he reads for his own pleasure rather than to impart knowledge
> or correct the opinions of others. Above all, he is guided by an
> instinct to create for himself, out of whatever odds and ends he
> can come by, some kind of whole—a portrait of a man, a sketch
> of an age, a theory of the art of writing.[6]

The common reader is the "recreatory reader" of the 1930s or the "ludic reader"[7] of the 1980s—the reader bent on pleasure. Common readers are neither professional nor technical readers, as critics and scholars are. They are likelier to be "gluttonous readers," or "text gobblers," for whom books offer an "endless supply of nourishment."[8] Yet like critics and scholars, common readers are interpreters; they continuously select their objects of attention as they work their way through texts. Phenomenologically, they typify the objects of their experiences so as to fit them into their streams of consciousness, thus protecting themselves from the innumerable tugs a situation can make on consciousness.[9]

Like people stepping into any other role, readers need to know how to perform and in what spirit. Although they expect to build up closure as they progress, readers come ill-prepared to their novels if they expect narrators to tell them everything they want to know about specific characters, events, and outcomes. The occasion demands a receptive, accommodating spirit but sometimes vigilance and skepticism as well. Like the world of everyday life, the world of literature comprises unclear claims, inadequate accounts, mistaken identities, mixed motives, and abbreviated utterances. Under those circumstances skepticism curtails confusion. Trusting their own judgments enough to question others' claims and accounts, skeptical readers feel "no need or compulsion to suppress [their] subjective view . . . but on the contrary bring it to the clearest possible expression. . . . "[10] Readers can and sometimes do "watch" themselves getting involved in texts, often sensing how their streams of experience take shape with the turning pages.[11] Less self-consciously, they suspend their everyday preoccupations and bracket their pragmatic motives. To an extent, readers also suspend some disbeliefs in favor of a receptive spirit. Beginning a novel, they take some of the narrative at face value, allow for some coincidences, make way for bare plausibility, and accommodate characters who deviate from what their own typifications readily allow.

Readers' imaginative acts at two levels sweep away the apparent paradoxes of reading fiction. In order to secure a stream of meaningful experiences readers explore the same possibilities their novelists did, albeit less deeply and originally. At another level they explore the possibilities of misreading; that is, being taken in unawares by casually dismissing actual possibilities novelists have built into their fictional worlds. Readers must attune their imaginations to irony, then. As in their everyday lives, they interpret acts in contexts that either permit or disallow taking them at face value.[12]

Mapping the diversity among common readers necessitates distinguishing adequate responses to novels from appropriate ones.[13]

The latter responses entail knowledge of a world of literature and suspension of enough everyday baggage to engage one's self in a "good story." Appropriate responses include laughing, crying, and sighing as well as suspense, anger, or dismay. The most appropriate of responses remains, however, pleasure or enjoyment. Appropriate responses to novels mostly involve imaginative acts tightly governed, on the one hand, by the conventions delineating the world of literature and defining the novel and, on the other hand, by the guidance built into the specific text uniquely actualizing those conventions and definitions. With some novels, appropriate responses are also adequate. Formulaic and subcultural works characteristically demand no responses that are appropriate without also being adequate. Since debunking plays no central part in these novels, the reader's immersion in a good story itself exhibits both characteristics. Occasionally, best-selling novels exhibit the same readerly characteristics; their debunking may be sufficiently soft-pedaled that adequate responses readily surface alongside appropriate ones among most readers.

Other works invite or even demand more from readers than knowledge of and relative conformity to novelistic conventions; their authors provide less clear-cut guidance through the text. Such novels, generally best-selling and canonical works, often allow for an enjoyable reading consisting mostly of appropriate responses, for example, *Mansfield Park, Uncle Tom's Cabin, Daisy Miller, The Grapes of Wrath, One Flew Over the Cuckoo's Nest,* or *The Women of Brewster Place.* When the enjoyment of such novels revolves narrowly around their "good stories," however, the reader's response is less than adequate. These works invite more. They are relatively open, multivocal texts whose authors proffer meanings at many levels, whose characters and plots cast intriguing light on actual worlds or untapped possibilities, whose ironies are none too obvious. In some sense, adequate responses to these novels requires measuring up to the text, meeting it on its own as well as one's own terms.

In large measure, all readers want to end their reading with a self-satisfied "I got it." No one likes feeling overwhelmed or defeated by a text, which is why virtually all readers avoid some kinds of texts. The most interdisciplinary of scholars ignores texts in some fields; ardent lovers of fiction pass over texts from some cultures or time periods; savvy critics find some texts beyond the reach of their publishable analyses. Readers choose the texts their past experiences prepare them for and their current interests recommend. Distinguishing between those whose preferred texts exhibit relative openness of meaning and those whose preferred texts hold out relative closure is no easy matter, yet the distinction is essential to understanding readers as cultural types.

Originally, I had considered labeling the former readers "avocational" and the latter "consumerist." My labels exploded with elitist connotations, and I never felt at ease with them. I came to realize that their connotations were empirically insupportable—a fate likely common, if not inevitable, among elitist stances. "Avocational" connotes a seriousness of purpose, a steadiness of commitment, and a purity of motive inapplicable to many, perhaps most, readers of open-ended texts. In fact, many such readers treat novels as cultural goods they must consume as proper denizens of society's privileged strata. Some literary scholars pick at novels as if they were gourmet morsels capable of yielding their connoisseurs more publications and greater stature; some social scientists use novels as teaching tools picked up at the hardware store of literature; many professional people delight in exhibiting greater literary taste than those around them. A consumerist ethic lands these seemingly avocational types on a terrain where literature serves social respectability, career advancement, or cultural snobbery.

We dare not use any label that insistently connotes the superiority of these readers over those who prefer texts more readily yielding closure. Yet labels that appear to be value-neutral are like happiness—once one tries to mastermind them, their value-neutrality starts slipping away. In class societies like ours, people seem unable to abjure status connotations when naming their fellow creatures. That said, I suggest that readers broadly constitute two cultural types, generalist and specialist. *Generalist readers* tend to sample the array of available literature extensively. They favor best-selling as well as canonical works; formulaic and subcultural novels hold *relatively* little appeal for them except insofar as they identify with one or more subcultures; they are inclined to enjoy some nonfiction such as biography, history, travel, art criticism, or contemporary affairs; many read book reviews, at least occasionally. Historically, these were general-interest readers with considerable schooling and fairly catholic interests. *Specialist readers* tend to sample the array of available literature intensively. They favor formulaic and best-selling novels as well as those portraying subcultures they identify with; they read little book-length nonfiction; book reviews are unlikely to treat the books that most interest them so they typically ignore reviews. Historically, these were illiterate individuals with no effective access to schooling and life experiences generally breeding parochial interests.

Generalist and specialist readers come to their reading prepared for and seeking distinct, though related, experiences. The generalist reader comes prepared to accommodate ambiguity, chase meanings, express and further discover a self, and enjoy the expression of as well as communication from another human being. The specialist reader comes prepared to follow a fairly unambiguous lead, largely accept narrators' words at face value, experience the types of selves they already know, and enjoy a story.

Rarely do people read every word narratives offer. Yet specialist readers largely stick with one style of reading that exposes them to nearly all a text's words. The speed of their reading varies little; its intensity is fairly constant. Unconcerned with the immediate integrity of a text and unrestricted by a single style of reading, generalist readers skip and skim. They not only stand among the third or more of ludic readers who skim while reading but also vary their attention according to their interests as individuals and their needs as readers, for example, reducing their reading speed on "most-liked passages."[14] Generalist readers personalize their reading more than specialist readers do.

In part, individuals read differently because they read different types of novels; in part, they read different types of novels because they read differently. The two-way relationship between what people read and how they read presupposes that texts make different demands on readers, inviting different sorts of participation. Samuel Beckett's novels or the *nouveau romans* of Alain Robbe-Grille and Ivy Compton-Burnett, for example, invite intense effort. Like other readers, critics disagree about novels peddling ambiguity. Henry James saw the need to explain an artistic work as a mark of failure. Similarly, Gore Vidal says the difficulty of reading *Gravity's Rainbow* is probably greater than Pynchon's difficulty writing it. Vidal concludes, "This is entropy with a vengeance."[15] Granville Hicks says, though, that novels making for difficult first readings usually end up justifying the demands they make, and American book reviewers today would seem to agree.[16] Critics nevertheless do disagree about ambiguous novels, showing that the world of literature does attract different types of readers. When they read, those individuals seek meaning, not absurdity. That they have in common. The kinds of meaning they seek and their willingness to exert themselves for it differentiate them, though.

Like criticism, reading comprises acts of deciding, and "what it tries to decide is meaning."[17] Historical or contemporary, generalist or specialist, all readers ask "that same old question: 'What's it supposed to mean?'"[18] At root, meaning concerns *what* an object of experience is, not how or why it presents itself as it does. Establishing meaning thus involves naming the objects of one's experiences. Early in *The Scarlet Letter* a reader may consider Hester Prynne a sinner; later, a saint. Or a reader may alternate between considering *Lolita's* Humbert Humbert an unforgivable roue and a love-torn deviate. At the same time a reader might consider Hester a heroine, a victim, or an emblem of an age-old double standard, just as Humbert Humbert might appear as an unreliable narrator, a nontraditional hero, or a master of irony. Always from the world of everyday life and sometimes from the world of literature, individuals bring types to their reading that let them establish meaning. Generalist readers are likely to bring knowledge about other novels and some sense of literary devices like irony or authorial intrusion; specialist readers are less likely to bring either type of literary knowledge.

Meaning inheres in a text no more than in a rosebud or a statistic. Rather, individuals establish meaning as they typify the stuff of their experiences. Yet no text offers as many meanings as it has readers. Since readers draw their typifications from a social stock of knowledge and texts guide readers' interpretive activities, readers establish "essentially the same" meanings for their less demanding texts. For their more demanding texts, they come up with several competing interpretations; for example, Dickie controls his own voice or Nada controls it in *Expensive People*.

While reading, though, individuals do face the challenge of deciding what particular details mean. At this level readers share a common fate. They know "some statements cannot be understood without rejecting what they seem to say."[19] Although the taste for irony is weak among specialist readers, many texts offer big enough gaps between characters' words and actions that most readers' typifications take that gap into account. Generalist readers may typify such gaps with literary names; for example, stable irony. The meanings they seek concern the work as well as the story. After reading a novel, generalists are likelier than specialists to live a while longer with Hester or Humbert Humbert or Dickie. They are likely to explore not only the inner horizon of the novel—its own aspects—but also its outer horizon, the objects connected with it in the reader's field of experience, for example, other novels by the same author, others with similar themes, or others of the same period. Unlike specialist readers, generalist readers may reread novels to enlarge the meanings they seek.

Specialists mostly gear their imaginations to explicit elements of the text. Sometimes they lack the experiences necessary for making multiple associations and appreciating subtlety. They may not know about a work's historical context and thus, at times, misread explicit elements of a text.[20] Or they may lack exposure to the literary context of a novel; they may miss connections like those between John Barth's *The Sot-Weed Factor* and eighteenth-century novels. Generally, though, specialist readers scarcely suffer as a result, since (like other readers) they choose novels largely offering what they want. Among ludic readers, Victor Nell has found many specialist readers. He reports that "fiction reading accounts for the most ludic reading," with formulaic fiction being its "primary vehicle." Moderate in difficulty and high in predictability, such fiction satisfies one of the antecedents of ludic reading for many individuals; it "provides rewards sufficient to sustain the reading process." Like Radway's romance readers, Nell's ludic readers are aware of and more or less responsive to qualitative differences among works of fiction. They are aware that most of their pleasure reading involves "trash" in the eyes of cultural authorities such as English teachers. Nell found that among students, librarians, and professional critics alike, "merit and preference rankings are inversely related," perhaps because readers share the Protestant-ethic vision that "pain and virtue are allied."[21] In search of pleasure, many common readers thus appear to forego the virtue of reading "serious" fiction. Yet their rank-orderings of thirty novelists from most to least readable include Charles Dickens, Somerset Maugham, Henry James, Jane Austen, and Graham Greene in the top half, together with Louis L'Amour, Hunter S. Thompson, and Ian Fleming. In spite of the association they make between merit and difficulty, these readers know a good story when they read one—whether it incorporates the comic irony of a Jane Austen or follows the spy-thriller formulas refined by an Ian Fleming.

Thus, the preference of many ludic readers for formulaic fiction needs always to be understood in the context of their interests as much as their skills or tastes. With striking frequency, individuals turn to fiction not to heighten consciousness but to dull it,[22] at least in terms of their subjective experiences. Yet that pattern is amenable to a less jaundiced description offering greater psychological and cultural meaning.

Following John C. Cawelti, we can regard each novel as a unique amalgam of conventions and inventions serving different cultural functions. To wit, "Conventions represent familiar shared images and meanings, and they assert an ongoing continuity of values; inventions confront us with a new perception or meaning which we have not realized before." Each novel falls on a continuum between two ideal-typical poles, the one "a completely conventional structure of conventions" and the other "a completely original structure which orders inventions." Cawelti cites a "Lone Ranger" episode and *Finnegan's Wake* as respective examples of these poles. A formula, then, is a "conventional system for structuring cultural products," a device not for intensifying but for relaxing or entrancing the consciousness of those who experience the works it governs. Such works may, as Cawelti suggests, serve "certain unconscious or repressed needs."[23] At the same time, they are likely to serve conscious needs —above all, the need for recreation or relaxation which most readers report is the purpose of "much" of their voluntary reading.[24]

Whether their most powerful motives are conscious or not, specialist readers have little taste for ambiguous or otherwise "difficult" fiction. Faced with an unduly difficult novel, they experience boredom or dismay. Reading a book outside their typical repertoire, specialist readers are disinclined to finish it. Like subjects responding to ethnomethodologists' breaching experiments, their exasperation often leads them to insist, in effect, on bringing their experiences back into the world of comfortable familiarity. Generalists are, of course, likely to exhibit the same reaction under similar circumstances. Their educational and other advantages leave them less vulnerable, though, to such frustrations while reading.

Texts and Constitutive Demands

All texts make constitutive demands on their readers. Of necessity, they comprise "missing elements that are said to occupy 'empty slots' in the text." To some degree, then, readers must engage in "text elaboration."[25] A literary text fluctuates around two poles besides the conventional-inventional ones. Its artistic pole is the author's own creation; its aesthetic pole is the reader's realization of the text.[26] Novels inviting minimal involvement offer, by definition, few aesthetic possibilities. Yet this scarcely means only academic or experimental novels are aesthetically rich. *Don Quixote* asks a lot of its readers, as do eighteenth-century novels like *Humphrey Clinker* and *Tristram Shandy*.

Unraveling textual demands widens the grounds for distinguishing among types of readers and types of novels. Reading is obviously interpretive, as we have seen, since readers must continuously select specific details for more or less attention, reflection, and judgment. What they select partly derives from cues the text offers; for example, one is hard pressed to disattend Dickie's italics and quotation marks in his first chapter. Yet readers also rely on their knowledge and interests for guidance.

The first type of constitutive demand concerns readers' knowledge. Reading means naming the objects of experience in a novel so as to situate them in the stream of the reader's own consciousness. Novelists' words and their contexts offer only partial sense; readers apply their knowledge so as to more or less complete that sense. Proper names alone illustrate that process. In the first two chapters of Erich Segal's *Love Story*, Oliver Barrett the narrator refers to Bach, Mozart, the Beatles, Harvard, Radcliffe, Preppie, Comp. Lit. 105, the Renaissance, the *Crimson*, Dartmouth; also to Phillips Exeter, the National Anthem, Deerfield, Mem Church, Cambridge, and Nate Pusey. Oliver does not flag those names as referents to an actual world. By virtue of their past experiences some readers know that Harvard and Radcliffe are, in fact, in Cambridge and that their buildings have the names Oliver uses. Some also know "Nate" Pusey was president of Harvard and so forth. Lacking some of that knowledge, other readers need not think about whether the names refer to actual objects. Although their experiences reading the first two chapters will differ from those of readers bringing more knowledge to the novel, the constitutive demand to recognize is mild here. Nearly every reader is capable of recognizing the names Harvard and the Beatles. Beyond that, some readers' knowledge amplifies the meanings they constitute but remains unnecessary for establishing sense.

The first two chapters of *Expensive People* offer proper names of a different sort: Aristotle, Cadillac, Wren, Nietzschean, *Peter Lully*, Flaubert, Louise Colet, Chaucerian, *Macbeth*, Stendhal, Bobbie Hunter, and West Bend, Indiana. Here many readers might have trouble determining whether Dickie is showing off or faking it. Other terms in the first chapters of these novels illustrate the same point. Oliver offers "eye the cheese," "A minus on the exam," "sandwich joint," "screaming for blood," " the ref," "jock," "dish it out," "horny bastards," and "up yours." Dickie offers "novelistic architecture," "the shrewd passivity of that phrase," "this memoir is a hatchet," "irony is an unpleasant character trait," "psychoanalytic literary critics," and "a photostat of a lithograph." Readers unable to meet Oates's (or any other's) demand for recognition are likely to experience "unaccommodated awareness . . . which pulls against what one takes to be the intention of the work or the authorial point of view."[27]

A second kind of demand involves imaginative inferences. Like participation in everyday life, reading a novel requires filling in blanks. Reading intensifies everyday versions of inferring intentions and completing pictures only partially sketched during interaction. The intensification derives from being lifted out of everyday life where other individuals often offer feedback on one's interpretations. It also comes from needing to infer within a field of far-flung possibilities rather than narrow probabilities.

How frequently and elaborately readers must infer differentiates texts and the readers they attract. All novels require "continuous oscillation between involvement and observation."[28] Some, though, demand abrupt shifts between prereflective and reflective involvement. They pull the reader back and forth between prepredicative experiences where characters, actions, and events are simply "given" and predicative experiences where the reader consciously judges textual elements. Such novels "produce a specific form of tension that leaves [the reader] suspended, as it were, between total entanglement and latent detachment. The result is a dialectic—brought about by the reader himself—between illusion-forming and illusion-breaking."[29] *Lolita* produces the tension characteristic of novels with high demands for imaginative inferences, partly because of its entrancing language.

A third kind of demand concerns familiarity. The familiar is that segment of experience currently needing no further investigation.[30] Familiarity rests on continuous syntheses of recognition; people experiencing it synthesize their recognitions of selfsameness (identity) or of similarity (type). Sufficient familiarity means having "established a type of such a degree of anonymity or concreteness so as to satisfy the interpretational requirements necessary to determine the topic at hand."[31] As they read, individuals oscillate not only between involvement and detachment but also—and correlatively—between familiarity and unfamiliarity. Although pleasurable reading requires unfamiliarity as a source of engagement, prolonged experiences of the unfamiliar border on the meaningless. Thus, readers perform "balancing operations" as they find familiarity in jeopardy; they compare "the fictitious characters with [their] own experience[s] and attempt to bring them into line with [their] own familiar world."[32] Iser says that

> The repertoire of the familiar—whether it be literary tradition, contemporary "Weltanschauung," or social reality—forms the background of the novel. The familiar is reproduced in the text, but in its reproduction it seems different, for its component parts have been altered, its frame of reference has changed, its validity has, to a degree, been negated.[33]

Yet novelists at least hint at *possible* ways to typify various aspects of their novels. Novels like *Love Story* offer a heavy dose of familiarity. Even though Harvard is no average setting and becoming a widower in one's twenties is far from typical, college romances and the loss of one's first love lie close to what people are familiar with. For many readers, Harvard rather than Boston University and losing a young spouse by death rather than a young lover by default defamiliarize the familiar enough to spark interest.[34] *Expensive People*, on the other hand, holds out details about attending a private boys' school, writing memoirs and novels, and living in suburbs where people chew Sweet Peach gum while keeping themselves tan and trim year round. Although most Americans have types available that keep privileged living and creative writing from being alien, many lack any experiences that allow them to meet the interpretational demands the overall picture makes. Dickie's unreliability exacerbates that circumstance. *Expensive People* demands the predicative constitution of familiarity much more than *Love Story* does.

The last of the basic demands is meaning. All novels demand meaning-intention, or the prepredicative grasping of *what* its specific details are. Novels low on the demand for meaning ask little more from readers. Most novels, however, also demand meaning-fulfillment, or the active constitution of meaning. Meaning-fulfillment requires "polythetic reconstruction," that is, attending to the steps whereby the individual grasped an object as this or that and fitted it into his or her stream of conscious life. At any point in the text what the reader has worked into familiar shape can be bent out of shape by shifting circumstances or fresh revelations. Such eventualities represent demands for meaning-fulfillment where the reader must actively constitute the meaning of past or even just-past experiences of the text. The reader's retrospective glances recur as the novel progresses. The interplay between elements of the text currently being experienced and the reader's prior meaning-intentions necessitates those pauses for meaning-fulfillment. While reading, then, "there is a continual interplay between modified expectations and transformed memories."[35]

Readers secure meaning by repeatedly combining and recombining textual elements.[36] They thus fill in textual blanks and vacancies; in a sense they complete the text. Barthes's analysis of reading Balzac's *Sarrasine* illustrates meaning-intention and meaning-fulfillment among readers. Barthes broke *Sarrasine* into short, contiguous pieces, often less than a sentence in length. Called "lexias," those fragments represent units of reading that "have at most three or four meanings to be enumerated."[37] Barthes intersperses the lexias with descriptions of the denotations, connotations, and ambiguities each presents. In the process he illustrates in detail a reader's constitution of meaning.

Iser offers truncated illustrations of the same processes but more rigorous accounts of how they occur. Using Edmund Husserl's findings about experience and meaning, Iser generalizes that at every moment reading involves retentions, protentions, and horizons. Retentions are the expectations built up from past acts of consciousness, whether prepredicative or predicative; protentions are the correlative expectations conditioning imminent acts of consciousness. Thus, when individuals experience objects, their awareness comprises a "horizon of expectation" built up from prior experiences. Every object of consciousness has a horizon, a set of possibilities for making more precise determinations of that object.[38] Novelists control those possibilities for their readers. After readers have finished a novel, however, that horizon remains as an amplitude of possibilities governed solely by the reader's past experiences (including those of having read the given novel), interests, and imagination. Thus, meaning-fulfillment often continues after readers have returned novels to their shelves. Periodically, for example, I still ponder the problems *Expensive People* poses.

Although novels make many other sorts of demands on readers, the demands for recognition, inferences, familiarity, and meaning offer sound starting points for describing what reading entails. Furthermore, these demands point to the intersubjective stuff shaping interaction between novelists and readers. What novels demand of their readers points, in short, to the social character of reading.

❦ Novel Making, Novel Reading, and Literary Interaction

I have always believed in letting my reader sink or skim.

Lawrence Durrell, *Balthazar*

Literary Communication, Expression, and Interaction

Reading literature is an engagement in interaction structured by the demands novelists make on their readers. Canonical novels make the keenest demands. Then come best-selling novels, followed by subcultural and formulaic novels. Literary artists and intellectuals largely attract generalist readers; literary chroniclers and reporters, specialist readers. These patterns imply different sorts of literary interaction. Broadly, generalist readers incline toward what Erving Goffman calls strategic interaction; specialist readers, toward what he calls teamwork.

A one-to-one situation "remains the essential condition of prose fiction."[1] Although it departs from the face-to-face situation, reading does instantiate dyadic interaction centered on a common situation. The reader and the novelist share an "intersubjective motivational context" where their motives "complement and validate each other as objects of reciprocal attention."[2] Although influence flows from novelist to reader, reciprocity stamps the novelist's and the reader's attention to Other.

Today fascination with The Text focuses attention on a text-reader dynamic, not an author-reader connection. Sociologically and phenomenologically, that stance is problematic. It diminishes readers' and writers' actual experiences by treating The Text as a linguistic gestalt stimulating little more than cognitive, solitary exercises. As Joyce Carol Oates points out, though, what academicians treats "as 'texts' (that most sinister of terms) . . . were written as urgent human documents" capable of "lifting the veil that separates one consciousness from another."[3] Similarly, Jeffrey L. Sammons approaches the text "as 'full' of life and reality and concern. . . . " He insists on "treating literature in its real, local context of human relations and social construction of consciousness. . . . "[4] That insistence requires grappling with reader-author interaction without dismissing the profound ways texts overflow their creators' conscious intentions. The sociologist Juan E. Corradi observes that writing began

> in social life, when those conditions emerged that gave literary practice its place and its function in a determinate social formation. Once in motion, writing proceeds according to patterns that "pass through," but also exceed, the writer. And writing does not cease with the accomplishment of a final *opus*, nor with the social consumption of the text, for the consumption is almost inexhaustively renewed, and, in some instances, itself productive of new texts.[5]

Texts are objective social facts shaped by more than the intentions of their authors. Like all human achievements, they carry consequences no one intended and give way to meanings no one foresaw. Yet to reify texts is no less unfortunate than to reify any other part of the social and cultural world. Above all, literary texts are gifts from social creatures bent on expressing some measure of uniqueness and achieving some form of communication through the conventions governing their work. The human will to speak and be heard, human agency in the service of a shared culture, human individuality forging ahead within the sociohistorical confines of objective culture—these are the animate realities issuing forth in literary texts, realities that scarcely disappear once a text appears as a cultural commodity on booksellers' shelves. Reading a novelist for the first time means meeting a new person; reading that novelist's other works furthers an agreeable association. Using Dickens's and Faulkner's works, for example, Guerard demonstrates that every strong novelist uses a variety of voices, including a personal voice unmistakably stamping his or her work. He also finds that novelists differ in the intimacy they cultivate with readers.[6] Authors' selves peek through their texts. They cannot vanish from their narratives; supposing they would want to distorts their actual experiences. Thus, authorial presence is a constant. Its forms and degrees imply the interactional variety available to readers.

From the eighteenth century well into the nineteenth century, novelists explicitly indicated the kind of interaction they sought with their readers. Their artifices revolved around direct statements to readers that sometimes crop up in contemporary novels. Often direct addresses facilitate readers' efforts at recognition. "The reader will be pleased to remember . . . ," says the narrator in *Tom Jones*.[7] In *The Wealth of Mr. Waddy*, the narrator reminds readers about prior allusions to "a Mr. Kipps" and cites the situations where he appeared. The narrator goes on: "The manifest intention of the author has been to arouse interest and curiosity in this person, to provoke the reader to ask, what the devil has Kipps to do with it?"[8] When novelists address their readers in these ways, they underscore their originative roles while implying a helping stance.

Novelists also directly address readers so as to facilitate their inferential activities. In *Pendennis*, the narrator remarks that "ours, as the reader has possibly already discovered, is a Selfish Story. . . . " In Williams Styron's *Set This House on Fire* the narrator says, "If this story has a hero it is [Cass], I suppose, who fits the part."[9] Though more tentative than Thackeray's narrator, Styron's nevertheless indicates the direction readers' inferences should take. Whether narrators point toward definite or tentative inferences, their remarks help to constitute both their own and their readers' roles. They imply that although authors demand imaginative inferences from their readers, they tailor their demands to reasonableness by helpfully stepping to the narrative fore.

Similar stances occur in connection with the demand for familiarization. Sometimes narrators step forward to alert readers about when to pause and familiarize themselves with details and when to push forward for details on the horizon. In *Joseph Andrews*, the narrator refers to "a speech on charity, which the reader, if he is so disposed, may see in the next chapter. . . . " Here the narrator advises the reader that the speech is unnecessary to familiarizing oneself with the fictional world at hand. *Jane Eyre's* narrator reminds readers that new chapters often mean new occasions for familiarization: "A new chapter in a novel is something like a new scene in a play; and when I draw up the curtain this time, reader, you must fancy you see a room in the George Inn at Millcote. . . . "[10]

Novelists also intrude so as to make reasonable their demands for establishing meaning. In *Tom Jones* the narrator says, "As this is one of those deep observations which very few readers can be supposed capable of making for themselves, I have thought proper to lend them my assistance. . . . "[11] Fielding does here what most novelists do at some points, namely reinforce the elements necessary for meaning-fulfillment. In *Joseph Andrews* Fielding's narrator says the "sagacious reader . . . can see two chapters before him."[12] The reader stands alerted, in other terms, to the need for alertness. Sometimes narrators address meaning-fulfillment by referring explicitly to other of their own works. In *Phineas Redux* Trollope refers to the heroine of *The Eustace Diamonds*, an earlier volume in his Palliser series. In *Mr. Crewe's Career* Churchill refers to a character from *Coniston*, another of his novels.[13] Such references pinpoint the retentions readers may use to fulfill some meanings of the text.

Sometimes narrators tell readers where to pursue meaning-fulfillment within the text itself. "Whether I shall turn out to be the hero of my own life, or whether that station will be held by anybody else, these pages must show," announces the narrator in the first sentence of *David Cooperfield*. Early in *Mr. Crewe's Career*, its narrator makes a similar move: "Without burdening the reader with a treatise on the fabric of a system, suffice it to say that something was continually going on that was not law. . . ."[14] *Realms of Gold* offers additional examples: "The fact that she was doing this, as she was some twenty-three pages ago, does not indicate that no time has passed. . . . " Similarly, the narrator says,

And that is enough, *for the moment*, of Janet Bird. More than enough, *you might reasonably think*, for her life is slow, *even slower than its description*, and her dinner party seemed to go on too long for her, *as it did to you*. Frances Wingate's life moves much faster. (Though it began rather slowly, in these pages—*a tactical error, perhaps*, and the idea of starting her off in a more manic moment has frequently suggested itself, but *the reasons against such an opening are stronger, finally, than the reasons for it*.)[15] (Emphasis added.)

Here the narrator makes five major points abut meaning-fulfillment. First, we will return to Janet Bird; second, the attention given Janet appears inordinate, but think of it as an emblem of her dull life; third, your experiences reading about Janet's party correlate with her experiences enduring it; fourth, perhaps I should have contrasted Wingate's faster-paced life with Janet's sooner (what do you think?); finally, what advantages might outweigh the disadvantages of having postponed that contrast? The narrator both reassures and queries the reader here while guiding meaning-fulfillment.

Authors' direct intrusions also concern what they themselves are taking for granted and what they assume their readers are capable of taking granted. Rather than give specific details, authors sometimes invoke readers' stock of knowledge. Fielding makes the move in both *Joseph Andrews* and *Tom Jones*, for example, "O reader! conceive if thou canst the joy which fired the breasts of these lovers on this meeting." In *Mr. Crewe's Career* the narrator claims, "We are so used in America to these tremendous rises that a paragraph will suffice to place Mr. Flint in his Aladdin's palace."[16] Instances like these show authors invoking readers' knowledge at hand while readying them for the next detail of interest.

Novelists as Interactants: Resources, Roles, and Selves

Understanding literary interaction mandates understanding the role of author including the resources it presupposes, the sorts of behavior it prescribes and proscribes, and the latitude it offers for expression.

Among authors' resources is *Verstehen*, "the experiential form of commonsense knowledge of human affairs."[17] Novelists use *Verstehen* to draw imaginative lines between interpreting their own experiences and interpreting others' meaning-contexts.[18] The novelist's others are fictional characters, or unembodied types, whose behavior he or she interprets while fitting it into a coherent fictional world. Artistic *Verstehen* proscribes baldly stereotyping characters. Defamiliarizing the familiar, or debunking, means novelists cannot duplicate commonsense typifications. Rather, they need to subvert those typifications (defamiliarization) without disregarding them (plausibility). Achieving that balance means applying *Verstehen* not by systematically investigating others' experiences but by imaginatively exploring the possible motives, outcomes, and identities that pertinent types of individuals experience. Novelists thus use *Verstehen* to create characters inhabiting a world readers enter with some ease, that is, a world readers can familiarize.

Novelists' other resources derive from print. Although they cannot wink at their readers or pat them on the back, writers command advantages unavailable in the face-to-face situation such as punctuation, capitalization, and footnotes. Such resources let writers control the emphasis given each element of their narratives, thus providing them some of the options gestures and glances provide speakers. Writers' resources also allow for what Goffman calls "parenthetical elaboration," a feature of all communication. Although novelists routinely exercise their option for revising, their texts nevertheless show them

exercis[ing] the right to introduce parenthetical statements, qualifying, elaborating, digressing, apologizing, hedging, editorializing, and the like. These passing changes in voice, these momentary changes in footing, may be marked in print through bracketings of some kind—parenthetical signs, dashes, etc. Or

the heavy-handed device of footnotes may be employed. . . .
Through all of these devices, the writer briefly changes footing
relative to his text as a whole. . . . These elaborations ordinarily
extend the "production base" for the reader, giving him more of
a grounding in the writer's circumstances and opinions than the
naked text might allow.[19]

Text-parenthetical comments also

convey qualifying thoughts that the speaker appears to have
arrived at just at the very moment. It is as if the speaker here
functioned as a broker of his own statements, a mediator
between text and audience, a resource capable of picking up on
the non-verbally conveyed concerns of the listeners and
responding to them in the light of the text and everything else
known and experienced by the speaker.[20]

Writers cannot, of course, pick up nonverbal cues from readers, but
they can use *Verstehen* to infer readers' likely needs and responses. They
understand that direct intrusions, apparent asides, and other momentary shifts in footing make their printed texts like spoken stories.

As self-revelatory storytellers, novelists also rely on resources for
directing readers and committing themselves to specific courses. Novels contain both *directives* concerning how to recognize, infer, and
familiarize and *commissives* "comprising promises, pledges, threats,
offerings, and the like." Aware of those sorts of moves, novelists also
know "A text allows a speaker a cover for the rituals of performance."[21]
Texts cover maneuvers people are hard pressed to hide in everyday life
including blushes, grimaces, and chuckles. To varying degrees they
also cover deliberate moves to implicate readers in temporary doubt or
confusion. Texts also remove authors from speakers' vulnerability to
interruptions and queries. Novelists can, in short, tightly control readers' responses to indeterminacies.

The conventions most affecting novelists deal with those indeterminacies. The most problematic indeterminacies concern the interactions among fictional characters and the interaction between novelist
and reader. In Goffman's terms, "The first issue is . . . frame," where
frame organizes specific activities like reading a novel.[22] The rules
enjoin novelists to use framing procedures that make their printed
words accessible as "a novel" while making accessible the world they
are portraying. At the same time novelists must arrange matters so
that readers can join them in "a ratified, joint, current, and running

claim upon attention, a claim which lodges them together in some sort of intersubjective . . . world." Thus, they must constitute "a sustained strip or tract of referencings, each referencing tending to bear, but often deviously, some retrospectively perceivable connection to the immediately prior one." Thereby the novelist puts forth "a particular definition of the situation, this representing, as it were, his claim as to what reality is."[23] Masterminding that definition without boring or exhausting readers necessitates controlling readers' information states; that is, what they know "of why events have happened as they have, what the current forces are, what the properties and intentions of the relevant persons are, and what the outcome is likely to be." Like all communication, literary communication presupposes that "the controlling and openly avowed (if not actual) purpose of the sender is to impart correct, adequate information to the recipient. . . . "[24] In a novel what constitutes correct information often depends on whose viewpoint is filtering the information, but what constitutes adequate information is less open: Readers must have enough information for meaning-intention and meaning-fulfillment.

Like all interactants, novelists may use "cues, tests, hints, [depicted] expressive gestures, status symbols" and other "predictive devices."[25] They may also change their footing momentarily, break frame, or set up virtual barriers to perception as long as they neither destroy the frame nor violate plausibility. Novelists work in a large playground, creating one of those "situations where an observer is dependent on what he can learn from a subject . . . and the subject [is] oriented to frustrate this assessment or facilitate it under difficult circumstances."[26] Literary interaction means the novelist (subject) and the reader (observer) continuously negotiate participation statuses relative to each lexia and move in the narrative, the one while writing and typifying the reader and the other while reading and typifying the novelist. Conjointly, novelists and their readers build up a participation framework that codifies their participation statuses.[27] As long as that virtual framework remains intelligible and conduct falls inside the range deemed appropriate, novelists may freely manipulate their readers' assessments.

Intermeshed with these interactional indeterminacies is a web of indeterminacies concerning the novelist as a public performer. Every performance involves "expressive identifiability": "From any and all of our dealings with an individual, we acquire a sense of his personality, character, quality as a human being. We come to expect that all his acts will . . . be stamped in a unique way."[28] Yet individuals cannot disclose their full personhood in social situations. Rather, they have "special selves" appropriate to specific sorts of occasions.[29] Following Goffman, we expect novelists to exhibit occasion-appropriate "special selves" no less than individuals in other roles. Among literary critics that expectation revolves around the problematic notion "persona," as Robert C. Elliott has shown using Goffman's principles.[30]

Wayne C. Booth says literary performances involve six aspects of the novelist. First is the *person or self*, the subject of a unique stream of experiences or a unique biography never completely suspended in the world of literature. Minimally, it centers the writer's stream of conscious experiences. When the novelist takes up a pen or turns on the microcomputer, the *author* comes into play—one who writes or composes. The author is the individual acting in a specific world with specific motives, plans, and projects diffusely related to those of the commonsense person he or she is. Once a work is available to readers, its originator becomes a performer at two levels. The *dramatized author* exhibits a unique self readers encounter in passages smacking of "Dear Reader" or "I, the author"; the *implied author* is the sum total of the impressions readers develop about the author *qua* author through a specific novel. The implied author derives from subtleties in the interaction between a novelist and a reader through a given work. When they experience an implied author, readers experience a person. They infer what sort of individual opts to write about the world at hand, treats characters in this fashion, uses language in these ways, and so forth; they infer, for instance, a cynical or a kindhearted sort of person. Inevitably for many readers, authors thus present an *implied self* that appears near the end of a novel and takes full shape in the aftermath of reading. So does the *novelist* as the reader's typification and assessment of the author *qua* author.[31] When the reader has read only one of an author's works, the novelist is the dramatized and the implied author of that novel as typified and assessed by the reader.

Describing literary interaction thus means examining the moves dramatized and implied authors make so as to evoke the countermoves whereby readers constitute the novelist and his or her implied self. It also involves examining those performances where authors take their specialist readers in, virtually refusing to dramatize and imply an author. Such authors engage their readers in teamwork rather than strategic interaction.

Reading as Strategic Interaction

Goffman's concern with the social forms of communication and how selves find expression in and through those forms makes his insights singularly valuable for illuminating interaction. A fruitful starting point is the generalist readers whose ideal-typical characteristics imply Goffman's model of strategic interaction, tending to correlate with what he ascribes to observers during such interaction.

Goffman defines *action* as "activities that are consequential, problematic, and undertaken for what is felt to be their own sake." It is "a species of activity in which self-determination is celebrated."[32] Novels such as *Our Mutual Friend* or *Expensive People* that attract generalist readers are problematic by virtue of their unreliable narrators, subtle ironies, intricate psychologies, or sheer complexity. Mastering such works is consequential when people's identities hinge on their analytical prowess. Such novels make reading an exercise of power as well as a gathering of pleasure, an opportunity for action alongside aesthetic experiences.

More capable today than ever before, most generalist readers perform as well as collaborate; they know when to move with and when to resist the text. Generalists know involvement with a text cannot be free-wheeling immersion: "A correct view of a scene must include the viewing of it as part of it."[33] Their tension of consciousness derives partly from the dialectic between thoroughgoing involvement and self-distancing observation and partly from distinctive features of the literary situation. Unlike members of an audience, the reader sits alone with a performer who is not directly perceptible and is often ironic.

The generalist's tension of consciousness is that of a participant in strategic interaction. Literary strategic interaction typically engages the literary artist or intellectual and the generalist reader. The author's interests lie in expressing himself or herself, communicating so as to please and stimulate, and becoming a novelist respected among generalist readers and literary critics. The generalist reader's interests lie in expressing himself or herself, mastering indeterminacies so as to experience pleasure and stimulation, and becoming a reader other generalist readers respect and critics and novelists presuppose in their works. The dramatized and implied authors must alternately appear to help and hinder "their" readers; "they" must manipulate indeterminacies without either giving the show away or making it a nonsensical exercise. That means orienting their performances to the typical reader's capacities by imaginatively inferring what sorts of people find appeal in their invitations to interact. Similarly, the reader orients his or her responses to the capacities dramatized and implied authors must be assumed to possess as the sort of person making these specific moves with word choices, shifts in the scene or point of view, and so forth. Author and reader engage, therefore, in a contest of assessment that provides readers an occasion for expressing their selves, for it is only *"against something* that the self can emerge."³⁴ Strategic interaction engages selves, not role-players as such.

Such interaction eventuates under several conditions:

> Two or more parties must find themselves in a well-structured situation of mutual impingement where each party must make a move and where every possible move carries fateful implications for all of the parties. In this situation, each player must influence his own decision by his knowing that the other players are likely to try to dope out his decision in advance, and may even appreciate that he knows this is likely. Courses of action or moves will then be made in the light of one's thoughts about the other's thoughts of oneself. . . . One part of strategic interaction consists of concrete courses of action taken in the real world that constrain the parties; the other part . . . consists of a special kind of decision-making—decisions made by directly orienting oneself to their situation as they would seem to see it, including their giving weight to one's own.³⁵

Strategic interaction activates the ability to acquire, reveal, and conceal information.³⁶ By its very nature novelist-reader interaction always is strategic to some extent, then. Robert Frost illustrates the point: "I understand the poem all right, but please tell me what is behind it? . . . The answer must be 'If I had wanted you to know, I should have told you in the poem.'"³⁷

In strategic interaction the subject adopts the viewpoint of the observer and then assesses his or her own activity in order to control it. The control that eventuates grows out of a series of *moves*, or "structured courses of action . . . which, when taken, objectively alter the situation of the participants." Moves affect both participants' states of information and the effective courses of action available to them as interaction continues.³⁸ A move comprises any number of gestures, words, and so forth that position the other party for the time being, that is, affect the other's framework of possible moves and their likelihood of success.³⁹ During strategic interaction individuals adopt *strategies*, or frameworks of different courses of action linked in advance to a possible choice of the opponent such that howsoever the opponent acts, the subject will be able to reply immediately.⁴⁰ Between novelist and reader immediate replies are impossible so novelists' strategies rely heavily on ambiguity. Unable to adapt their moves to unexpected but consequential "replies" from their readers, novelists need ambiguity to provide for imaginative forays with their characters (and thus a good show) and keep readers active (and thus involved in the show).

An *authorial move* is any stretch of narrative that "has a distinctive unitary bearing on some set or other of the circumstances" between the author and the reader he or she typifies. Such a move might evoke a distinctive emotion or mood, puzzle or illuminate, introduce a new character, or omit what the reader might be supposed to have expected. An author's move may be as short as a sentence or phrase and as long as several successive paragraphs or a chapter. In most instances a chapter comprises a series of moves, each chapter being a fresh round of strategic interaction. An author's moves incorporate both statements and replies, since authors must respond, more or less reflectively, to absent readers whose supposed responses shift the novelist's position from one move to the next. A *statement* is "a move characterized by an orientation to some sort of answering to follow"; a *reply* is "a move characterized by its being seen as an answering of some kind to a preceding matter that has been raised."[41] Consider Dickie Everett beginning his narrative:

Statement 1:	I was a child murderer.
Reply 1:	I don't mean child-murderer
Statements:	(2) though that's an idea.
	(3) I mean child murderer,
Replies:	(2) that is a murderer who happens to be a child,
	(3) or a child who happens to be a murderer.
Statement:	(4) You can take your choice.

Although authors enjoy a diversity of possible moves, the actual regress of moves and virtual countermoves (from the typified reader) is quite limited. Prior moves narrow the range of effective moves at any point, and pressing one's luck too far in that regard is likely to be ruinous.

Sometimes authors aim to position their readers quite specifically *and* to expose their intention. Whenever their statements or replies direct the reader's attention or commit the dramatized author to an imminent course of action, authors are using directives and commissives. Early in a novel, such moves win the reader's trust while facilitating access to the fictional world at hand. Sometimes directives and commissives rescue the reader from ambiguity and intricate detail. Authors also use directives and commissives as farewells for ending their novels. All authors use these moves. When strategically interacting with their readers, though, they use them alongside other techniques that put readers on guard or catch them off guard. Functioning much like directives and commissives is *accentuated revealment* whereby dramatized or implied authors emphatically provide details or insights.[42] Short moves of accentuated revealment fix the reader's attention, often functioning as an indirect directive. Longer moves of this sort enhance the dramatized or implied author's credibility while heightening readers' sense of reality.

Dramatized and implied authors also use *asides*, brief text-parenthetical statements or replies with diverse functions. An aside provides a short respite from the narrative's frame, thereby accentuating the frame it violates. It also lets the author appear spontaneous or accessible, shoring up readers' sense of collaborating in the show they are, in part, figuring out. Asides also let authors sneak crucial information into their texts, testing the reader's alertness while positioning themselves to surprise the reader later. *Reservations*, or qualified statements and replies, function similarly. Used occasionally, they serve as virtual breaks from frame or shifts in footing, casting the author as a human figure who is, after all, far from omniscient. Reservations also let authors introduce information without taking all the wind out of it in one fell swoop. Finally, reservations give authors the opportunity to later withdraw from standpoints and their implications.[43] Thus, they lend mystery to implied authors and implied selves for readers trying to determine against whom they are playing.

Authors also make seductive moves. *Ironic seduction* occurs when the "author conveys to his reader an unspoken point, . . . creat[ing] a sense of collusion against all those, whether in the story or out of it, who do not get that point." Irony seduces readers by making them feel they have earned their favored position. *Ideological seduction* involves invoking norms that make readers feel the dramatized or implied author shares their values. *Social seduction* involves treating readers like trusted colleagues or literary companions, making it likelier they will go along with the dramatized or implied author. Sometimes social seduction involves ritualizing another participation framework; that is, introducing the sorts of demeanor associated with another sort of interaction.[44] Directly addressing the reader as "friend" is an example, as are appeals to readers for their judgments (the collegial stance). Such ritualization pays off in enriched deference, landing readers in a position where the author can more readily dupe them.

Innuendo can snap readers to attention while creating tentative expectations that keep interest lively. Often, it relieves the author of responsibility for having misled readers. *Innuendo* is readily deniable communication that lets one "profit from lies without technically telling any."[45] More generally, authors can use nearly any *ambiguity* as a move. Often when readers are left confused or doubtful, the dramatized or implied author has opted for this sort of move. Sometimes ambiguity builds up as the author's moves accumulate, that is, ambiguity can be a strategy. Kafka, Beckett, and Robbe-Grillet, for instance, let readers learn about situations, in effect, at the same time as their narrators.[46] As a strategy, ambiguity may incorporate any of the aforementioned moves. It may also include moves like disqualifying oneself, omitting crucial information, making control moves, and fabrication.

Like other interactants, dramatized and implied authors can use *disqualification* of their status to mislead readers.[47] Hysterical illness like the sort Dickie Everett claims is illustrative. *Crucial omissions* sometimes serve a similar function. The absence of what is expected can serve as an alarm. If the reader is not expecting specific information, however, its absence goes unnoticed. Thus, crucial omission can help readers by alerting them or hinder them by providing an incomplete view.

More subtle than crucial omissions, even after the fact, are *control moves*, or the "intentional effort . . . to produce expressions that [the subject] thinks will improve his situation if they are gleaned by the observer."[48] Ford Madox Ford says authors must sometimes "*appear* to digress. This is the art which conceals your Art. So you will provide [the reader] what he thinks are digressions—with occasions on which he thinks he may let his attention relax."[49] The one place where Dickie Everett appears to slip and call his memoir a novel may illustrate a control move. His slipup may be a guise he expects the reader to latch onto; it may be a snare to deepen confusion about who actually controls Dickie's voice. Control moves are tantamount to *fabrication*, "the intentional effort . . . to manage activity so that a party . . . will be induced to have a false belief about what it is that is going on."[50] Unlike control moves, fabrication misleads, rather than confuses, readers for a time by leaving them unaware their current viewpoint is distorted or downright wrong. Apparent directives, commissives, and related moves can actually be fabrications.[51] Authors can execute all these moves through statements or replies. With statements alone, they can execute the *set-up*, a statement likely to evoke a response to which the author can then reply with the desired move.[52] Here authors obscure their purposes by indirection.

Thus, authors' statements and replies constitute moves ranging from directives and commissives, on the one end, to fabrications and set-ups, on the other end. In no way, however, does an author's every phrase or sentence constitute a move. Not every element of a narrative alters the reader's or the author's position, that is, the state of either's information or available courses of action. Authors are likely to make *unwitting moves* "unoriented to the assessment an observer might be making."[53] Given the surfeit of moves they purposefully make, authors are probably taken in by their own acts at some junctures. Given that they are literary artists and intellectuals, though, their unwitting moves are limited together with their spontaneity.

Authors use guises for dramatizing and implying themselves to readers. Often the narrator is the author's principal medium for self-revelation. Often, too, one or more of the (other) characters stand in for the author. Thus, the author faces many choices for the presentation of a self to readers. The range and depth of that presentation distinguish authors from one another.

When they choose the capacity in which they themselves are to act, authors "select (or attempt to select) the capacity in which [readers] are [to be] present. . . ."[54] Eighteenth-century novelists pinpointed their readers' roles so that the dramatized or implied author could guide their activities closely, whether directly or indirectly. Nineteenth-century authors let their readers "discover" the roles prescribed for them and adopt a critical attitude toward them.[55] Under those circumstances readers find themselves involved in expression games where "The observer [reader] imagines the likely consequence of the subject [author] discovering that he is being assessed, and attempts to offset the likely control of impression before it has had a chance to occur successfully."[56] The skepticism of generalist readers aims to offset the implied author's moves by detecting them as they occur in the text. Such readers know success "depends on inferences about what the author could assume" not only in framing a fictional world but also in typifying his or her readers.[57] They understand that their authors engage them in occasions of strategic interaction.

While many authorial moves are virtual or tacit, all readers' moves have that character by virtue of their inability to generate responses from authors.[58] Yet readers' responses are moves, inasmuch as they assess the dramatized and implied authors and take the author's point of view, just as the author tends to adopt (typified) readers' points of view while writing. Among readers' moves are those lying on the border between moves and nonmoves; namely *naive moves*, or

> the assessment an observer makes of a subject when the observer believes that the subject can be taken as he appears, that is, that he is involved in an unwitting move. The subject is assumed to be in clear text, readable by anyone with technical competence to see.[59]

A series of naive moves can, in and of itself, lull readers away from their skeptical stances, making them likelier to misread an innuendo, miss a crucial omission, or fall prey to social seduction. Thus, generalist readers get suspicious when a text apparently invites an abundance of naive moves; alternatively, they get bored.

Readers also make *uncovering moves* comprising attempts "to crack, pierce, penetrate, and otherwise get behind the apparent facts in order to uncover the real ones."[60] Uncovering moves involve meaning-fulfillment, while naive moves involve only meaning-intention. Uncovering moves mean the reader is "on," or self-conscious, reflective, and calculating.[61] During naive moves the reader is "off," or involved, prereflective, and spontaneous. In ideal-typical terms the author's unwitting moves evoke naive moves from readers; their covering moves evoke uncovering moves. Actually, authors sometimes give themselves away unwittingly and readers sometimes get taken in beyond the point that provides pleasure and stimulation. Like all interactants, actual authors and actual readers are, on occasion, unwittingly unwitting.

Readers' efforts at meaning-intention and meaning-fulfillment require some sense of *who* the author is, as dramatized and implied in the narrative. Typifying the author involves skills used in everyday life to meet parallel challenges. People constitute sense from others' actions by inferring the motives associated with observed courses of action. As Alfred Schutz showed, their observations presuppose *course-of-action types* that guide meaning-intention when they see specific expressive processes or their products. That two characters "fall in love" in a novel's opening chapter has, for example, "obvious" meaning by virtue of the romantic-love ideology governing "lovers" as a social type in our society. Moving from a course-of-action type to typical motives establishes a *personal type*. Basically, the observer takes a completed act as a starting point, determines what type of action produced it, and establishes what type of person must have acted so and with what motives. That one of the characters is about to come into a large inheritance and the other is a desperately poor artist may lead to the determination that the love they share is less than fully mutual. Yet these characters lack much specific individuality. Their behavior necessitates "reading" contexts and inferring "*more* about . . . beliefs, knowledge, intentions, and understanding" than was expressly communicated or otherwise indicated by their actions.[62]

Everyday life thus sets the stage for readers' activities, but generalist readers take less for granted than commonsense actors. The author remains profoundly inaccessible; the meanings of things shift as their typical contexts are abandoned; the reader lacks the cues other individuals routinely provide in everyday life. Under these conditions prereflective experiences become less common. In order to experience best-selling and canonical texts as meaningful, readers must do their recognizing, inferring, and familiarizing more or less reflectively. The reader's participation status hinges on tacit queries about what the author means by this or that and what type of individual the author is.

The reader's tacit moves consist, then, of virtual queries to and inferences about the author. The reader does have a measure of "production tolerance" that allows for some flaws, slipups, digressions, and long-windedness.[63] Moreover, the reader's immediate interest lies mostly, though not exclusively, with the story. "Getting" the story and enjoying its unfolding mean, however, listening to its teller and supposing, often reflectively, what sort of person fashioned it.

The moves generalist readers make are nearly impossible to differentiate beyond naive and uncovering moves. Yet the experiences motivating either type of move are susceptible to preliminary breakdown. Basically, experiences of irrelevance and fortuitousness lean readers toward naive moves; experiences of conflict, suspicion, and doubt lean them toward uncovering moves. *Irrelevance* stamps readers' experiences when, either prereflectively or reflectively, they disattend elements of the text as unimportant for purposes at hand. *Fortuitousness*, on the other hand, means sensing that significant elements can be "incidentally" produced and straightforwardly presented.[64] Experiencing either irrelevance or fortuitousness involves prepredicative judgments; that is, judgments made without benefit of reflectively predicating anything.

The experiences that incline readers toward uncovering moves involve predicative judgments based on reflective experiences of textual elements. Conflict is perhaps the most common among them. *Observed conflict* is the reader's awareness of incongruity among textual elements, for example, between what a character says and does.

The other principal type of conflict is *cognitive-affective conflict* involving dissonance between the reader's sympathies and judgments.[65] On the one hand, the reader may sympathize with Dickie Everett, the apparent victim of parents who should have loved him more assuringly; on the other hand, Dickie presents the jumbled memories of a disturbed consciousness, virtually guaranteeing that the reader's judgments pull against his or her sympathies.

Another experience that leads to uncovering moves is *suspicion*, believing "that the strip of activity [the reader] is involved in has been constructed beyond his ken and that he has not been allowed a sustainable view of what frames him."[66] Early on, for instance, *Emma* raises readers' suspicions when Emma's matchmaking efforts seem unrealistically ambitious. Suspecting trouble, the reader is likelier to experience more fully the conflict between what Emma says and what she does. Such uncovering moves brace the reader for the mishaps that ensue. Sometimes the reader experiences *doubt*, or uncertainty about the framework or key that applies to specific elements of the narrative.[67] For contemporary readers Fielding's direct intrusions sometimes produce doubt. Is he sincere? Sarcastic? A spotty artist? Those uncovering moves shift the reader into reflective experiences of the text.

Thus, the interaction between literary artists and intellectuals and generalist readers fulfills most of the conditions of strategic interaction. Such readers understand that literary works attempt to capture consciousness and that readers can choose the terms of their surrender.[68] Their reading often promotes critical understanding as do their rereadings. As E. M. Forster insists, though, "The final test of a novel will be our affection for it, as it is the test of our friends, and of anything else which we cannot define."[69] That test raises the question of how teamwork shifts readers' experiences and on what social-psychological terrain that shift lands them.

Reading as Teamwork

Authors take account of readers in different ways. Those who write canonical novels, together with some who write best-selling and subcultural novels, write as individuals addressing individuals; those who write formulaic novels, together with some who write best-selling and subcultural novels, write more as role-players communicating to other role-players. In the first instance authors imply selves, leave clear-cut room for readers' interpretive activities, express as well as communicate, and stimulate as well as entertain. In the second instance authors barely imply their selves, monopolize the interpretive work, and thus spend their energies mostly communicating and entertaining.

Although all imaginative writers work self-consciously, their premises differ radically. Some authors find out what readers want and give it to them, applying their imaginations more to marketing than literature. Some novelists not only typify their readers' knowledge and interests but also typify them as passive recipients of communications largely duplicating that knowledge and sympathetically addressing those interests.

William H. Whyte, Jr. says, "It is a churlish critic who would gainsay people the solace of fairy tales. But good fairy tales tell the reader that he is about to enter the land of make-believe; current slick fiction proclaims itself as realistic slices of life."[70] Such works "are to be faulted not for resembling one another so closely but because . . . as a whole [they] so little resemble anything" beyond themselves.[71] In other terms, formulaic and some subcultural and best-selling novels abstract from the interpretive schemes already used by their readers, offering them not simplification as such but schematization; they offer "readers' digests."[72] From the reader's side the attraction of such experiences is their ease. Meaning-intention largely suffices, with familiarization requiring little effort to the extent that the characters are often clichés and stock figures.

Between the authors and readers of such fiction what occurs is a variant of teamwork. As Goffman indicates, in many situations the "natural unit" is the *team* sustaining together a given definition of the situation. Some authors typify their readers not in order to challenge their competence but to entertain them as virtual teammates. Nevertheless the author-reader team does involve different participation statuses with the author monopolizing both dramatic and directive dominance—controlling the dramatic action and directing the other member of the team.[73] The author usually exercises those prerogatives unobtrusively, however.

Goffman observes that "Teammates tend to be related to one another by bonds of reciprocal dependence and reciprocal familiarity. . . . " Although the author and reader do have distinct participation statuses, together they are "cooperators" who "contribute to a single overall definition of the situation which involves not so much a real agreement as to what exists but rather a real agreement as to whose claims concerning what issues will be temporarily honored." Teammates thus arrive at a *working consensus* whereby they tacitly agree to maintain a "proper tone of voice, vocabulary, and degree of seriousness. . . . " Typically, teammates maintain a "surface of agreement" or "veneer of consensus."[74]

Authors who successfully recruit readers for their teams not only apprise themselves of readers' interests and dominate them obliquely but also show them deference in specific sorts of ways. Broadly, deference comprises avoidance rituals and presentational rituals. For the sake of the team, authors use both types but favor the former variety. *Avoidance rituals* "lead the actor to keep at a distance from the recipient and not violate" the person's privacy by inappropriate language or any other intrusive behavior.[75] Formulaic novels, along with some subcultural and best-selling ones, are elaborate systems of avoidance rituals. For most of their readers, they preserve the social-psychological space granted to individuals in public places, at least in societies like ours. When readers join the teams headed by the authors of such novels, they hardly open themselves to virtual scrutinization by dramatized or implied authors. Rather, their beliefs, values, and other private holdings gain support or respectful avoidance. *Presentational rituals* involve the individual in "specific attestations to recipients concerning how he regards them and how he will treat them."[76] Authors who use elaborate avoidance rituals can scarcely turn around and intrude on their readers by dramatizing themselves through gestures of concern or explicit moves to help or hinder. Rather, their presentational rituals are few, and those are extended obliquely. Like the originators of other mass communications, formulaic authors obscure their selves in narrow roles.

Not surprisingly, the joint activity of such a team fails to absorb "all of the team's energies and constitut[e] their sole social reality; the performance is something the team members can stand back from, back far enough to imagine or play out simultaneously other kinds of performances attesting to other realities." Thus, author-reader teamwork comprises *uneventful moments* "that are not consequentially problematic."[77] Neither author nor reader risks exposing weaknesses, slipping up, or feeling overwhelmed. The safe territory where their teamwork occurs consists of predictable occasions, not virtual encounters for challenging interactions.

Like all social occasions, formulaic fiction does comprise a distinctive ethos or emotional structure as well as an agenda of activity, an allocation of management functions (to the author), a preestablished unfolding of events, and a highpoint.[78] Unlike all but the most formal occasions, however, formulaic fiction rigidly fixes those elements. The highpoint will be the hero and heroine consummating their enduring love, the hero or heroine seizing the murderer, the secret agent outwitting his or her enemies by abruptly turning the tables on them. Readers entering such worlds not only spend uneventful moments there but also *killed moments* more often than not. Like uneventful moments, killed time is inconsequential. In addition, it

> does not spill over into the rest of life and have an effect there. Differently put, the individual's life course is not subject to his killed moments; his life is organized in such a way as to be impervious to them. Activities for killing time are selected in advance as ones that cannot tie up or entangle the individual.[79]

Reading formulaic fiction is a *removal activity* that "provides something for the individual to lose himself in, temporarily blotting out all sense of the environment which, and in which, he must abide."[80] Formulaic fiction offers that opportunity by exploiting fixed formulas that map out the reader's experiences quite specifically and lay out a world quite clearly. Such fiction blots out the perplexities taxing readers' typifications to some degree in everyday life. In their teamwork with authors, such readers become "true believers," temporarily pure and unassailable. Formulaic fiction thus involves teamwork that provides readers clear-cut roles where decisions are unnecessary, meaning is not at issue, and selfhood need not be demonstrated. It offers subjectively satisfying release from the everyday world by exploiting highly conventionalized schemes that wash away its most gnawing challenges and painful disappointments.

Specialist readers pick up their novels mostly prepared for naive moves whose easy appropriateness signals the minimal indeterminacy their authors manipulate. Their reading occasions few inferences about the selves authors imply and few imputations of intentions to the authors minimally dramatized and barely implied in the narratives they read. Their reading revolves around meaning-intention and psychological removal from everyday life. While they read, specialists are mostly prereflective, involved, and "off." Their texts leave them little room for spontaneity, however. Since the parts assigned them are considerably cut and dried, readers' participation statuses provide little space for the self to romp in at will. Rather, their texts offer specialist readers experiences that may be infrequent in their daily lives—mystery, romance, triumph, emotional reciprocity, or (above all) reasons to hope and to persevere.

Yet specialist readers have their favorite authors within the specific types of fiction they enjoy, as Radway found.[81] Specialists do glean the distinctive voices at work in the narratives they read, even though they are disinclined to impute motives and infer authorial intentions as much as generalist readers do. Specialists do favor works "said to be 'easier' forms psychologically"—works likely, however, to evoke powerful "archetypal responses."[82] Moreover, the same works yield other "occasional riches" to readers whose literary expectations diverge from those of "formalist critics." Oates observes that since the structure of formulaic works "appears to be a given, it is in *parts*, and rarely in structural *wholes*, that we find evidence of fresh insights and imaginative writing. . . . "[83] As Italo Calvino puts it,

Literature can work in a critical vein or to confirm things as they are and as we know them to be. The boundary is not always clearly marked, and . . . on this score the spirit in which one reads is decisive: it is up to the reader to see to it that literature exerts its critical force, and this can occur independently of the author's intention.[84]

In readers' terms, this means that

The authors who matter to us, whom we read with passionate engagement . . . , seem to confirm what we most need to hear. We find in them a more perfect expression of our own inchoate desires and resentments, a magic mirror that gives us back an ideal image of ourselves. They become powerful allies in our continuing project of finding support from others for the more angular, less easily acceptable parts of ourselves.[85]

Generalist or specialist, readers have in common such standing needs and their prospective fulfillment in literary interaction.

8

❦ Literary Socialization

[Lopez] knew that his hoped-for father-in-law had been reading a novel.
He had not suspected such weakness, but argued well from it for the
business at hand.

Anthony Trollope, *The Prime Minister*

In *Northanger Abbey* (1818) the narrator observes that

There seems almost a general wish of decrying the capacity and
under-valuing the labour of the novelist, and of slighting the
performances which have only genius, wit, and taste to recommend them. "I am no novel reader—I seldom look into novels—Do not imagine that *I* often read novels—It is really very
well for a novel." Such is the common cant.[1]

In general, remarks like those of Jane Austen's narrator helped to
institutionalize the novel by socializing its fledgling readers. Such
comments offered readers grounds for justifying their reading.

During the nineteenth century no other institution existed to
socialize literate individuals into readers of novels. While carving out
their own identities, novelists had to socialize the readers required for
institutionalizing the novel. Early novelists used artifices like
verisimilitude, the excursus, prefaces, chapter titles, and direct
addresses for such purposes. Those devices not only gave the novel
palpable form but also instructed readers about what to expect from
novels and how to read them. The nature of the novel guarantees
readers always need socializing to some extent. Novelists share with
other imaginative writers a struggle to burst the forms their predecessors developed.[2] As a form of encoding, then, the novel changes faster
than forms like law and theology.[3] Its considerable dynamism necessitates socializing readers more or less continuously.

Once the novel was institutionalized, novelists could more subtly instruct their readers. Yet the rise of the penny press, popular magazines, and newspapers renewed the need to socialize readers. As the forms of mass culture gained popularity, literary artists and intellectuals had to instruct their readers about why to read their canonical works. Later, radio and movies and television imposed similar burdens. Literary themes rather than literary artifices became the primary vehicle for informing readers about the benefits of canonical novels. As the seeds of mass culture began sprouting, readers began appearing often as characters in canonical novels. Those characters provided unobtrusive grounds for extolling the virtues of such novels. Thus, the novel illustrates not only how a changing institution accommodates its participants to its dynamism but also how it responds to competition from institutions apparently serving the same broad purposes.

Literary Artifices and Socialization

Novelists' artifices serve social as well as literary functions. Those characterizing the novel during any period serve, in particular, to tell readers *how* to read and, often enough, *what* to expect from the novel at hand. Over time, the proliferation of reviewers and critics, interpretive guidance on book jackets, and literature courses diffused the burden of socializing readers. Nonetheless novelists continue bearing some of that burden. That they socialize their readers more and more subtly makes them no less important as instructors in the art of reading.

Historically, verisimilitude was a potent socializing device. The first modern novelists offered their readers "histories." Henry Fielding's *Joseph Andrews* (1742) is subtitled *The History of the Adventures of Joseph Andrews and his Friend Mr. Abraham Adams*. Fielding also wrote *The History of Tom Jones: A Foundling* (1749). There he tells his readers that "truth distinguishes [these] writings from those idle romances which are filled with monsters, the productions . . . of distempered brains. . . . "[4] While dissociating themselves from romantic storytellers and associating themselves with venerable historians,[5] novelists like Fielding were also telling readers to approach their stories in roughly the same way they were accustomed to reading histories.

More generally, fiction "has traditionally . . . borrowed its forms from letters, journals, diaries, autobiographies, histories, travelogues, news stories. . . . It has simply pretended to be one or other of them."[6] All that "pretending" represents a search not only for fictional forms but also for ways to socialize readers. When Samuel Richardson chose the epistolary form, he selected a versatile "means of self-revelation" as well as a meaningful form for readers involved in the cult of writing letters.[7] The epistolary novel socialized readers in much the same ways novelists' "histories" did. Similarly, when novelists adapted the forms characteristic of seventeenth-century conduct books or, later, the forms associated with autobiographies and biographies, they provided implicit instruction on how to read their works. Throughout the eighteenth and nineteenth centuries travelogues also gave novelists grounds for socializing their readers. In fact, some novelists' travelogues are nearly indistinguishable from their fiction; for example, Herman Melville's *Typee* (travel book) and his *Omoo* (novel).[8]

Like other originators of the modern novel, Fielding used an eclectic approach. *Tom Jones* "is only part novel"; it is also "picaresque tale, comic drama, occasional essay."[9] Fielding's "occasional essays" illustrate another technique of instructing readers. Fielding introduces each "Book" of *Tom Jones* with an obvious excursus as the introductory chapter. Here socialization is fairly manifest. The first chapter of Book I, entitled "The introduction to the work, or bill of fare to the feast," serves as a sweeping philosophical introduction. Book II begins with "Showing what kind of a history this is: what it is like, and what it is not like." In Book VII, Fielding's introductory essay is "A comparison between the world and the stage." The next two introductory essays are "A wonderful long chapter concerning the marvellous; being much the longest of all our introductory chapters" and "Of those who lawfully may, and of those who may not, write such histories as this." Critics are the target of the next two introductory essays: "Containing instructions very necessary to be perused by modern critics" and "A crust for the critics." Throughout these essays Fielding defines himself as author, explores the nature of the novel, discusses critical standards, and philosophizes on the themes of *Tom Jones*. All the while he suggests how to read and evaluate his own and other novels.

Subsequent novelists followed in Fielding's wake. Their socializing shows up in prefaces to their novels and in brief excursuses punctuating their narratives. In his preface to *Pendennis* (1848–50), for example, William Makepeace Thackeray scolds the critics of his moral realism and instructs readers, in effect, to approach his fiction as an expression of moral earnestness. Charles Dickens's preface to *David Copperfield* (1849–50) serves parallel functions. When he writes, "No one can ever believe this Narrator in the reading more than I believed it in the writing," Dickens alludes to the novel's autobiographical dimension.[10] Neither novelist adopts guises as exaggerated as Fielding's. Rather, they presuppose some familiarity with the genre and comment on how readers might extend that familiarity to Thackeray's and Dickens's own works.

During the nineteenth century novelists further institutionalized the novel by weaving their instructional materials more tightly into the fabric of their texts. Narrators, obliquely related to authors, offered this subtler instruction; authors had begun standing at a remove from their texts. In *The Professor* (1857), Charlotte Brontë begins Chapter XIX with "Novelists should never allow themselves to weary of the study of real life." The narrator thus sets the tone for the chapter while informing readers about the aesthetic priorities governing the novel. Similarly, the narrator in George Eliot's *Adam Bede* (1859) comments at length on the cultural responsibilities and aesthetic aims of novelists. In Chapter XVII the narrator argues for attention to the stuff of everyday life. Such comments provide Eliot a platform for her aesthetics while telling readers how to appreciate her work.

Throughout the eighteenth and nineteenth centuries chapter titles also served socializing functions. *Tom Jones* has 208 short chapters, providing the reader frequent stopping points. Each has a title, sometimes lengthy, pinpointing the chapter's main focus. Read consecutively, the chapter titles show the structure of the novel and summarize its plot. Chapter titles exhibit an uneven history, however. As early a novelist as Austen did not use them.

A final artifice with clear-cut socializing functions is direct addresses to readers. All forms of "Dear Reader" evoke readers' attention to themselves, priming them for helpful hints about reading the novel at hand or for instruction in the art of reading. *Joseph Andrews* and *Tom Jones* are shot through with such addresses. Some direct addresses in *Tom Jones* help the reader with the text at hand; for instance, "The reader will be pleased to remember. . . . "[11] Others further familiarize readers with the role of reader, as when the narrator says he is passing over many of Little Benjamin's character traits since "the reader will himself very easily perceive them on his farther acquaintance with this extraordinary person."[12]

Directly addressing readers so as to socialize them into specific texts or further socialize them into the role of reader is a common artifice among Fielding's successors. In *Pendennis* the narrator lends a hand by acknowledging "what perhaps some persons are anxious to know, namely who little Laura is, who has appeared more than once before us. . . . " The narrator in *David Copperfield* is similarly helpful: "Whether I shall turn out to be the hero of my own life, or whether that station will be held by anyone else, these pages must show. . . . " The narrator in *Barchester Towers* periodically underscores the need for imaginative inferences to fill narrative gaps. Trollope's narrator asks, for example, "How shall I sing the divine wrath of Mr. Slope. . . ?" He also reports, "Not being favorites of the tragic muse, we do not dare to attempt any description of Eleanor's face when she first heard the name of Mrs. Slope. . . . "[13]

Today novelists continue clarifying points for their readers and introducing narrative interludes where they comment on their genre and their art (and thus on the role of reader to some extent). Although they favor subtler devices for achieving those ends, novelists sometimes still address their readers directly while socializing them. In *The Embezzler* the narrator says, "If the reader is astonished, . . . let him remember. . . . " In *The Good Soldier* the narrator remarks, "But I guess I have made it hard for you, O silent listener, to get that impression." Similarly, "Is all this digression or isn't it? Again, I don't know. You, the listener, sit opposite me. But you are so silent." In *Breakfast of Champions* the narrator says, "And now comes the spiritual climax of this book. . . . "[14] Such instances attest to novelists' continuing concern with socializing their readers by showing them how to read specific texts and instructing them about their role.

Contemporary novelists thus continue the socializing that originators of the novels initiated. Unlike their earliest predecessors, novelists now concern themselves more with winning or renewing readers' commitment to the canonical novel than with assisting them or further defining their roles. Since the middle of the nineteenth century, in particular, cultural competition has led novelists to socialize their readers about why to read their novels more than how to read them.

Literary Themes, Cultural Competition, and Literary Socialization

Mary McCarthy notes that novels often dramatize the "evil effects of reading."[15] Cultural competition underlies the pattern she finds inexplicable. Canonical novelists have always faced competition—first from other writers and later from the nonprint media. Survival necessitated winning readers' commitment over successive generations of competition. Novelists needed, in short, to socialize readers about why to read canonical novels.

Novelists often pursued that task by making reading a theme or subtheme in their works. Broadly, literary artists and intellectuals use three techniques to socialize readers through such themes. First, they contrast characters who read canonical works with those who read "inferior" fiction. Second, they associate the canonical novel with "high" culture and draw invidious contrasts with the forms and values of mass culture. Third, they imply that where science and technology become dominant institutions, literature suffers. In each case the theme is defensive: It invites commitment to a beleaguered institution, the canonical novel.

The first technique of thematizing reading dates back to Cervantes. From its beginnings the canonical novel faced competition from romances and gothic novels. *Don Quixote* (1605, 1615) implies a contrast between itself and the romances on knight-errantry that led to Don Quixote's nearly fatal misperceptions. Similarly, in *Northanger Abbey* Austen parodies Gothic works that fill readers with "nonsense and stuff."[16] In many respects the novel's heroine is a female Don Quixote engaged in misadventures because she reads the "wrong" sort of fiction. Both works imply the value of canonical novels by dramatizing the hazards of reading unworthy works.

Thackeray also thematizes reading by contrasting characters who read canonical novels with those who read inferior fiction. In *Pendennis* Madame Frisby, who had read more cheap novels than anyone in town, "had got to be so absurdly sentimental that in her eyes life was nothing but an immense love match. . . . "[17] Fanny, who "devours" novels, compares a prospective lover with "all the heroes of all those darling greasy volumes" she has read (p. 483). By contrast, Missy "improved her mind by a sedulous study of the novels of the great modern authors of the French language" (p. 226). The narrator condemns many penny-press publications (pp. 317–18) while defending novels like his own as "moral" and "edifying" (p. 148).

The first technique of socializing readers about the benefits of canonical fiction also finds a practitioner in E. M. Foster. In *A Room with a View* (1908) two characters—Miss Lavish and Cecil—serve as reference points for other characters portrayed in part by their reading habits. Touring Italy, Lucy Honeychurch and Charlotte Bartlett meet Miss Lavish who is writing a work about "love, murder, abduction, revenge. . . . "[18] She flatly confesses, "We literary hacks are shameless creatures" (p. 56). Other characters regard her as a "shoddy lady writer" seeking "notoriety by print" (pp. 69, 160). Cecil, one of Lucy's suitors, is a discerning reader; inferior novels offend his sensibilities. Cecil talks easily in literary terms: "I . . . have won a great victory for the Comic Muse. George Meredith's right—the cause of Comedy and the cause of Truth are really the same. . ." (p. 134).

As readers, the other characters gravitate toward the poles Miss Lavish and Cecil exemplify. Mrs. Honeychurch admits she is "neither artistic nor literary nor intellectual nor musical. . . . " (p. 160). When Lucy has to tell her mother that "We weren't talking of real fences,"

Mrs. Honeychurch replies, "Oh, I see, dear—poetry" (p. 112). Beyond "paving" her empty trunk with books (p. 90), Charlotte apparently has little use for them. Lucy herself only supposes that some of her ideas "come out of some book" or other (pp. 123, 145). When her brother Freddy confronts a "sitting-room . . . blocked with books," he asks whether the people he is visiting are "great readers. Are they that sort?" Freddy whispers (p. 144). Mr. Beebe, a rector and family friend, recognizes the name Byron on the bookshelves but cannot identify *The Way of All Flesh*. Seeing volumes by Schopenhauer, Nietzsche, and others, he concludes that the younger generation "knows its own business" (p. 144). Taken together, these characters imply that not all people appreciate "solid literature" (p. 173), and some even fail to appreciate books.

The second technique of socializing readers about the importance of canonical works is to link them with "high" culture while drawing invidious contrasts with mass culture. As we saw, George Eliot uses this technique in *Middlemarch* (1872). Henry James's *The Tragic Muse* (1890) is also illustrative. In the first chapter Lady Agnes questions her son Nick about the merits of looking at works of art. Lady Agnes condones such activities only when they further her daughter Biddy's development or some other social purpose.[19] Nick, who aims to be a portrait artist, says his mother finds art "pardonable" only as an infrequent diversion (p. 18). Lady Agnes represents the tastelessness associated with mass culture; Nick, the artist trying to understand and fulfill his vocation; Biddy, the naive layperson facing a panoply of cultural forms and wanting to discriminate among them.

Paralleling Lady Agnes is Mrs. Dallow who reads whatever "people are talking about" because "one has to know" (p. 292). She finds the arts uninteresting. Mrs. Rooth "delight[s] in novels, poems, perversions, misrepresentations, and evasions. . ." (p. 240). She reads "greasy volumes" of romances—"dirty old novels" from the circulating library that help her pass the time (pp. 219, 252, 630). Like Lady Agnes and Mrs. Dallow, Mrs. Rooth lacks aesthetic sense.

Paralleling Nick is his friend Gabriel Nash. Nash has disowned his one published novel and seeks his artistic vocation in life itself (p. 35). Literature, he says, "is for the convenience of others" and "requires the most abject concessions" (p. 36). Nash does read novels "when they are extraordinarily good" (p. 73), and he enjoys the work of portrait artists (p. 460). He also admires poets whose words are "enchanting collocations and unforgettable signs" (p. 191). Nash considers theater "the lowest of the arts" and the English theater, in particular, "puerile and barbarous" (pp. 60, 131).

Biddy wants to believe that art is "necessary to the happiness" and "greatness of a people"; that it is "manly and honorable"; that "the artist—the conscientious, serious one—is as distinguished a member of society as anyone else" (p. 718). Biddy's cousin Peter Sherringham, who shares her sentiments, knows Shakespeare and the great lyric poets (pp. 247, 364). He says the theater is his "sole vice" (p. 87). His confession signals his aesthetic immaturity inasmuch as he tries to treat popular plays as artistic achievements, even though he sees continual signs that the theater largely lacks an aesthetics. Sherringham understands that Miriam, his favorite actress, is no "priestess of art" but "a female gymnast, a mountebank at higher wages" (p. 208).

Miriam the actress is Mrs. Rooth's daughter. The themes at hand make her the novel's focal character. Like Nick and Nash, she feels a sense of vocation and disciplines herself in pursuit of it. Like Biddy and Sherringham, she wants to be aesthetically discriminating but lacks confidence in her judgments. Like Lady Agnes and Mrs. Dallow and Mrs. Rooth, she promotes mass culture. Miriam knows her art involves "parad[ing] one's body and one's soul" (p. 176). Yet she goes "from continent to continent and clime to clime; with populations and deputations, reporters and photographers, placards and interviews and banquets, steamers, railways, dollars, diamonds, speeches, and artistic ruin all jumbled into her train" (p. 619).

Miriam's is the world of the theater. In *The Tragic Muse* that world represents a burgeoning mass culture infected with commercial values, run by hucksters, and patronized by dandies and bored crowds (pp. 69–70). That world is heavily advertised and commonly reviewed in the newspapers (pp. 215, 755). In fact, "deafening newspaperism" is pervasive (p. 619), with "unpleasant phrasemongers" and "worldly, semi-smart" people being decisive influences (pp. 429, 543, 839). Under such conditions the "aesthetic element—the sense of form" withers, and "certainty of eye" fades (pp. 19, 242). James's indictment of mass culture is severe: *The Tragic Muse* is a richly ironic title.

Willa Cather uses similar techniques in *The Professor's House* (1925). Professor Godfrey St. Peter thinks about Euripedes, quotes Marc Anthony, and remembers scenes from Henry James's novels.[20] The opera soothes him, and he thinks often of Brahms' Requiem (pp. 92–93, 257–58). St. Peter believes "Art and religion (they are the same thing, in the end, of course) have given man the only happiness he has ever had" (p. 69). His wife has "fastidious tastes in literature" (p. 50), and his best friend appreciates Indian folk art and reads the Latin poets (pp. 118, 245, 251). St. Peter, his wife, and his friend contrast with Blake who does read newspapers but sees education as "some kind of hocus-pocus that enable[s] a man to live without work" (pp. 187, 188). They also contrast with St. Peter's son-in-law who writes newspaper editorials and jingles (pp. 38, 44). The sharpest contrast is with St. Peter's daughter Rosamond who shares her mother's literary sensibilities but succumbs to conspicuous consumption when circumstances make her an heiress. The novel denigrates her values while extolling the arts as pathways to full living. *The Professor's House* invidiously contrasts literary values with the values of a commodity culture where consumption undergirds most social bonds.

Virginia Woolf's *To the Lighthouse* (1927) treats literature in much the same way as Cather's novel. Its characters "scatter about, in attics, in bedrooms, on little perches of their own, reading, writing, putting the last smooth to their hair, or fastening dresses. . . . [They have] little odds and ends on their washing-tables and dressing-tables, and . . . novels on the bed-tables, and . . . diaries."[21] In this world reading, writing, and introspection take their place alongside activities like grooming oneself.

Together, the husband and wife in the novel dramatize the satisfactions of reading. Mr. Ramsay forgets "his own bothers and failures completely" as he reads literature. His reading brings "astonishing delight," a "feeling of vigor," and occasions for pondering morality (p. 180). Sometimes—as with "one of old Sir Walter's" novels—reading moves him "very much" (p. 176). As she reads, Mrs. Ramsay experiences herself "climbing, . . . shoving her way up under petals that curved over her" (pp. 178–79). "How satisfying! How restful! All the odds and ends of the day stuck to this magnet; her mind felt swept; felt clean" (p. 181). Contrasting with the Ramsays are acquaintances whose attitudes imply the influence of mass culture. Charles Tansley's criticisms of Sir Walter Scott and Austen and Tolstoy are vehicles for "I-I-I"; Tansley chronically wonders what impression he is making (pp. 160, 162–63). Minta Doyle says "she [does] not believe anyone really enjoy[s] reading Shakespeare" (p. 162). Symptomatically, Minta once "left the third volume of Middlemarch in the train" and, therefore, "never knew what happened in the end. . ." (p. 148). Paul Rayley says one's childhood reading "lasts," but Paul is "stupid" about books (pp. 162–63).

Walker Percy also uses the second technique of socializing readers. In *The Moviegoer* (1961) the main character is a thirty-year-old stockbroker. Binx had once loved music and read only "fundamental" books, . . . such as *War and Peace*, the novel of novels. . . . "[22] During that time he had "lived in [his] room as Anyone living Anywhere and . . . only for diversion took walks around the neighborhood and

saw an occasional movie" (p. 60). Now, however, Binx is embarked
on a "search" that leads him toward mass culture (pp. 16, 171). Binx
cares little for television, which offers only "little nightcaps" of programs (pp. 39, 89). He reads liberal and conservative periodicals at
the library; the hatred the various camps bear one another "enlivens"
him (p. 83). He also reads the *Reader's Digest* his landlady shares with
him. Like her, he finds the articles "cute and heartwarming" (p. 65).
Most often, Binx goes to movies. As he narrates his story, he recalls
stars and scenes from his favorite films. Movies "certify" places for
Binx, making it possible "to live, for a time at least, as a person who
is Somewhere and not Anywhere" (p. 55).

Throughout his narration Binx also refers to books. Binx's
cousin Kate had discovered "the world of books and music and art
and ideas... " (p. 42), but her unsteady world cannot support an artis-
tic-intellectual lifestyle (p. 145). Nell, another cousin, claims "books
and people and things are endlessly fascinating" (p. 84)—fascinating
enough that she and her husband relinquish television one night, turn
on the phonograph, and read *The Prophet* together (p. 84). Also symptomatic of her tastes is Nell's anger at "a celebrated novel which...
takes a somewhat gloomy and pessimistic view of things" (pp. 83–84).
When he becomes an invalid, Binx's father begins reading mystery
novels (p. 123). Sharon, Binx's secretary and would-be lover, reads
Peyton Place but tries to conceal it. Significantly, Binx thinks she
should forego that "kind of stuff" (p. 58).

Near the end of the novel Binx observes a "romantic" reading
The Charterhouse of Parma on a bus and wonders whether the young
man's motives are literary or social. Binx recognizes his fellow traveler as "a moviegoer" who "does not go to movies" (p. 171). Binx contrasts him with a salesperson on the bus who "like many businessmen
... is a better metaphysician than the romantic" (p. 171). Percy's novel
concerns diverse contemporary means for alleviating ennui and
meaninglessness. Literature is a good bet, it implies, but few people
enjoy it in exhilarating, meaningful ways. Literature has become, in
effect, a tiny facet on the dazzling jewel of mass culture.

Frederick Exley also uses the second technique of socializing
readers. The narrator of *A Fan's Notes* (1968) identifies himself as a
"fan." The New York Giants are his "delight," "folly," "anodyne," and
"intellectual stimulation."[23] The fan is a high school teacher, would-be
novelist, and sexual gadfly. His story reads like a memoir punctuated
with football lore culled from sports columns. The narrator's addic-
tion to football serves as a guise making his critical posture toward
mass culture less blatant.

Like other novelists using this second technique, the fan often refers to canonical writers and their works. He mentions Pope, Keats, Milton, Wordsworth, and Yeats as well as Dickens, Joyce, Dostoevski, Capote, Mailer, Hemingway, and McCarthy (among others). Four works win the fan's recurrent attention: *The Scarlet Letter*, *The Adventures of Augie March*, *Lolita*, and *Catcher in the Rye*. Each concerns estrangement and identity; each speaks to the themes of *A Fan's Notes* that emerge as the canonical references accrue alongside the fan's portrayal of the mass media and his observations about reading.

A Fan's Notes portrays television as a droning medium (pp. 169, 180) The fan criticizes religious programs, science fiction shows, soap operas, and quiz shows that "imprison" people in an "illiterate and banal orbit" (p. 182). He sees television aerials as "monuments to . . . isolation" (p. 180). The fan is no less critical of movies and magazines. He thinks today's movies treat reality superficially (p. 41), and he damns Hollywood (and Herman Wouk!) for warping his capacity to love (pp. 156–57). The fan does read *Time*, *Newsweek*, *Sports Illustrated*, *Harpers Magazine*, *The Atlantic*, and *The New Yorker*. *True Detective* with its "sappy sadism" belongs in another category, however (p. 241). Similarly, the fan questions "intellectual habits" like *Movie Screen* or *Reader's Digest* (p. 130), and he loathes hearing from his mother "what *McCall's*, *Woman's Day*, and the *Ladies Home Journal* had to say about fatness" (p. 337).

In general, the fan esteems books and reading, even though he no longer has an overflowing library. The fan reads to allay boredom and to feel the "consolation of other men's grief" (p. 55). He vaguely laments people's ignorance of such rewards and their "facile misreading" of authors' intentions (p. 225). He observes people pretending to read works like *From Here to Eternity* or priding themselves on reading "serious" works like *The Caine Mutiny* (pp. 152, 257). Such observations convey the fan's pessimistic vision of mass culture.

The fan thinks "writing best-sellers" is just a "way to make a living like any other" (p. 17). Today's "mock-epic hero" is the salesperson (p. 271) capable of "wedg[ing] a place" in people's minds and thus "becom[ing] unavoidable" (p. 305). The fan understands many people try to "commit to paper . . . their joy, their grief, their passion" (p. 128), but he also knows artistic accomplishment requires "the very longing" people often try to repress (p. 34). In the end the fan sympathizes with illiterates "confront[ing] things they do not understand" (p. 28); their "groping search for words" touches him (p. 105). The fan is no elitist. Rather, he is a frustrated writer alienated from a culture that denigrates his craft and at odds with a society where the marketplace debases literacy and literature.

A final work illustrating this technique of socializing readers is John Irving's *The World According to Garp* (1978). Irving contrasts Garp, his mother Jenny, and his wife Helen as readers and writers. As a boy Garp's "way with a story was to find one he liked and read it again and again."[24] Garp regards reading as a demanding pleasure, but he reads rather little as an adult. His priorities lie with "making up" stories (p. 190). Since "imagining something is better than remembering something" (p. 605), he denigrates autobiographical fiction (p. 457). Garp regards literature as a "luxury item," wishing it were "more basic" but hating it when it is (p. 252). He claims art is basically useless, but his stance is ironic. What Garp actually considers useless is the mass media stifling people's imaginations. Garp loathes the tastelessness of popular movies, and television strikes him as a "cancer insidious and numbing, putting the world to sleep" (p. 280). He loathes thinking that "whenever the television glows there sits someone who isn't *reading*" (p. 280). Not surprisingly, Garp the writer is uninterested in becoming a "household product"; he is not "that kind of writer" (p. 195). Garp rejects fiction that reads like an "X-rated soap opera" and resists techniques eliciting readers' "cheap but immediate attention" (p. 471).

Unlike her son Garp, Jenny is an avid reader—until her feminism leads to social activism. Jenny read so much that people found it strange: "What was she reading . . . for?" (p. 36) Jenny's books—Twain, Conrad, Melville, Dickens, Hemingway—displace *Sports Illustrated*, *Time*, and *Newsweek* in the infirmary where she works. Yet Jenny's "taste for literature was never keen" (p. 170). At bottom, Jenny reads to oversee her son's education and inform herself about current affairs. Like her son, though, Jenny becomes a writer. Her one book is an autobiography entitled *A Sexual Suspect*. Although the "serious journals" criticize it, the mass media respond "warmly" (p. 185). Jenny's work supposedly "bridge[s] the usual gap between literary merit and popularity," but Garp says it has "the same literary merit as the Sears, Roebuck catalog" (p. 13). As a reader and a writer, Jenny stands closer to popular tastes than Garp. She reads for down-to-earth purposes and writes to convey a message.

Helen, Garp's wife, is "a good and nonstop reader" who grew up "devouring" the bookstore and library at the school where her father worked (pp. 79, 80). Helen earned her Ph.D. in English literature at the age of twenty-three and began an academic career. Her writing thus contrasts with Garp's and Jenny's. Helen writes papers on the narrative techniques of Conrad and Woolf, for example. She hates movies and dislikes television. Helen lives in a world removed from Jenny's and distinct from Garp's.

Around these three characters revolve other readers and writers. Mr. Tinch finds so-called metafiction perplexing. Michael Melton discusses Woolf but "only pretend[s] to have read *Mrs. Dalloway.*" Mrs. Ralph finds Dostoevsky's *The Eternal Husband* "a sick story"; she wonders "what's so special about Dostoevsky" (p. 257). John Wolf, Garp's editor, feels obliged to reject the "slop" that crosses his desk even if "people *do* want to read" it (p. 168). An unnamed novelist cashes in on a radical feminist movement: "The novel was written by a man, of course. His previous novel had been called *Confessions of a Porn King,* and the one before that had been called *Confessions of a Child Slave Trader.* . . . He was a sly, evil man who became something different about every six months" (pp. 585–86). All these characters support the novel's subthemes concerning literature. Together, they imply the differences between "serious" and "popular" works (p. 456) and the people who read each type.

The third technique of socializing readers is to suggest that in the extreme science and technology threaten the canonical novel. Kurt Vonnegut uses this technique in *Player Piano* (1952). The hero of the novel is Paul Proteus, an engineer who moves on "only one plane and along one line."[25] Proteus's "job, the system, and organizational politics had left him variously annoyed, bored, or queasy" (p. 15). Even though he had never been a reader, Proteus finds himself "developing an appetite for novels" (p. 135). Yet Proteus lives in a world where reading fiction is acceptable only as a means of "pleasant relaxation" (p. 135). Proteus's is a mechanized world where music is cheap (a nickel in the player piano), and television addicts display a book like *Tarzan* to show that they read. Proteus's is a futuristic world where few people see that machines cannot recognize artistry, let alone "appreciate it, foster it, sympathize with it" (p. 172). Collecting books is an affront to such a world, and serious writers have no place in it. A National Council of Arts and Letters approves manuscripts for publication and assigns them to one of twelve cost-efficient book clubs established for the major types of readers.

Max Frisch uses the same technique to socialize readers. In *Homo Faber* (1959) the main character cannot read novels, which bore him as much as dreams do.[26] Nor does Walter Faber know "classical names" like Hardy and Tolstoy. Faber does not care for folklore, symphonies, painting, theater, opera, or museums. His sole connection to the world of artistic expression is his camera, but he often finds himself with "absolutely nothing to film" (pp. 20, 25). Faber regards the arts as "womanish" and the imagination and emotions as insignificant (p. 101). He considers himself a "technologist . . . accustomed to seeing things as they are" (p. 22). The only books he values concern cybernetics, probability, and related matters. Not surprisingly, his former wife called Walter "homo faber" (p. 46). Together, his distaste for the arts and his denigration of human emotions mark him as an alienated denizen of a machine-ridden world.

Other novelists who use the third technique of socializing readers include Ray Bradbury, George Orwell, and Aldous Huxley. Bradbury's *Fahrenheit 451* (1967) portrays a totalitarian society where electronic technology reigns, and firemen's main job is burning books. "Parlour families" inhabit every house—three walls of screens televising "what to think."[27] Montag, the novel's hero, risks his life for books. Mildred his wife is addicted to the electronic world where she feels safe but empty. When Montag reads Mildred and two of her friends "Dover Beach" from a book he obtained illegally, one friend begins crying uncontrollably. The other friend uses the incident to illustrate how poetry and "silly words" create "awful feelings" and hurt people (p. 98). Mildred simply wants to turn "the family" on and "be cheery" (p. 99). The novel portrays a cultural battle between the print media and the electronic media where literature stands to lose as electronic technology gains ground. Bradbury's themes resonate with those in *Animal Farm, 1984,* and *Brave New World.*

When novelists treat reading as a profound pastime, contrast literary forms and values with those of mass culture, and portray technological threats to literature, they reinforce their readers' commitment to the canonical novel. Treating literature in these ways extends their concerns well beyond the ken of those who treat reading as an indicator of class position; for example, William Dean Howells in *The Rise of Silas Lapham* (1885). Thematic attention to reading differs, in short, from referential interest in it as a sign of social differentiation.

The phenomenon at hand raises questions about author's intentions. *The Tragic Muse, A Fan's Notes,* and *Player Piano* virtually force the interpreter to infer that the novelist intended the socializing his novel furthers. With novels like *The Professor's House* and *To the Lighthouse,* however, reading and related matters are subthemes subordinated to other events constituting the story line. In those cases one wonders whether or not the novelists intended the socializing their novels accomplish. Paralleling those considerations is the question of how much readers are aware of the subthemes affecting their responses to a novel. Once McCarthy's observations piqued my curiosity, I reread the novels treated here expecting to find few instances of what she had noticed. I could not remember having come across these themes and subthemes at all, yet they leapt out at me once I began rereading. As Albert Guerard notes, innumerable differences obtain between first and subsequent readings of a novel.[28] Sociologists of literature could, I suspect, begin accounting for those differences by developing models of interaction between authors and readers. The data at hand have additional theoretical import centered on the framing issues Erving Goffman raised. Literary socialization concerns the subtleties of framing and the taken for grantedness bred by whatever frames interaction and experience. If the "serious" reader takes for granted the frames most novelists construct, Goffman's ideas about framing merit closer attention as scholars continue exploring aesthetic responses.

Carla L. Peterson occupies a prominent place among scholars tackling these sorts of issues. In *The Determined Reader* she focuses on nine French and British novels spanning the nineteenth century: *Corinne of Italy, Louis Lambert, Jane Eyre, David Copperfield, The Red and the Black, Lamiel, Madame Bovary, The Mill on the Floss,* and *Jude the Obscure.* Peterson analyzes the "reader-protagonists" in these novels. Often orphans or half-orphans, these readers seek in books—fictional and nonfictional, religious and secular—bases for securing their identities. Their efforts usually fail since they seek not only literary socialization but also all the other varieties of socialization necessary for establishing a full-blown identity. They seek, among other things, gender identities. As Peterson points out, the nineteenth-century debate over reading books—particularly novels—"was specially directed against young women. . . . " Historically, the female reader-protagonist appeared to be abandoning "her natural sphere of domesticity and entering into the alien world of culture, conceived as essentially masculine. . . . " Her search for identity is more difficult than that of her male counterpart. Often faced with "male-authored texts . . . and thus likely to come across male images with which she cannot identify," the female reader-protagonist faces the further indignity of ridicule—not unlike what working-class males encounter as reader-protagonists. A message takes shape: "Book learning in the nineteenth-century novel is natural to the formation of middle-class males alone."[29] Embedded in canonical novels like those Peterson analyzed, that message suggests novelists themselves have played a part in canon formation.

In other terms, some novelists appear to have framed their novels so as to help canonize men's literature in the process of inveighing against a popular culture associated mostly with women. In the 11 novels examined here that pattern holds sway. Cecil, Binx, "the fan," Garp, Proteus, and Montag serve as guardians of literary culture; Miss

Lavish, Miriam, Nell and Sharon, Jenny, and Mildred are uninterested
in or incapable of discriminating between "serious" literature and its
country cousins. Interestingly, in Cather's and Woolf's novels both
female and male characters enjoy worthwhile literature, and both are
vulnerable to the ravages of popular culture. Peterson herself suggests
that "the particular perspectives of both male and female writers"[30]
may condition literary interaction, including literary socialization.

Peterson analyzes how narrators "comment not only on the relationship of literary forms to their characters' lives but also on the cultural values that underlie these forms" and how they "manipulate
their account of the reader-protagonists so as to evoke specific
responses from the readers of the novels."[31] Peterson thus illustrates
how attention to framing in literary texts also illuminates the cultural
context wherein authors and their readers find one another. Her study
shows that framing means constituting from the cultural terrain the
specific grounds necessary for people to secure shared experiences in
relatively effortless, decidedly immediate ways.

Novelists as Canon Makers

Engaged in literary socialization and cultural competition,
literary artists and intellectuals are also often engaged in more narrowly self-interested projects. Particularly during the nineteenth century when "novelist" was an emergent identity in the literary world,
laying implicit claim to the role of critic meant novelists could bolster
their literary identities while shaping critical standards for the novel.
At the same time such novelists were setting their own novels up for
canonization by invidiously contrasting them with those presumably
reflecting lesser talent, taste, and imagination. Novelists themselves
have thus participated in canon formation. As Paul DiMaggio has
noted, artists often shape the "artistic classification systems" wherein
"genre distinctions are created, ritualized, and eroded and . . . tastes
are produced as part of the sense-making and boundary-defining
activities of social groups." Such *professional classification* results from
artists' attempts to develop reputations. . . ."; it "emerge[s] out of
struggles among artists for status and material success."[32]

In the case of novelists we find professional classifications often
woven into the narratives they set forth as artistic creations. That circumstance makes for problems. As Italo Calvino observes, when it
tries to educate (or socialize), literature tends to fail "except for the
reader who strips it of the hoax" and sees "the text within the social
framework from which it emerged."[33] The history of the novel com-

prises cultural hoaxes of sorts—hoaxes aimed at translating what is culturally arbitrary and narrowly self-interested into what is objectively meritorious and universally worthy.

Those hoaxes involved, as DiMaggio's work predicts, the twin processes of sense-making and boundary-defining. What male novelists had to make sense of was the enormous popularity of fictions written by women. At the same time, though less obviously, they had to make sense of the deviant femininity many of those women exhibited. They also had to make sense of women's virtual monopolization of lucrative opportunities that, by virtue of a separate-spheres system of sexual inequality, should have belonged to men. Historically, making sense of those matters meant defining the "serious" novel while demonstrating its superiority in and through their own works, thereby drawing the social boundaries of an elite group of novelists—solid literary men whose company admitted only the most exceptional of women.

Robert Scholes emphasizes that Cervantes's masterpiece was an "anti-romance,"[34] and we saw earlier how Fielding took pains to distinguish his work from "idle romances." In large measure the novel arose and continued taking shape in reaction against women's popular fiction. The politics of lifestyles may have played a role alongside the politics of cultural forms (and, of course, the politics of gender itself). As Ellen Moers points out, "the earliest women romancers, of the Restoration or early eighteenth century, of whom Aphra Behn is the best-known, . . . were sexually experienced, highly literate, short of money, and indifferent to respectability."[35] Unconstrained by traditional femininity, these women may have seemed fair game culturally. What more effective way to condemn their lifestyles than to reject their literary efforts as "idle" or "greasy"? As Joyce W. Warren observes, "There is no place in our society for the woman who chooses to expand and absorb. She, by definition, is the one to be absorbed."[36] With "deviant" women like the early romancers, where social absorption is impossible without social change, extreme cultural trivialization may have to serve.

Over time adjectives like "idle" and "greasy" tend to disappear from the epithets wielded against popular female novelists. In part, the gradual erosion of such class-loaded terms may reflect (at least in the American case) the entry of more solidly middle-class females into novel making. Ann Douglas sampled thirty middle-class, nineteenth-century women who "were among the leading literary propagandists for a sentimentalized culture"—individuals like Louisa May Alcott, Harriet Beecher Stowe, and Fanny Fern (Sara Payson Willis). A third of the women were the daughters of ministers, and several married ministers; these were "well-bred" women. Yet their gender status was less solid than their class status. Barely half of them married; only about half of those bore children.[37] What to make of their works? Where "greasy" might not do, "non-serious" might.

In fact, the invidious contrasts literary artists and intellectuals draw between their own works and those of more popular novelists center on the notion of seriousness. As a claim to literary merit, that notion commonly incorporates a "patriarchal didacticism . . . often used to denigrate the popular women's genres."[38] Most of the adjectives used to applaud or lambast fiction are gender-loaded along the serious/nonserious continuum; for example, consequential, rigorous, powerful, seminal, demanding versus silly, light, weak, obvious, simple. "Serious" and its critical correlatives seem masculinist weapons wielded against women writing "nonserious" fiction. The novels surveyed here, for example, rarely mention "nonserious" male-authored fiction. Were men not writing such fiction? Is women's commercial success more wounding than men's? It would seem so, at least on the surface of "serious" novelists' narratives.

In any case, many women wrote against the literary mainstream, garnering enormous popularity in the process. "More than a third of American fiction published before Cooper's *Precaution* in 1820 was by women and the average was still higher in England."[39] Before 1840, half or more of British novelists were women, according to Tuchman with Fortin.[40] Women's "sentimental 'domestic' novels . . . dominated the literary market in America from the 1840s through the 1880s."[41] During the 1850s, for instance, "women wrote practically *all* the popular books in America."[42] Hawthorne and Melville published three books each during that decade, but none "sold the way the women's books did."[43] Similarly, "a host of women novelists emerged in Britain during that decade," and their minor domestic novels "flourished."[44] Given their male counterparts' sense-making and boundary-defining projects, perhaps these circumstances favoring female novelists meant that prose fiction needed chastening by realism; that heroines needed less idealized portrayals; that heroes needed toughening up; that high culture needed separating from popular culture.

Habegger argues that "Women's fiction posed a challenge to men, a challenge taken up in a definitive way in realistic [American] fiction of the 1870s and 1880s."[45] Less definitive responses to the challenge pervaded nineteenth-century British and American fiction, but "realism" was the common rallying cry integrating those responses. Tuchman, with Fortin, looks at men's appropriation of the British canonical novel in three stages: 1840–79, when men invaded novel making in large numbers; 1880–99, when they redefined the novel along canonical lines; and 1901–17, when they institutionalized the canonical novel.[46] Before invasion, however, came mobilization; thus, the period antedating 1840 merits passing examination. As George Levine observes, "In the vigor of the dismissal of earlier literature, particularly of the popular novels by women at the end of the eighteenth century, . . . is an implicit consensus that literature had to be relocated."[47] Its relocation was from a feminine to a masculine realm.

Since reading and writing books were no longer reliable indicators of privilege, "elite men who had once claimed th[ese] marks[s] of distinction began insistently to differentiate their literature from the literature of others."[48] Who were women to be publicizing their consciousness, making money, winning fame, and otherwise stepping beyond the personal sphere where middle-class femininity properly resided? Early on, the works of men like Charles Brockden Brown and Sir Walter Scott caused few ripples compared with the waves of reaction women's popular fiction evoked. Brown's *Wieland* was perhaps the first gothic novel in American literature, the first of six gothic romances he published between 1798 and 1801; Poe and Hawthorne, among others, praised his fictions.[49] Writing only somewhat later, Scott took pains to distinguish between the romance and the novel but nearly always described his work as "light" literature. Like later "realists" (mostly males), Scott "pokes fun at a certain kind of busybody novel reader"; like his popular contemporaries (mostly females), though, he "reflects no unease about giving the public what it wants."[50] Like Fielding, Scott nonetheless lays a masculine claim to "realism," which arose as an anti-gothic gesture directed "against the excesses . . . of various kinds of romantic, exotic, or sensational literature."[51] Mobilization thus began along ambiguous lines likely to be drawn more clearly as women continued writing popular works beyond the literary mainstream.

Before the century was half over, the novel was clearly becoming the "prototypical genre of the bourgeois age."[52] Yet during the first four or five decades of the century that literary form was feminine in the popular imagination—women wrote novels, women read them, women's concerns pervaded them. The time for invasion had come. In England, "the treatment of their subject, not their subject" served to distinguish serious from popular fiction; in America, subject matter tended to divide the two, as "serious" novelists like Melville portrayed "men involved in economically and ecologically significant activities," while popular novelists favored domestic matters.[53] Both

American and British realists shared a problematic rhetoric, however.
Although "romance" had many meanings in nineteenth-century
America, the men who practiced it (most notably Hawthorne and
Melville) are seen today as constituting an "experimental tradition" of
the romance.[54] Their approach often endowed the romance with a
realistic dimension foreign to its gothic versions. Hawthorne used the
American past as his conduit to a measure of realistic representation.
The Scarlet Letter, for instance, invokes the Puritan world by citing
actual places and events and incorporating historical figures like John
Winthrop and John Wilson. Melville's conduit to realistic representation was the insider's viewpoint, based on his own seafaring experiences, that supports his intricate depictions of the sea and whaling.
The "experimental" romance thus shared with realism a reaction
against the imaginative excesses adjudged to pervade popular fictions. An empiricist stance colored that reaction.

As Levine has noted, literary realism "was a method consonant
with empirical science. . . . " Its epistemology was empiricist; its language partly derived from science; it joined modern science in depriving Nature of "divine meaning and order" and setting about the business of "domesticating" it.[55] Bent on describing "reality itself,"
determined to pursue more than "wish fulfillment," and preoccupied
with particulars capable of deflating the ideal, realists were dis-
enchanters.[56] Their rhetorical stances made "writing novels seem an
important enough activity to engage the best, the brightest, and the
most talented—men."[57]

The rhetoric of realism included jabs at novel readers as well as
novel makers of the popular ilk. In Thackeray, Levine concludes, one
finds a "contemptuous rejection of the reader's unreflecting assumptions about narrative."[58] Similarly, Hawthorne "complained bitterly
about the low tastes of the feminine reading public,"[59] and Melville
counseled that works like *Moby Dick* were for men's, not women's,
enjoyment. By the 1850s, publishers were hiring readers to evaluate
the manuscripts submitted to them, and most of those readers were
men.[60] Literary journals and other periodical literature were also gaining cultural force at midcentury, their content often mirroring the
stances of novelists like Thackeray, Hawthorne, and Melville. These
new influences dovetailed with the novelistic themes examined earlier. The invasion involved, in short, multifaceted efforts to institutionalize masculine standards of taste by denigrating the feminine reading public and the female authors who commanded its attention.

Elaine Showalter suggests the invasion was self-conscious insofar as literary women's successes did threaten their male counter-

parts, who saw women "dominating because of superior numbers rather than superior abilities."[61] Tuchman, with Fortin, observes that during the 1840s and 1850s critical articles explicitly addressed the "woman question" in literature.[62] Ann Douglas argues that popular female writers were aware of "the hostility emanating from their clerical and literary brethren, and they returned it with interest,"[63] thus feeding the invaders' self-consciousness. Less directly, the relative inattention paid to popular male writers also suggests willfulness. As Douglas shows, some male sentimental writers were extremely popular; in her judgment they even "played a crucial role in making the periodical literary scene a testing ground for covert social and sexual hostilities."[64] Yet their work was never the target of widespread cultural trivialization. Apparently, the boundary defining under way did have as much to do with masculinity as with Literature. To wit, masculinity is more clear-cut when the Others are exclusively females. Constituting them as such requires upholding polite standards towards members of one's own sex; it requires what Goffman calls "civil disattention."

Not surprisingly, rhetoric substantially informed the progression into realism, sometimes involving denials of the demonstrable similarities between realists' and romancers' works. Levine shows that in Thackeray's work excess repeatedly "reasserts itself against the realist style imagined to deny it" and that "however elaborately Thackeray's novels resist the entrapment of romance, they cannot entirely avoid it."[65] More generally, Levine demonstrates that "The antiromantic realist, enthusiastically rejecting the falsification of earlier narrative forms, cannot very long remain true to the elements of the realistic."[66] Habegger offers a complementary argument about Henry James's work, which bridges the period of invasion and the period of redefinition. Like Thackeray, James carried much of the baggage of women's fiction into realism's buggy. Habegger cites the secret-plot as illustrative. Seemingly "formulaic and subliterary, the stock-in-trade of cheap romance, melodrama, or detective fiction," the secret-plot appears in all of James's best works. Similarly, his novels suggest that James "was much more the daydreamer and theory-spinner than the sharp-eyed observer he often thought he wanted to be."[67]

By the century's end—well into the period of redefinition—the divergences between realism as literary principles and realism as literary practices were becoming blatant. Conrad's fiction seems "a more sophisticated development of the texture of *Frankenstein*"; "the world that had been the realist's subject had become all illusion as well."[68] In American literature, the successors of James and Howells

were realists "(superficially called naturalists) who pushed the exploration of American masculinity much further"; for example, Theodore
Dreiser, Frank Norris, Stephen Crane.[69] What realism often involved
in practice, then, was putting men—characters and writers alike—in
sure charge of the bourgeois genre they wanted to qualify for entry
into the literary canon. Its rhetoric of masculinity couched in anti-fem-
inine, scientific terms served that end. As Habegger points out, "realistic" fiction presupposes "independent knowledge of the society in
question."[70] Lacking that knowledge, nineteenth-century realists were
prone toward serving as rhetoricians for a male-dominated literature.

At the same time, realists were prone toward de-idealizing heroines and toughening up heroes in their novels. As an "adversary" of
women's fiction, which comprised an idealized heroine and a lot of
domestic details,[71] realism of necessity took heroines down from their
pedestals or diluted their gumption while relegating domesticity to a
lesser place or no place at all in its fictions. The realistic novel "see[s]
all people and things within large containing social organizations"; it
focuses on a "single character . . . implicated in a world of the contingent who must make peace with society and nature or be
destroyed."[72] Confined mostly to home and church, realists' female
characters are in no position to demonstrate their capacity for tri-
umphing in a large-scale social world. Their need for male protection
displaces their capacity for effective action. Similarly, the pedestal
where popular heroines often stood either gets toppled or reduced to
dollhouse proportions. The toppling derives from treating female
characters in more or less individualistic ("realistic," by bourgeois
standards) terms; the reduction derives from subordinating domesticity to politics, business, and other male-dominated pursuits. In Thackeray's novels, for example, women either have no access to the worldly knowledge men have or, "educated about the world, they rather
quickly become threatening or villainous. . . . "[73] Elizabeth Ermarth
concludes that "consciousness of an alternative world cannot be
grounded within the realistic economy." Realism breeds "the literary
convention of consensus," emphasizing "a world of common agreements." The result is female "casualties": "The heroine participates in
this common system as a sacrifice not a survivor."[74] Thus, as we have
seen, women like Eliot subverted some of the literary agreements
governing the realistic novel.

The hero, on the other hand, emerges as the modern individualist. His outcomes uncertain and his challenges ambiguous, he asserts
himself as a singular individual finding his way in a world fraught
with competition and change. As Alan Swingewood puts it, the hero

of the modern novel is "alone in the world, to work out his own personal salvation."[75] In popular American fiction, the tomboy made frequent appearances during the 1860s. During the 1870s and 1880s, however, "boy books" took over.[76] The contrast between those books and women's bestsellers of the 1850s is telling. The latter portray female orphans facing the "ultimate pain" of "devot[ing] [themselves] for the entire narrative to reconstituting a domestic life. But in the boy books, the heroes ran away from home, preferring to take their chances in the world."[77] Such is the realistic hero, a product of novelists like Thackeray who lamented that "no writer of fiction among us has been permitted to depict to his utmost power a MAN."[78]

According to Tuchman, with Fortin, the redefinition and institutionalization of the masculinist novel also meant fashioning "high culture": "By 1870 men of letters were using the term *high culture* to set off novels they admired from those they deemed run-of-the-mill." Late in the nineteenth century, "men used their control of major literary institutions to transform the high-culture novel into a male preserve."[79] Criticism played a role in that connection, but not until Henry James's prefaces and Percy Lubbock's *The Craft of Fiction* (1921) did critical standards for the novel begin getting systematized.[80] Overall, novelists played the major role in touting high culture, deflating the cultural value of women's popular fiction, and defining the canonical novel while making it their own. Late to pay systematic attention to the novel, critics left it to novelists to override what belonged mostly to women in favor of what must belong mostly to men.

Nineteenth-century literary change thus illustrates that woman is, as Simmel put it, "the being in relation to whom man has the right to make demands and to pass judgments from the pinnacle of objective norms."[81] At the same time, such change shows "objective" norms in the process of being made perceivedly so. It also discloses "genre" as a cultural tool designating novels as particular "kinds of objects" and validating certain of them as artistically meaningful.[82] Nineteenth-century novelists were, among other things, showing that genres are "socially constructed organizing principles that imbue artworks with significance beyond their thematic content and are, in turn, responsive to structurally generated demands for cultural information and affiliation." As DiMaggio goes on to emphasize, we "cannot afford to take artistic categories as given or to treat taste as exogenous." DiMaggio advances two principles central to interpreting the data surveyed here. First, the "intended meaning [of artworks] may be sociologically less important than the ways in which they signify group affiliation." Second, "social groups use distinctive forms of cultural expertise to define themselves and to recognize members and outsiders."[83] Keeping those principles at the fore means putting the novel squarely into the sociohistorical world where biographical individuals give it culturally contingent shape. It also means seeing novels as multivocal documents capable of furthering canon formation.

9

🐝 The Business of Literature

The bookseller is concerned with a more noble form of merchandise
than any other merchant.

Levin L. Schucking, *The Sociology of Literary Taste*

George Webber, the protagonist in Thomas Wolfe's autobiographical *You Can't Go Home Again*, largely lives for writing. When he
lands in the literary marketplace, his vocation gets tempered somewhat for the sake of reaching an audience. *You Can't Go Home Again* is
a virtual memoir dramatizing the interplay between vocation and
marketplace.

In the novel's second chapter, "Fame's First Wooing," George's
literary agent sends him to James Rodney & Company to meet the
editor Foxhall Edwards who is interested in George's first novel. Rodney's "is" Charles Scribner's Sons; Foxhall Edwards "is" Maxwell
Perkins; George's first novel "is" *Look Homeward, Angel*. George's initial experiences with Edwards forecast a long-term intimacy, while
Rodney's unveils "the unknown world of publishing and the people
who inhabit it." Gradually, George finds himself working "among all
the crawling fashions of this world of lice."[1] His disillusionment eventuates in switching to another publisher. In the last four chapters of
You Can't Go Home Again George shares the letter declaring his professional independence from Edwards.

Those chapters also detail nine years of legendary collegiality
between Wolfe and Perkins. George writes that he had been "picked
up and sustained just when [his] spirit reached its lowest ebb, . . .
given life and hope, the restoration of [his] self-belief, the renewal of
[his] faith by the assurance of [Edwards's] own belief." For George,
Edwards is "Ecclesiasticus—noble, wise, eloquent, truthful."[2] As
Perkins saw it, Wolfe sought another publisher because of his notorious dependence on Perkins' editing. Perkins says that by dedicating

Of Time and the River to him "in most extravagant terms," Wolfe jeopardized their working relationship: "That dedication ... gave shallow people the impression that Wolfe could not function as a writer without collaboration. . . . "[3] Although such reactions strained their working relationship to the breaking point, their kindredness persisted. Wolfe designated Perkins his literary executor.

Hamilton Basso's *The View from Pompey's Head* portrays similar actual personalities. The novelist Garvin Wales "is" the playwright Eugene O'Neill; his editor Phillip Greene "is" Saxe Commins, who introduced Basso to Eugene and Carlotta O'Neill in 1947. Basso then interviewed O'Neill "over a period of months, prior to writing the three-part profile of [O'Neill] which appeared in *The New Yorker* in 1948."[4] *The View from Pompey's Head* appeared in 1954, a year after O'Neill's death. Its narrator says Wales and Greene's friendship had "become one of the legends of American publishing." Acquaintances seemed unable "to discuss [that] friendship . . . without becoming almost reverent." Seemingly, "no two men could have possibly been closer." Their separation may have stemmed partly from perceptions that "Garvin was incapable of writing a book without Phil. . . . " Phillip Greene's reputation allowed for that inference. He had won the loyalty of many gifted writers and had "more 'discoveries' to his credit than any other editor in the business, with the possible exception of Maxwell Perkins ... at Charles Scribner's Sons."[5]

Wolfe's and Basso's novels portray a business world comprising literary agents, publishers, reviewers, and lawyers as well as writers and editors. Both novels depict a marketplace based on commercial relationships, economic motives, and cultural commodities. The progression from manuscript to book thus conjoins two powerful archetypes—the artist and the businessperson.[6] The one is commonly romanticized, though unappreciated; the other, though respected, is seen as leading "the great intellectually unwashed of America," as Henry Luce put it.[7] Defoe considered writing a "very considerable branch of English commerce."[8] His observation underscores how decisively the world of business, like the world of everyday life, conditions writers' experiences and thus shapes our literature and its forms. As Howard Becker puts it, "Art works always bear the marks of the system which distributes them. . . . "[9]

Instruments of Mediation

Walter Abish laments the aesthetic ramifications of literary commerce:

I think the book's production—the reality principle of publishing, book merchandising—actually comes between the reader and myself. If I am to be aware of one, why not be equally aware of the other? One is as important as the other. The readers are there, as are the reviews, the critics, the interviews, the bookstores, the shelf life. How can one keep all of this in mind? Almost everything is an impediment to further work.[10]

As C. Wright Mills repeatedly emphasized, contemporary artists work within increasingly complex organizations and social *milieux.* Such individuals appear to exemplify freedom from the tangles of bureaucracy; their work seems to ensure autonomy and promote individuality. Yet making that work "available to circles, publics, and masses" requires the "cultural apparatus" standing between them and their audiences. In other terms, out of the patronage system of earlier centuries came the nineteenth-century "bourgeois public" accompanied by the cultural worker as an entrepeuneur selling "cultural commodities to anonymous publics."[11] As Per Gedin puts it, "The transformation from an aristocratic, court-dominated society to a middle-class capitalistic society meant the creation of a *market* for culture."[12] It meant, in Robert Escarpit's terms, that "the writer proposes and the public disposes."[13] Yet today's publics are "intensively cultivated into the condition of a receptive mass."[14]

The transformation of a writer with a manuscript into a novelist with a book and an audience thus involves producers, distributors, and promoters constitutive of a cultural apparatus beyond the writer's control yet essential to his or her purposes. Between writer and reader stand socially structured, "aesthetically irrelevant forces." In Arnold Hauser's terms, "a whole series of mediators and instruments of mediation" stands between creator and recipient; these "remove and alienate" artist and recipient from each other even while linking them.[15] Mediating institutions make art less awesome and more accessible, but the demystification built into modern mediation involves a "deformation of the [artist's] creative vision." Thus, although mediators are "neither 'for' nor 'against'" artists, in the aggregate they often undercut artists' aesthetic priorities.[16]

Steven C. Dubin's study of CETA's Artists-in-Residence (AIR) program illustrates how mediating institutions affect artists. Looking at artists "grounded within a network of producers and production constraints," Dubin details how this one program "normalized" its artists and how they regulated themselves in order to secure their continuing participation.[17] As Dubin points out, "It is not a matter of freedom *or* control, but how much of each can be discerned in a concrete situation." Such discernment is difficult to come by, however, since over time self-regulation can and probably does become part of most artists' work habits. Dubin observed, for instance, that "Self-imposed restraint followed directly from AIR's procedural requirements. . . . "[18] Such restraint is probably as common as the forms of restraint successfully inculcated in most participants in any institutional order. Most young people apparently slip past the question of whether or not to marry, instead focusing on the problem of whom to marry; most intellectuals seeking fellowships instinctively propose something along the apparent lines of the granting agency's thematic focuses, even when their keenest interests lie elsewhere. No less than other people, writers face socially structured opportunities and rewards as well as culturally structured conventions and values. Like others, artists are inclined to take for granted huge pieces of the institutional landscape structuring their options and outcomes. Many, if not most, novelists may by now take for granted that they must latch onto a literary agent, that they must be available for promotional activities, and so forth. Less consciously perhaps, many probably also take for granted that their relative autonomy presupposes some self-restraint as to subject matter, style, vocabulary, and other essentially artistic matters. Becker summarizes that "most artists, wanting their work distributed, do not make what the system will not handle."[19]

The experiences of Salman Rushdie illustrate how mediating institutions like bookstores themselves make choices based on readers' reactions and media attention. The Corcoran's decision to cancel the exhibition of Robert Mapplethorpe's photographs illustrates how perceptions of funding prospects and concern about institutional reputability may affect mediators' decisions about providing public access to specific artworks. The furor over one of Andres Serrano's works shows how concerns about good art and good taste continue to intermingle. These news-making, debate-provoking instances dramatize what artists must to some extent take for granted: Interposed between them and their prospective audiences are taste and decision makers capable of determining their outcomes. Unattached to those mediators, artists stand essentially alone with their cultural goods, lacking effective means of reaching those whose enjoyment fulfills the artistic enterprise.

Granted, artists vary dramatically in their practical capacities to control the instruments of mediation. Modern systems for producing and distributing cultural goods have given rise to the "star system" throughout the artistic world. The Star, says Mills, is "a person whose productions are so much in demand that, to some extent at least, he is able to use distributors as his adjuncts."[20] Thus, James Michener enjoys considerable independence from promotional tours, television talk shows, and other marketing activities. Similarly, Tom Robbins can by now "keep away from literary politics and the sort of social contacts that can put the wrong emphasis on one's work."[21] Yet, as Mills notes, Stars can get trapped in aesthetic molds seen as sealing their fame and lucrative outcomes.

Here Weber's distinction between living off and living for an activity (in the external sense) reasserts itself. On the face of things it would seem that those artists living for their work—those not dependent on it for their income—are less prone to the whims of mediating institutions. Yet those artists who do work at something else to secure their livelihood are likely to be in the employ of a mediating institution. As we saw, novelists are often university professors. In that role they are no less subject to institutionalized controls, largely informal in nature, over their work than novelists wholly dependent on their writing for income. Despite its emphasis on academic and related freedoms, academe often applies extraintellectual, extra-aesthetic standards to its members' work. Anthropologist Derek Freeman's criticisms of Margaret Mead's Samoan field work unleashed, for instance, not only "profound intellectual disagreements" but also "turf wars between schools of thought, ideologically and politically motivated maneuvering, all obscured by personal animus."[22] Similarly, the release of the National Research Council's *A Common Destiny: Blacks and American Society* evoked charges about the "politically conservative bent of some members of the committee" commissioned for the study.[23] Fearful that social class might overshadow race as an explanatory factor, some scholars registered essentially political reactions to the report. Imagine, then, the latitude available to scholars and administrators reacting to artistic works governed by more fluid criteria. In any event, novelists living for writing are on average just as consequentially subject to mediating institutions as those living off writing are.

For novelists, the principal mediators include literary agents, publishers, editors, critics, reviewers, and booksellers. The interplay among them structures novelists' individual and collective situations. Other institutional systems serve less obviously as instruments of mediation. Today film companies and television networks are capable of mightily enlarging novelists' audiences and fattening their bank accounts. Think of Ken Kesey's *One Flew Over the Cuckoo's Nest* or Alice Walker's *The Color Purple*. Educational institutions also mediate the relationship between novelists and readers. Pierre Bourdieu observes that "the higher one rises in the social hierarchy, the more one's tastes are shaped by the organization and operation of the educational system, which is responsible for inculcating the 'programme' . . . which governs 'cultivated minds. . . . '"[24] Schools tell students whom to read and what kinds of things to say about texts. Curricula emphasize some works enough "that they become institutionalized as canonical literature. Within that broad canon, . . . those admitted but read only in advanced courses, commented upon only by more or less narrow specialists, are subjected to the further tyranny of 'major' versus 'minor.'"[25] All the while, educators' book orders help to determine which books stay in print and which enjoy repeated printings. The "cultivation of minds" simultaneously involves schools in taste making, canon making, and market making alongside the business of certifying people for social mobility.

Over time, the instruments of mediation "achieve their full sense and real meaning only in relationship to one another."[26] Thus, canon formation has an interpersonal side to it only hinted at earlier. The interpersonal dynamics of canon formation are rooted in the unequal access novelists have to those individuals who staff the mediating institutions, as we will soon see.

Publishers, Agents, and Editors

The book industry includes publishers, literary agents, book manufacturers, reviewers and critics, advertising agencies, warehouses and wholesalers, bookstores and book departments of other stores, and buyers of subsidiary rights.[27] The publishing sector of the industry is its hub. A publishing firm is itself a complex division of labor comprising editors, managers, artists, designers, publicity and sales people, and readers serving as in-house critics. The most powerful publishers concentrate on trade books; that is, those for nonprofessional readers. Such publishers represent a recent development in the political economy of culture.

Around 1825 printing, publishing, and selling books began emerging as distinct sectors of the literary marketplace.[28] The century also saw the establishment of publishing firms successful enough to survive as profitable enterprises today. In 1807, Charles Wiley began publishing in downtown New York. His firm helped to establish James Fenimore Cooper with *The Spy* in 1821; it also published Poe, Hawthorne, and Melville.[29] In 1817 four Harper brothers traded farming on Long Island for a printing business in New York City. Soon they began publishing, turning out a title a week by 1830. By the late 1870s Harper & Brothers was paying Dickens for advance sheets of his novels, thus defeating literary pirates. Harper & Brothers published Lew Wallace's *Ben-Hur*, Owen Wister's *The Virginian*, and R. D. Blackmore's *Lorna Doone* as well as works by Henry James, William Dean Howells, Mark Twain, Zane Grey, and Booth Tarkington.[30] British publishing firms also rose to prominence during this period. Dickens, for example, began with Chapman and Hall and eventually returned to their fold; Trollope started out with Longmans and eventually switched to Chapman and Hall; Meredith stuck with Chapman and Hall where he eventually succeeded Forster as their literary advisor.[31] Publishers were competing for authors, and authors were playing publishers off against one another. By the end of the century more than 400 British publishing houses were in business.[32]

The proliferation of publishers was due, in part, to the technological innovations and growing literacy that made cheap books highly profitable. In 1860, Beadle & Company introduced the dime novel published in numbered series.[33] Before its demise more than 3,100 titles had appeared. The firm's writers-for-hire, often using pseudonyms, turned out a novel every few weeks for $150 to $300.[34] Louisa May Alcott earned money that way with Thomas & Company, which published her pseudonymous thrillers among its Ten Cent Novelettes.[35] Later in the century, "best-sellers" made their appearance when that term was "seemingly coined for the lists that *The Bookman* began publishing in 1895. . . . "[36]

During the last two decades of the nineteenth century, pocket-sized paperbacks emerged and quickly flourished. Paperback publishing subsided during the next several decades. In 1935, though, a softcover revolution began when "Penguins" entered the cheap reprint market. Pelican Books appeared in 1937, quickly followed by Penguin Classics and Pocket Books.[37] After World War II publishers understood softcover books were here to stay. Among the first clues was $35,000 paid for reprint rights against earned royalties for Norman Mailer's *The Naked and the Dead*. By now, original paperbacks that become bestsellers are reprinted in hardcover editions.[38] In fact, "Stephen King, Sidney Sheldon, John Jakes, and Danielle Steele are all creations of the paperback; that is, these novelists achieved hardcover success by building paperback success and an audience that crossed over to hardcover buying."[39]

The book industry has grown dramatically during this century. By 1981 American publishers were annually producing about 45,000 new titles and new editions.[40] Textbooks and encyclopedias, followed by book clubs and children's books, dominate the industry with adult trade books (including novels) representing less than ten per cent of the books published.[41] Publishing remains intensely competitive. Before World War II, about 400 American publishers competed; by 1982, the number was 1,300.[42] One reason for the absence of oligopoly is that huge size carries few competitive advantages; both small and large publishers may benefit from the efficiencies of the same printer.[43] Although most publishing firms remain privately owned, over the past twenty years conglomerates have been buying publishing houses, in part to capitalize on the "learning industry."[44] One effect is rising profit expectations, as publishing firms face pressures to perform as well as other companies on the stock exchanges.[45] Although some such firms—Knopf and Harper & Row, for example—are increasingly active in literary publishing, most maximize profits by curtailing their ventures with canonical novels.[46]

Publishing trends challenge novelists trying independently to establish reputations and earn income from writing. In general, entrepreneurial writers have three options. They may try to submit manuscripts to big-name, high-stakes publishers. Such writers find, though, that McGraw-Hill, Simon and Schuster, Putnam's, William Morrow, Dell, and Doubleday reject unsolicited manuscripts.[47] Alternatively, novelists may turn to smaller publishing companies knowing that most bestsellers lists include at least one volume from a small publisher.[48] For authors of best-selling and formulaic novels, small publishing houses may be a good bet. Since those novels appeal to large, heterogeneous audiences, the money spent promoting them stands to bring decent returns. The prospects for canonical works are less good since they are far riskier for small-capitalization firms. A third option is self-publication through companies publishing authors' works for fees (subsidy publishers), such as Exposition Press, Dorrance and Company, and Vantage Press.[49] Although a few reputable writers did begin as self-published authors, self-publication is economically unattractive and professionally unpromising.[50]

The nature of publishing makes it troublesome to nearly every novelist starting out. Although publishers like James Laughlin and Sir Stanley Unwin regard their work as self-expressive and literary, most others subordinate such interests to market imperatives.[51] Their identities override notions of belonging to the "service class of literature" and pursuing the "last honorable form of commerce."[52] Most publishers are tough-minded gatekeepers. In general, the publishing world is "stacked against the writer" despite the lucrative deals some novelists make.[53]

Not until the second quarter of the nineteenth century was the royalty system even introduced. Before that, publishers bought manuscripts outright. Today, authors get royalty statements at the end of June and December based on sales estimates. Since booksellers can return undamaged books to their publishers, though, publishers often pay no royalties until after the first or second statement.[54] Thus, authors are eager for advances. Besides, advances make publishers more actively promote their recipients' books.[55] Most advances are modest, but established authors command stupendous figures such as Barabara Taylor Bradford's three-million-dollar advance from Doubleday for her next two novels.[56] A highly competitive market comprising fast-sellers, steady-sellers, and mass-circulation books among its best-selling works[57] allows substantial returns on such investments. Besides royalties and advances, authors also earn income from the sale of subsidiary rights including first and second serial rights, book club rights, translation and foreign publication rights, reprint rights, movie and television rights, and rights for extracts, anthologies, and abridged editions.[58] Subsidiary rights sometimes sell for millions of dollars. Advances, royalties, and income from the sales of subsidiary rights to *Jaws* earned Peter Benchley more than ten million dollars, and Bantam paid over three million dollars for paperback rights to Krantz's *Princess Daisy.*[59] Significantly, these novels fall mostly into the best-selling, not the canonical, category.

Since they get 50 percent of the money from selling subsidiary rights, publishers often depend on the "successful exploitation of subsidiary rights" for high profits.[60] Even though novels represent a small fraction of their titles, the income they generate is often considerable. That circumstance provides lucrative opportunities for authors of best-selling and formulaic fiction. The tendency of first novels to lose money limits those opportunities, however. By now, "the economics of publishing are such that 'high' literature ... depends on the money produced by best-sellers. ... "[61]

The search for a publisher among the 1,300 houses and the challenge of negotiating a contract with the publisher lead many writers to literary agents. Such representatives have figured prominently in publishing since World War I.[62] The effective agent is a business manager and advisor who protects the writer's rights while maximizing the writer's income.[63] Like editors, literary agents often get intensely involved in their clients' personal and professional lives. Nadine Gordimer describes the "fatherly relationship" her agent had with her when she was a young, unknown, divorced mother of a small child. He urged her forward whenever anyone bought one of her pieces and got her "sufficient money... to live on" by pushing Simon and Schuster for a small advance on her first novel and then another advance when she was again short of money.[64]

Predictably, many literary agents are former editors.[65] Editors acquire the "inside" information and contacts literary agents need. For their services most literary agents get a 10 percent commission; the top ones command 12 or 15 percent. That commission applies to clients' royalties, advances, and sales of subsidiary rights. Like publishers, literary agents stand to gain a lot by making a novelist a "property," or a name with high commercial value.[66] Conversely, agents can ill afford to sign clients whose work has little such value. The top agents accept new clients only by referral.

Once a writer has, with or without an agent, found a publisher, his or her most crucial contact is the editor who sees the manuscript through all the phases necessary for getting it on the market. An editor must collaborate with the author at some level. William Goyen says editors' functions include "really caring for authors" and "letting them know that he cares."[67] Perkins was sufficiently adept at such concern that Ernest Hemingway once said, "I cared so much for Max Perkins that I have never been able to accept that he is dead."[68] Commins was equally magnetic. Besides his well-known bond with O'Neill, he enjoyed a close relationship with Faulkner. After Faulkner brought the manuscript of *Absalom, Absalom!* to Random House in 1936, Commins and he worked together closely until Commins died in 1958. When Faulkner won the Pulitzer Prize for *A Fable*, Commins represented him at the ceremony; when he won the Nobel Prize, Commins rented his suit and silk hat. Going overseas, Faulkner vested Commins with "complete and absolute power of attorney" and designated him his literary executor in the event of his death.[69]

Before he died, Commins saw publishing "becoming a high-pressure business with the emphasis on large volume, quick turnover, and sure profit...."[70] By now, some publishing houses assess editorial performance by the net profits of the books editors recommend.[71] That development dovetails with publishers', agents', and editors' increasing significance "as midwives of ritual classifications...." Together with advertisers, reviewers, and booksellers, they mastermind *commercial classifications* or "boundaries imposed upon artworks by profit-seeking entrepreneurs and firms in market societies." Such classifications segment markets "for distinct clusters of artistic work," thus "creat[ing] differing degrees of awareness of and access to genres among different segments of the public." For market-related reasons, commercial classifications "yield broader, more weakly framed genres than does ritual classification," such as literary critics pursue. Paul DiMaggio goes on to conclude that "commercial producers try to expand markets even at the risk of reducing the ritual value of the products they sell."[72]

In the process, novelists' works can take on lives that were never authorially intended. Recall Dean R. Koontz lamenting the early pigeonholing of Dick Francis's work. Ursula Le Guin has experienced similar difficulties. She says her work "didn't sell until it was given to a science fiction editor." Her work sells beyond that category by now, seemingly "because once you get published it is easier to get published again and again and to enlarge that pigeonhole you've been put in." Today Le Guin asks, "Is it science fiction? Is it fantasy? Who cares?"[73] Commercial classifiers aiming for profits must to some extent care about such matters. Their classifications exacerbate the problems novelists face getting published, particularly if they work with what Le Guin calls "hybrid forms." At the same time, commercial classifications may feed specialist readers' inclination to limit their fiction reading to one genre by visibly underscoring generic labels on book jackets as well as in bookshops, advertisements, and book reviews. In the process, Simmel's insight that culture's "ultimate purpose . . . can only be in the enrichment of individuals" gets diluted.[74]

Critics, Reviewers, and Sellers

A book's reception depends on how publishers promote it, how enthusiastic national booksellers are about it, how often its author makes public appearances, how timely the work is, and how strong its author's reputation is. Many of these factors strongly correlate, and most also correlate with the number and character of the reviews a book gets. In a competitive marketplace reviews serve, in Kurt Lang's terms, as "an extension of industry promotion."[75]

Modern criticism emerged in the eighteenth century when Samuel Johnson made it a literary genre.[76] The growth of periodicals during that century was crucial to its institutionalization. As a literary and social force the review gave critics a forum for working out the terms of their work and establishing their audiences. It became a major force when the *Edinburgh Review* appeared in 1802.[77] During the nineteenth century, the lecture also emerged as a vehicle for criticism, first for public audiences and later for university classes. Eighteenth- and nineteenth-century critics were practical interpreters of literature and culture. They oriented themselves toward some part of the increasingly differentiated reading public and felt responsible for applying "prevailing standards (usually moral) to [their] judgment[s] of literature."[78] They felt, then, some responsibility for linking authors and readers by cultivating a broad cultural consensus among literate people.

By the 1920s, literary critics began separating themselves from book reviewers,[79] making the academic and popular versions of criticism more distinct. Today criticism is mostly the turf of university professors, a circumstance involving mounds of critical output as well as "an unprecedented self-consciousness."[80] What distinguishes contemporary criticism is its insistence on treating works in relation to literature and art, not in relation to everyday life, mass leisure, or consumption.[81] In practical terms, this means the twentieth-century critic "feels no responsibility toward a public, either to express its standards or to shape its taste. If anything, he imposes his standards on his public."[82] Since criticism is "discourse about discourse,"[83] such imposition is easily established. Criticism can become a language game played more to gain academic tenure and intellectual reputation than to promote critical literacy or heighten aesthetic awareness.

In any event literary criticism (as well as highbrow reviewing) "creates communities of meaning"[84] where the reputations of both critics and authors are made while readers' expectations and tastes are shaped. Like the other arts, literature requires a "special institution which serves [its] reception," and criticism and reviews are the institutions serving either to raise or lower the plane where readers receive their novels.[85] Yet the academic appropriation of criticism removes it from the reach of all but a few generalist readers. That circumstance notwithstanding, art is for laypeople, "people who at first have nothing to do with it even if they eventually learn to have a great deal to do with it. It should be within reach of people who have a need for it. . . . "[86] In the best of all cultural worlds, critics would stretch the aesthetic reach of people needing art; in the confines of actual cultural worlds, they appear bent on constricting that reach. All the while, the critic or highbrow reviewer remains an influential interpreter, albeit one mostly addressing other critics and reviewers.

Needless to say, cultural contingencies shape critical works,[87] as do critics' social networks and biographical situations. Criticism is "the expression of personal perceptions, ideas, and illusions, just as [imaginative] literature is."[88] What a critic says about a text "is inextricably bound up with the kinds of questions . . . ask[ed] of that text" and with what "seems best suited to articulate one's felt experience."[89] Critics interpret their literary experiences, then, in part by drawing on the same social stock of knowledge and the same systems of relevances used to interpret their other experiences. One interesting illustration is

Constance Fenimore Woolson, now "consigned to oblivion." Henry James cited Woolson and William Dean Howells as "the only English-language novelist[s] he read," and "he included a sketch of her along with those of de Maupassant, Turgenev, Emerson, George Eliot, Trollope, Daudet, and Stevenson in *Partial Portraits* (1888)." Woolson remained "anthologized throughout in 1920s." Cheryl B. Torsney cites a "decidedly male critical bias" as one of the reasons for Woolson's literary demise. Her work "disappears from the anthologies of American short stories just about the time that the canon of American literature comes into being." Like many other female Americans of her generation, Woolson got relegated to the ranks of "regionalists and local colorists."[90] As Diane Johnson puts it, there is no "equal right of imperfection"[91] for writers of the "wrong" sex, color, ethnicity, or social class. The work of Tuchman with Fortin demonstrates that absence by showing how in-house reviewers and literary critics gradually appropriated the high-cultural novel, denying all but the most exceptional of women even the right to serious attention.

The most singular study of critical biases belongs, however, to Wendy Griswold, who emphasizes that reviewers constitute their critical meanings partly out of what they themselves deem significant and partly out of "what *they think* their readers will find significant." (emphasis added) Examining American, British, and West Indian reviews of the West Indian George Lamming's novels, Griswold finds stunning cross-cultural divergences. The three cultural groupings differ in their attention to literary style, the literary context wherein they considered the novels, and the number and kinds of literary references they made. American reviewers mentioned race about three fourths of the time, their attention varying with time period; the West Indian reviewers mentioned it only about a fourth of the time, the British mentioning it even less frequently. The British reviewers, on the other hand, were "conspicuously silent" about colonialism despite its thematic relevance in Lamming's fiction. Griswold concludes that "different literary meanings may be woven from the same literary symbols interacting with the concerns of distinct sets of readers insofar as these concerns highlight different aspects of a multivocal text."[92]

More recently, Marjorie L. DeVault has shown how gender conditions critics' and reviewers' interpretations along lines paralleling nationality. Examining critical reactions to Nadine Gordimer's *The Late Bourgeois World*, she finds that the early reviewers (1966–67), mostly men, typically relied on "common stereotypes of women" to account for the heroine's behavior. During the late 1970s literary critics, addressing more specialized audiences and concerned more with aesthetics, "seem to have expected a more traditional story, with an active male hero"; few of them saw the heroine at the story's center. One feminist critic deviates markedly from that pattern, able to "place at the center of the story what is clearly a peripheral element for the other, mostly male, readers." DeVault advises skepticism toward "the power of something 'in' the text." She favors the question implicit in the broader considerations at hand; specifically, "Powerful for whom?"[93]

As cultural enterprises, criticism and reviewing thus tend to express the relevances of their practitioners. Literary criticism remains overwhelmingly white, male, and upper-middle class. Had feminist criticism and black and ethnic studies not emerged, it would probably be more skewed in those directions. In all likelihood, reviewing involves a more heterogeneous aggregate of individuals, yet even among reviewers biases seem far from absent. Recently, I picked up two issues of *The New York Times Book Review* I had at hand. Together, the two (July 30 and August 6, 1989) reviewed eleven novels—six male- and five female-authored works. Men wrote eight of the reviews, reviewing all but one of the male-authored novels and all but two of the female-authored ones. Should that pattern prove representative, it means men are entitled to review novels written by either sex while women are entitled mostly to review novels by women. Simmel would have predicted no less.

Interesting, though woefully anecdotal, are the adjectives reviewers use to characterize the novels. The three men reviewing females' novels find them (1) "charming" and "witty"; (2) "fine," "absolutely nothing regional," and "a bit choppy"; and (3) "stylish," "endearing," "mild," "obvious," "one-dimensional," and "essentially flimsy."[94] Contrast those terms with the ones Desmond Ryan uses to describe Donald E. Westlake's *Sacred Monster:* "witty, venomous, and knowing"; "devastating"; "pungent, right-on-the-money"; and "cleverly entwined."[95] Thinking I might be onto a research project to share with undergraduates, I picked up the *New York Review of Books* (August 17, 1989) closest at hand. It reviewed only four novels, all male-authored; the reviewers were men. Of particular interest was Brad Leithauser's review of Nicholson Baker's first novel *The Mezzanine.* In Leithauser's judgment its energy derives from "keen-eyed attention"; it is "dextrously and wittily delineated ...;" its author is a "precisionist" who has "finessed his way through a remarkable debut."[96]

Phillip Goldberg pioneered the study of how an author's (apparent) sex affects readers' reactions to a text.[97] Like Griswold, he looked at "the interaction between a cultural object and its recipients ... by holding one side of the relationship constant while allowing the other to vary."[98] While awaiting more such studies, we would do well to bear in mind the preliminary findings, surveyed in Chapter 5, showing how gender itself conditions reading. Those findings, like Goldberg's and Griswold's and DeVault's, attest to how social location, cultural context, and biographical situation interplay in a practical hermeneutics that knows no absolutes but nonetheless seeks them in a flight from ambiguity. In Becker's terms, aesthetics is "an activity rather than a body of doctrine." That activity takes shape within a system where differentiation "into subgroups—by ethnicity, age, sex, and class, at a minimum—makes it likely that each group will lack some of the conventional knowledge necessary to understand art works aimed at some other group."[99] Conventions like genres thus represent broadly social as well as narrowly literary codes[100] structuring aesthetic activities that routinely, though perhaps not intentionally, maintain the stratification benefiting some while depriving and excluding others. The long, slow trek toward such understandings has already begun with debates over the literary canon. Out of those debates have come revisionist insights about such things as how Hawthorne's work got shifted from the popular to the canonical realm and how Melville's *Moby Dick* was classified as cetology, travel, or adventure "as late as the 1920s."[101] As awareness of the social constitution of literary merit grows, critics and reviewers alike may give up their exclusionary stances for inclusionary visions that serve readers and novelists alike. Mediating may yet become their forte.

In the meantime, novelists must bear the brunt of the unevenness criticism and reviewing exhibit. Some, like Bernard Malamud, dislike critics, particularly those concerned "not with what the writer has done but how it fits, or doesn't fit, the thesis they want to develop." Others, like May Sarton, lament that their "kind of writing" fails to "present an exciting tool for analysis by young professors who might want to make a name for themselves." Others, perhaps a majority, share Thomas McGuane's perception: "The critics don't understand how much influence they can actually have on a writer, how much a writer's feelings can be hurt, how much they can deflect his course. . . . "[102] Kurt Vonnegut is the rare novelist willing to admit such personal experiences, saying "I never felt worse in my life" than after reading the reviews of *Slapstick*.[103]

Yet most authors would savor the opportunity for such anguish. The competition for reviews is fierce. Only about ten percent of new books gets reviewed for retail buyers. The novels least likely to be reviewed are formulaic works, original softcover works, novels published by small companies, and those written by unknowns whose publishers have not "hyped" their works.[104] Even negative reviews are better for sales than no reviews, it seems. Apparently, reviews do influence booksellers, all the more so when "critical acclaim" enters the picture. Even a mention in a news story or feature article may increase a book's sales.[105] Since bestsellers lists derive from bookstores' sales figures, anything that gets books into bookshops raises sales potential.

During the nineteenth century most major American publishers established their own bookstores. Yet prior to World War I fewer than 500 bookstores operated in the United States. That number quadrupled before World War II.[106] By 1982, at least 9,000 general bookstores sold to American readers.[107] A fairly recent development is national bookstore chains like B. Dalton (475 stores) and Waldenbooks (640) that appeal to readers intimidated by less impersonal, small bookshops.[108] The chains may create more book buyers, make booksellers more aggressive, and help certain books onto the best-seller lists.[109] But if they stimulate more aggressive stances among booksellers, do they also raise their competitors' costs; for example, advertising expenses? Do the bookstore chains expect higher profits? If so, do they minimize the space devoted to books with low sales volumes? Which novels bookstores stock, how they display them, whether or not they advertise them, and how often clerks recommend them all influence sales. And those sales determine the makeup of best-sellers lists. The rate, not the overall volume, of bookstores' sales lands books on those lists.[110] What booksellers report as sales figures thus determines the fate of many books.

Mail-order businesses, most prominently book clubs, are today's other major form of bookselling. Such businesses began on the assumptions that some readers are unable or unwilling to go to bookstores and that specialized audiences are more effectively reached with a direct approach.[111] Although mail-order booksellers operated during the nineteenth century, the Book-of-the-Month Club (BOMC) originated the successful book club, together with the Literary Guild, begun the next year in 1927. Today about eighty book clubs sell to American readers with clubs' editions usually selling for somewhat less than publishers' original editions.[112] Besides access to books, what the clubs sell are guidance, review, and preselection, according to BOMC chairman Edward Fitzgerald and Macmillan Book Club president William Houghton.[113] The selections vary from club to club; with its predominately female membership the Literary Guild offers, for example, a high proportion of historical and romantic fiction.[114] Critics charge that the BOMC favors candidates for the bestsellers lists, tending to ignore contemporary canonical novels. Fitzgerald counters that besides novelists like Michener and Wouk, the BOMC has furthered the exposure of writers like Solzehnitsyn, Grass, and Camus.[115] Janice Radway's findings lend credence to Fitzgerald's contention. She found that although BOMC editors and readers include commercial considerations among their relevances, they select many works on the basis of how much they themselves like them or how firmly they believe in their merit, notwithstanding the small number of members likely to order them.[116]

Gatekeeping, Mentoring, Networking: Interpersonal Relations and Canon Formation

For writers as well as literary agents, publishers, and editors, contacts are invaluable. Increasingly important for writers is a media personality and the willingness to let image makers exploit it. As James Michener points out, such images serve "a society that [does] not want artists but [does] want some kind of cabalistic reassurance that it [has] artists among its people." The "Ernest Hemingway solution" is common in such societies: "The artist is consciously built up into a public figure whose image stands for something almost concrete and whose life work fulfills that image."[117] For acclaimed novelists, though, image making is far from inevitable. James Gould Cozzens and J. D. Salinger demonstrate that, as does Michener himself whose work in the publishing business led him to regard it as a "hilarious, harmless but not altogether honest racket" that markets authors while trying to make them feel like authors. Michener knows few authors and publishers and no critics; he gives no lectures or seminars; he does not work in Hollywood; he leaves the country when his books are being released.[118] The pressures inviting such a solution represent one more challenge for the writer with a literary vocation. The same pressures likely affect female and male novelists differently, paralleling the different outcomes they are likely to experience as a result of different contacts and professional experiences. The same generalization might be extended to writers of color and others whose social identities deflate their effective participation in the interpersonal spheres anchoring literary organizations.

Let us first dispose of publicity pressures. Virtually no systematic research exists about novelists' participation in image-making via promotional tours, television talk shows, and related activities, if only because they have gotten institutionalized only recently. Undoubtedly, self-promotional activities have preoccupied any number of novelists from time immemorial. Dickens was a master of that art. So, too, were Edgar Allen Poe and Frances Sargent Osgood who went about during the 1840s "dramatizing themselves as romantic hero and heroine" while advancing "their own and one another's careers."[119] Oscar Wilde's "sensational lecture tours of America in 1882" promoted a "taste of art, beauty, and good design,"[120] but Wilde was also promoting Oscar Wilde. By now, we take such activities more or less for granted.

According to Kenneth C. Davis, Jacqueline Susann was central to their institutionalization. She was "a genius at self-promotion."[121] Andy Warhol is Susann's male counterpart. One thinks, too, of Truman Capote, Barbara Cartland, Jackie Collins, and Norman Mailer. Given the double standard of aging in societies like ours and the abiding connections between femininity and physical attractiveness, it would seem that female novelists on average face lesser odds than male novelists of successfully establishing an appealing media image. More than their male counterparts, they face pressures to present a glamorous self; for them, being interesting or even titillating is unlikely to be quite enough. Granted, the mystique of "artist" and the power of a "hot bestseller" undercut such tendencies, but they are probably insufficient to wash away sex differences along these lines. One thinks here of female newscasters like Diane Sawyer and Connie Chung who would seem to have met standards never applied as rigorously to men in their field.

Although they may be relatively handicapped in the media-based, self-promotional arena, women's handicaps in the literary marketplace foremostly derive—like those of minority-group members generally—from their relative dearth of effective contacts. The publishing world offers an obvious starting point. We have already seen that a number of novelists have pursued editorial and journalistic work that expands their circle of acquaintances in the publishing world. Albert Camus was an editor at Gallimard; William Goyen at McGraw-Hill; E. L. Doctorow at Dial Press and New American Library. Currently, Toni Morrison is an editor at Random House. A generation ago, though, her chances of getting such a position would have been woefully smaller than today. No female editor has achieved the stature of Max Perkins or Saxe Commins. Historically, sexual and racial discrimination in publishers' hiring effectively barred female and minority individuals from making contacts capable of furthering their careers as writers or even literary agents.

Equally important are mentors whose own contacts often serve the interests of aspiring writers. Lisa Pater Faranda indicates that "mentorial relationships were part of the social reality of the nineteenth-century literary world. There was a network of writers and publishers who not only influenced what was written but what was published and then was reviewed." Clubs formalized such networks, but "very few intellectual clubs with a powerful and influential membership . . . included women."[122] Shirley Marchalonis's anthology *Patrons and Protegées: Gender, Friendship, and Writing in Nineteenth-Century America* documents such patterns. Among the specific relationships examined therein are those between Margaret Fuller and Ralph Waldo Emerson, Fanny Fern and Walt Whitman, and Charlotte Perkins Gilman and William Dean Howells. Those relationships commonly turned on a patriarchal axis, and literary historians have tended to miniaturize the female and lionize the male in each case.

Friendship, whether built out of a mentorial relationship or taking nurture from collegiality and acquaintances in common, often serves novelists' careers. Within the literary establishment, where friendships can gain novelists access to decision makers and secure them places in the mainstream literary community, men are generally more advantaged than women. As Alfred Habegger remarks, "It is worth remembering that Mark Twain got an incalculable boost from his friend W. D. Howells. The one respectable literary friend and power-broker Mrs. Emma D. E. N. Southworth knew was John Greenleaf Whittier, and he wasn't worth so very much." In fact, Whittier tried to redirect Southworth's work along canonical, masculinist lines. *Ishmael*, the resultant novel, is "dull" and "didactic."[123] Worse than no powerful friends at all, perhaps, are those who misdirect one's energies, in part by applying inappropriate criteria to works they cannot (or care not to) appreciate. Sometimes women are the beneficiaries of such bonds, as when Gore Vidal "forced" Anaïs Nin's work on E. P. Dutton.[124] More typically, women tend to share their closest friendships with other women and to benefit less on average from their friendships with men than their male counterparts do.

One can scarcely help but notice that female novelists are usually the ones having felt shut out of or isolated within the literary establishment, though only a few publicly report such experiences. May Sarton has felt that way, claiming "I've never had any kind of power behind me." Rebecca West felt similarly: "I never met anybody with whom I could have discussed books before or after"—not even an editor.[125] Virginia Woolf felt similarly shut out despite her connections with influential intellectuals and artists.

Yet one factor continues favoring for female novelists—the predominance of women among novel readers. Particularly for women talented at writing the sorts of works read almost exclusively by women, the gatekeepers get enthusiastic and networks become more permeable. Gothic romances, for instance, were "proven moneymak-

ers" through the late 1960s, and historical romances were "the publishing sensation of the seventies." Such circumstances apparently
correlate with "the emergence of women as editors in the paperback
field," most notably in the romance area.[126] For talented females writing nonformulaic fiction, however, data like these seem disheartening
in terms of the sex-segregated patterns they suggest; namely, that
female authors, female editors, and female readers somehow constitute their own separate (and inferior) cultural sphere. Then, too, as we
have seen, book review editors may be inclined to assign female
reviewers mostly to female-authored works. Dubin notes that "the
marketplace for the enthusiastic reception of ideas is not directed by
an 'invisible hand': rather, the active role of gatekeepers in the production and distribution processes helps determine market success."[127] So, too, the success of female and male novelists; the visible
hands are dirtied to some extent by double standards.

For artists and intellectuals, female or male, literary market conditions are gloomy. The decline of traditional patronage and the rise of
the book industry complicate their writing lives. Helpful to some of
them, though, are fellowships and grants offered by private corpora-
tions, foundations, or governments. National Institute of Arts and Letters grants have supported Baldwin, Bellow, Capote, Heller, Mailer,
McCarthy, Nabokov, O'Connor, Percy, Roth, and Vonnegut. The Ford
Foundation has helped Baldwin, Bellow, O'Connor, and Roth as well
as others. Dos Passos got three Guggenheim Fellowships; Porter and
Welty, two each. Guggenheim has also supported writers as diverse as
Bellow, Kosinski, Nabokov, and Wolfe.[128] E. L. Doctorow wrote *Ragtime*
with fellowships from the Guggenheim Foundation and the Creative
Artists Program Services. During its first twenty years (1966–85), the
Literature Program of the National Endowment for the Arts (NEA)
supported nearly 1,600 writers with fellowships and awards of various
kinds. The NEA emphasizes the diversity of the writers it has supported. Yet during its first twenty years, women apparently received less
than a third of the fellowships and awards the Literature Program
handed out. Of the 1,598 writers listed in a volume celebrating the
twentieth anniversary of the Literature Program,[129] 67 names leave one
unsure of the individual's sex. Among the remaining 1,531 writers, 463
(30.2 percent) are women; the ratio of male to female recipients is 3.3 to
1. Those figures may reflect fewer applications from women, the
underrepresentation of women among academically fashionable writers, the tendency of judges to take women's work less seriously, less
enthusiastic letters of recommendations, or any number of other circumstances. The fact is that over the years, women's writing has gar-

nered less support through the Literature Program than men's.

In any event, literary artists and intellectuals can be distinguished from their more popular counterparts by such awards, which in turn trigger other "selecting mechanisms" favoring these writers.[130] They enjoy, for example, greater chances for the free room and board available at the dozen or so writers' colonies in the United States. Despite the conflict between their literary interests and the commercial interests of the marketplace, writers with literary vocations do have opportunities to take the edge off their frustrations. Nevertheless, they live with more than a little awareness that "most of the cost of developing ideas is borne by artists who hope the industry will take them and distribute them."[131] Writers can scarcely escape the sense that "anyone who makes something where nothing was before provides occupation and profit for so many others."[132] And those others are the contacts writers need in order to reach their audiences and thereby complete their works.

As Lucien Goldmann saw, modern conditions thus jeopardize "efficacious action by those trying to use mass media toward effectively creative, cultural ends."[133] More recently, Jeffrey C. Goldfarb has argued that in societies like ours where the market is capable of keeping artists' freedom of expression unfulfilled, cultural freedom requires making the "unmarketable" accessible to the public. It requires seeing that economic constraints on artists are neither "natural" nor "unavoidable" and that the free market wedges itself between artists' consciousness and publication. Where markets and marketing determine artists' outcomes, according to Goldfarb, "successful creators are more likely to work on material with specific outlets in mind before the act of creation." In the American case, the relative paucity of federal support for the arts coupled with tightening connections between trade publishing and the mass entertainment industry virtually guarantee that "the struggle over the production and reception of culture and the politics of interpretation" will remain intense. Although that struggle is inevitable, its degree needs tempering for the sake of cultural freedom, which "centers on the freedom of expression and reception, that is, the freedom of relatively unconstrained public discourse." Book-loving, freedom-minded individuals who value such discourse need to remember that cultural freedom thrives on a "pluralism of supports yield[ing] pluralistic constraints, which can be manipulated."[134] In the absence of social action based on such recognitions, books will join other discursive vehicles as mere instruments of a mass culture marketed along lines denying the diversity that makes our collective life adaptive and rich.

10

❦ The Art of Social Worlds and the Science of Social Worlds

Sociology has undoubtedly acquired today something of the same intel-
lectual-synthetic function that the literary and historical imaginations
claimed in the last century.

Malcolm Bradbury, *The Social Context of Modern English Literature*

The setting of Randall Jarrell's *Pictures from an Institution* is Benton
College whose president Dwight Robbins is a smooth-talking sociologist. Temporarily at Benton is Gertrude Johnson, a novelist who teaches
creative writing. Robbins and Johnson show what living off sociology
and living off literature mean in practical terms. Jarrell's novel tells the
story of a sociologist and a novelist bent on self-aggrandizement.

"President Robbins was so well adjusted to his environment that
sometimes you could not tell which was the environment and which
was President Robbins."[1] Robbins habitually charms and cajoles people into liking him. Not even "evolved to the stage of moral development at which hypocrisy is possible" (p. 67), he manipulates his beliefs
as readily as he manipulates people: "About anything, anything at all,
Dwight Robbins believed what Reason and Virtue and Tolerance and a
Comprehensive Organic Synthesis of Values would have him believe.
And about anything, anything at all, he believed what it was expedient
for the President of Benton College to believe" (p. 17).

In balder ways than Robbins, Johnson is a misanthrope. Exploiting people as she goes about "Collecting for the Book" (p. 59), Johnson
is polite to "material" (p. 37). Her novels rest on facts churned through
her mechanically analytical mind. Johnson turns the novel's debunking tradition into a pseudo-sociological project meant to appeal to
experimentalist writers and alienated readers. She stands without
beliefs: "All clichés, slogans, fashions, turns of speech, details of dress,
disguises of affection, tunnels or by-passes of ideology, gravestones of

rationalization and cant live in Gertrude as in nutrient broth; and Gertrude nourished them unharmed, knowing all, believing none" (p. 119). Johnson lacks the values and methods that transform mere observations into sociological insights. Although she fantasizes about sociologists' approval (p. 182), those Johnson pictures represent a grotesque extreme that few sociologists approach.

"President Robbins never had time to be human, Gertrude had never wanted to be ... " (p. 146). Both characters are preeminently role-players who go awry by rejecting the humanistic character of their disciplines. Their outcomes imply that fulfilling a vocation means transcending the roles associated with its pursuit, and their experiences imply the linkages between sociology and novels as cultural forms.

Two Cultural Arrays: The Art and the Science of Social Worlds

The originators of the novel and sociology responded to upheavals wrought by urbanization, industrialization, and political revolutions. The novel and sociology grew on the shambles of taken for grantedness and the banner of progress, both centering their concerns on human agency, social order, freedom, and fulfillment. Among nineteenth-century novelists and sociologists, social classes, occupations, religions, and bureaucracies garnered attention as "a traumatizing acute sense of the making and breaking of connections came over Western Man and culture."[2]

Bruce Mazlish considers nineteenth-century cultural life in terms of that pervasive concern with connections. By and large, he shows that philosophers, novelists, and poets lamented the breakdown of traditional connections, but the forces of social change blunted their capacity to chasten the felt loss of meaningful, stable connections. In fact, their "literary lamentation is transformed into (presumed) scientific analysis," most strikingly in the form of a nascent but ambitious sociology. During the 19th century, then, a cultural struggle ensues "between those who cherish connections—by which they mean the old connections—and those who detest them, as chains." In the end, the latter individuals appear to triumph as the former's voices get "scientized" in sociology. Central to the cultural battles constituting that apparent victory was George Eliot, whose novels "are a bridge to the development of early sociology." Influenced by Comte's positivism and committed to the notion of "natural sympathy," Eliot conjoined the changing literary and the emergent sociological worlds of the Victorian era. Mazlish generalizes that "statisticians thought 'hard facts' would be more persuasive than imaginative depictions of the breakdown of affective ties; that science, based on statistics, rather than sympathy, based on sensibility, was the remedy for social disease." Eliot steered a cultural course between those stances, one that makes profound sense among those who see the fundamental kinship between the two worlds being institutionalized as distinct spheres. As Mazlish puts it, we need to consider "in the end whether, seeking science, [early sociologists] emerge only with myth, that is, with a new form of literary rather than scientific expression. Or, is it that a science of society must necessarily resemble myth and metaphor more than it does equations and general laws?"[3] Put differently, is sociology a cultural form fundamentally akin to the modern novel as a cultural form?

During the last century, pointed convergences between the two forms suggest so. Balzac and Flaubert were central to those convergences, as were nineteenth-century critics who frequently commented on society and culture as well as literature. With the "realistic" novel came self-conscious concern with social representation. Eliot subtitled *Middlemarch* "A Study of Provincial Life"; Harriet Beecher Stowe used southern newspapers and personal records to document *Uncle Tom's Cabin*; Charles Kingsley relied on newspaper reports about the London poor while writing *Alton Locke*.[4] Himself an author of lyric poetry and an unfinished comic novel, Marx wrote about literature and used literary data in his other studies. Sir James Frazer, whose *Golden Bough* deeply influenced modern literature, pursued such literary projects as preparing editions of Addison's essays and Cowper's letters.[5] Twentieth-century social and behavioral scientists extended such convergences. Freud, whose impact on literature is incalculable, said, "The poets and philosophers before me discovered the unconscious. What I discovered was the scientific method by which the unconscious can be studied."[6] Freud entitled criticism "to find in the material of dreams the stuff from which literature is made."[7] Psychoanalytical criticism emerged, and psychological criticism like that of I. A. Richards won respect. Karl Mannheim's work influenced T. S. Eliot and Phillip Rahv, and in his cultural studies Eliot adopted "the point of view of the sociologist."[8] As the anthropologist James Clifford notes, "Malinowski's authorial identifications (Conrad, Frazer) are well known," as perhaps are Weber's in *The Protestant Ethic*—John Keats and Matthew Arnold, among others.[9] Mead, Sapir, and Benedict "saw themselves as both anthropologists and literary artists," and sociologists as different as Peter L. Berger and Richard Sennett have published novels.[10] Contemporary critics like Harold Bloom, Wolfgang Iser, and Barbara Herrnstein Smith cite Erving Goffman.[11] By now, though, reciprocal influence between social scientists and literary individuals has waned, deepening the historical divergences between the two groups while masking their convergences.

From the seventeenth century, literary individuals saw science as a threat, and science "excluded certain expressive modes from its legitimate repertoire"—modes deemed rhetorical, fictional, and subjective that then got "localized in the category of 'literature.'"[12] Lennard J. Davis argues that 1700 to 1750 was "a crucial [period] in the separation of factual narratives from fictional ones," a separation central to the social constitution of fiction as a "specialized discourse that has been canonized and valorized as aesthetic, and therefore removed from the world of public events"[13] and the world of science. Cultural wedges were being driven between what Stephan Fuchs calls "aesthetic-expressive discourse" and "theoretical discourse."[14] In the latter discourse "Polyvocality was restrained and orchestrated . . . by giving one voice a pervasive authorial function. . . . "[15] Thus, the modern sciences, like the modern novel, emerged by articulating a rhetoric of differences and institutionalizing means of exclusion. Like the anti-romance and experimental-romance novelists, the first generations of modern scientists excluded not only "lay audiences" but also "competing knowledge-producing organizations . . . from 'legitimate' and 'serious'" discourse in their realm.[16] Over time, the differences drawn *between* literature and science engendered a "repression of differences" *within* each pursuit.[17]

In the case of literature and sociology, from the mid-nineteenth century each claimed "to offer the key orientation to modern civilization . . . ," as Wolf Lepenies has shown. Trying to establish their academic relevance and scientific promise, sociologists "distance[ed] themselves from the early literary forms of their discipline," thus feeding the "conflict between cold reason and the culture of feeling" while constituting a "'secret history' of the modern social sciences [where] so significant a role is played by women. . . . "[18] In stunning detail, Lepenies links the efforts of Auguste Comte, Émile Durkheim, Gabriel Tarde, Herbert Spencer, Beatrice Webb, Karl Marx, Wilhelm Dilthey, Max Weber, Georg Simmel, and Karl Mannheim with those of John Stuart Mill, H. G. Wells, Matthew Arnold, F. R. Leavis, T. S. Eliot, Stefan George, and Thomas Mann. He emphasizes competitive linkages in France, England, and Germany. As all sociologists worth their salt understand, keen competition entails reciprocal influence. Between the lines of Lepenies's text, then, runs a rich commentary on how literature and sociology impinged on one another.

Nonetheless cultural rivalry persists, obfuscating the similarities

between the sociological and literary vocations. Academic overspe-
cialization, the low status of interdisciplinary studies, and competition for enrollments tighten the blinders that keep sociologists, novelists, and literary critics from experiencing their kinship. So, perhaps,
does C. P. Snow's notion of "two cultures."[19] Snow's thesis is valid.
Literature and the sciences are different worlds. Yet both presuppose
the commonsense world and have their origins there. Thus, "there
can be no divorce between science and technology, on the one hand,
and art, on the other, any more than there can be a divorce between
art and the forms of social life. Works of art, psychological forms, and
social forms all reflect each other, and change with each other."[20] Put
differently, no world has "favored relations" with reality.[21]

In fact, the literary and sociological versions of rationality
strongly complement one another. Both assume "we cannot begin to
see things as they are until we see how we see," and both use "criteria
of economy, congruence and consistency, elegance, originality, and
scope."[22] Both "organize experience into formal structures."[23] Both the
literary and sociological versions of rationality allow for imagination
and intuition; both distinguish between discovery and demonstration.
Even though literary rationality affirms the imagination more than
sociological rationality does, it nevertheless recognizes only those
accomplishments that "manage to get themselves fully embodied in
the text."[24] Both varieties of rationality also comprise disinterested-
ness based on distinctive means for achieving distance from the
world of everyday life. The paramount tension of consciousness for
novelists derives from disjunctures between commonsense speech
and literary language; for sociologists, between commonsense experiences and sociological explanations.

In the worlds of literature and social science both actualities and
possibilities demand attention. The novelist fashioning a plausible
imaginary world molds possibilities into shapes limited only by what
is conceivable, yet the conceivable is a modalization of the actual.
Thus, imaginative writers work against a backdrop of actualities.
Inversely, the social scientist manipulates actualities against a backdrop of possibilities. Unless seeking no more than an exact replication
of others' findings, the social scientist shapes actualities by assessing
the range of possibilities wherein controls function, variables correlate, subjects behave, and data make sense. Moreover, when social scientists study actual power structures or poverty or dual-career couples, they often aim to disclose possibilities like decentralization,
economic justice, and egalitarian marriage.

Literature and sociology rest on the "desire to comprehend the . . .

world, to reduce its apparent complexity, even chaos, to some kind of ordered representation."[25] Both advance models of social action, though they formalize their models to different degrees and in different forms. Both also advance distinctive interpretive schemes meant to illuminate selves and social worlds. Together, the worlds of literature and social science thus curtail "the dilemma of either the predicable or the ineffable."[26] Since literature occupies a "debatable ground" between the applied arts like architecture and the nonutilitarian arts like music, it concerns the predicable as well as the ineffable.[27] Sociology accepts the scientific ideals of logical deductions and controlled research, but it also accepts the artistic ideals of subjective interpretation and sympathetic understanding. To that extent sociologists concern themselves with the ineffable as well as the predicable. Social worlds draw novelists and sociologists onto the same terrain where "significant works of the imagination ... speak with equal power to the consoling piety that we are all like one another and to the worrying suspicion that we are not."[28]

Their different methods give novelists and sociologists different stances toward social worlds. Sociologists' stances make for a "reduced, emasculated, and docile" subject matter.[29] Less negatively, sociologists stabilize their subject matter,[30] abstracting from people's experiences only those elements deemed pertinent to their investigation. Novelists do much less abstracting. In their fictions, experiences retain their integrity, the emotions remain lively, consciousness darts hither and yon, the ins and outs of relationships disclose fluid selves. Not surprisingly, many individuals look to novelists for what sociologists fail to give them. Consider, for example, "Max Weber, who discussed eroticism with great understanding and some sympathy, but from a point of view totally alien to it, and irreconcilable with it."[31]

Like individuals in the world of everyday life, novelists and sociologists typify the objects of their experiences and use *Verstehen*. They typify reflectively, however, by applying the rationality institutionalized in their respective worlds. *Verstehen* lets novelists understand their characters enough to portray them credibly and their readers enough to stimulate them adequately. Sociologists understand their subjects' behavior in similar ways. Only *Verstehen* allows them to get beyond statistics and flat statements about the obvious. Both groups take prereflective activities fundamental to everyday life and reflectively exploit them for the sake of understanding people's lived experiences. "Understanding another person" requires grasping the other's own meaning-contexts.[32] Yet when they investigate female labor force participation rates, population growth, or crime rates, sociologists often ignore the subjectively meaningful activities and subjective meaning-contexts underlying their statistical data. In those instances sociologists constitute objective meaning-contexts by applying social-scientific relevances to their object of inquiry so as to fit it into their stream of social-scientific experiences. Here the researcher's point of view reigns. Novelists, in no position to establish objective meaning-contexts, cannot ignore subjective meaning-contexts. They try to engender in readers "the illusion of more or less direct apprehension of subjective meaning," while sociologists try to objectify subjective meaning-contexts.[33] Both, however, reduce their subjects' "freedom." Narrative forms themselves reduce characters' freedom.[34] As Alfred Schutz notes, sociologists' models produce similar effects.

> These models of actors are not human beings living within their biographical situation in the social world of everyday life. . . . [The social scientist] has created these puppets or homunculi to manipulate them for his purpose. A merely specious consciousness is imputed to them. . . . The puppet and his artificial consciousness is not subjected to the ontological conditions of human beings. . . . He is not free in the sense that his acting could transgress the limits his creator, the social scientist, has predetermined. . . . He cannot choose, except among the alternatives the social scientist has put before him. . . .[35]

Both novelists and sociologists undercut subjectivity as people experience it in actual worlds. Thereby the practical challenges of freedom are rendered less complex, but its roots become more accessible to consciousness.

Together, novelists' and sociologists' findings offer keener insights into social worlds than either group offers by itself. Yet literary individuals commonly remain critical of science. Many sense that "The difference between a practical rule of thumb that is true eighty-five percent of the time and a genuine universal is not a mere fifteen percent. It is an unbridgeable abyss."[36] Virginia Woolf says, "A history of modes and manners . . . is not a history of ourselves, but of our disguises. The poets and the novelists are the only people from whom we cannot hide."[37] Other novelists and critics concede that ours is "the century of sociology, the century of matrices."[38] Malcolm Bradbury observes that as literature oscillates "between the styles of realism and aestheticism," those opting for realism claim "art as a species of knowledge analogous to sociology or science."[39] As Henry W. Wells put it more than seventy years ago, "In our own times the relation of any branch of thought to science generally constitutes one of its chief problems. The rule holds good for art and literature."[40]

Whatever their stances toward sociology, novelists from the eighteenth century onward have pursued projects similar to those of sociologists. Similarly, some sociologists treat literature as a neglected complement of sociology. Robert Nisbet says none of sociology's principal themes "was ever reached through anything resembling what we are today fond of identifying as 'scientific method.'" Indeed, says Nisbet, artists often recognize cultural shifts before sociologists.[41] Morroe Berger says sociologists who treat literature as inferior social science "compare the achievement of the novel with the unfulfilled promise of social science. If the achievements of both are compared, the gap considerably narrows."[42] Richard Harvey Brown argues that "an aesthetical view of sociological knowledge—a poetic for sociology—can contribute greatly to resolving methodological . . . contradictions confronting the human studies today."[43] More recently, he has argued that "Reality is *imagined* as literal and objective, whereas symbols are seen as metaphoric and subjective" (emphasis added). Such a stance, which invites a quick leap to the last section of this chapter, has led Brown to revisit the topic of "Literary Form and Sociological Theory."[44]

That broad topic has concerned more than a few scholars over the past several decades, and the concern is growing. Even though two to three hundred years of tradition buttress the cultural walls dividing literature and science, those walls are weakening. One sign of their weakening is literary analyses of sociological narratives. Nearly thirty years ago, Stanley Edgar Hyman looked at Marx as well as Darwin, Frazer, and Freud as imaginative writers. About ten years later, Frederic Jameson undertook a literary analysis of Weber's writings. Later still, John Lofland and Peter K. Manning each tackled the matter of style in Goffman's works. More recently, Tomoko Masuzawa has approached Durkheim's *Elementary Forms* along literary axes, and Robert Paul Wolff has analyzed the literary structure of Marx's *Capital*. By far the most ambitious of such analyses is Bryan S. Green's literary examination of Simmel's and Weber's works.[45]

Green's analytical *tour de force* leaves little doubt that "sociological theory is a form of literary activity . . . " and that its "classical texts" are "literary organizations of reading responses."[46] In Simmel's works Green finds an analogical approach to exposition, dialectical writing, allegorical devices, and a distinctly modernist voice; in Weber's he finds above all the casuistic tradition. In great detail Green shows what most scientists are wont to overlook—the expression of personal voices in and through narratives cast in transpersonal, objective tones.

Green thus finds *style*, which should come as little surprise to readers who celebrate Goffman's as much as they bemoan Parsons's. Yet science has insisted on "univocal discourse" where a single voice belonging to a faceless, objective narrator reigns from beginning to end. As "realistic" discourse, it has insisted on "the deliberate effacement of the traces of producers and consumer," as Jameson puts it; "the viewing eye, faced with representational discourse, has a vested interest in ignoring its own presence. . . . "[47] Yet, the voice of a person seeps through such narratives. After all, "Artifice is as natural to [human beings] as spontaneity."[48] It is narratively inevitable and relatively open to choice. Ironically, it often takes a non-sociologist such as the linguist Roger Fowler to remind us that Goffman himself showed that "the construction of a persona is an inevitable strategy . . . ," thus guaranteeing that "authorial silence is an unattainable goal in any circumstances."[49] To that extent polyvocality is inescapable in representational discourse, even in those of its forms where mathematical symbols and statistical tables are central.

Clifford stresses that literary "discourse, repeatedly banished from science, but with uneven success, is incurably figurative and polysemous."[50] Like all great imaginative writers, all acclaimed (or at least widely cited) sociologists exhibit a dramatically distinctive style—not only Marx, Durkheim, Weber, and Simmel but also Homans, Mills, Garfinkel, and Giddens. In part, this circumstance may reflect Raymond Boudon's insight that sociology exhibits "a higher degree of polymorphism than the other sciences" or, less kindly put, that "sociology" is a "somewhat elastic term."[51] In part, it may also derive from some sociologists' striving for distinction, wanting to stand out from the twentieth-century herd comprising thousands of sociologists, even more social scientists, and yet more intellectuals. As Pierre Bourdieu observes,

The sense of distinction . . . is affirmed not so much in the manifestos and positive manifestations of self-confidence as . . . in the innumerable stylistic or thematic choices which, being based on the concern to underline difference, excel all the forms of intellectual (or artistic) activity regarded at a given moment as inferior. . . . [52]

Similarly, the polysemous character of sociological narratives may sometimes reflect the desire to have one's scientific work "thought of as both esoteric and socially useful in the long run. Esoteric work carries status probably because it symbolizes freedom—in the form of distance from the dictatorial marketplace."⁵³ Wendy Griswold makes a related argument about ambiguity in fiction. She notes that reviewers, in particular, value it as an occasion "for exercising their interpretive skills." At the same time Griswold allows for the possibility that writers may value it as an inducement to reviewers and other interpreters. She stresses that "certain cultural works, but not others, possess the capacity to stimulate a wide, but not random, variety of interpretations." Significantly, multiple interpretations correlate with attributions of aesthetic value.⁵⁴ A parallel situation may cover sociology where polyvocality may yield continual, competing interpretations which in turn constitute "classic" or "significant" works.

In any event, style stamps sociological narratives, and polyvocality in practice displaces univocality in principle. Green concludes that style is "a methodologically central feature of sociology." Yet it involves a great deal more than the expression of a singular voice. Style is a "compositional activity" organizing readers' responses.⁵⁵ It emanates not only from the tastes of the narrative strategist but also from his or her purposes and subject matter. Green observes that Simmel's style, for example, may derive from Simmel's interest in short-circuiting "a univocal, uniform way of questioning social life." In terms used earlier, purposes hovering around *defamiliarization* sometime shape a narrator's style. Simmel's work "conspicuously lacks the usual apparatus of footnotes and references through which discourse is conventionally tied to intellectual traditions"; that lack is a stylistic "means of suspending normative authorial authority."⁵⁶ At the same time the dearth of conventional scholarly markers also serves defamiliarizing functions by depriving readers of those citations capable of "restricting the text's connotations. . . . "⁵⁷ Insofar as intellectuals may be prone to "believe in the representation . . . more than in the things represented . . . ,"⁵⁸ such defamiliarizing is as central to strong science as to strong fiction. In both realms it feeds readers' reflective consciousness; in both realms it may elicit (among professional readers) new models of representation.

Conceptions of subject matter also shape style. Jameson implies that Weber's portrayal of Luther broadly illustrates that connection. Wolff more pointedly addresses how conceptions of one's object of inquiry condition the selection of literary devices to delineate that object.⁵⁹ Interestingly, Elizabeth Langland advances a parallel argument about portrayals of society in novels. Examining the "writer's need to create a society consonant with the formal ends of the work itself," Langland concludes that novelists' depictions of society "depend as much on artistic needs as on unconscious influences."⁶⁰

How novelists think about and develop their protagonists—victim, rebel, outcast, leader, deviate—bears on the shape society can effectively take in their novels, for example. Similarly, how sociologists think about society bears on the figurative options effectively available to them. An obvious example is sociologists who think of society as conflictual; organismic metaphors will not serve them well, if at all. Yet how sociologists think about society or other topics is often from the beginning vividly metaphorical. As Boudon points out, the "analogical paradigm" is a "particularly important form" in sociology.[61] Such a paradigm, built up by adapting the concepts and principles from another body of knowledge, effectively restricts how its users may conceptualize their subject matter. Society-as-drama and society-as-text surely condition how Goffman and Brown, respectively, may talk about society. No matter which came first—the vividly metaphorical or the apparently literal conception—once the metaphor is put to paradigmatic use, what the theorist can reasonably say is limited.

Style derives not only from personal predispositions, narrative purposes, and conceptions of subject matter but also from what Green calls the "constraint of generic recognizability": "All writing is performed under the constraint of being a recognizable genre of writing within some cultural array."[62] Goffman's work is illustrative. *Asylums* is subtitled "Essays on . . . "; *Stigma* is "Notes on . . . "; *Frame Analysis* is "An Essay on. . . . " Goffman's subtitles and his textual references to them allude to the constraint of generic recognizability. It would seem that Goffman struggled against that constraint less by stretching or bursting the forms of the scientific monograph or research report than by abandoning them in favor of the essay. *Webster's Seventh New Collegiate Dictionary* defines that form as "an analytic or interpretive literary composition usu[ually] dealing with its subject from a limited or personal point of view," and Green himself emphasizes that the essay is an "art form."[63] Given his powers as a wordsmith, it seems unlikely that Goffman labeled his narratives haphazardly. Rather, he eluded the constraint most of us take for granted when we tailor our style to the demands of scientific genres.

This is all to say that imaginative writers and scientific writers are commonly situated, even though their purposes diverge as well as dovetail. Two final considerations support that broad conclusion. Bourdieu pinpoints the first consideration: "In the case of the social sciences, scientific discourse cannot ignore the conditions of its own reception. This depends at all times on the state of the prevailing social problematic, which is itself partly defined by the reactions to an earlier form of that discourse."[64] As with literary discourse, scientific discourse gets varying receptions. In both cases the reception varies, as Griswold suggests, with "the symbolic capacities of the object itself and . . . the perceptual apparatus of those who experience the object."[65] The perceptual inclinations of literary and scientific readers differ less widely than might be thought, even though groupings of specialized readers do constitute cultural communities. Barbara Herrnstein Smith says, for example, that literary professionals and students "tend to forget how relatively homogeneous a group we are, how relatively limited and similar our experiences of verbal art, and how relatively confined and similar are the conditions under which we pursue the study of literature."[66] She might just as well have been talking about sociologists and their students.

In readers' terms, the constraint of generic recognizability is the freedom of generic taken for grantedness, which grows out of the perceptual homogeneity bred among specific communities of readers in schools, through book reviews, and so forth. The systems of relevances such readers bring to their texts are more or less comparable, revolving as they do around generic recognizability. The reception of "deviant" texts across various fields lays bare that comparability. Green found, for example, that "canonical" or "receptive epithets" dot the comments sociologists make about their colleagues' texts, and those epithets are commonly literary; for example, "dazzling," "colorful," "well written," "slippery," "elusive," or "charming." (Here another study of book reviews suggests itself.)

Thus, while reading, individuals stubbornly remain readers first and sociologists or literary critics second. When their expectations get frustrated or disappointed, they predictably receive their texts differently. At the most fundamental level that happens when genre becomes problematic; that is, when the narrator's voice is too personal (in science) or too impersonal (in literature), when his or her purposes seem out of place, or when subject matter seems trivial or inappropriate. We now see that "style" and "genre" concern different levels of analysis,[67] not mutually exclusive sets of textual features. Style is the configuration of strategies a writer uses to stamp his or her text as a *unique* instance of some *genre*; above all, it guides readers' responses in those directions. A style offering insufficient such guidance (by community standards) is liable to evoke responses ranging from puzzlement to condemnation.

At the same time, of course, such a style attracts interpreters interested in seeing their own stars rise within a given cultural community. That circumstance leads us to the second consideration exposing similarities between imaginative and scientific writers.

Again, Bourdieu opens the door when he observes that "the mode of expression characteristic of a cultural production always depends on the laws of the market in which it is offered."[68] Like novelists, though not nearly to the same degree,[69] most sociologists work within a system where academic and commercial publishers market "sociology lines," where unpublished writers trying to "break in" labor at a disadvantage, where topics run from hot to cold, where individuals may tailor their work to what the market is currently trafficking in scholarly goods. Unlike novelists, however, tenured sociology professors (at least for the time being) have secured middle-class incomes for themselves. Gaining that security minimally requires, however, entering the intellectual marketplace of scholarly journals and often the intellectual/economic marketplace overseen by editors, publishers, and reviewers. Moreover, even the tenured among them share with novelists and other culture-makers an interest in "accumulat[ing] reputational capital"[70]—less for the sake of income and more for the sake of credibility, it would seem. Sociologists' training as researchers inculcates the notions that solid, innovative work gets published and recognized and that the best and brightest scholars rise to the top—not of the bestseller lists but of the higher-education, intellectual hierarchy. Like novelists, sociologists can build up their reputations only if their work "provides a resource for other members of the professional community," and the likelihood of that happening largely derives from the "organizational structures controlling scientific production."[71] As with literature, so with sociology: "The genteel tradition remains exactly the same sort of thing it has always been—a superior counterculture that defines itself against the ordinary . . . [and] insists as it has always done on [itself] as something separate, something vastly more distinguished."[72] As Bourdieu's work delineates, making such distinctions is a solidly collective enterprise. Thus, between scientists and their audiences stand mediating institutions paralleling those wedged between novelists and their readers.

Am I not citing the obvious? In practical terms, it would seem not. As Stanley Aronowitz notes, the sociology of science "forms the backdrop of the effort to turn sociology into a science."[73] By exposing science as a socially structured, culturally shaped enterprise, sociologists have constituted the grounds for linking science with literature and other types of knowledge or culture production. The sociology of science routinely skirts such linkages, though. It is more oriented toward exposing the natural and physical sciences as institutions conditioned by the same sociocultural factors as sociology. Such efforts constitute a common ground where sociology joins the other sciences as a cognitively superior, albeit culturally contingent, pursuit. Symptomatic here is the commonplace separation between the sociology of science and the sociology of knowledge, which feeds a "refusal of self-reflection" among sociologists.[74] That refusal keeps sociologists from experiencing their kinship with literary artists and intellectuals. So, too, do sociologists' typical ways of writing.

Texts are "the only 'true' result of any research."[75] As the art of words, literature is thus the informing discipline for the social sciences.[76] In fact, worthy social-scientific works have a strong literary quality, for example, the works of Kai T. Erikson. Most sociologists write in anti-literary ways, however, thus weakening their credibility and inviting other scholars to illuminate sociological topics. Such writing stymies their discipline while feeding the divide between the two cultures.

Sociologists join professors of education and psychology as academe's "worst noun-stringers."[77] In his *Dictionary of Modern English Usage*, H. W. Fowler devotes an entry to "sociologese," an abuse of language that seems "deliberately employed for the purpose of making what is simple appear complex."[78] Instead of common words, sociologists favor what Malcolm Cowley calls "Socspeak."[79] Correlatively, "love of the long word" reigns: "alternative" for "other," "proportion" for "part."[80] Further, some terms become popular enough that using them is nearly required in sociological papers: "parameter," "nexus," "interface," and "subsume" have exhibited such popularity. Apparently, Jerrold Whittaker, a sociology professor at Jarrell's Benton College, illustrates more than a stereotype. Whittaker

> always hesitated before he spoke, like a child who has to translate everything from the vernacular into English; but with him, of course, it was the other way around. He was every inch a sociologist.

> He talked the way a windmill would talk, the way a sentence would talk—as he spoke, English seemed to have been dead for many centuries, and its bones to have set up a safe, staid, sleepy system of their own, in respectable secession from existence.[81]

C. Wright Mills, among others, believed sociologists write so as to bolster their scientific claims. Quantitative methods also influence their writing. The fetish of method that overcomes many sociologists as they "gather" data has a counterpart in the fetish of figures that overtakes them as they write. For many, *the* substance of their reports lies in tables and graphs. As Michel Foucault notes, "The recourse to mathematics . . . has always been the simplest way of providing . . . a scientific style, form, and justification."[82] Their statistical manipulations also put sociologists in a position demanding probabilistic, wordy terminology. Finally, the bureaucracies employing sociologists encourage faulty writing. "Bureaucratese" lets people abuse language for the sake of self-protective ambiguity. People already misusing language are particularly susceptible to that influence.

Fortunately, neither subject matter nor science necessitates sluggish prose. Berger's, Erikson's, Goffman's, and Mills's works illustrate the stylistic range sociologists command. Their writing demonstrates that powerful expression and communication correlate, that sociological principles require no linguistic contortions, that clear thinking and clear writing are inseparable. Yet standard sociological prose denies those connections. It quietly feeds a rhetoric of differences distancing sociology from literature and the other humanities while seeming to draw itself closer to the natural and physical sciences. The fact remains, however, that writing joins the worlds of literature and sociology, and language largely decides their participants' outcomes.

Literature, Sociology, and Facts

The boundary traditionally dividing literature and social science concerns fiction and fact. Yet imaginative writers have long based their fictions on facts. Dostoevsky claimed, "An artist is bound to make himself acquainted, down to the smallest detail, . . . with everything . . . relating to that reality which he designs to show forth."[83] Howard Nemerov pinpoints why: "All this never happened, but it is essential to be accurate about how."[84] Plausibility steers imaginative writers toward facts bursting the limits their biographies otherwise impose.

More than ever before, the boundaries between the worlds of literature and social science defy the divide between fact and fiction. The "literature of fact," in particular, dramatizes that circumstance. Its rise also implies sociology's cultural shortcomings, such as its neglect of timely topics, its institutionalization of weak writing, and its reliance on academic journals for reporting its findings. At the same time the literature of fact suggests some literary individuals are trying to regain their predecessors' cultural authority by moving onto the sociological and journalistic terrains without compromising their distinctive uses of language. In the process they show how every topic, however investigated and wherever reported, allows for literary expression.

The literature of fact (also known as faction, journalistic novels, or nonfiction novels) parallels the new journalism (also known as parajournalism, subjective journalism, or consumer journalism).[85] Broadly, the two spheres are divided by form and by their practitioners' professional backgrounds. The literature of fact retains some of the novel's traditional form; for example, Truman Capote's *In Cold Blood*. The new journalism breaks from traditional journalism over viewpoint, objectivity, and vocabulary but does retain some features of narratives reporting factual matters; for example, Hunter Thompson's *Hell's Angels*. To some extent the literature of fact represents the logical culmination of the realistic novel; the new journalism, a logical culmination of muckraking journalism. The practitioners of the former are usually novelists or essayists; the practitioners of the latter are usually news reporters or writers. Although new journalists like Tom Wolfe and Gay Talese are both sociological and literary, my concern is the literature of fact where literature and sociology bare their standing intersections.

The Armies of the Night exemplifies the literature of fact intellectually, artistically, and culturally. Mailer divides the work into Book One, "History as a Novel: The Steps of the Pentagon," and Book Two, "The Novel as History: The Battle of the Pentagon." Both treat the same events; namely, a 1967 anti-war march on the Pentagon that landed Mailer in jail briefly. Book One reads like a novel. Its limited, third-person point of view belongs to Norman Mailer, the novel's protagonist. Its plot revolves around his anxieties about participating in the demonstration and his ambivalence toward the judicial system that let him off the hook. The first pages of Book One strand the reader between the book's novelistic form and its factual basis. Form overtakes facts, however. Gradually, the reader "forgets" Mailer is both actual author and fictional character. The reader slips into a novel, albeit one evoking a distinctive tension of consciousness.

Book Two, roughly the last quarter of *The Armies of the Night*, also uses a limited, third-person point of view. Here, though, the point of view shifts to an anonymous, "objective" observer. Book Two comes across as the work of a careful journalist, sociologist, or historian. The facts at hand now seem bald. About halfway through Book Two, the narrator temporarily abandons the historian's artifices. Having made subjectivity a fugitive, he experiences difficulty treating the complex data.

Forget that the journalistic information available from both sides is so incoherent, inaccurate, contradictory, malicious, even based on error that no accurate history is conceivable. More than one historian has found a way through chains of false fact. No, the difficulty is that the history is interior—no documents can give sufficient intimation: the novel must replace history at precisely that point where experience is sufficiently emotional, spiritual, physical, moral, existential, or supernatural to expose the fact that the historian in pursuing the experience would be obliged to quit the clearly demarcated limits of historic inquiry. . . . The collective novel which follows, while still written in the cloak of an historic style, . . . will now unashamedly enter that world of strange lights and intuitive speculation which is the novel.[86]

In other terms, social scientists' methods reduce their chances of capturing the full weight of events and their entire network of ramifications. Unlike Dwight Robbins and his ilk, however, social scientists need not act as mere role-players. The precocious among them can illuminate the subjectivities making history and bearing its imprints. Kai T. Erikson exemplifies such social scientists.

In 1973, Erikson found himself in a situation not unlike Mailer's. He had traveled to Buffalo Creek, West Virginia, to survey the wreckage from a disastrous flood. Erikson went at the request of a law firm seeking his recommendation of a sociologist as a consultant. His experiences there inspired Erikson to volunteer his services to the law firm. Faced with a traumatic situation, Erikson the sociologist made professional decisions paralleling Mailer's. His rejection of a narrow role was the birth of a sociological masterpiece. *Everything in Its Path* illustrates the sociological imagination at hard work. Erikson tried to imagine the flood's horror by reconstructing those of its features that "touch the senses." He also confronted the need for and hazards of metaphors that tap subjective meanings.[87] *Everything in Its Path* deals with community, taken for grantedness, language, trauma, and commonsense experience. That range provides the theoretical space for treating a contemporary event without shortchanging the subjective features making it a *human* disaster. Still, Erikson's work is thoroughly sociological.

Like pathbreaking sociological works, the literature of fact exposes close connections as well as distinct discontinuities between literature and sociology. Subject matter links the two. Crime, capital punishment, political unrest, war, and social change attract nonfiction novelists like Tom Wolfe, Truman Capote, and Norman Mailer. Their purposes also link them. Objectively understanding subjective meanings aligns nonfiction novelists with sociologists, especially symbolic interactionists and phenomenological sociologists. Further, their methods partially overlap. Nonfiction novelists use approaches similar to participant observation, direct observation, and case studies. Unlike sociologists, however, they are unconcerned with the samples, controls, and statistical manipulations that make evidence scientific and allow for causal analysis. The two groupings also use different narrative techniques. Broadly, sociological reports narrate action; literary reports dramatize it.[88] Sociologists lean toward summary, or generalization; nonfiction novelists lean toward scene, or "undigested data."[89] The former generally presuppose distance between the study's subjects and its readers, while the latter generally minimize that distance. Correlatively, sociologists use little dialogue in their reports, while nonfiction novelists include a great deal. Then, too, narrators' voices vary a lot among nonfiction novelists, while sociologists largely reject such variability.[90] At the same time they dismiss many linguistic options.

Their lesser attention to language means, perhaps, sociologists are ill-prepared to understand that "writers are always selling somebody out."[91] Ironically, sociologists may be slower than novelists to accept in practical terms that "Every discipline is made up of a set of restrictions on thought and imagination. . . . "[92] Every discipline, in short, promotes ideology. Debunking is no cure-all for ideology, particularly the ideology supporting one's own vocation or craft.

Literature, Sociology, and Ideology[93]

Inescapably, commonsense individuals face the nasty outcomes of domestic disharmonies, job dissatisfaction, violence, and scarcity. Apart from the unavoidable suffering wrought by sickness, injuries, and loss of loved ones, common-sense individuals routinely struggle for dignity and self-esteem. As partitions of the world of everyday life, all social worlds somehow address the dissatisfactions commonsense individuals continually face. Intentionally or not, every social world espouses methods of coping with dissatisfactions and solving society's problems. American advertisers imply that dissatisfactions derive from having too few products or having the wrong ones. Educators imply that dissatisfactions derive from ignorance. The leisure industry implies that dissatisfactions come from taking the world too seriously or neglecting the need for fun. Religious spokespersons imply that dissatisfactions derive from too little concern with the afterlife. Sexual experts imply that dissatisfactions derive from sexual repression and ignorance. A host of voluntary associations—civic, political, social, and cultural—imply their own distinctive notions about why life is trying. In other terms, every world spawns ideologies.

As different interpretations of the same commonsense world, ideologies compete with one another in pluralistic societies. An *ideology* is an interpretive scheme that orders experiences, lending them coherence and meaning. The experiences it addresses are standing problems in the everyday world, whether experienced directly or indirectly. The core of an ideology is several generalizations its adherents take as self-evident and relevant to their problematic experiences. Almost anything may focus an interpretive scheme that reduces the perplexities people experience in their worlds. Yet relatively few ideologies compete in a society, if only because the powerful are equipped to spread their messages while undercutting (consciously or not) those ideologies inimical to their interests.

Most worlds generate several competing ideologies that reflect major divisions among their participants. Literature is no exception. Its novelists produce four types of works, each implying a distinctive ideology. As they portray problems like divorce, corruption, and loneliness, different types of novels imply different ideologies independently of what their authors' styles, plots, and characters imply. Formulaic novels imply an ideology of mass entertainment promoting entertainment as a respite from the disappointments powerlessness imposes and romanticizing leisure as a means of counteracting painful realities. Authors of formulaic novels treat literature like an institution of mass entertainment. For them, the novel institutionalizes possibilities to reinforce readers' values and alleviate their anxieties by temporarily overriding their everyday worries.

Best-selling novels also imply the benefit of entertainment, but an ideology of knowledge overshadows the ideology of entertainment in these works. Best-selling novels imply that the root cause of human problems is inadequate knowledge leading to misunderstanding, insensitivity, and injustices. They also imply that knowledge alleviates personal frustrations and social problems. The literary ideology of knowledge emphasizes clearheaded thinking and critical stances toward the powerful and the privileged. Best-selling novels express an ideology that favors knowledge lying somewhere between the academic and commonsense varieties. Those who write such novels treat literature like an institution of mass education. For them, the novel institutionalizes possibilities for readers to know themselves and their worlds.

Subcultural novels imply more concern with communication than knowledge. Such novels rest on an ideology akin to a "quasi-theory of communication."[94] They imply that open communication is necessary for satisfactory societies, harmonious relationships, and personal fulfillment. The literary ideology of communication implies that the root cause of human problems is misleading or restricted communication that spawns misunderstanding, insensitivity, and injustices. Authors of subcultural novels treat literature like an institution of mass communication. For them, the novel institutionalizes people's possibilities for openly communicating with one another.

Canonical novels emphasize the correlation between communication and knowledge. They imply that the root cause of human problems is the failure to recognize and temper ideologies, thereby undermining people's possibilities for empathy and justice. Using literary language to debunk social worlds engenders an ideology of ideology. Debunking implies the value of knowledge based on skepticism and critical thinking; its contrast with everyday speech and scientific jargon makes literary language a potent means of disclosing how people communicate. Together, the definitive features of canonical novels imply that all knowledge is social. To wit, people's knowledge reflects the interests of their partners in communication and the structure of the communications themselves and vice versa. Implying that two-way relationship, canonical novels also imply that people continuously constitute the social stock of knowledge and, therefore, never overcome ideology.

To the extent that the uses of language and the portrayal of social worlds in novels imply ideologies, novels' themes vary with novels' types. Ideological underpinnings act, in short, as a restraint on the themes a novel can credibly sustain. The themes of formulaic novels with their ideology of mass entertainment generally concern conformity to group expectations, particularly sex-role expectations and class standards. Best-selling novels with their ideology of mass education generally concern adjustment, or the continual negotiation of one's identity on the terrain lying between group expectations and personal preferences. The themes of subcultural novels with their ideology of mass communication generally concern group pride, where the grouping may be religious, ethnic, sexual, or socioeconomic. The themes of canonical novels with their ideology of ideology usually concern authenticity, or the continual struggle to maintain one's personal integrity across the public and private spheres of life.

Like other forms of social action, imaginative writing rests on networks of values and purposes. Its different types of novels express taken-for-granted ideals—entertainment, knowledge, communication, and relative freedom from ideology. The institutionalization of any action engenders interpretive schemes that make it meaningful and significant. Inescapably, social action rests on an ideological infrastructure that goes unnoticed until individuals find their world under attack. Critical or skeptical outsiders may spur them to "rationalize consensus" so that elements of the ideological infrastructure surface.[95] Ordinarily, though, a world's most solid ideological grounds remain tacit. Taken for granted and unnoticed, such grounds reflect the collective constitution of interpretive schemes that make specific forms of social action "obviously" sensible and worthwhile.

Thus, every form of social action is potentially propagandistic. Ideology deteriorates into propaganda when individuals use forms of social action institutionalized for other purposes to maintain or extend their own or their group's power. Propagandizing on the grounds of an ideology of ideology would strain the canonical novel beyond the limits of sense. Best-selling and formulaic novels are not very susceptible to propagandizing either. The former are constrained by potential paradoxes like those canonical novels face; the latter, by the incompatibility between entertainment and propaganda. The novelists most likely to propagandize write subcultural novels; those authors belonging to the groups they portray are most vulnerable. Subcultural novelists do not debunk the worlds they treat. Thus, they are vulnerable to propagandizing on behalf of the worlds they portray. Fiction and literary language undercut the temptation by removing a writer from the practical sphere where propaganda proves or defeats itself. Nonetheless those novelists inclined toward realism but disinclined to debunk are vulnerable to propagandizing.

The forms of social action making up sociology also rest on ideological infrastructures. Like novelists committed to one or another type of novel, sociologists largely stick with one methodology while pursuing their vocations or crafts. More than the specific topics they investigate, a sociologist's methodology implies his or her ideological inclinations. Qualitative sociologists imply an ideology of empathic understanding. Their methods presuppose that such understanding is necessary for personal and professional satisfaction as well as for social progress. Some qualitative sociology emphasizes the communication subcultural novelists tacitly advocate, but the sociological ideology of emphatic understanding insists on careful field work or theorizing as routes to the ends it implies. Qualitative sociologists treat their discipline like an institution of social enlightenment. For them, sociology institutionalizes people's possibilities for mutual understanding and tolerance. In contrast, quantitative sociologists imply an ideology of scientific rationalism. Their methods presuppose that the scientific study of human behavior is necessary for rationally controlling human affairs and alleviating social problems. Quantitative sociology implies that subjectivity, undisciplined by scientific methods and uninformed by scientific knowledge, is the major impediment to social progress and personal fulfillment. Yet the sociological ideology of scientific rationalism endorses knowledge less sweepingly than the literary ideology of mass education. Quantitative sociologists treat their discipline like an institution of scientific education. For them, sociology institutionalizes people's possibilities for rationally managing their interdependence and alleviating their problems.

Scientific methods and terminologies limit sociologists' susceptibility to propagandizing just as fiction and literary language limit novelists' susceptibility. Nonetheless sociological reports can be propagandistic. Qualitative sociologists are likelier to issue such reports inasmuch as the scientific canons governing their work are less restrictive than those governing quantitative work. Qualitative sociologists increase their vulnerability when they study groups with whom they identify or sympathize. Quantitative and qualitative sociologists alike are likelier to propagandize when the organizations employing or funding them are interest groups with public-relations concerns or other vested interests. In that respect some sociologists encounter intellectual and political temptations few novelists face.

Unlike ideology, propaganda is typically an object of thought and discussion. Its users do not take it for granted any more than they take for granted their power or lack thereof. The principal link between ideology and propaganda is rhetoric, those methods used to maintain or extend support for an interpretive scheme the speaker or writer accepts as true or useful. Rhetoric pervades social worlds. Its applications at least hint at a world's ideological infrastructure and imply the limits wherein propaganda is likely to be effective.

In the world of literature rhetoric commonly takes two forms. The *literary rhetoric* of fiction comprises all those artifices making fictional worlds and characters plausible, on the one hand, and entertaining or stimulating, on the other. Literary rhetoric is all those moves, both intended and unintended, a novelist makes in strategic interaction or teamwork with readers. The *social rhetoric* of novels consists of all those moves that together persuade readers to adopt a viewpoint, even though the author apparently did not intend those cumulative effects. Readers persuaded by *Pictures from an Institution* that novelists and sociologists are sometimes narcissistic or that academicians are sometimes petty are responding to the novel's social rhetoric. When they recognize Dwight Robbins as a slick functionary or when they try to fulfill the meaning of the narrator's leaving his wife nameless, they are responding to its literary rhetoric. Similarly, when *Expensive People* persuades readers that the line between mental health and mental illness cannot be pinpointed or that posh suburban living is sometimes vacuous and tragic, its social rhetoric is at work. When the novel leads readers to reflect on whether or not Dickie intended the slipup where he calls his memoir a novel, its literary rhetoric is at work.

Although both types of rhetoric function throughout a novel, their effects have different temporal structures. Ordinarily, the literary rhetoric of a novel stimulates pauses, reflection, and predicative judgments while reading. It fuels readers' alternations between being on and being off as they read. Usually, the social rhetoric stimulates little reflection while readers are playing their texts. Its effects accrue in readers' post-textual reflections (if any). In fact, when a novel stimulates readers' reflections about its messages, propaganda rather than social rhetoric is probably at work. Of course, a reader may stand alerted to a novel's social rhetoric from early on when it opposes his or her cherished beliefs or proffers alien notions. When the social rhetoric of a novel has that effect on a cross-section of readers, though, propaganda is in the wings.

Sociological reports exhibit parallel forms of rhetoric. Their *sociological rhetoric* comprises all those data presented, statistics reported, and interpretations advanced that sociologists use to make their research generically recognizable. Sociological rhetoric consists mostly of moves institutionalized as necessary for constituting evidence and furthering scientific knowledge. The *social rhetoric* of sociological reports consists of all those moves that together persuade readers to adopt a viewpoint, even though the author apparently did not intend those cumulative effects. Readers persuaded by *Everything in Its Path* that the federal government was sorely ineffectual in helping flood victims or that businesses are sometimes woefully negligent are responding to the report's social rhetoric. When they reflect on the concept of trauma and the difficulties of studying it, they are responding to its sociological rhetoric. Similarly, when *Strategic Interaction* persuades readers that people are often calculative or that trust is sometimes a fool's achievement, its social rhetoric is at work. When the report leads readers to consider how people infer motives in everyday life or how one might study expression games across different cultures, its sociological rhetoric is at work.

Like their literary counterparts, sociological rhetoric and social rhetoric have different temporal structures for readers. When sociological reports strike a cross-section of readers as biased, propaganda is probably infiltrating the report. In both the world of literature and the world of social science colleagues, critics, and readers mostly evaluate the technical rhetoric that distinguishes prose in that world. The social rhetoric receives peripheral attention or at least informal attention unless propaganda looms as a possibility.

Thus, the art of social worlds and the science of social worlds resonate as finite provinces of meaning. The worlds of literature and of social science do differ yet they are as similar to one another as each is to the world of everyday life. All worlds leave their most alert participants wondering how what is said relates to what is. No less than novels or everyday conversations, sociological reports leave that potential provocation intact. Under routine circumstances art, everyday life, and science rest on a blend of facts their participants reflectively or prereflectively constitute and fictions they most often take for granted. And so we arrive at post-structuralism, postmodernism, postempiricism, deconstructionism, narratology, and all the other critical developments hovering around the terrific gap between what we say and what we mean to have said, between what we mean to have represented and what we represent. Here the briefest of citations must suffice; another book must continue saying what I can only preface here. (That book concerns narrative frames in social theory.)

Narratives, Representation, and Cultural Forms

"By what route," asks Italo Calvino, "is the soul or history or society or the subconscious transformed into a series of black lines on a white paper?"[96] Calvino's question assumes that society and other things are "out there" in the "real" world, that writers establish methods for crossing whatever distance separates "out there" from "in here," and that that crossing is a transformative activity. Postmodernists reject these assumptions. They largely regard "the" world as a textualized construction giving way to a multiplicity of other such constructions. Foucault, for instance: Knowledge consists "in relating one form of language to another form of language; in restoring the great unbroken plain of words and things; in making everything speak." Its proper function "is not seeing or demonstrating; it is interpreting." Discourse, then, "is merely representation itself represented by verbal signs." People "believe that their speech is their servant and do not realize that they are submitting themselves to its demands."[97]

But what is interpretation? Whence come the demands of speech? Stanley Fish: Interpretation "is the source of texts, facts, authors, and intentions." It arises out of and draws it sustenance from "interpretive communities" that are "neither objective nor subjective":

An interpretive community is not objective because as a bundle of interests, of particular purposes and goals, its perspective is interested rather than neutral; but by the very same reasoning, the meanings and texts produced by an interpretive community are not subjective because they do not proceed from an isolated individual but from a public and conventional point of view.[98]

Stephan Fuchs: "True sentences do not fit into nature; rather they fit into the cultural possession of particular goods of professional knowledge producers." Thus, "truth is a contingent label . . . we attach to practices and sentences that are conventionally shared and accepted by particular social groups." Scientific knowledge is "the cultural property of professional groups. . . . "[99] Frederic Jameson: Textuality is a "methodological hypothesis" supplanting the realities or existents studied in the human sciences with "so many texts that we *decipher* and *interpret*. . . . " Those texts exude stories; "the very structure of language itself shows a deep functional vocation for storytelling, which must then be seen, not as some secondary pastime, to be pursued around the fireside when praxis is over, but rather as a basic and constitutive element of human life."[100]

Barbara Herrnstein Smith: Narratives are "verbal acts consisting of *someone telling someone that something happened*." One might reasonably ask why "someone has chosen (or agreed) to tell someone else that something happened and why the latter has chosen (or agreed) to listen." (But "what happened" is itself textual, linguistically constructed, interpreted in the happening—as we have "seen.") Thus, "the formal properties of an individual narrative would be regarded as *functions of . . . multiple interacting conditions* rather than as *representations* of specific, discrete objects, events, or ideas."[101] Hayden White: "Narration and narrativity [are] the instruments by which the conflicting claims of the imaginary and the real are mediated, arbitrated, or resolved in a discourse. . . . " The "value attached to narrativity in the representation of real events arises out of a desire to have real events display the coherence, integrity, fullness, and closure of an image of life that is and can only be imaginary."[102]

Richard Harvey Brown: "Literal scientific discourse must pretend that there is a bedrock of nonlinguistic experience to which words are tethered." Yet what the human sciences study are "interpretations, or more precisely the objectifications of the interpretation of other persons." A narrative is no more than "an account of an agent [read "scientist" in this context] whose character or destiny unfolds through events in time." (We return to stories. Sociologists tell theirs by saying what happened to them.) "Realistic art or science is not convincing because it is realistic, instead it is realistic because we have already been convinced." (We belong to interpretive communities.) "The relation between the literal and the metaphoric is dialectical. Like essence/appearance and factual/fictional, each term presupposes and implies the other."[103] (And each refers to some "reality" central to the telling of good stories.) James Clifford: In anthropology, a dominant ideology persists in "claiming the transparency of representation and the immediacy of experience." But "what appears as 'real' . . . is always analyzable as a restrictive and expressive set of *social* codes and conventions" (emphasis added). Thus, "interest in the discursive aspects of cultural representation draws attention not to the interpretation of cultural 'texts' but to the relations of production." Like much (all?) else, "Ethnography is a hybrid textual activity; it traverses genres and disciplines."[104] (It belongs to multiple interpretive communities.)

Genres are specifiable codes widely shared within an interpretive community; they tell what activities—substantive and formal—constitute stories for community members; they provide for distinguishing among stories. Jacques Derrida: "Can one identify a work of art, of whatever sort, but especially a work of discursive art, if it does not bear the mark of a genre, if it does not signal or mention it or make it remarkable in any way?" (The remarkable concerns the boundaries between interpretive communities as well as those between kinds of stories.) "As soon as the word 'genre' is sounded, as soon as it is heard, as soon as one attempts to conceive it, a limit is drawn."[105] Paul DiMaggio: Genres rest on "perceived similarities." "The challenge for the sociology of art is to understand the processes by which similarities are perceived and genres enacted."[106] Victor Turner: "I like to think of ritual essentially as *performance*, as *enactment* . . . "; thus, "performative genres" and (within limits) "performative plenitude."[107] Richard Bauman: *Story, Performance, and Event: Contextual Studies of Oral Narrative* (Bloomington: Indiana University Press, 1986).

Thereafter, I pulled from my shelves of theory books a story called *Constructing Social Theories* (which, by the way, begins in a remarkable way until one reads the closing paragraph of its preface). There I found, "The first requirement for a concept is that it accurately reflects the forces actually operating in the world." Also: "As the science advances, it progressively redefines its concepts until they accurately represent the phenomena in the world."[108] There I initially experienced the somnambulism members of more than one interpretive community have institutionalized. I picked up another story, Norman K. Denizen's "Postmodern Social Theory," to reread the passage where the narrator reminds the reader that "American social theory has not theorized language. . . ."[109] Indeed, it had done little of that; it needs to do more.

It cannot, however, do in practice what postmodernism demands of it in principle. Social theory can be deconstructed, as can all efforts at representation, communication, and expression. Deconstructive and related stances toward such performances enlarge our insights by telling us stories about ourselves as storytellers. But theory-making cannot itself become a deconstructive effort. Trying to make it so means trying to settle for metatheory or metanarration as a postmodern substitute for (as well as corrective to) theory's traditional forms—narrative forms whose life derives as much from the structure of language, the conventions of interpretive communities (especially generic conventions), and the inevitability of storytelling as from the imaginative reflections of individual theorists. Yet, as Foucault points out, "modern thought has been unable to avoid . . . searching for the locus of a discourse that would be neither of the order of reduction nor of the order of promise. . . ."[110] Metatheory belongs to the order of reduction; modern social theory, to the order of promise. Neither will do.

Postmodern metatheory revolves around what Jeffrey L. Sammons calls "the fictionalization of everything, the transformation of all reality into a literary text." Literature thus disappears. "If there is no tension between imagination and reality," Sammons emphasizes, "there is no category of the imagination; there is only a blooming and buzzing epistemological anarchy. . . ."[111] Metatheory must serve theory, not displace it, and theory must express in some fashion the tension between imagination and reality that brings it into being in the first place.

Naming the narrative signs of the postmodern, theoretic expression of that tension is a task beyond my purview here. As Foucault implies, however, theory can no longer promise what it cannot deliver; it can no longer claim to be what it cannot be. "Phallo-logo-ethno-centrism" needs chastening, but so does "the labyrinth of indeterminacy, non-interference and self-referentiality post-structuralism has built for itself."[112] The deconstructive project of undoing the "structures of absolute knowledge and value in ways that prevent—deliberately and programmatically—reconstruction" is in the end excessive and impractical. We storytellers need "deconstruction in the service of reconstruction."[113] Of necessity, literature reenters the picture here. As "encounters [with] the untamed, imperious being of words,"[114] as unashamed storytelling, as expressions of self-conscious imaginers lodged in concrete worlds, as a world that never goes away yet never remains quite the same, literature *is* the informing discipline for the sciences. Literature reminds us that when taken to the experiential extreme, self-consciousness can only become solipsistic snobbery. It reminds us that all saying must in the end be listening, that narratives presuppose interlocutors bound together across time and space by faith in the fictive. In the postmodern world that faith must be self-conscious and critical. At the same time it must be indefatigable and affirmative of the speakers/listeners whose stories secure shared worlds. In practical terms, a vivid sense of the fictive is what separates postmodern literature and sociology from their modern counterparts.

11

❦ The Fictive

Whenever the golden thread of pleasure enters that web of things which our intelligence is always busily spinning, it lends to the visible world that mysterious and subtle charm which we call beauty.

George Santayana, *The Sense of Beauty*

Among their themes Saul Bellow's *Dangling Man* and John Barth's *Sabbatical* include the fictive. Bellow's novel deals with the fictive in everyday life; Barth's, with the fictive in the world of literature. Together, the two works imply how the fictive illuminates the unity of knowledge and the integrity of experience by bridging the divide between fiction and fact.

Dangling Man is the journal of Joseph, a young man awaiting military induction. When he begins his journal in December, 1942, Joseph has been perched on a bureaucratic limb for seven months. Problems with his file and blood tests, coupled with changing regulations, leave him ample time to ponder his fate as well as the human condition in Western societies. While he writes and worries, his wife Iva supports them.

Above all, Joseph's four-month journal considers the competing claims of individuality and sociality. Like his contemporaries, Joseph dangles between the need to express himself as a self-determining creature and the need to express himself as a conscientious member of society. Joseph uses "craters of the spirit" as a metaphor for what irreducibly seals a person's individuality. He supposes that a transcendental teleology governs the craters of individuals' spirits: "to know what we are and what we are for, to know our purpose, to seek grace."[1] That teleology demands more than rugged individualism, however. It requires a "colony of the spirit" forbidding spite, bloodiness, and cruelty (p. 27). Actual social structures sometimes preclude a colony of the spirit (p. 27), but fulfilled individuality nonetheless requires humane sociality. Like goodness, individuality "is achieved not in a vacuum but in the company of other men, attended by love" (p. 61).

Joseph sprinkles his journal with insights into how individuality and sociality dovetail. He understands that forbidding people to communicate with one another means forbidding them to think. He sees in mundane objects—billboards, houses—analogues of people's interiority, and he looks for "clear signs of... common humanity" (p. 18). Like it or not, Joseph belongs to the world that wearies him. He sees that even his face is "a register of [his] ancestors, a part of the world, and simultaneously, the way [he] received the world, clutched at it, and the way, moreover, in which [he] announced [him]self to it" (p. 51). Joseph knows he cannot establish his individuality by denying his sociality.

He further understands that their imaginations equip people to negotiate their ways between the claims of individuality and those of sociality. Yet modern culture stultifies the imagination. Pondering possible substitutes for the imagination, Joseph confronts an ironic conclusion: Alternatives "grow only on imaginary trees" (pp. 56, 61). In the first half of his journal Joseph wearily affirms that conclusion, while insisting that only imaginative consciousness can disclose the craters of the spirit and improvise a workable colony of the spirit.

In the second half of his journal, another perspective emerges. It concerns the Western weariness with life that incapacitates the imagination. Joseph considers the ramifications of a culture premised on "Look out for yourself, and the world will be best served" (p. 72)—a culture equating "business wisdom" with the general welfare and spawning entrepreneurs for every need (p. 73). Such a culture dehumanizes people. They "learn to be unfeeling toward [themselves] and incurious" (p. 79). They are hard put to experience "the notion of center, of balance, of order... " (p. 75). People become quarries; the detritus of evil abrades their hearts; they inhabit a "peeling environment" (pp. 59, 61, 79, 101). Like Joseph, they dangle. A dialectic swings them back and forth as they forego personal growth for lack of imagination.

That dialectic is the opposition between the unprecedented possibilities and the woeful actualities of Western societies. Joseph most clearly portrays that dialectic in the interior dialogues he carries on with himself. The dialogues pit Joseph, the weary product of a misguided culture, against the Spirit of Alternatives, the imaginative self Joseph struggles to nurture. During the first dialogue Joseph's two sides discuss the inevitable distance between ideals and actualities, also touching on how ideals can generate obsession or exhaustion. Between the first and the second dialogues, Joseph decides that the worthiest ideals "unlock the imprisoning self" (p. 102). Joseph affirms ideals that keep people from undertaking "quests" (p. 102), activities breeding zeal. About a week later, Joseph describes a Christian Scientist woman who proselytizes in his neighborhood. Although the nameless individual is physically wasting away, she continues mouthing memorized words about the "true science" (p. 107). She not only epitomizes the potential destructiveness of ideals but also shows that ideals alone cannot resolve the dialectic troubling Joseph.

In the second "dialogue" Joseph recognizes that "everybody else is dangling, too" (p. 110). Still unable to decide whether or not each individual has a "separate destiny," Joseph nevertheless ends the dialogue with "I'm all right" (p. 112). During the next week he experiences the wonder of spring, the satisfaction of helping a neighbor, and fresh wrinkles on his face. He accepts those experiences with pleasurable equanimity. The next day, however, Joseph has nasty encounters with Iva and four other people. That night he sends a request for earliest possible induction.

Several days after his blood test, Joseph visits his childhood room and finally confronts the "ephemeral agreements by which we live and pace ourselves" (p. 126). He reports,

Such reality, I thought, is actually very dangerous. It should not be trusted. And I rose . . . , feeling that there was an element of treason to common sense in the very objects of common sense. Or that there was no trusting them, save through wide agreement, and that my separation from such agreement had brought me perilously far from the necessary trust, auxiliary to all sanity. . . . To be pushed upon oneself entirely put the very facts of simple existence into doubt (p. 126).

Thus, Joseph sees that human beings constitute a world together. In the process he confronts the fictive. Joseph now knows every world presupposes tacit agreements that let individuals take its foundations for granted, even though they themselves silently constitute those foundations. People agree, at bottom, to act as if the realities they constitute together are obvious givens.

Although Joseph's insights along those lines cannot dissolve his dialectic, they soften it. At the end of his journal Joseph sees that individuality as well as sociality rests on the fictive. Individuals establish identities, make plans, and pursue projects by deciding, in effect, to act as if their actions add up to a consistent self, as if both the world and other individuals are fundamentally reliable, as if the projects they undertake have obvious meaning and entail obvious means and outcomes. Individuality and sociality do sometimes press competing claims on people. Continuously, though, the two complement one another. In modern worlds neither disposition exists without the other; in all worlds both rest on the fictive.

Barth's *Sabbatical* portrays the fictive in the world of literature. The novel's main characters are Susan Seckler, an English professor, and her husband Fenwick Turner, a former officer in the Central Intelligence Agency whose current interest is writing fiction. *Sabbatical* is the story of Susan's sabbatical spent with Fenwick on their sailboat while writing a novel together. The novel is mostly about their sabbatical ventures which, of course, center on their writing the story of their sabbatical ventures. Barth's novel more than alludes to the fictive. It continuously exposes the as-if agreements underlying fiction.

Like many novels, *Sabbatical* includes authorial intrusions directly addressing readers.[2] Barth uses that device in a distinctively ironic way, though. Whereas most such occasions remind readers they are reading a work of fiction, intrusions in *Sabbatical* occasion readers' few experiences of taking for granted that they are reading a *real* novel. Barth so repeatedly uses devices that keep readers aware of reading a fiction that when he uses a traditional artifice serving that function, readers enjoy a fleeting respite from the fiction making that otherwise steadies their attention. Barth makes readers aware of how fiction depends on tacit agreements between authors and readers to act *as if* a story somehow has some autonomy apart from its teller.

Several devices achieve that effect. Unlike most storytellers, Susan and Fenn remain at the foreground. The most continuous way they make their presence felt is rapid shifts in voice, sometimes even within a sentence. First- and third-person narration intermingle: "Fenwick stops talking to the log-book—he wrote while steering with tiller between thighs as Susan secured the anchor on its roller chock, and thus we've managed to run aground . . ." (p. 244). Sometimes Susan speaks in the first person, sometimes Fenn; sometimes the two together. At other points a third-person narrator takes over: "Done? Okay? Well! Hum! Why, that's some tall order, Susan, Fenn!" (p. 207) Such shifts continuously signal that a fiction is being created and that its authors have to work at their project, making many decisions and relieving one another of narrative burdens. A second device is having Susan and Fenn include in their story comments about its plot and structure.

> So what else needs doing in this chapter, Suse?
> Pardon?
> Part Two of our story.
> Oh. Well. If this is really Part Two, there's a lot to be done yet (p. 124).

Does this go into the story or not? (p. 219)

This chapter, Fenwick says into her hair, would make a novel by itself.

Our story needn't be about us. You and I may not even be in it. I like that, Fenn. We're not for public consumption (p. 356).

Another device is extended dialogues where Susan talks about literary artifices. *Sabbatical* includes, for instance, "A Dialogue on Diction," "The Literary Marvelous," and "On Narrative Viewpoint, Selectivity, and Advancement of the Action."

Thus, the novel continuously loops back on itself like a "sawed-off simile" (p. 11). The novel is (like) a novel. It takes reflexivity toward its literary limit by keeping readers aware of the fictional authors its author created to tell a story about storytelling. It also keeps readers aware that these fictional authors and their creator fit into a world of other authors whose own stories socialize readers about storytelling. References to Cervantes, Kafka, Michener, and other storytellers feed such awareness. Similarly, references and allusions to Barth's other works keep the ideal-typical reader aware of Barth as the storyteller masterminding this story. Susan's dissertation treated Ebenezer Cooke as well as other Maryland authors (p. 46), and Cooke gets a reference in a footnote as well as several allusions. Cooke is the protagonist of Barth's *Sot-Weed Factor*. *Sabbatical* also alludes to Barth's *Lost in the Funhouse* and *Chimera*. All its major artifices make the novel a story whose point "is that the point of [another] story is that the point of [another] story . . ." and so forth (p. 365). The regression is psychologically infinite; its point concerns finitude, however. No author escapes or transcends the historical moment given him or her to write. The author may burst some limits past storytellers faced, but no author can suspend history.

Though less explicitly than *Dangling Man*, *Sabbatical* also treats the fictive in the world of everyday life. Barth implies the continuity of art and life by labeling incidents in characters' everyday lives as stories. Thus, *Sabbatical* includes "The Story of Fenwick Turner's Boina," "The Story of Miriam's *Other* Rapes," and "A Legendary Sea-Monster Swims Through Our Story." By setting those stories off within the chapters of his reflexive novel, Barth implies that "stories" constitute everyday life; the fictive lurks there. Similarly, he points toward the fictive at work beneath facts of all sorts. *Sabbatical* is replete with footnotes referring to newspaper stories and books that apparently exist as cited. Moreover, one story in the novel reports

"The Strange True Case of John Arthur Paisley" (pp. 86–105). The "account is composed entirely of excerpts from ... the *Baltimore Sun* ... most of them written by ... Mr. Tom Nugent and Mr. Steve Parks, with whose kind permission, and that of the *Sun*, we quote" (p. 86). Barth's uses of apparent facts hints at "apparent facts," or the reliance of facts on the fictive. His novel thus tumbles readers into the realm of the fictive where literature, everyday life, and other worlds have their foundations and where fictions and facts ultimately rest their cases.

Underlying every human world are shared but implicit agreements to act as if some matters are true, obvious, or at least plausible enough not to necessitate questioning. Although questioning pervades modern worlds, it presupposes the "obvious" things that provoke it. What appears obvious or given rests atop a series of implicit statements, declaring "Let's act as if . . . . " The fictive is a deeply but silently social "Let's pretend." A "we" establishes the fictive, thus distinguishing it from the fantastic.[3]

Games and stories readily illustrate the fictive. When people play a frantic game of "tag" or a heated tennis match, they enter a world resting on as-if agreements: Let us act as if whether or not I tag you is fateful; let us act as if "love" is having zero on the scoreboard and hitting balls back and forth across a net is a serious adult activity. In our games the fictive allows us to get on with the "really" important issues like whether or not touching people's hair counts for tagging them and whether or not one's opponent crossed the baseline while serving. In order to occupy themselves with matters at hand in the world of games or any other world people must "forget" the arbitrary agreements underlying that world. Establishing a world means masking its fictive foundations. For all *practical* (but not deconstructive) purposes, worlds consign the fictive to the margins of consciousness.

Unlike inhabitants of other worlds, imaginative writers make the fictive an object of consciousness. As "fiction" itself implies, some individuals enact and elaborate the fictive through forms establishing a world of literature. Every novel is a *text*, a written document susceptible to competing interpretations. Every novel also has a *subtext* consisting of the fictive arrangements between readers and novelists. Although readers take subtextual agreements for granted as they pick up their texts, those understandings between readers and writers remain operative; for example, let us act as if the text portrays real individuals' experiences. The form the fictive assumes here is character. Similarly, let us act as if those individuals face sharply problematic experiences they will gradually resolve; enacting this fictive arrangement means experiencing plot. Further, let us act as if one or

more of those individuals or some observer can coherently recon-
struct their experiences; here the fictive arrangement concerns point
of view. In these basic forms the fictive anchors fiction.

The as-if underlies readers' very movement towards texts. Fiction proffers worlds, and individuals enter them with startling ease.
Characters may seem too inconsistent; coincidence may weigh too
heavily in the plot; points of view may seem unclear or—in a
sense—unduly omniscient. Yet readers facing such problems question
neither subtextual agreements nor the world of literature. The fictive
arrangements remain intact when readers criticize or even reject
aspects of specific texts.

Less obvious are the fictive arrangements underlying the world
of science. Although people often contrast that world with the world
of literature, both are cultural forms with the fictive at their base. By
and large, as postmodernists contend, science rests on fictive agreements like acting as if the spatial, temporal world objectively exists;
acting as if that selfsame world has an inherent order; acting as if the
meaning of intersubjective agreement were straightforward. In the
social sciences the as-ifs compound. Social scientists mostly agree to
act as if human beings are basically rational. Moreover, their methods
incorporate the fictive agreement that given words and sentences
mean essentially the same thing to different respondents. More baldly,
many social scientists agree to act as if a small set of questionnaire
items measures prejudice, religiosity, or self-esteem.

The world of everyday life also has fictive roots. Paramount
among the institutions ordering the world of everyday life are the
family, work, and government. Within those institutions fictive
understandings let people take much for granted while going about
their business with little confusion, apprehension, or even thought. In
many societies people implicitly agree to act as if children are their
parents' property and paid work is the hallmark of maturity. Similarly, many people agree to act as if government serves "the people," the
majority rules, or the "common good" routinely gets served.

In their daily lives people's activities presuppose the fictive
agreements underlying commonsense routines. Like the fictive agreements undergirding all human worlds, the implicit understandings
allowing for everyday life are not necessarily untrue. What distinguishes them is that they are not known to be true but are enacted as
if they were true or at least not problematic. Indeed, people's common-sense beliefs rest on bases similar to those Don Quixote used for
making decisions; namely, "documents, monuments, authenticated
accounts by witnesses, and uninterrupted tradition."[4] In other terms,

individuals unavoidably steer a course "between the instinct of observation and the perplexities of circumstances."[5] What they negotiate in
the process is the shape of the fictive.

In *Hard Times* Charles Dickens points out some of the "fictions"
pervading everyday life in Coketown, the setting of his story. Dickens's comments illustrate how writers, among others, disclose the
arbitrary arrangements underlying shared worlds of action. They also
illustrate the continuity the fictive can exhibit; that is, some of these
as-ifs persist more than a century later. Finally, Dickens shows that
some fictive elements of a common world are intentionally created
and sustained. Dickens writes that

> "What one person can do, another can do." This ... was among
> the fictions of Coketown. Any capitalist there who had made
> sixty-thousand pounds out of sixpence always professed to
> wonder why the sixty-thousand nearest Hands [manual work-
> ers] didn't each make sixty-thousand pounds out of sixpence,
> and more or less reproached them every one for not accomplish-
> ing that little feat. What I did you can do.[6]

About the Hands, the capitalist Bounderby says,

> "Show me a dissatisfied Hand, and I'll show you a man that's fit
> for anything bad, I don't care what it is." Another of the popular
> fictions of Coketown which some pains had been taken to dis-
> seminate—and which some people really believed.[7]

The fictive can be disclosed, then. Once aware of it, people can,
if they have the will and the power, alter the arrangements underlying their worlds. In fact, planned social change premises the desirabil-
ity of shifting the fictive understandings supporting a shared world.
Proposing a better way or a new world, individuals propose alternative fictive arrangements. Every world or proposed world presupposes such arrangements. As Wallace Stevens put it, "The structure of
reality ... is ... an adult make-believe."[8]

That human worlds rest on arbitrary understandings does not
mean those understandings are unimportant. Many people apparently delight in dismissing others' beliefs as ill-based and arbitrary. For
some, debunking is a snobbish pastime. To have a world means,
though, to live atop arbitrariness. Those who press for change or
debunk others' worlds advocate, at bottom, displacing one kind of
arbitrariness with another. Understanding that need not dampen

enthusiasm for or commitment to change. It only tempers the spirit of advocacy with a sense of common humanity. Understanding the fictive and one's own commitments to given fictive arrangements means identifying universal ingredients of humanness.

Within the world of everyday life, appreciating the fictive might enhance tolerance by helping people see that the fictive arrangements readily discerned in alien cultures also inform their own cultures. Appreciating the fictive also makes people more aware of their daily choices. Many abide by the rhetoric that says they "have to do" this or that. Social arrangements offer, however, considerable latitude, particularly to those privileged with considerable education and income. An abiding awareness of the fictive nurtures people's sense of freedom by loosening the hold of conventional wisdom on their imaginations.

In the world of science people can disclose the fictive and examine its utility. Such disclosures often mark scientific breakthroughs, for instance, the discovery of the quark or the self-fulfilling prophecy. In the world of literature, awareness of fictive arrangements also leads to breakthroughs like new approaches to characterization or fresh varieties of literary criticism. The genius of a Virginia Woolf or a William Faulkner illustrates the innovations arising from insights into past fictive understandings.

Debunking means, at root, unveiling the fictive by undermining reification. Among all social institutions, literature most reminds people that the fictive is not only "natural" but also colorful, instructive, and sometimes moving. Writers' explorations of the fictive address individuals' marginal awareness of what underlies their worlds. In that sense literature is a call homeward. It underscores the imaginative consciousness Joseph clung to while dangling—the consciousness that not only shapes the arbitrary agreements people take for granted but also discloses those agreements as people debunk in search of meaning and freedom. Novelists ply a trade that illuminates the grounds of every world. By applying their imaginations to the fictive, they show how pliable it is or, alternatively, how versatile human consciousness is.

Literature thus offers grounds for reintegrating contemporary experiences. It provides readers opportunities to see that when they pass from one world to another, they are shifting from one set of fictive arrangements to another. It heightens awareness of the continuity among all worlds. It serves as a potential antidote to the pessimism that says we cannot understand those who inhabit worlds different from our own. It implies the scientist can understand the artist and vice versa. It implies, too, that the commonsense person can become attuned to the integrity of the human world.

We may live in different worlds, but we need not forget what lies beneath each of them. We need not forget the fictive. Literature short-circuits that eventuality by nurturing a sensitivity akin to that of paleo-agricultural peoples:

> Among [them] the essential duty is the periodic evocation of the primordial event which inaugurated the present condition of humanity. All their religious life is a commemoration, a re-memorizing. The Remembrance, reenacted ritually . . . plays the decisive part: one must take the greatest care not to forget what happened *in illo tempore* (i.e., at the time of the beginnings). The real sin is forgetfulness.[9]

Literature is a dam against forgetfulness. It is also a home away from home, whatever the specific world that lodges each of us most assuredly. As Ursula K. Le Guin puts it, "In the tale, in the telling, we are all one blood."[10]

🍎 Appendix

Additional Novels in the Sample

The following lists of bestselling and canonical novels supplement Table 1 (p. 60). These lists constitute the remainder of my sample of novels.

Bestselling Novels

Lisa Alther, *Other Women*
Sherwood Anderson, *Winesburg, Ohio*
Hamilton Basso, *The View from Pompey's Head*
Pearl S. Buck, *The Good Earth*
Eugene Burdick and Harvey Wheeler, *Fail-Safe*
Taylor Caldwell, *This Side of Innocence*
Kate Chopin, *The Awakening*
Winston Churchill, *Mr. Crewe's Career*
James Gould Cozzens, *By Love Possessed*
Patrick Dennis, *Auntie Mame*
E. L. Doctorow, *Ragtime*
Lloyd C. Douglas, *Magnificent Obsession*
Arthur Conan Doyle, *The Hound of the Baskervilles*
Allen Drury, *Advise and Consent*
Frederick Exley, *A Fan's Notes*
Ian Fleming, *Goldfinger*
Paula Fox, *A Servant's Tale*
John Galsworthy, *One More River*
Ernest K. Gann, *The High and the Mighty*
Shirley Ann Grau, *The House on Coliseum Street* and
    The Wind Shifting West
Doris Grumbach, *The Ladies*
Arthur Hailey, *Hotel*
James Hilton, *Good-bye, Mr. Chips*
Mac Hyman, *No Time for Sergeants*
Vicenta Biasco Ibanez, *The Four Horsemen of the Apocalypse*

Shirley Jackson, *Hangman*
Pamela Hansford Johnson, *Winter Quarters*
James Jones, *From Here to Eternity*
Frances Parkinson Keyes, *Dinner at Antoine's*
Judith Krantz, *Scruples*
John LeCarré, *Tinker, Tailor, Soldier, Spy*
Sinclair Lewis, *Babbit* and *Arrowsmith*
Mary McCarthy, *The Group*
John P. Marquand, *The Late George Apley* and *Point of No Return*
Edwin O'Connor, *The Last Hurrah*
John O'Hara, *A Rage to Live*
James Purdy, *Mourners Below*
Erich Maria Remarque, *All Quiet on the Western Front*
George Santayana, *The Last Puritan*
William Saroyan, *The Human Comedy*
Dorothy Sayers, *Murder Must Advertise*
Jane Schwartz, *Caught*
Erich Segal, *Love Story*
Irwin Shaw, *Rich Man, Poor Man*
Charles Monroe Sheldon, *In His Steps*
Max Shulman, *Rally Round the Flag, Boys!*
Joan Silber, *Household Words*
Isaac Bashevis Singer, *Shosha*
Betty Smith, *A Tree Grows in Brooklyn*
Irving Stone, *Love Is Eternal*
Mary-Ann Tirone Smith, *The Book of Phoebe*
Thomas Tryon, *Lady*
Anne Tyler, *The Accidential Tourist*
Evelyn Waugh, *Brideshead Revisited*

Canonical Novels

Margaret Atwood, *The Handmaid's Tale*
Julian Barnes, *Flaubert's Parrot*
Donald Barthelme, *The Dead Father*
Charlotte Brontë, *Jane Eyre*
Rita Mae Brown, *Rubyfruit Jungle*
Willa Cather, *The Professor's House*
Jerome Charyn, *Darlin' Bill*
Allen Cheuse, *The Grandmothers' Club*
Pat Conroy, *The Prince of Tides*
Stephen Crane, *The Red Badge of Courage*

Don DeLillo, *White Noise*
Ralph Ellison, *Invisible Man*
Louise Erdrich, *Love Medicine*
Ford Madox Ford, *The Good Soldier*
John Fowles, *The French Lieutenant's Woman*
Elizabeth Gaskell, *Wives and Daughters*
Ellen Glasgow, *Vein of Iron*
Nadine Gordimer, *The Burger's Daughter*
Elizabeth Hardwick, *Sleepless Nights*
Joseph Heller, *Catch-22*
Zora Neale Hurston, *Their Eyes Were Watching God*
Randall Jarrell, *Pictures from an Institution*
Diane Johnson, *The Shadow Knows*
Pamela Hansford Johnson, *The Survivors of the Fittest*
Ken Kesey, *Sometimes a Great Notion*
Doris Lessing, *The Four-Gated City*
Sinclair Lewis, *Main Street*
Henry Miller, *Tropic of Cancer* and *Tropic of Capricorn*
Toni Morrison, *Beloved*
Penelope Mortimer, *The Pumpkin Eater*
Iris Murdoch, *An Accidental Man* and *The Good Apprentice*
Vladimir Nabokov, *Invitation to a Beheading* and *Lolita*
Flannery O'Connor, *The Violent Bear It Away*
Jayne Anne Phillips, *Machine Dreams*
Sylvia Plath, *The Bell Jar*
J. B. Priestley, *Angel Pavement*
Tom Robbins, *Still Life with Woodpecker*
Marilynne Robinson, *Housekeeping*
Lee Smith, *Oral History*
Wallace Stegner, *Crossing to Safety*
William Styron, *Set This House on Fire*
Harry Swados, *Celebration*
Mark Twain, *Adventures of Huckleberry Finn*
Anne Tyler, *Dinner at the Homesick Restaurant*
Gore Vidal, *Burr*
Robert Penn Warren, *All the King's Men*
H. G. Wells, *The Wealth of Mr. Waddy*
Edith Wharton, *The House of Mirth*
Thornton Wilder, *The Bridge of San Luis Rey*
Owen Wister, *The Virginian*
Tom Wolfe, *Bonfire of the Vanities* and *The Electric Kool-Aid Acid Test*

❧ Notes

Chapter One

1. Annie Dillard, "Write Till You Drop," *The New York Times Book Review* (May 28, 1989), 23.

2. George Santayana, *The Sense of Beauty: Being the Outline of Aesthetic Theory*, New York, Dover Publications, 1955, p. 4.

3. Italo Calvino, *The Uses of Literature: Essays*, New York, Harcourt Brace Jovanovich, 1986, tr. Patrick Creagh, pp. 7, 10, 16; cf. Robert C. Elliott, *The Literary Persona*, Chicago, University of Chicago Press, pp. xi-xii.

4. Robert Boyers, "The Old-Fashioned Critic That Never Was" (Review of Robert Alter's *The Pleasures of Reading*), *The New York Times Book Review* (June 25, 1989), 22.

5. Mary F. Rogers, "Everyday Life As Text" in Randall Collins (ed.), *Sociological Theory*, San Francisco, Jossey-Bass, 1984, pp. 165–86.

6. Georg Simmel, *On Women, Sexuality, and Love*, New Haven, Yale University Press, 1984, tr. Guy Oakes, p. 90.

7. Alfred Schutz, *Collected Papers I: The Problem of Social Reality*, ed. Maurice Natanson, The Hague, Martinus Nijhoff, 1973, pp. 230–31, 212.

8. *Ibid.*, p. 233.

9. Simmel, *op. cit.*, pp. 90–91.

10. Remy C. Kwant, *Phenomenology of Expression*, Pittsburg, Duquesne University Press, 1969, p. 57.

11. Maurice Merleau-Ponty, *In Praise of Philosophy*, Evanston, Northwestern University Press, trs. John Wild and James M. Edie, 1963, p. 55.

12. Virginia Woolf, *The Death of the Moth and Other Essays*, New York, Harcourt Brace Jovanovich, 1974, p. 204.

13. Mary McCarthy, *Ideas and the Novel*, New York, Harcourt Brace Jovanovich, 1980, pp. 31, 43–44.

14. Gerald Graff, *Literature Against Itself: Literary Ideas in Modern Society*, Chicago, University of Chicago Press, 1979, p. 179.

15. Lionel Trilling, *Beyond Culture: Essays on Literature and Learning*, New York, Harcourt Brace Jovanovich, 1965, p. 89.

16. Leslie Fiedler, "Giving the Devil his Due," *Journal of Popular Culture* 12 (Fall, 1979), 207. The first quotation belongs to W. H. Auden, as reported in William Van O'Connor, "The Novel in our Time" in William Van O'Connor (ed.), *Forms of Modern Fiction*, Bloomington, Indiana University Press, 1961, p. 3.

17. Joyce Carol Oates, *(Woman)Writer: Occasions and Opportunities*, New York, Dutton, 1989, p. 380.

18. Virginia Woolf, *The Years*, New York, Harcourt Brace and World, 1937, p. 192; Lawrence Durrell, *Justine*, New York, Dutton, 1961, p. 215; Shirley Jackson, *Hangman*, New York, Ace Publishing Company, 1951, p. 9; Ken Kesey, *Sometimes a Great Notion*, New York, Bantam, 1965, p. 233; John Hawkes, *The Blood Oranges*, New York, New Directions, 1971, p. 37.

19. Jean Kennedy Smith and George Plimpton, "The Creative Uses of Disability, The Restorative Functions of Art," *The New York Times*, Section 2 (June 11, 1989), 6, 26.

20. Wayne Booth, *Critical Understanding: The Powers and Limits of Pluralism*, Chicago, University of Chicago Press, 1979.

21. Lionel Trilling, *The Liberal Imagination: Essays on Literature and Society*, Garden City, NY, Doubleday Anchor Books, 1950, p. 47.

22. Irving Howe, *The Critical Point: On Literature and Culture*, New York, Delta Books, 1975, p. 118.

23. Bernard Bergonzi, *The Situation of the Novel*, Pittsburg, University of Pittsburg Press, 1972, p. 7.

24. Theodor Adorno, "Lyric Poetry and Society," *Telos* 20 (Summer, 1974), 56–71.

25. Trilling, *Liberal Imagination*, pp. 250, 257.

26. *Ibid.*, p. 200.

27. *Ibid.*, pp. 204, 249.

28. C. Wright Mills, *The Sociological Imagination*, New York, Oxford University Press, 1959, Ch. 4.

Chapter Two

1. William Makepeace Thackeray, *The History of Pendennis: His Fortunes and Misfortunes; His Friends and His Greatest Enemy*, New York, Clarke, Given,

and Hooper, University Edition, n.d., pp. 361, 414. Subsequent references are to this edition.

2. Max Weber, "Politics as a Vocation" and "Science as a Vocation" in *From Max Weber: Essays in Sociology*, New York, Oxford University Press, trs. and eds. H. H. Gerth and C. Wright Mills, 1958, pp. 77–128; 129–56.

3. Eudora Welty in Charles Ruas, *Conversations with American Writers*, New York, Alfred A. Knopf, 1985, p. 9.

4. Susan Sontag in *ibid.*, p. 19; Bernard Malamud in George Plimpton (ed.), *Writers at Work: The Paris Interviews*, Sixth Series, New York, Viking Press, 1984, p. 154; Katherine Anne Porter in Van Wyck Brooks (ed.) *Writers at Work: The Paris Review Interviews*, Second Series, New York, Viking Press, 1965, p. 140; Lawrence Durrell in *ibid.*, p. 260; John Gardner in Plimpton, *op. cit.*, p. 395.

5. Nadine Gordimer in *ibid.*, p. 248; Joyce Carol Oates, *(Woman)Writer: Occasions and Opportunities*, New York, Dutton, 1989, p. 348.

6. Gore Vidal in Ruas, *op. cit.*, pp. 59, 60.

7. Gordimer in Plimpton, *op. cit.*, pp. 249, 251.

8. Kurt Vonnegut, Jr. in *ibid.*, p. 218; Porter in Brooks, *op. cit.*, p. 141.

9. Gardner in Plimpton, *op. cit.*, pp. 394–95.

10. Ralph Ellison in Brooks, *op. cit.*, p. 320.

11. Saul Bellow, "Distractions of a Fiction Writer" in Granville Hicks (ed.), *The Living Novel: A Symposium*, New York, Collier, 1962, p. 18.

12. "Catastrophe of vocation" comes from Harold Bloom, *A Map of Misreading*, New York, Oxford University Press, 1975, p. 14.

13. Truman Capote in Ruas, *op. cit*, p. 39.

14. D. H. Lawrence, *Selected Literary Criticism*, New York, Viking, ed. Anthony Beal, 1966, p. 16; James E. Miller, Jr., *World, Self, Reality: The Rhetoric of Imagination*, New York, Dodd, Mead & Company, 1974, p. 7; Sylvia Plath, *Letters Home: Correspondence 1950–1963*, New York, Harper & Row, 1975, pp. 57, 207, 211, 305, 308.

15. Ernest Hemingway in Brooks, *op. cit.*, p. 223.

16. Vidal in Ruas, *op. cit.*, p. 61.

17. Oates, *op. cit.*, p. 20.

18. Aldous Huxley in Brooks, *op. cit.*, p. 206.

19. Porter in *ibid.*

20. Stephen Spender, *The Struggle of the Modern*, Berkeley and Los Angeles, University of California Press, 1965, p. 164; Joseph Conrad, *A Personal Record*, Chapter V (1912), excerpted in Miriam Alott (ed.), *Novelists on the Novel*, New York, Columbia University Press, 1959, p. 126.

21. Conrad in *ibid.*, p. 152.

22. John Gardner in Joe David Bellamy (ed.), *The New Fiction: Interviews with Innovative American Writers*, Urbana, University of Illinois Press, 1974, p. 189.

23. Porter in Brooks, *op. cit.*, p. 149; Miller in *ibid.*, p. 180.

24. Terry Eagleton, *Exiles and Emigrés*, 1970, cited by John Hall, *The Sociology of Literature*, New York, Longman, 1979.

25. Barth in Bellamy, *op. cit.*, p. 16; Mary Kathleen Benet, *Writers in Love*, New York, Macmillan, 1977, p. 5.

26. Ellen Moers, *Literary Women*, Garden City, NY, Anchor Books, 1977, p. 16.

27. "Researchers Link Manic–Depressive Illness and Artistic Creativity," *The Chronicle of Higher Education* XXXV (June 21, 1989), A6.

28. *Ibid.*

29. E. M. Forster, "The Raison d'Etre of Criticism in the Arts" (1948) in *Three Cheers for Democracy* (1951), excerpted in Allott, *op. cit.*, p. 158.

30. Preface to the 1850 edition of *Wuthering Heights* reprinted in *ibid.*, p. 154; Henry Miller in Brooks, op. cit., p. 171.

31. Virginia Woolf, *Moments of Being: Unpublished Autobiographical Writings*, ed. Jeanne Schulkind, New York, Harcourt Brace Jovanovich, 1976, p. 122.

32. *Ibid.*, pp. 67, 72.

33. *Ibid.*, p. 81.

34. Alex Zwerdling, *Virginia Woolf and the Real World*, Berkeley and Los Angeles, University of California Press, 1986, p. 178.

35. Doris Lessing, *A Small Personal Voice*, New York, Vintage, 1975, p. 69.

36. Oates, *op. cit.*, p. 19.

37. In Bellamy, *op. cit.*, pp. 21, 22, 26.

38. Oates, *op. cit.*, p. 370.

39. In Bellamy, *op. cit.*, pp. 27–28, 30.

40. Goyen in Plimpton, *op. cit.*, pp. 185, 199, 202–03.

41. Frank Kermode, "Introduction" in *ibid.*, p. xi.

42. Gail Godwin, "Keeping Track" in *Ariadne's Thread: A Collection of Contemporary Women's Journals*, New York, Harper & Row, ed. Lyn Lifshin, 1982, p. 75.

43. Gordimer in Plimpton, *op. cit.*, pp. 265, 275, 276.

44. Oates, *op. cit.*, p. x.

45. E. L. Doctorow in Ruas, *op. cit.*, pp. 203, 200.

46. J. W. Cross, *George Eliot's Life as Related in Her Letters and Journals*, (1884), Ch. XIX, excerpted in Allott, *op. cit.*, p. 155; Plath, *op. cit.*, p. 333.

47. Bellow cites the Whitman quotation in "Distractions," p. 21; Virginia Woolf, *Books and Portraits*, New York, Harcourt Brace Jovanovich, ed. Mary Lyon, 1977, Tolstoy in a letter to I. S. Aksakov, 8/28/1850, *Letters* (1914), tr. Ethel Colburn Mayne in Allott, *op. cit.*, pp. 149–50; Albert Guerard, *The Triumph of the Novel: Dickens, Dostoevsky, Faulkner*, Chicago, University of Chicago Press, 1976, p. 7; Upton Sinclair, *The Cup of Fury*, New York, Hawthorn Books, 1956, p. 46.

48. In Brooks, *op. cit.*, pp. 221–22, 282; Vonnegut in Plimpton, *op. cit.*, p. 220.

49. Ted Bartimus, "Best-Selling Author Lives a Tale of Romance," *Pensacola News Journal*, August 16, 1981; N. Anderson, "Author Becomes Producer," *Las Vegas Sun*, September 24, 1982.

50. Bill Lyon, "Expatriate Writer Frank Yerby Is Grousing Even Though His 30th Best-Seller Is Coming Up," *People Magazine* 15 (March 30, 1981), 99+.

51. Jack Garner, "Author Is Slower, But Better with His Novels," *Pensacola News Journal*, August 20, 1981.

52. David Handler, "Former Jockey Pens 21st Novel," *Las Vegas Review-Journal*, May 23, 1982, 10J.

53. Dean R. Koontz, *How to Write Best-Selling Fiction*, Cincinnati, Writer's Digest Books, 1981, pp. 119, 285–86, 111.

54. *Ibid.*, p. 1.

55. *Ibid.*, p. 43–44.

56. John Gross, *The Rise and Fall of the Man of Letters: A Study of the Idiosyncratic and the Humane in Modern Literature*, New York, Macmillan, 1969, p. 200.

57. Ralph Daigh admits parts of his book are autobiographical; see *Maybe You Should Write a Book*, Englewood Cliffs, NJ, Prentice-Hall, 1977, p. 16.

58. Ken Purdy, "The Fruit of the Bittersweet" in Aron M. Mathieu (ed.), *The Creative Writer*, Cincinnati, Writer's Digest, Second Revised Edition, 1972, p. 273.

59. Marian Gavin, *Writing Short Stories for Pleasure and Profit*, Boston, The Writer, 1973, p. 9.

60. Erskine Caldwell, *Writing in America*, New York, Phaedra, 1957, p. 133.

61. Patrick Anderson, "King of the 'Techno-Thriller,'" *The New York Times Magazine*, (May 1, 1988): 85.

62. The phrase comes from Jack Woodford, *How to Write and Sell a Novel*, New York, Woodford Press, 1948, pp. 114–15.

63. Alan Devoe, "Literary Discipline" in Trentwell Mason White, *How to Write for a Living*, New York, Reynal & Hitchcock, 1937, p. 272; Koontz, *op. cit.*, pp. 11–12, 13–14.

64. Hallie and Ivy Burnett, *Fiction Writer's Handbook*, New York, Harper & Row, 1975, p. 177; White, *op. cit.*, pp. xiii, 226.

65. Woodford, *op. cit.*, p. 278; Robert Newton Peck, *Secrets of Successful Fiction*, Cincinnati, Writer's Digest Books, 1980, p. 100.

66. Harford Powel, Jr., "The Author's Second Trade" in White, *op. cit.*, p. 254.

67. Peck, *op. cit.*, p. 101.

68. Barbara Cartland, *I Search for Rainbows*, New York, Bantam, 1977, pp. 153, 277, 290; Matt Wolf, "Barbara Cartland, at 86, Is Still a Whirlwind of Words," *Pensacola News Journal*, January 7, 1988, 5D.

69. Koontz, *op. cit.*, pp. 18–19, 22, 23, 25.

70. Yet some strong writers do quickly complete manuscripts. Between 1929 and 1939, Faulkner wrote *Sartoris*, *The Sound and the Fury*, *As I lay Dying*, *Sanctuary*, *Light in August*. Durrell admits to writing "at a terrific speed"; he wrote *Bitter Lemons*, *Balthazar*, and *Clea* each in six to seven weeks; Richard H. Rovere, "Introduction" in William Faulkner, *Light in August*, New York, Modern Library, 1950; Lawrence Durrell in Brooks, *op. cit.*, pp. 267, 270.

71. Koontz, *op. cit.*, p. 259.

72. Ayn Rand, *The Romantic Manifesto: A Philosophy of Literature*, New York, New American Library, Revised Edition, 1975, pp. 110–11.

73. John D. MacDonald quoted by Daigh, *op. cit.*, p. 136.

74. Maugham, *op. cit.*, p. 50.

75. Daigh, *op. cit.*, p. 94; Devoe, "Literary Discipline," p. 272; Koontz, *op. cit.*, p. 62; Somerset Maugham, *The Summing Up*, New York, Doubleday, Doran & Company, 1938, p. 81; Jean Z. Owen, *Professional Fiction Writing: A Practical Guide to Modern Techniques*, Boston, The Writer, 1974, p. 11.

76. Daigh, *op. cit.*, pp. 102, 129.

77. Woodford, *op. cit.*, pp. 124, 129.

78. Anderson, "King of 'Techno-Thriller,'" 55, 84, 85.

Chapter Three

1. Virginia Woolf, *A Room of One's Own*, New York, Harcourt Brace Jovanovich, 1963; *Three Guineas*, New York, Harcourt Brace Jovanovich, 1963.

2. David Gadd, *The Loving Friends: A Portrait of Bloomsbury*, New York, Harcourt Brace Jovanovich, 1974, pp. 47, 7.

3. Others include Arnold Bennet, Ian Fleming, James Jones, Frank Norris, J. D. Salinger, Nathaniel West, and Richard Wright. Except where noted, the biographical data in this section from Ann Evory (ed.), *Contemporary Authors*, Detroit, Gale Research Company, 1960; Stanley J. Kunitz (ed.), *American Authors 1600–1900*, New York, H. W. Wilson Company, 1938; Stanley J. Kunitz (ed.), *British Authors of the Nineteenth Century*, New York, H. W. Wilson Company, 1936; Abraham H. Lass (ed.), *Plot Guides to 100 American and British Novels*, Boston, The Writer, 1966; Lina Mainiero (ed.), *American Women Writers*, New York, Frederick Ungar, 1979; James Vinson and D. L. Kirkpatrick (eds.), *Great Writers of the English Language: Novelists and Prose Writers*, New York, St. Martin's Press, 1979.

4. Michele Murray, "Creating Oneself from Scratch" in Janet Sternberg (ed.), *The Writer and Her Work*, New York, Norton, 1980, pp. 78, 82–83.

5. Janet Burroway, *"Opening Nights: The Opening Days"* in Sternberg, *op. cit.*, pp. 185–86, 209.

6. Nadine Gordimer in George Plimpton (ed.), *Writers at Work: The Paris Review Interviews*, Sixth Series, New York, Viking Press, 1984, pp. 274, 261.

7. Doris Lessing, *A Small Personal Voice*, New York, Vintage, 1975, p. 26.

8. Arlie Hochschild, *Second Shift*, New York, Viking Press, 1989.

9. Rebecca West in Plimpton, *op. cit.*, pp. 15–16.

10. Katherine Anne Porter in Van Wyck Brooks (ed.), *Writers at Work:*

The Paris Review Interviews, Second Series, New York, Viking Press, 1965, pp. 158–59, 161.

11. Joyce Carol Oates, *(Woman)Writer: Occasions and Opportunites*, New York, E. P. Dutton, 1989, p. 176.

12. Nadine Gordimer in Plimpton, *op. cit.*, p. 275.

13. Alice Walker, *"One* Child of One's Own: A Meaningful Digression within the Work(s)"* in Sternberg, *op. cit.*, p. 140.

14. Anne Tyler, "Still Just Writing" in Sternberg, *op. cit.*, p. 11.

15. See, for example, Rae André, *Homemakers: The Forgotten Workers*, Chicago, University of Chicago Press, 1981; Nancy Chodorow, *The Reproduction of Mothering: Psychoanalysis and the Sociology of Gender*, Berkeley and Los Angeles, University of California Press, 1978; Ruth Schwartz Cowan, *More Work for Mother: The Ironies of Household Technology from the Open Hearth to the Microwave*, New York, Basic, 1983; Annagret S. Ogden, *The Great American Housewife: From Helpmate to Wage Earner, 1776–1986*, Westport, CT, Greenwood, 1986; and Susan Strasser, *Never Done: A History of American Housework*, New York, Pantheon, 1982.

16. Toni Cade Bambara, "What It Is I Think I'm Doing Anyhow" in Sternberg, *op. cit.*, p. 166; Katherine Anne Porter in Brooks, *op. cit.*, New York, Viking Press, 1965, p. 159; Oates, *op. cit.*, p. 378.

17. Patrick Anderson, "King of the 'Techno-Thriller,'" *The New York Times Magazine* (May 1, 1988), 55.

18. Gordimer in Plimpton, *op. cit.*, p. 277.

19. Alex Zwerdling, *Virginia Woolf and the Real World*, Berkeley and Los Angeles, University of California Press, 1986, pp. 98, 99.

20. *Ibid.*, pp. 177, 193, 255.

21. David Plante, "In the Heart of Literary London," *The New York Times Magazine* (September 11, 1988), 42.

22. Zwerdling, *op. cit.*, p. 225.

23. Jeffrey Meyers, *Married to Genius*, New York, Barnes & Noble, 1977, p. 167.

24. *Ibid.*, p. 117.

25. Gore Vidal in Charles Ruas, *Conversations with American Writers*, New York, Alfred A. Knopf, 1985, p. 64.

26. Rebecca West in Plimpton, *op. cit.*, p. 15.

27. "John Gardner" in *ibid.*, p. 375; Mervyn Rothstein, "Homegrown Fiction," *The New York Times Magazine* (May 15, 1988), 98.

28. "Ralph Ellison" in Brooks, *op. cit.*, p. 317.

29. Tom Dardis, *Some Time in the Sun*, New York, Scribner's, 1976, p. 84.

30. Zwerdling, *op. cit.*, pp. 12, 26, 113, 118, 199.

31. Georg Simmel, *On Individuality and Social Forms*, Chicago, University of Chicago Press, ed. Donald N. Levine, 1971, p. 180.

32. Georg Simmel, *On Women, Sexuality, and Love*, New Haven, Yale University Press, 1984, tr. Guy Oakes, p. 65.

33. Jane Austen, *Emma*, New York, Bantam, 1958, p. 164.

34. Richard Brautigan, *The Abortion: An Historical Romance 1966*, New York, Pocket Books, 1972, p. 85.

35. Saul Bellow, *Henderson the Rain King*, New York, Penguin, 1976, p. 271.

36. Mary Kathleen Benet, *Writers in Love*, New York, Macmillan, 1977, p. 143.

37. Virginia Woolf, *The Common Reader* First Series, New York, Harcourt Brace Jovanovich, 1953, p. 172.

38. Roger Dataller, *The Plain Man and the Novel*, Port Washington, NY, Kennikat, 1970, p. 81.

39. Meyers, *op. cit.*, p. 9.

40. Ellen Moers, *Literary Women*, Garden City, NY, Anchor Books, 1977, pp. 208–9.

41. Jenni Calder, *Women and Marriage in Victorian Fiction*, New York, Oxford University Press, 1976, p. 171.

42. Meyers, *op. cit.*, p. 18; Gadd, *op. cit.*, p. 165; John Gross, *The Rise and Fall of the Man of Letters: A Study of the Idiosyncratic and the Humane in Modern Literature*, New York, Macmillan, 1969, p. 92.

43. Meyers, *op. cit.*, p. 82.

44. Martin Green, *Transatlantic Patterns: Cultural Comparisons of England with America*, New York, Basic, 1977, p. 153.

45. Ralph Daigh, *Maybe You Should Write a Book*, Englewood Cliffs, NJ, Prentice-Hall, 1977, p. 53.

46. David Daiches, *The Novel and the Modern World*, Chicago, University of Chicago Press, Revised Edition, 1965, p. 83; Fiedler, *op. cit.*, p. 59.

47. Dardis, *op. cit.*, p. 113.

48. Meyers, *op. cit.*, pp. 59, 188, 205.

49. Walter L. Reed, *An Exemplary History of the Novel: The Quixotic versus the Picaresque*, Chicago, University of Chicago Press, 1981, p. 104.

50. Albert J. Guerard, "Notes on the Rhetoric of Anti-Realist Fiction," *TriQuarterly* 30 (Spring, 1974), 31.

Chapter Four

1. Ruth apRoberts, *The Moral Trollope*, Athens, Ohio University Press, 1971, p. 166.

2. See C. B. Macpherson, *The Political Theory of Possessive Individualism: Hobbes to Locke*, London, Oxford University Press, 1962.

3. Anthony Trollope, *The Way We Live Now*, Indianapolis, Bobbs-Merrill, 1974, p. 732. All references are to this edition.

4. Peter Berger and Stanley Pullberg, "Reification and the Sociological Critique of Consciousness," *History and Theory* IV (1965), 207.

5. Karl Marx, *Capital*, Vol. 1, New York, International Publishers, tr. Samuel Morse and Edward Aveling, 1967, p. 75; Joseph Gabel, *False Consciousness: An Essay on Reification*, New York, Harper Torchbooks, trs. Margaret A. Thompson and Kenneth A. Thompson, 1978, pp. 148–51, 313.

6. *Ibid.*, pp. 150–51.

7. Mary F. Rogers, "Taken for Grantedness," *Current Perspectives in Social Theory: A Research Annual* 2 (1981): 133–55.

8. The examples come from (1) William Makepeace Thackeray, *Vanity Fair: A Novel without a Hero*, New York, Signet, 1962, p. 497; (2) Thomas Hardy, *Jude the Obscure*, New York, Penguin, 1978; (3) George Santayana, *The Last Puritan: A Memoir in the Form of a Novel*, New York, Scribner's, 1936, p. 227; (4) Frank Yerby, *Pride's Castle*, New York, Dial, 1949, pp. 1–2; (5) Ralph Ellison, *Invisible Man*, New York, Vintage, 1972, p. 563.

9. James Joyce, *A Portrait of the Artist as a Young Man*, New York, Penguin, 1976, pp. 62, 166–67, 179, 189.

10. William Faulkner, *As I Lay Dying*, New York, Vintage, 1957, pp. 163, 164, 165.

11. William Faulkner, *The Sound and the Fury*, New York, Vintage, 1954, p. 145.

Notes 227

12. John Barth, *Giles Goat-Boy*, New York, Fawcett, 1967, pp. xv–xvi.

13. William Faulkner, *The Hamlet*, New York, Vintage, 1956, p. 261; Thomas Pynchon, *Gravity's Rainbow*, New York, Bantam, 1974, p. 263.

14. Eudora Welty, *Losing Battles*, New York, Vintage, 1978, p. 12; John Dos Passos, *Nineteen-Nineteen*, Vol. II in *U.S.A.*, New York, Modern Library, 1937, p. 127; Vladimir Nabokov, *Lolita*, New York, Berkeley, 1966, p. 69.

15. Howell Raines, *Whiskey Man*, New York, Viking, 1977, p. 63; Raymond Queneau, *The Bark Tree*, New York, New Directions, tr. Barbara Wright, 1971, p. 172.

16. Allen Wheelis, *The Desert*, New York, Basic, 1970, p. 104; Charles Dickens, *David Copperfield*, New York, Modern Library, 1950, p. 348; Virginia Woolf, *The Years*, New York, Harcourt Brace and World, 1937, p. 267; Anthony Burgess, *The Long Day Wanes: A Malayan Trilogy*, New York, Ballantine, 1966, p. 517.

17. These examples are from Elizabeth Hardwick, *Sleepless Nights*, New York, Random House, 1979, p. 69; Ken Kesey, *Sometimes a Great Notion*, New York, Bantam, 1965, p. 79; Vladimir Nabokov, *Invitation to a Beheading*, Greenwich, CT, Fawcett, tr. Dmitri Nabokov with Vladimir Nabokov, 1960, p. 30.

18. These examples are from D. H. Lawrence, *Lady Chatterly's Lover*, New York, Grove Press, 1962, p. 77; Joseph Heller, *Catch-22*, New York, Dell, 1978, p. 85; Edna Ferber, *Showboat*, New York, The Book League of America, 1926, p. 33.

19. Grace Metalious, *Peyton Place*, New York, Dell, 1957, pp. 7, 8.

20. Cf. Michael Zeraffa, "The Novel as Literary Form and as Social Institution" in Elizabeth and Tom Burns (eds.), *Sociology of Literature and Drama: Selected Readings*, Harmondsworth, Middlesex, England, Penguin, 1973, p. 36.

21. What is at issue here is the focus of the fiction, not the subculture of its readers. Each type of novel tends, as Chapters 5 and 6 imply, to associate itself with a distinctive subculture.

22. Georg Simmel, *On Women, Sexuality, and Love*, New Haven: Yale University Press, tr. Guy Oakes, 1984, pp. 72, 81, 83.

23. Joseph Allen Boone, *Tradition Counter Tradition: Love and the Form of Fiction*, Chicago, University of Chicago Press, 1987, pp. 65, 66, 67.

24. Simmel, *op. cit.*, p. 103.

25. Alex Zwerdling, *Virginia Woolf and the Real World*, Berkeley and Los Angeles, University of California Press, 1986, p. 251.

26. Boone, *op. cit.*, pp. 131, 280–81; cf. Nina Auerbach, *Communities of Women: An Idea in Fiction*, Cambridge, Harvard University Press, 1978.

27. Ellen Moers, *Literary Women*, Garden City, NY, Anchor Books, 1978, pp. 187, 189, 191, 192, 228, 235.

28. Northrop Frye, *The Secular Scripture: A Study of the Structure of Romance*, Cambridge, Harvard University Press, 1976, pp. 24–28.

29. Janice A. Radway, *Reading the Romance: Women, Patriarchy, and Popular Culture*, Chapel Hill, University of North Carolina Press, 1984, pp. 134, 165, 168–9.

30. Michael Davitt Bell, *The Development of American Romance: The Sacrifice of Relation*, Chicago, University of Chicago Press, 1980, p. 35.

31. Richard Chase, *The American Novel and Its Traditions*, Baltimore, Johns Hopkins University Press, 1957, p. 11.

32. Robert N. Bellah, Richard Madsen, William M. Sullivan, Ann Swidler, and Steven M. Tipton, *Habits of the Heart: Individualism and Commitment in American Life*, New York, Perennial Library, 1986.

Chapter Five

1. George Eliot, *Middlemarch: A Study of Provincial Life*, New York, Oxford University Press, 1953, pp. 2, 3.

2. Charles Dickens, *Bleak House*, New York, New American Library, 1964, pp. 307–8.

3. Jack Goody and Ian Watt, "The Consequences of Literacy," *Comparative Studies in Society and History* 5 (Fall, 1963), 338.

4. Jorge Luis Borges, "Libraries, Books, and Reading" in Robert Karlin (ed.), *Reading for All: Proceedings of the Fourth International Reading Association World Congress on Reading*, Newark, DE, International Reading Association, 1973, p. 3.

5. Frank Hatt, *The Reading Process: A Framework for Analysis and Description*, London and Hamden, CT, Clive Bingley and Linnet Books, 1976, pp. 51–52.

6. Elizabeth L. Eisentein, "Some Conjectures about the Impact of Printing on Western Society and Thought: A Preliminary Report" in Harvey J. Graff (ed.), *Literacy and Social Development in the West: A Reader*, Cambridge, Cambridge University Press, 1981, pp. 56–66.

7. Michael T. Claunchy, "Literature and the Illiterate; Hearing and Seeing: England 1066–1307" in Graff, *op. cit.*, p. 40.

8. Leslie Shepard, *The History of Street Literature: The Story of Broadside Bal-*

lads, Chapbooks, Proclamations, News-Sheets, Election Bills, Tracts, Pamphlets, Cocks, Catchpennies, and Other Ephemera, Detroit, Singing Tree Press, 1973, p. 110.

9. Kenneth A. Lockridge, "Literacy in Early America 1650–1800" in Graff, *op. cit.*, p. 183.

10. Shepard, *op. cit.*, pp. 14, 23, 36.

11. Hatt, *op. cit.*, p. 36.

12. See Jonathan Cobb and Richard Sennett, *The Hidden Injuries of Class,* New York, Vintage, 1973; Randall Collins, *The Credential Society: An Historical Sociology of Education and Stratification,* New York, Academic Press, 1979.

13. Lauren B. Resnick and Betty H. Robinson, "Motivational Aspects of the Literacy Problem" in John B. Carroll and Jeanne S. Chall (eds.), *Toward a Literate Society: The Report of the Committee on Reading of the National Academy of Education,* New York, McGraw-Hill, 1975, p. 262.

14. National Committee on Reading, "Report of the Committee on Reading, National Academcy of Education" in Carroll and Chall, *op. cit.*, p. 8. This is roughly the ability to understand a magazine like *Newsweek*.

15. Lawrence C. Stedman and Carl F. Kaestle, "Literacy and Reading Performance in the United States, From 1880 to the Present," *Reading Research Quarterly* XXII (Winter, 1987), 42.

16. On "simple" and "higher" illiteracy, see Francis S. Chase, "Demands on the Reader in the Next Decade" in Martha L. King, Bernice D. Ellinger, and Willavene Wolf (eds.) *Critical Reading,* New York, J. B. Lippincott, 1967, p. 6.

17. Douglas Waples, Bernard Berelson, and Franklyn R. Bradshaw, *What Reading Does to People: A Summary of the Evidence on the Social Effects of Reading and a Statement of Problems for Research,* Chicago, University of Chicago Press, 1940, pp. 13, 74–80.

18. *Ibid.*, pp. 25, 29.

19. Shepard, *op. cit.*, pp. 39–40.

20. Henry C. Link and Harry Arthur Hopf, *People and Books: A Study of Reading and Book-Buying Habits,* New York, Book Industry Committee, Book Manufacturers' Institute, 1946, pp. 57, 58.

21. William S. Gray and Ruth Munroe, *The Reading Interests and Habits of Adults: A Preliminary Report,* New York, Macmillan, 1930, p. 262.

22. Amiel T. Sharon, "What Do Adults Read?" *Reading Research Quarterly* IX, No. 2 (1973–1974), 150, 158.

23. *Ibid.*, p. 150, 157.

24. Link and Hopf, *op. cit.*, pp. 58–67.

25. Douglas Waples, *Research Memorandum on Social Aspects of Reading in the Depression*, New York, Arno Press, 1972, p. 99.

26. Gray and Munroe, *op. cit.*, p. 263.

27. Sharon, "What Do Adults Read?" 162; Waples, *op. cit.*, p. 197.

28. Janice A. Radway, *Reading the Romance: Women, Patriarchy, and Popular Literature*, Chapel Hill, University of North Carolina Press, 1984, p. 58.

29. Link and Hopf, *op. cit.*, pp. 91, 111, 117, 124.

30. Waples, *op. cit.*, pp. 85, 154–55, 168, 169, 178.

31. James D. Hart, *The Popular Book: A History of America's Literary Taste*, New York, Oxford University Press, 1950, p. 214.

32. Paul DiMaggio, Michael Useem, and Paula Brown, *Audience Studies of the Performing Arts and Museums: A Critical Review*, Washington, DC, National Endowment for the Arts, Research Development Report No. 9, November, 1978, p. 15.

33. Victor Nell, "The Psychology of Reading for Pleasure: Needs and Gratifications," *Reading Research Quarterly* XXIII, No 1 (Winter, 1988), 25.

34. Karen C. Beyard-Taylor and Howard J. Sullivan, "Adolescent Reading Preferences for Type of Theme and Sex of Character," *Reading Research Quarterly* XVI, No. 1 (1980), 111, 114.

35. Joanne M. Golden and John T. Guthrie, "Convergence and Divergence in Reader Response to Literature," *Reading Research Quarterly* XXI (Fall, 1986), 419, 420.

36. Patrocinio P. Schweickart, "Reading Ourselves: Toward a Feminist Theory of Reading" in Elizabeth A. Flynn and Patrocinio P. Schweickart (eds.), *Gender and Reading: Essays on Readers, Texts, and Contexts*, Baltimore, Johns Hopkins University Press, 1986, p. 45; Judith Fetterly, "Reading about Reading: 'A Jury of Her Peers,' 'The Murders in the Rue Morgue,' and 'The Yellow Wallpaper'" in Flynn and Schweickart, *op. cit.*, p. 152.

37. *Ibid.*, p. 159.

38. Joseph Allen Boone, *Tradition Counter Tradition: Love and the Form of Fiction*, Chicago, University of Chicago Press, 1987, pp. 101, 102, 111.

39. David Bleich, "Gender Interests in Reading and Language" in Flynn and Schweickart, *op. cit.*, pp. 260, 261.

40. Elizabeth A. Flynn, "Gender and Reading" in Flynn and Schweickart, *op. cit.*, p. 273.

41. Madonne N. Miner, "Guaranteed to Please: Twentieth-Century Women's Bestsellers" in Flynn and Schweickart, *op. cit.*, p. 191.

42. Radway, *op. cit.*, pp. 56, 59, 60.

43. Nell, "The Psychology of Reading...," p. 42.

44. Radway, *op. cit.*, pp. 66, 67, 179.

45. *Ibid.*, pp. 193, 195, 196.

46. Victor Nell, *Lost in a Book: The Psychology of Reading for Pleasure*, New Haven, Yale University Press, 1988, p. 146.

47. *Ibid.*, pp. 228, 229.

48. Radway, *op. cit.*, p. 66.

49. Nell, *op. cit.*, p. 252.

50. Radway, *op. cit.*, p. 197.

51. *Ibid.*, p. 59.

52. *Ibid.*, pp. 61, 91, 101.

53. *Ibid.*, pp. 61, 63.

54. Nell, *op. cit.*, p. 238.

55. Douglas Waples and Ralph W. Tyler, *What People Want to Read About*, Chicago, University of Chicago Press, 1931, p. 5.

56. Harold V. Bonny, *Reading: A Historical and Psychological Study*, Gravesend, England, Alex J. Philip, 1939, pp. 68–69.

57. Waples *et al.*, *op. cit.*, p. 24.

58. Holbrook Jackson, *The Reading of Books*, New York, Scribner's, 1947, p. 18.

59. Shepard, *op. cit.*, p. 110.

60. William Ryan, *Blaming the Victim*, New York, Vintage, 1976.

61. Nell, *op. cit.*, p. 5.

62. William Makepeace Thackeray, *The History of Pendennis: His Fortunes and Misfortunes; His Friends and His Greatest Enemy*, New York, Clarke, Given and Hooper, University Edition, n.d. (orig. 1848–50), p. 147.

63. George Santayana, *The Last Puritan: A Memoir in the Form of a Novel*, New York, Scribner's, 1936, p. 7; Henry James, *The Portrait of a Lady*, New York, Modern Library, 1959, p. 287.

64. Jean-Paul Sartre, *Nausea,* New York, New Directions, 1964, p. 67; Henry James, *The Tragic Muse,* New York, Crowell, 1975, p. 98.

65. John Cheever, *Falconer,* New York, Knopf, 1977, p. 59; May Sarton, *The Small Room,* New York, Norton, 1976, p. 61.

66. Sartre, *op. cit.,* p. 144; Lawrence Durrell, *Justine,* New York, Dutton, 1961, p. 87.

67. Richard Sennett, *The Frog Who Dared to Croak,* New York, Farrar, Straus & Giroux, 1982, p. 137.

68. Henry James, *The Portrait of a Lady,* New York, Modern Library, 1951, p. 288.

69. Jean Rhys, *Quartet,* New York, Vintage, 1974, p. 22.

70. Muriel Spark, *The Prime of Miss Jean Brodie,* New York, Dell, 1966, p. 133.

71. Lawrence Durrell, *Clea,* New York, Dutton, 1961, pp. 98–99.

72. Ralph Ellison, *Invisible Man,* New York, Vintage, 1972, p. 494.

73. Vladimir Nabokov, *Invitation to a Beheading,* Greenwich, CT, Fawcett, tr. Dmitri Nabokov with Vladimir Nabokov, 1960, p. 88; Vladimir Nabokov, *Lolita,* New York, Berkeley, 1966, pp. 15–16.

74. Walker Percy, *Lancelot,* New York, Avon, 1978.

75. Saul Bellow, *Mr. Sammler's Planet,* New York, Fawcett, 1971, p. 7.

76. Lawrence Durrell, *Mountolive,* New York, Dutton, 1961, p. 53.

77. E. M. Forster, *Where Angels Fear to Tread,* New York, Vintage, 1958, p. 127.

78. Stendhal, *The Red and the Black,* New York, Signet, 1970, p. 76.

79. Charles Dickens, *Great Expectations,* New York, Holt Rinehart Winston, 1966, p. 22.

80. Jean-Paul Sartre, *The Age of Reason,* New York, Vintage, 1973, p. 101.

81. Hermann Hesse, *Demian,* New York, Bantam, 1970, p. 97.

82. James Joyce, *A Portrait of the Artist as a Young Man,* New York, Penguin, 1976, p. 203.

83. Bellow, *op. cit.,* p. 213.

84. The examples are from (1) E. M. Forster, *A Passage to India,* New York, Harcourt, Brace & World, 1952, p. 70; (2) Cheever, *op. cit.,* p. 29; (3) Henry James, *The Ambassadors,* New York, Washington Square, 1963, p. 151; (4) E. M. Forster, *Howards End,* New York, Vintage, 1954, pp. 186–87.

85. Philip Roth, *Portnoy's Complaint*, New York, Bantam, 1970, p. 88.

86. Virginia Woolf, *To the Lighthouse*, New York, Harcourt Brace Jovanovich, 1927, p. 51.

87. Max Frisch, *I'm Not Stiller*, New York, Vintage, 1958, p. 242; Ken Kesey, *Sometimes a Great Notion*, New York, Bantam, 1965, p. 472; Lawrence Durrell, *Balthazar*, New York, Dutton, 1961, p. 26.

88. Durrell, *Mountolive*, p. 48.

89. André Gide, *The Immoralist*, New York, Vintage, tr. Dorothy Bussy, 1970, p. 43.

90. The examples come from (1) Ivan Turgenev, *Fathers and Sons*, New York, Signet, 1972, p. 91; (2) Roth, *op. cit.*, p. 114; (3) John Updike, *Couples*, New York, Fawcett, 1968, p. 111; (4) Jean-Paul Sartre, *Troubled Sleep*, New York, Vintage, 1973, p. 193; (5) Margaret Drabble, *A Summer Bird-Cage*, New York, Popular Library, 1977, p. 41.

91. Donald Barthelme, *The Dead Father*, New York, Farrar, Straus and Giroux, 1975, p. 46.

92. E. M. Forster, *Where Angels Fear to Tread*, New York, Vintage, 1958, p. 55.

93. Jerzy Kosinski, *Blind Date*, New York, Bantam, 1978, p. 228.

94. Ford Madox Ford, *The Good Soldier*, New York, Vintage, 1955, p. 54.

95. Sarton, *op. cit.*, p. 223.

96. Charles Dickens, *Our Mutual Friend*, New York, Signet, 1964, p. 225.

97. André Malraux, *The Temptation of the West*, New York, Jubilee Books, tr. Robert Hollander, 1974, p. 13.

98. Frisch, *op. cit.*, p. 281.

99. The examples come from (1) Henry Fielding, *The History of Tom Jones: A Foundling*, New York, Modern Library, 1950 (orig. 1749), p. 256; (2) Margaret Drabble, *The Needle's Eye*, New York, Popular Library, 1977, p. 33; (3) John Cheever, *The Wapshot Chronicle*, New York, Perennial Library, 1973, p. 257; (4) Mary Wollstonecraft, *Mary: A Fiction*, New York, Schocken, 1977, p. 91; (5) Anthony Trollope, *Phineas Finn*, New York, Oxford University Press, 1973, p. 109.

100. The examples come from D. H. Lawrence, *Women in Love*, New York, Bantam, 1969, p. 271; Updike, *op. cit.*, p. 147; Saul Bellow, *Henderson the Rain King*, New York, Penguin, 1976, p. 339.

101. Fielding, *op. cit.*, p. 433.

102. Thackeray, *op. cit.*, p. 64.

103. Joseph Conrad and Ford Madox Ford, *Romance*, New York, Signet, 1968, p. 156.

104. John Barth, *Lost in the Funhouse: Fiction for Print, Tape, Live Voice*, New York, Bantam, 1969, p. 4.

105. Diane Johnson, *The Shadow Knows*, New York, Vintage, 1982, p. 106.

106. Doris Lessing, *The Four-Gated City*, New York, New American Library, 1976, p. 10.

107. Durrell, *Balthazar*, p. 121.

108. The examples come from (1) *ibid.*, p. 249; (2) Frank Norris, *McTeague*, New York, Signet, 1964, p. 147; (3) Rhys, *op. cit.*, p. 118; (4) Anthony Trollope, *Barchester Towers*, New York, New American Library, 1963, p. 227; (5) William Faulkner, *Light in August*, New York, Modern Library, 1950, p. 275; (6) Iris Murdoch, *An Accidental Man*, New York, Warner, 1973, p. 219; (7) Thackeray, *op. cit.*, p. 133; (8) Philip Roth, *My Life as a Man*, New York, Bantam, 1975, p. 174.

109. Daniel Defoe, *Moll Flanders*, New York, Pocket Books, 1952, p. 62.

110. Alfred Schutz, *Collected Papers I: The Problem of Social Reality*, ed. Maurice Natanson, The Hague, Martinus Nijhoff, 1973, pp. 67–68.

111. Paul DiMaggio, "Classification in Art," *American Sociological Review* 52 (August, 1987), 443. Interestingly, Radway reports that the romance readers she studied enjoy the "pleasure of regular discussions of books with other women"; Radway, *op. cit.*, p. 96.

Chapter Six

1. Joyce Carol Oates, *Expensive People*, New York, Fawcett, 1968, p. 81. All references are to this edition.

2. James Phelan, *Worlds from Words: A Theory of Language in Fiction*, Chicago, University of Chicago Press, 1981, p. 9.

3. Wallace Martin, *Recent Theories of Narrative*, Ithaca, NY, Cornell University Press, 1986, p. 152.

4. Deborah Wells Rowe and Lawrence Rayford, "Activating Background Knowledge in Reading Comprehension Assessment," *Reading Research Quarterly* XXII (Summer, 1987), p. 161.

5. Walter Slatoff, *With Respect to Readers: Dimensions of Literary Response*, Ithaca, NY, Cornell University Press, 1970, pp. 178–79.

6. Virginia Woolf, *The Common Reader: First Series*, New York, Harcourt Brace Jovanovich, 1953, p. 1.

7. William Gray and Ruth Munroe, *The Reading Interests and Habits of Adults: A Preliminary Report*, New York, Macmillan, 1930, p. 268; Victor Nell, "The Psychology of Reading for Pleasure: Needs and Gratifications," *Reading Research Quarterly* XXIII, No. 1 (Winter, 1988), p. 6–50.

8. *Ibid.*, p. 42.

9. Harold Bloom, *A Map of Misreading*, New York, Oxford University Press, 1975, p. 74.

10. Hermann Hesse, *My Belief: Essays of Life and Art*, New York, Farrar, Straus and Giroux, tr. Denver Lindley, 1975, pp. 166–67. Here Hesse is commenting on the genuine critic.

11. Wolfgang Iser, *The Act of Reading: A Theory of Aesthetic Response*, Baltimore, Johns Hopkins University Press, 1978, p. 134.

12. Wayne C. Booth, *The Rhetoric of Irony*, Chicago, University of Chicago Press, 1975, p. 93.

13. Cf. Slatoff, *op. cit.*, p. 38.

14. Nell, "The Psychology of Reading...," pp. 18, 20.

15. Gore Vidal, *Matters of Fact and Fiction: Essays, 1973–1976*, New York, Random House, 1977, p. 123.

16. Granville Hicks, "Afterword: The Enemies of the Novel" in Granville Hicks, *The Living Novel: A Symposium*, New York, Collier's, 1962, p. 212; Wendy Griswold, "The Fabrication of Meaning: Literary Interpretation in the United States, Great Britain, and the West Indies," *American Journal of Sociology* 92 (March, 1987), 1111.

17. Bloom, *op. cit.*, p. 3.

18. Iser, *op. cit.*, p. 8.

19. Booth, *op. cit.*, p. 1.

20. Wolfgang Iser, *The Implied Reader: Patterns of Communication in Prose Fiction From Bunyan to Beckett*, Baltimore, Johns Hopkins University Press, 1974, p. 38; Booth, *op cit.*, pp. 96–97, 222–23.

21. Nell, "The Psychology of Reading...," 8, 20–21, 28, 30–31.

22. *Ibid.*, 41.

23. John Cawelti, "The Concept of Formula in the Study of Popular Literature" in Sherman Paul (ed.), *Criticism and Culture: Papers of the Midwest*

Modern Language Association, No. 2, Iowa City, Midwest Modern Language Association, 1972, pp. 118, 119, 122.

24. Gray and Munroe, *op. cit.*, p. 61.

25. Nita Sundbye, "Text Explicitness and Inferential Questioning: Effects on Story Understanding and Recall," *Reading Research Quarterly* XXII (Winter, 1987), 83, 84.

26. Wolfgang Iser, *Implied Reader*, p. 9.

27. Slatoff, *op. cit.*, p. 71.

28. Iser, *Act of Reading*, p. 128.

29. *Ibid.*, p. 127.

30. Alfred Schutz, *Reflections on the Problems of Relevance*, New Haven, Yale University Press, ed. and ann. Richard M. Zaner, p. 27.

31. *Ibid.*, p. 57.

32. Iser, *Implied Reader*, pp. 160–61.

33. *Ibid.*, pp. 34–35.

34. As Herbert J. Gans points out, Oliver Barrett IV's and Jennifer Cavilleri's romance also makes for some appealing fantasies about social mobility; see his "*Love Story:* A Romance of Upward Mobility," *Social Policy* 2 (May–June, 1971), 34–36.

35. Wayne C. Booth, *Critical Understanding: The Powers and Limits of Pluralism*, Chicago, University of Chicago Press, 1979, p. 242; Iser, *Act of Reading*, p. 111.

36. Cf. *ibid.*, pp. 184–5.

37. Roland Barthes, *S/Z*, New York, Hill and Wang, tr. Richard Miller, 1974, pp. 13–4.

38. Edmund Husserl, *Cartesian Meditations: An Introduction to Phenomenology*, The Hague, Nijhoff, tr. Dorian Cairns, 1970, p. 45.

Chapter Seven

1. Rachel Trickett, "Vitality of Language in Nineteenth-Century Fiction" in Gabriel Josipovici (ed.), *The Modern English Novel: The Reader, the Writer, and the Work*, London, Open Books, 1976, p. 39.

2. Alfred Schutz, *The Phenomenology of the Social World*, Evanston, Il,

Northwestern University Press, tr. George Walsh and Frederick Lehnert, 1967, p. 159.

3. Joyce Carol Oates, *(Woman)Writer: Occasions and Opportunities*, New York, Dutton, 1989, pp. 191, 42.

4. Jeffrey L. Sammons, *Literary Sociology and Practical Criticism: An Inquiry*, Bloomington, Indiana University Press, 1977, pp. xi, xii.

5. Juan E. Corradi, "Textures: Approaching Society, Ideology, Literature," *Ideologies & Literature* 1 (February–April, 1977), 19.

6. Albert J. Guerard, *The Triumph of the Novel: Dickens, Dostoevsky, Faulkner*, Chicago, University of Chicago Press, pp. 136–8, 145–50, 205, 226–34.

7. Henry Fielding, *The History of Tom Jones: A Foundling*, New York, The Modern Library, 1950, p. 75. In these and the following examples I assume the narrator is often the author's stand-in or at least that readers respond to most narrators as if that were so. This paragraph as well as the following one derive from my "Literary Socialization and Literary Interaction: Novelists on Reading Novels," *Current Perspectives in Social Theory: A Research Annual* 6 (1985), 272.

8. H. G. Wells, *The Wealth of Mr. Waddy*, Carbondale, Southern Illinois University Press, 1969, p. 56.

9. William Makepeace Thackeray, *The History of Pendennis: His Fortunes and Misfortunes; His Friends and His Greatest Enemy*, New York, Clarke, Given, and Hooper, n.d., p. 566; William Styron, *Set This House on Fire*, New York, Signet, 1961, p. 8.

10. Henry Fielding, *Joseph Andrews*, New York, The Modern Library, 1939, p. 274; Charlotte Brontë, *Jane Eyre*, New York, Modern Library, 1950, p. 98.

11. Fielding, *Tom Jones*, pp. 12–13.

12. Fielding, *Joseph Andrews*, p. 40.

13. Anthony Trollope, *Phineas Redux*, New York, Oxford University Press, 1973, p. 38; Winston Churchill, *Mr. Crewe's Career*, New York, Macmillan, 1908, p. 130.

14. *Ibid.*, p. 24.

15. Margaret Drabble, *The Realms of Gold*, New York, Popular Library, 1977, pp. 121, 174; emphasis added.

16. Fielding, *Joseph Andrews*, p. 320; Churchill, *op. cit.*, p. 13.

17. Alfred Schutz, *Collected Papers I: The Problem of Social Reality*, The Hague, Nijoff, ed. Maurice Natanson, 1973, p. 57.

18. I rely here on Schutz; see *Phenomenology*, pp. 112–13.

19. Erving Goffman, *Forms of Talk*, Philadelphia, University of Pennsylvania Press, 1981, pp. 176–77. This paragraph as well as the following one derives from Rogers, "Literary Socialization," 272-73.

20. *Ibid.*, p. 177.

21. *Ibid.*, pp. 63, 194. "Commissives" comes from J. R. Searle; Goffman defines performance as "all the activity of a given participant on a given occasion which serves to influence in any way any of the other participants"; see *The Presentation of Self in Everyday Life*, New York, Anchor Books, 1959, p. 15.

22. Erving Goffman, *Frame Analysis: An Essay on the Organization of Experience*, New York, Harper Colophon Books, 1974, pp. 127, 247.

23. Goffman, *Forms of Talk*, pp. 170–71, 72; Goffman, *Presentation of Self*, p. 85.

24. Goffman, *Frame Analysis*, pp. 133–34; Erving Goffman, *Strategic Interaction*, Philadelphia, University of Pennsylvania Press, 1969, p. 7.

25. Goffman, *Presentation of Self*, p. 249.

26. Goffman, *Strategic Interaction*, pp. 13–14.

27. Cf. Goffman, *Forms of Talk*, p. 3.

28. Goffman, *Frame Analysis*, pp. 288, 290, 293.

29. Erving Goffman, *Interaction Ritual: Essays on Face-to-Face Behavior*, New York, Anchor Books, 1967, p. 52.

30. Robert C. Elliott, *The Literary Persona*, Chicago, University of Chicago Press, 1982.

31. Wayne C. Booth, *Critical Understanding: The Powers and Limits of Pluralism*, Chicago, University of Chicago Press, 1979, pp. 268–71.

32. Goffman, *Interaction Ritual*, pp. 185, 214.

33. Goffman, *Frame Analysis*, p. 85. This section of the chapter relies heavily on Rogers, "Literary Socialization," 274-76.

34. Erving Goffman, *Asylums: Essays on the Social Situation of Mental Patients and Other Inmates*, New York, Anchor Books, 1961, p. 320.

35. Goffman, *Strategic Interaction*, pp. 127–28.

36. *Ibid.*, p. 4.

37. Robert Frost, *Robert Frost on Writing*, New Brunswick, NJ, Rutgers University Press, ed. Elaine Barry, 1973, p. 122.

38. Goffman, *Strategic Interaction*, p. 182.

39. *Ibid.*, p. 126.

40. *Ibid.*

41. Goffman, *Forms of Talk*, p. 24.

42. The phrase is Goffman's; *Strategic Interaction*, p. 18.

43. Goffman, *Forms of Talk*, p. 73.

44. Wayne C. Booth, *The Rhetoric of Fiction*, Chicago, University of Chicago Press, 1961, p. 304; Goffman, *Strategic Interaction*, pp. 47–48; Goffman, *Forms of Talk*, p. 153.

45. Goffman, *Presentation of Self*, p. 62.

46. George H. Szanto, *Narrative Consciousness: Structure and Perception in the Fiction of Kafka, Beckett, and Robbe-Grillet*, Austin, University of Texas Press, 1972, pp. 12–13.

47. Goffman, *Frame Analysis*, p. 190.

48. Goffman, *Strategic Interaction*, pp. 15–16.

49. Ford Madox Ford, *It Was the Nightingale*, Part II, Chapter ii (1934), excerpted in Miriam Allott (ed.), *Novelists on the Novel*, New York, Columbia University Press, 1959, p. 271; emphasis added.

50. Goffman, *Frame Analysis*, p. 83.

51. See Wayne C. Booth, *A Rhetoric of Irony*, Chicago, University of Chicago Press, 1975, p. 55. He offers examples from Gerhardie's *Futility*, Durrell's *Balthazar*, and Nabokov's *Lolita*.

52. Erving Goffman, *Relations in Public: Microstudies of the Public Order*, New York, Harper Colophon Books, 1971, p. 173.

53. Goffman, *Strategic Interaction*, p. 15.

54. Goffman, *Forms of Talk*, p. 145.

55. Wolfgang Iser, *The Implied Reader: Patterns of Communication in Prose Fiction from Bunyan to Beckett*, Baltimore, Johns Hopkins University Press, 1974, p. xiii.

56. Goffman, *Strategic Interaction*, p. 60.

57. Booth, *Rhetoric of Irony*, pp. 99–100.

58. Goffman defines virtual or tacit moves using George Herbert Mead's principles: "adapting to the other's response before it has been called forth. . . . " See *Strategic Interaction*, p. 60.

59. *Ibid.*, p. 15.

60. *Ibid.*, p. 22.

61. Erving Goffman, *Stigma: Notes on the Management of Spoiled Identity*, Englewood Cliffs, NJ, Prentice-Hall, 1963, p. 14.

62. Jeff Coulter, "Transparency of Mind: The Availability of Subjective Phenomena," *Philosophy of the Social Sciences* 7 (December, 1977), 337, 338.

63. The phrase is Goffman's; *Forms of Talk*, p. 230.

64. Cf. Goffman, *Frame Analysis*, p. 33.

65. Guerard, *op. cit.*, p. 49. The phrase is mine.

66. Goffman, *Frame Analysis*, p. 122.

67. *Ibid.*

68. On the "capture of consciousness," see William H. Gass, *Fiction and the Figures of Life*, New York, Vintage, 1972, p. 33.

69. E. M. Forster, *Aspects of the Novel*, New York, Harcourt Brace Jovanovich, 1955, p. 23.

70. William H. Whyte, Jr., "Literature in an Organization Society" in Irving Deer and Harriet A. Deer (eds.), *The Popular Arts: A Critical Reader*, New York, Scribner's, 1967, p. 61.

71. Abraham Kaplan, "The Aesthetics of the Popular Arts" in Deer and Deer, *op. cit.*, p. 320.

72. Cf. Wolfgang Iser, *The Act of Reading*, Baltimore, Johns Hopkins University Press, 1978, p. 83; Kaplan, "Aesthetics," p. 321.

73. Goffman, *Presentation of Self*, p. 104. Significantly, the author-reader team has no audience; it is a distorted version of the teams Goffman analyzes.

74. *Ibid.*, p. 83; Goffman, *Asylums*, p. 189; Goffman, *Presentation of Self*, pp. 9–10; *ibid.*, p. 10.

75. Goffman, *Interaction Ritual*, p. 62.

76. *Ibid.*, p. 171.

77. Goffman, *Presentation of Self*, p. 207; *Interaction Ritual*, p. 174.

78. Goffman, *Behavior in Public Places: Notes on the Social Organization of Gatherings*, New York, Free Press, 1963, p. 19.

79. Goffman, *Interaction Ritual*, p. 162.

80. Goffman, *Asylums*, p. 309.

81. Janice A. Radway, *Reading the Romance: Women, Patriarchy, and Popular Literature*, Chapel Hill, University of North Carolina Press, 1984, pp. 120–22.

82. Joyce Carol Oates, *(Woman) Writer: Occasions and Opportunities*, New York, Dutton, 1989, p. 120.

83. *Ibid.*, p. 192.

84. Italo Calvino, *The Uses of Literature: Essays*, New York, Harcourt Brace Jovanovich, tr. Patrick Creagh, 1986, p. 26.

85. Alex Zwerdling, *Virginia Woolf and the Real World*, Berkeley and Los Angeles, University of California Press, 1986, p. 35.

Chapter Eight

1. Jane Austen, *Northanger Abbey*, New York, Dell, 1967, p. 55.

2. See Harold Bloom, *Kabbalah and Criticism*, New York, Seabury Press, 1975; *A Map of Misreading*, New York, Oxford University Press, 1975; also Walter L. Reed, *An Exemplary History of the Novel: The Quixotic Versus the Picaresque*, Chicago, University of Chicago Press, 1981, p. 265.

3. On encoding, see Orrin Klapp, *Models of Social Order: An Introduction to Sociological Theory*, Palo Alto, CA, National Press Books, 1973.

4. Henry Fielding, *The History of Tom Jones: A Foundling*, New York, Modern Library, 1950, p. 106.

5. Masao Myoshi, *The Divided Self: A Perspective on the Literature of the Victorians*, New York, New York University Press, 1969, p. 4.

6. William Gass in Joe David Bellamy (ed.), *The New Fiction: Interviews with Innovative American Writers*, Urbana, University of Illinois Press, 1974, p. 43.

7. Wolfgang Iser, *The Implied Reader: Patterns of Communication in Prose Fiction from Bunyan to Beckett*, Baltimore, Johns Hopkins University Press, 1974, p. 62; Ian Watt, *The Rise of the Novel: Studies in Defoe, Richardson and Fielding*, Berkeley and San Francisco, University of California Press, 1957, p. 189.

8. Mary McCarthy, *Ideas and the Novel*, New York, Harcourt Brace Jovanovich, 1980, p. 43.

9. Watt, *op. cit.*, p. 288.

10. Charles Dickens, *David Copperfield*, New York, Modern Library, 1950.

11. Fielding, *op. cit.*, p. 75.

12. *Ibid.,* p. 346.

13. William Makepeace Thackeray, *The History of Pendennis: His Fortunes and His Misfortunes; His Friends and His Greatest Enemy,* New York, Clarke, Given and Hooper, University Edition, n.d., p. 74; Dickens, *op. cit.,* p. 1; Anthony Trollope, *Barchester Towers,* New York, New American Library, 1963, pp. 289, 406–7.

14. Louis Auchincloss, *The Embezzler,* Boston, Hougton Mifflin, 1966, p. 123; Ford Madox Ford, *The Good Solider: A Tale of Passion,* New York, Vintage, 1955, p. 12; Kurt Vonnegut, *Breakfast of Champions,* New York, Dell, 1974, p. 218.

15. McCarthy, *op. cit.,* p. 56. The bulk of this part of the chapter is only a slight revision of ideas I first formulated in "Literary Socialization and Literary Interaction: Novelists on Reading Novels," *Current Perspectives in Social Theory* 6 (1985), 261–78.

16. Austen, *op. cit.,* p. 68.

17. Thackeray, *op. cit.,* p. 148.

18. E. M. Forster, *A Room with a View,* New York, Vintage, 1961, p. 57.

19. Henry James, *The Tragic Muse,* New York, Crowell, 1975, p. 57.

20. Willa Cather, *The Professor's House,* New York, Vintage, 1973, pp. 150, 156, 169–70.

21. Virgina Woolf, *To the Lighthouse,* New York, Harcourt Brace Jovanovich, 1927, p. 125.

22. Walker Percy, *The Moviegoer,* New York, Avon, 1980, p. 125.

23. Frederick Exley, *A Fan's Notes: A Fictional Memoir,* New York, Pocket Books, 1977, pp. 1–2.

24. John Irving, *The World According to Garp,* New York, Dutton, 1978, p. 111.

25. Kurt Vonnegut, Jr., *Player Piano,* New York, Dell, 1974, p. 41.

26. Max Frisch, *Homo Faber,* New York, Harcourt Brace Jovanovich, tr. Michael Bullock, 1971, pp. 12, 72, 79.

27. Malcolm Bradbury, *The Social Context of Modern English Literature,* New York, Schocken, 1971, p. 84.

28. Albert J. Guerard, *The Triumph of the Novel: Dostoevsky, Dickens, Faulkner,* Chicago, University of Chicago Press, 1976, pp. 33–36.

29. Carla L. Peterson, *The Determined Reader: Gender and Culture in the Novel from Napoleon to Victoria,* New Brunswick, NJ, Rutgers University Press, 1987, pp. 19, 33–34.

30. *Ibid.*, p. 3.

31. *Ibid.*, p. 2.

32. Paul DiMaggio, "Classification in Art," *American Sociological Review* 52 (August, 1987), 441, 449, 451.

33. Italo Calvino, *The Uses of Literature: Essays*, New York, Harcourt Brace Jovanovich, tr. Patrick Creagh, 1986, pp. 36, 68.

34. Robert Scholes, *Fabulation and Metafiction*, Urbana, University of Illinois Press, 1979, p. 30.

35. Ellen Moers, *Literary Women*, Garden City, NY, Anchor Books, 1977, p. 219.

36. Joyce W. Warren, *The American Narcissus: Individualism and Women in Nineteenth-Century American Fiction*, New Brunswick, NJ, Rutgers University Press, 1984, p. 71.

37. Ann Douglas, *The Feminization of American Culture*, New York, Avon Books, 1978, pp. 94, 112.

38. Nina Baym, "The Madwoman and Her Languages: Why I Don't Do Feminist Literary Theory," *Tulsa Studies in Women's Literature* 3 (Spring/Fall, 1984), 46.

39. James D. Hart, *The Popular Book: A History of America's Literary Taste*, New York, Oxford University Press, 1950, p. 57.

40. Gaye Tuchman with Nina Fortin, *Edging Women Out: Victorian Novelists, Publishers, and Social Change*, New Haven, Yale University Press, 1989, p. 7.

41. Douglas, *op. cit.*, p. 72.

42. Alfred Habegger, *Gender, Fantasy, and Realism in American Literature*, New York, Columbia University Press, 1982, p. ix.

43. Hart, *op. cit.*, p. 91.

44. Monica Correa Fryckstedt, "Defining the Domestic Genre: English Women Novelists of the 1850s," *Tulsa Studies in Women's Literature* 6 (Spring, 1987), 10.

45. Habegger, *op. cit.*, p. ix.

46. Tuchman with Fortin, *op. cit.*, pp. 7, 8.

47. George Levine, *The Realistic Imagination: English Fiction from Frankenstein to Lady Chatterly*, Chicago, University of Chicago Press, 1981, p. 13.

48. Tuchman with Fortin, *op. cit.*, pp. 7, 8.

49. Hart, *op. cit.*, p. 64; Michael Davitt Bell, *The Development of American Romance: The Sacrifice of Relation*, Chicago, University of Chicago Press, 1980, p. 41.

50. Levine, *op. cit.*, pp. 85, 89, 133.

51. *Ibid.*, p. 5.

52. Tuchman with Fortin, *op. cit.*, p. 7.

53. Douglas, *op. cit.*, p. 14.

54. Bell, *op. cit.*, pp. 7, 242.

55. Levine, *op. cit.*, pp. 11, 18, 204, 253.

56. *Ibid.*, pp. 8, 9.

57. Tuchman with Fortin, *op. cit.*, p. 10.

58. Levine, *op. cit.*, p. 133.

59. Douglas, *op. cit.*, p. 284.

60. Tuchman with Fortin, *op. cit.*, p. 66.

61. Elaine Showalter, *A Literature of Their Own*, Princeton, Princeton University Press, 1977, p. 75.

62. Tuchman with Fortin, *op. cit.*, p. 240.

63. Douglas, *op. cit.*, p. 293.

64. *Ibid.*, p. 283.

65. Levine, *op. cit.*, pp. 42, 140.

66. *Ibid.*, pp. 181–82.

67. Habegger, *op. cit.*, pp. ix, 252, 275.

68. Levine, *op. cit.*, pp. 317, 319.

69. Habegger, *op. cit.*, p. 65.

70. *Ibid.*, p. vii.

71. *Ibid.*, p. 106.

72. Levine, *op. cit.*, p. 56

73. *Ibid.*, p. 170.

74. Elizabeth Ermarth, "Fictional Consensus and Female Casualties" in Carolyn G. Heilbrun and Margaret R. Higonnet (eds.), *The Representation of*

Women in Fiction: Selected Papers from the English Institute, 1981, Baltimore, Johns Hopkins University Press, 1983, pp. 9, 10, 14.

75. Alan Swingewood, "Towards the Sociology of the Novel," Part Three in Diana T. Laurenson and Alan Swingewood, *The Sociology of Literature,* New York, Schocken Books, 1972, pp. 193–94.

76. Habegger, *op. cit.,* pp. 117, 172.

77. *Ibid.,* p. 205.

78. Cited in Levine, *op. cit.,* p. 157.

79. Tuchman with Fortin, *op. cit.,* pp. 3, 5.

80. Cf. Zahava Karl McKeon, *Novels and Arguments: Inventing Rhetorical Criticism,* Chicago, University of Chicago Press, 1982, p. 230.

81. Georg Simmel, *On Women, Sexuality, and Love,* New Haven, Yale University Press, tr. Guy Oakes, 1984, p. 106.

82. Cf. McKeon, *op. cit.,* p. 109.

83. DiMaggio, "Classification in Art," 441, 442, 448.

Chapter Nine

1. Thomas Wolfe, *You Can't Go Home Again,* New York, Dell, 1960, pp. 40, 459.

2. *Ibid.,* pp. 639, 661.

3. Maxwell Perkins, "Publishing Thomas Wolfe" in Bill Henderson (ed.), *The Art of Literary Publishing: Editors on their Craft,* Yonkers, NY, Pushcart Book Press, 1980, p. 249.

4. Dorothy Commins, *What Is an Editor? Saxe Commins at Work,* Chicago, University of Chicago Press, 1978, p. 85.

5. Hamilton Basso, *The View from Pompey's Head,* Garden City, NY, Doubleday, 1954, pp. 108–9, 32, 149, 26.

6. Doris Lessing, *A Small Personal Voice: Essays, Reviews, Interviews,* New York, Vintage Books, 1975, p. 29.

7. Cited by James Sloan Allen, *The Romance of Commerce and Culture: Capitalism, Modernism, and the Chicago-Aspen Crusade for Cultural Reform,* Chicago, University of Chicago Press, 1983, p. 225.

8. Cited by Diana T. Laurenson, "The Writer and Society," Part Two of

Diana T. Laurenson and Alan Swingewood, *The Sociology of Literature*, New York, Schocken Books, 1972, p. 131.

9. Howard S. Becker, *Art Worlds*, Berkeley and San Francisco, University of California Press, 1982, p. 94.

10. Walter Abish in Larry McCaffery and Sinda Gregory, *Alive and Writing: Interviews with American Authors of the 1980s*, Urbana, University of Illinois Press, 1987, p. 17.

11. C. Wright Mills, "The Cultural Apparatus" in Irving Louis Horowitz (ed.), *Power, Politics and People: The Collected Essays of C. Wright Mills*, New York, Oxford University Press, 1967, pp. 406, 407, 411.

12. Per Gedin, *Literature in the Marketplace*, London, Faber, tr. George Bisset, 1977, p. 17.

13. Robert Escarpit, *The Book Revolution*, London, George C. Harrap & Company, 1966, p. 151.

14. Mills, "Cultural Apparatus," p. 412.

15. Arnold Hauser, *The Sociology of Art*, Chicago, University of Chicago Press, tr. Kenneth J. Northcott, 1982, pp. 431, 489.

16. *Ibid.*, pp. 465, 467, 490.

17. Steven C. Dubin, *Bureaucratizing the Muse: Public Funds and the Cultural Worker*, Chicago, University of Chicago Press, 1987, pp. 26, 28, 138, 158.

18. *Ibid.*, pp. 156, 166.

19. Becker, *op. cit.*, p. 95.

20. Mills, "Cultural Apparatus," p. 419.

21. Tom Robbins in McCaffery and Gregory, *op. cit.*, p. 225.

22. Peter Monaghan, "Anthropologist Who Sparked Dispute by Criticizing Margaret Mead's Research on Samoan Life Finds New Backing for his Claims; Some Still Skeptical," *The Chronicle of Higher Education* (August 2, 1989), A4–A6.

23. Ellen K. Coughlin, "Report Blames Racism and a Sagging U.S. Economy for Stagnation in Progress of Black Americans," *The Chronicle of Higher Education* (August 2, 1989), A4–A5, A7.

24. Pierre Bourdieu, *Distinction: A Social Critique of the Judgement of Taste*, Cambridge, Harvard University Press, tr. Richard Nice, 1984, p. 67.

25. Lillian S. Robinson, "Treason Our Text: Feminist Challenges to the Literary Canon," *Tulsa Studies in Women's Literature* 2 (Spring, 1983), 67.

26. Hauser, *op. cit.*, p. 489.

27. Chandler B. Grannis, "Introduction: General View of a Diverse Industry" in Chandler B. Grannis (ed.), *What Happens in Book Publishing*, New York, Columbia University Press, Second Edition, 1967, p. 4.

28. John Tebbel, "A Brief History of American Bookselling" in Charles B. Anderson (ed.), *Bookselling in America and the World: Some Observations & Recollections*, New York, Quadrangle, 1975, p. 3.

29. Carolyn T. Anthony, "John Wiley at 175," *Publishers Weekly* 222 (September 24, 1982), 42.

30. Anna Lou Ashby, "Harper & Bros." in Madeleine B. Stern (ed.), *Publishers for Mass Entertainment in Nineteenth Century America*, Boston, G. K. Hall, 1980, pp. 153, 154; Cass Canfield "An Introductory Review of Harper Highlights" in Stern, *op. cit.*, pp. 147–49.

31. Frank Arthur Mumby, *Publishing and Bookselling*, London, Jonathan Cape, 1956, pp. 237–46.

32. John Gross, *The Rise and Fall of the Man of Letters: A Study of the Idiosyncratic and the Humane in Modern Literature*, New York, Macmillan, 1969, p. 199.

33. Lawrence Parke Murphy, "Beadle & Co." in Stern, *op. cit.*, pp. 41, 42.

34. *Ibid.*, pp. 44, 47.

35. Madeleine B. Stern, "Introduction" in Stern, *op. cit.*, p. xv.

36. James D. Hart, *The Popular Book: A History of America's Literary Taste* New York, Oxford University Press, 1950, p. 184.

37. Frank Arthur Mumby, *Publishing and Bookselling: A History from Earliest Times to the Present Day*, London, Jonathan Cape, Fourth Edition, 1956, p. 321; Freeman Lewis, "Mass Market Paperbacks" in Grannis, *op. cit.*, p. 379.

38. Ralph Daigh, *Maybe You Should Write a Book*, Englewood Cliffs, NJ, Prentice-Hall, 1977, pp. 16, 17, 26.

39. Kenneth C. Davis, *Two-Bit Culture: The Paperbacking of America*, Boston, Houghton Mifflin, 1984, p. 382.

40. Arthur Plotnik, "Book, Editors: A Special Breed," *Publishers Weekly* 222 (October 29, 1982), 22.

41. Dan Lacy, "The Economics of Publishing, or Adam Smith and Literature" in Jean Spealman Kujoth (compiler), *Book Publishing: Inside Views*, Metuchen, NJ, Scarecrow Press, 1971, pp. 35, 36.

42. Simon Michael Bessie, "Small Publishing—Is It Beautiful?" in Henderson, *op. cit.*, p. 114.

43. Lacy, "Economics of Publishing," p. 34.

44. John Fischer, "Myths about Publishing," in Kujoth, *op. cit.*, p. 66; Ted Solotaroff, "Publishers, Booksellers, Readers, and Writers: Some Straws in a Whirlwind" in Henderson, *op. cit.*, p. 84.

45. Jonathan Galassi, "The Double Agent: The Role of the Literary Editor in the Commerical Publishing House" in Henderson, *op. cit.*, p. 78.

46. Solotaroff, "Publishers," p. 4.

47. Bill Adler, *Inside Publishing*, Indianapolis, Bobbs-Merrill, 1982, p. 17.

48. Bessie, "Small Publishing," p. 113.

49. See Edward Uhlan, *The Rogue of Publishers' Row: Confessions of a Publisher*, New York, Exposition Press, 1975.

50. A less obvious (and relatively inaccessible, granted) option is to establish one's own publishing business, as Virginia and Leonard Woolf did with Hogarth Press. For a good survey of publishers' and authors' relative needs and problems, see Peter H. Mann, *Author-Publisher Relationships in Scholarly Publishing*, London, The British Library Research and Development Department, 1978.

51. Susan Howe and Charles Ruas, "New Directions: An Interview with James Laughlin" in Henderson, *op. cit.*, p. 39; Sir Stanley Unwin, *The Truth about Publishing*, London, George Allen & Unwin Ltd., Sixth Edition, 1950, pp. 329–30.

52. John Leonard, "Dedication—For Henry Robbins (1927–1979)" in Henderson, *op. cit.*, p. vii.

53. Harvey Swados, "The Image in the Mirror" in Granville Hicks (ed.), *The Living Novel: A Symposium*, New York, Collier, 1962, p. 177.

54. Daigh, *op. cit.*, p. 25.

55. Frank Swinnerton, "Authorship" in John Hampden (ed.), *The Book World*, London, Thomas Nelson, 1935, p. 14.

56. Adler, *op. cit.*, p. 56.

57. Escarpit, *op. cit.*, pp. 5–6, 130.

58. Joseph Marks, "Subsidiary Rights and Permissions" in Grannis, *op. cit.*, pp. 231–40.

59. Daigh, *op. cit.*, p. 82; Dean R. Koontz, *How to Write Best-Selling Fiction*, Cincinnati, Writer's Digest Books, 1981, p. 34. 68; Marks, "Subsidiary Rights," p. 230.

60. Solatoroff, "Publishers," p. 6.

61. John Hall, *The Sociology of Literature*, New York, Longman, 1979, p. 99.

62. John Farrar, "Securing and Selling the Manuscript" in Grannis, *op cit.*, p. 35.

63. John Oliver Brown, "Literary Agents" in Kujoth, *op. cit.*, p. 248.

64. Nadine Gordimer in George Plimpton (ed.), *Writers at Work: The Paris Interviews*, Sixth Series, New York, Viking Press, 1984, pp. 253–54.

65. Daigh, *op. cit.*, p. 70; Farrar, "Securing and Selling," p. 36.

66. Adler, *op. cit.*, pp. 12, 17, 58.

67. William Goyen in Plimpton, *op. cit.*, p. 183.

68. Ernest Hemingway in Van Wyck Brooks (ed.) *Writers at Work: The Paris Review Interviews*, Second Series, New York, Viking Press, 1965, p. 227.

69. Commins, *op. cit.*, pp. 195, 219–21.

70. *Ibid.*, p. 137.

71. Solotaroff says at least one company does this; "Publishers," p. 4.

72. Paul DiMaggio, "Classification in Art," *American Sociological Review* 52 (August, 1987), 446, 449, 450; also see Jacques Dubois and Pascal Durand, "Literary Field and Classes of Texts" in Phillippe Desan, Priscilla Parkhurst Ferguson, and Wendy Griswold (eds.), *Literature and Social Practice*, Chicago, University of Chicago Press, tr. Priscilla Parkhurst Ferguson, pp. 148–49.

73. Ursula Le Guin in McCaffery and Gregory, *op. cit.*, 1989, pp. 177, 187.

74. Georg Simmel, *On Women, Sexuality, and Love*, New Haven, Yale University Press, tr. Guy Oakes, 1984, p. 65.

75. Kurt Lang, "Mass, Class, and the Reviewer" in Milton C. Albrecht, James H. Barnett, and Mason Griff (eds.), *The Sociology of Art and Literature*, New York, Praeger, 1970, p. 460.

76. Patrick Parrinder, *Authors and Authority: A Study of English Literary Criticism and its Relation to Culture, 1750–1900*, Boston, Routledge & Kegan Paul, 1977, pp. 1, 5.

77. Gross, *op. cit.*, pp. 1–2.

78. Judith R. Kramer, "The Social Role of the Literary Critic" in Albrecht, Garnett, and Griff, *op. cit.*, pp. 439, 445.

79. Malcolm Bradbury, *The Social Context of Modern English Literature*, New York, Schocken, 1971, p. 196.

80. Kramer, "The Social Role...," p. 444.

81. Northrop Frye, *The Educated Imagination*, Bloomington, Indiana University Press, 1964, p. 105; *The Stubborn Structure: Essays on Criticism and Society*, Ithaca, NY, Cornell University Press, 1970, pp. 87–88.

82. Kramer, "The Social Role...," p. 446.

83. Zahava Karl McKeon, *Novels and Arguments: Inventing Rhetorical Criticism*, Chicago, University of Chicago Press, 1982, p. 231.

84. George Levine, *The Realtistic Imagination: English Fiction from Frankenstein to Lady Chatterly*, Chicago, University of Chicago Press, 1981, p. 4.

85. Hauser, *op. cit.*, pp. 490, 465.

86. *Ibid.*, pp. 435, 460.

87. McKeon, *op. cit.*, p. 74.

88. Hauser, *op. cit.*, p. 476.

89. McKeon, *op. cit.*, pp. 234, 111.

90. Cheryl B. Torsney, "The Tradition of Gender: Constance Fenimore Woolson and Henry James" in Shirley Marchalonis (ed.), *Patrons and Protegées: Gender, Friendship, and Writing in Nineteenth-Century America*, New Brunswick, NJ, Rutgers University Press, 1988, pp. 161, 162, 163.

91. Diane Johnson, *Terrorists and Novelists*, New York, Knopf, 1982, p. 21.

92. Wendy Griswold, "The Fabrication of Meaning: Literary Interpretation in the United States, Great Britain, and the West Indies," *American Journal of Sociology* 92 (March, 1987), 1082, 1093, 1094, 1096, 1097, 1101, 1105.

93. Marjorie L. DeVault, "Novel Readings: The Social Organization of Interpretation," *American Journal of Sociology* 95 (January, 1990), 898, 899, 906, 911, 917.

94. Eric Kraft, "At Last, a Boy to Toy With" (Review of *Second Fiddle* by Mary Wesley), *The New York Times Book Review* (July 30, 1989), 8; Howard Frank Moser, "Far from Kennebunkport" (Review of *Monkey Bay* by Elaine Ford), *The New York Times Book Review* (August 6, 1989), 9; Josh Rubins, "They All Want a Piece of the Legend" (Review of *Various Miracles* and *Swann* by Carol Shields), *The New York Times Book Review* (August 6, 1989), 11.

95. Desmond Ryan, "Sleeping His Way to the Middle" (Review of *Sacred Monster* by Donald E. Westlake), *The New York Times Book Review* (July 30, 1989), 12.

96. Brad Leithauser, "Microscopy" (Review of *The Mezzanine* by Nicholson Baker), *The New York Review of Books* (August 17, 1989), 15.

97. Phillip A. Goldberg, "Are Women Prejudiced Against Women?" *Trans-Action* 5 (1968), 28–30.

98. Griswold, "The Fabrication of Meaning," 1082.

99. Becker, *op. cit.*, pp. 131, 348.

100. Cf. Alain Viala, "Prismatic Effects" in Desan, Ferguson, and Griswold, *op. cit.*, p. 162.

101. Jane Tompkins, *Sensational Designs: The Cultural Work of American Fiction, 1790–1860*, New York, Oxford University Press, 1985; Gerald Graff and William E. Cain, "Peace Plan for the Canon Wars," *National Forum* LXIX (Summer, 1989), 9.

102. Bernard Malamud in Plimpton, *op. cit.*, p. 165; Dolores Shelley, "A Conversation with May Sarton," *Women & Literature* 7 (Spring, 1979), 34.

103. Kurt Vonnegut in Plimpton, *op. cit.*, pp. 225–26.

104. Cf. Carolyn T. Anthony, "Are Reviewers Fair to Trade Paperbacks?" *Publishers Weekly* 222 (October 15, 1982), 29–36.

105. William S. Gray and Ruth Munroe, *The Reading Interests and Habits of Adults: A Preliminary Report*, New York, Macmillan, 1930, p. 266.

106. Daigh, *op. cit.*, pp. 78, 79.

107. Plotnik, "Book Editors," 22.

108. Adler, *op. cit.*, p. 208.

109. G. Roysce Smith, "The Future of Bookselling" in Anderson, *op. cit.*, p. 139; Adler, *op. cit.*, p. 208.

110. Judith Appelbaum and Nancy Evans, *How to Get Happily Published*, New York, Harper & Row, 1979, p. 210.

111. John Tebbel, "Publishing Books to Sell by Mail" in Grannis, *op. cit.*, p. 400.

112. Marks, "Subsidiary Rights," p. 233.

113. S. J. Diamond, "Book Club Selling Methods Debated." *Las Vegas Review-Journal*, May 23, 1982, p. 10C.

114. Leo Gurko, *Heroes, Highbrows, and the Popular Mind*, New York, Charter Books, 1962, p. 147; Diamond, "Book Club Selling Methods."

115. Dean Bender, "How They Choose the Book of the Month," *The Pensacola Journal*, September 2, 1981, p. 4D.

116. Janice Radway, "The Book-of-the-Month Club and the General Reader: On the Uses of 'Serious' Fiction" in Desan, Ferguson, and Griswold, *op. cit.*, p. 161.

117. James Michener, "A Writer's Public Image" in Kujoth, *op. cit.*, pp. 193, 200.

118. *Ibid.*, pp. 197–98.

119. Mary G. DeJong, "Lines from a Partly Published Drama: The Romance of Frances Sargent Osgood and Edgar Allen Poe" in Marchalonis, *op. cit.*, p. 32.

120. Allen, *op. cit.*, pp. 38–39.

121. Davis, *op. cit.*, p. 344.

122. Lisa Pater Faranda, "A Social Necessity: The Friendship of Sherwood Bonner and Henry Wadsworth Longfellow" in Marchalonis, *op. cit.*, pp. 202, 206.

123. Alfred Habegger, *Gender, Fantasy, and Realism in American Literature*, New York, Columbia University Press, 1982, p. 177.

124. Gore Vidal in Charles Ruas, *Conversations with American Writers*, Alfred A. Knopf, 1985, p. 67.

125. Dolores Shelley, "A Conversation with May Sarton," *Women & Literature 7* (Spring, 1979), 33; Rebecca West in Plimpton, *op. cit.*, p. 27.

126. Davis, *op. cit.*, pp. 361–63; also see Janice A. Radway, *Reading the Romance: Women, Patriarchy, and Popular Literature*, Chapel Hill, University of North Carolina Press, 1984, pp. 18ff.

127. Dubin, *op. cit.*, p. 158.

128. These data are from James Vinson and D. L. Kirkpatrick (eds.), *Great Writers of the English Language: Novelists and Prose Writers*, New York, St. Martin's Press, 1979.

129. Scott Walker (ed.), *Buying Time: An Anthology Celebrating 20 Years of the Literary Program of the National Endowment for the Arts*, St. Paul, Graywolf Press, 1985.

130. Gedin, *op. cit.*, p. 188.

131. Becker, *op. cit.*, p. 126.

132. Fay Weldon, *The Hearts and Lives of Men*, New York, Dell Books, 1989, p. 187.

133. Goldmann, "Possibilities of Cultural Action . . . ," pp. 47–48, 49.

134. Jeffrey C. Goldfarb, *On Cultural Freedom: An Exploration of Public Life in Poland and America*, Chicago, University of Chicago Press, 1982, pp. 4, 26, 29, 32, 45, 112, 113, 123.

Notes   253

Chapter Ten

1. Randall Jarrell, *Pictures from an Institution: A Comedy*, New York, Avon, 1980, p. 50. Subsequent references in the text are to this edition.

2. Bruce Mazlish, *A New Science: The Breakdown of Connections and the Birth of Sociology*, New York, Oxford University Press, 1989, p. 12.

3. *Ibid.*, pp. 14, 48, 57, 103, 137, 23.

4. Ellen Moers, *Literary Women*, Garden City, NY, Anchor Books, 1977, pp. 29, 125; Roger Dataller, *The Plain Man and the Novel*, Port Washington, NY, Kennikat, 1970, p. 40.

5. Terry Eagleton, *Marxism and Literary Criticism*, Berkeley and Los Angeles, University of California Press, 1976, p. 1; Lionell Trilling, *Beyond Culture: Essays on Literature and Learning*, New York, Viking Press, 1965, p. 13.

6. Cited by Lionel Trilling, *The Liberal Imagination: Essays on Literature and Society*, Garden City, NY, Doubleday Anchor Books, 1950, p. 32.

7. Moers, *op. cit.*, p. 382.

8. T. S. Eliot, *Notes toward the Definition of Culture*, New York, Harcourt, Brace, 1949, p. 35; Philip Rahv, *Literature and the Sixth Sense*, Boston, Houghton Mifflin, 1969, p. viii; Eliot, *op. cit.*, p. 69.

9. James Clifford, "Introduction: Partial Truths" in James Clifford and George E. Marcus (eds.), *Writing Culture: The Poetics and Poltics of Ethnography*, Berkeley and Los Angeles, University of California Press, 1986, p. 3; Wolfe Lepenies, *Between Literature and Science: The Rise of Sociology*, New York, Cambridge University Press, tr. R. J. Hollingdale, 1988, p. 305.

10. Clifford, "Introduction," p. 3; Felix Fastian (aka Peter L. Berger), *The Enclaves*, Garden City, NY, Doubleday, 1965; Richard Sennett, *The Frog Who Dared to Croak*, New York, Farrar, Straus & Giroux, 1982.

11. See, for example, Harold Bloom, *Kabbalah and Criticism*, New York, Seabury Press, 1975, p. 81; Wolfgang Iser, *The Act of Reading: A Theory of Aesthetic Response*, Baltimore, Johns Hopkins University Press, 1978, p. 166.

12. Morroe Berger, *Real and Imagined Worlds: The Novel and Social Science*, Cambridge, Harvard University Press, 1977, p. 5; Clifford, "Introduction," p. 5.

13. Lennard J. Davis, "A Social History of Fact and Fiction: Authorial Disavowal in the Early English Novel" in Edward W. Said (ed.), *Literature and Society*, Baltimore, Johns Hopkins University, 1986, pp. 131, 145; also see Lennard Davis, *Factual Fictions: The Origins of the English Novel*, New York, Columbia University Press, 1985.

14. Stephan Fuchs, "The Social Organization of Scientific Knowledge," *Sociological Theory* 4 (Fall, 1986), 127.

15. Clifford, "Introduction," p. 15.

16. Stephan Fuchs and Jonathan H. Turner, "What Makes a Science 'Mature'?: Patterns of Organizational Control in Scientific Production," *Sociological Theory* 4 (Fall, 1986), 149.

17. Cf. Barbara Johnson, *The Critical Difference: Essays in the Contemporary Rhetoric of Reading*, Baltimore, Johns Hopkins University Press, 1985.

18. Lepenies, *op. cit.*, pp. 1, 14.

19. C. P. Snow, *The Two Cultures: And a Second Look*, New York, Cambridge University Press, 1969; also see Lepenies, *op. cit.*, pp. 155–58.

20. Susan Sontag, *Against Interpretation and Other Essays*, New York, Delta, 1967, p. 299.

21. Michael Polanyi and Harry Prosch, *Meaning*, Chicago, University of Chicago Press, 1975.

22. David Caute, "Commitment without Empathy: A Writer's Notes on Politics, Theatre, and the Novel," *TriQuarterly* 30 (Spring, 1974), 63; Richard H. Brown, *A Poetic for Sociology: Toward a Logic of Discovery for the Human Sciences*, New York, Cambridge University Press, 1978, p. 3.

23. Northrop Frye, *The Stubborn Structure: Essays on Criticism and Society*, Ithaca, NY, Cornell University Press, 1970, p. 44; Brown, *op. cit.*, p. 3.

24. Wayne C. Booth, *Critical Understanding: The Power and Limits of Pluralism*, Chicago, University of Chicago Press, 1979, p. 244.

25. Robert Nisbet, *Sociology as an Art Form*, New York, Oxford University Press, 1976, p. 15.

26. Roland Barthes, *Image-Music-Text*, New York, Hill and Wang, tr. Stephen Heath, 1977, p. 180.

27. Stephen Spender, *The Making of a Poem*, New York, Norton, 1962, p. 16.

28. Clifford Geertz, "Found in Translation: On the Social History of the Moral Imagination," *The Georgia Review* 31 (Winter, 1977), 796.

29. John Crowe Ransom, *Beating the Bushes: Selected Essays 1941–1970*, New York, New Directions, 1972, pp. 2–3.

30. Frye, *op. cit.*, pp. 40, 55.

31. Martin Green, *Transatlantic Patterns: Cultural Comparisons of England with America*, New York, Basic, 1977, p. 21.

32. Alfred Schutz, *The Phenomenology of the Social World*, Evanston, Northwestern University Press, trs. George Walsh and Frederick Lehnert, 1967, p. 113.

33. Peter C. Sederberg with Nancy B. Sederberg, "Transmitting the Nontransmissible: The Function of Literature in the Pursuit of Social Knowledge," *Philosophy and Phenomenological Research* 36 (December, 1975), 158.

34. Roland Barthes, *S/Z*, New York, Hill and Wang, tr. Richard Miller, 1974, p. 135.

35. Alfred Schutz, *Collected Papers I: The Problem of Social Reality*, The Hague, Nijhoff, ed. Maurice Natanson, 1973, p. 42.

36. E. D. Hirsch, Jr., *The Aims of Interpretation*, Chicago, University of Chicago Press, 1976, p. 59.

37. Virginia Woolf, *Books and Portraits*, New York, Harcourt Brace Jovanovich, ed. Mary Lyon, 1977, p. 27.

38. Wayne C. Booth, *A Rhetoric of Irony*, Chicago, University of Chicago Press, 1975, p. 234.

39. Malcolm Bradbury, *The Social Context of Modern English Literature*, New York, Schocken, 1971, pp. 78–79.

40. Henry W. Wells, *The Realm of Literature*, Port Washington, NY, Kennikat, 1966, p. 165.

41. Nisbet, *op. cit.*, pp. 3, 8, 9.

42. Berger, *op. cit.*, p. 235.

43. Richard H. Brown, *op. cit.*, p. 1.

44. Richard Harvey Brown, *Society as Text: Essays on Rhetoric, Reason, and Reality*, Chicago, University of Chicago Press, 1987, pp. 118, 172ff.

45. Stanley Edgard Hyman, *The Tangled Bank: Darwin, Marx, Frazer and Freud as Imaginative Writers*, New York, Atheneum, 1962; Frederic Jameson, "The Vanishing Mediator; or, Max Weber as Storyteller" in *The Ideologies of Theory: Essays 1971–1986*, Vol. 1 *Situations of Theory*, Minneapolis, University of Minnesota Press, 1988 (orig. 1973); John Lofland, "Early Goffman: Style, Structure, Substance, Soul" in Jason Ditton (ed.), *The View from Goffman*, London, Macmillan, 1980, pp. 24–51; Peter K. Manning, "Goffman's Framing Order: Style as Structure" in *ibid.*, pp. 252–284; Tomoko Masuzawa, "The Sacred Difference: On Durkheim's Last Quest," *Representations* 23 (Summer, 1988), 25–50; Robert Paul Wolff, *Moneybags Must Be So Lucky: On the Literary Structure of Capital*, Amherst, University of Massachusetts Press, 1988; Bryan S. Green, *Literary Methods and Sociological Theory*, Chicago, University of Chicago Press, 1988.

46. *Ibid.*, pp. vii, 13.

47. Jameson, *op. cit.*, p. 61.

48. Robert C. Elliott, *The Literary Persona*, Chicago, University of Chicago Press, 1982, p. 62.

49. Roger Fowler, *Literature as Social Discourse: The Practice of Linguistic Criticism*, Bloomington, Indiana University Press, 1981, pp. 94, 112.

50. Clifford, "Introduction," p. 5.

51. Walter H. Bruford, "Literary Criticism and Sociology," *Yearbook of Comparative Criticism* V (1973), Joseph P. Strelka (ed.), 3.

52. Pierre Bourdieu, *Distinction: A Social Critique of the Judgement of Taste*, Cambridge, Harvard University Press, tr. Richard Nice, 1984, p. 499.

53. Stanley Aronowitz, *Science as Power: Discourse and Ideology in Modern Society*, Minneapolis, University of Minnesota Press, 1988, p. 351.

54. Wendy Griswold, "The Fabrication of Meaning: Literary Interpretation in the United States, Great Britain, and the West Indies," *American Journal of Sociology* 92 (March, 1987), 1111, 1078, 1105.

55. Green, *op. cit.*, pp. 18, 28.

56. *Ibid.*, pp. 89, 90, 108.

57. Fowler, *op. cit.*, p. 103.

58. Bourdieu, *op. cit.*, p. 5.

59. Frederic Jameson, *The Ideologies of Theory: Essays 1971–1986*, Vol. 2 *Syntax of History*, Minneapolis, Columbia University Press, 1988, p. 24; Wolff, *op. cit.*, p. 24.

60. Elizabeth Langland, *Society in the Novel*, Chapel Hill, University of North Carolina Press, 1984, pp. ix, 218.

61. Raymond Boudon, *The Crisis in Sociology: Problems of Sociological Epistemology*, New York, Columbia University Press, tr. Howard H. Davis, 1980, p. 152.

62. Green, *op. cit.*, p. 59.

63. *Ibid.*, p. 99.

64. Bourdieu, *op. cit.*, p. 160.

65. Griswold, "The Fabrication of Meaning," 1079.

66. Barbara Herrnstein Smith, "Narrative Versions, Narrative Theories"

in W. J. T. Mitchell (ed.), *On Narrative*, Chicago, University of Chicago Press, 1981, p. 213.

67. Green, *op. cit.*, p. 27.

68. Bourdieu, *op. cit.*, p. xiii.

69. Lewis A. Coser, *Men of Ideas: A Sociologist's View*, New York, Free Press, 1970, p. 291.

70. Fuchs, "The Social Organization...," 131.

71. *Ibid.*, 131; Fuchs and Turner, "What Makes a Science 'Mature'?...," 148.

72. Alfred Habegger, *Gender, Fantasy, and Realism in American Literature*, New York, Columbia University Press, 1982, p. 302.

73. Aronowitz, *op. cit.*, p. 279.

74. Brown, *Society as Text*, p. 68.

75. Barthes, *Image*, pp. 198, 201.

76. Frye, *Stubborn Structure*, p. 45.

77. Sheridan Baker, *The Practical Stylist*, New York, Crowell, Second Edition, 1969, p. 53; Malcolm Cowley, "Sociological Habit Patterns in Linguistic Transmogrification," *The Reporter* 15 (September 20, 1956), 43.

78. H. W. Fowler, *A Dictionary of Modern English Usage*, New York, Oxford University Press, Second Edition, rev. Sir Ernest Gowers, 1965, p. 570.

79. Cowley, "Sociological Habit."

80. Fowler, *op. cit.*, pp. 344–45.

81. Jarrell, *op. cit.*, pp. 48–49,.

82. Michel Foucault, *The Order of Things: An Archaeology of the Human Sciences*, New York, Vintage, 1973, p. 351.

83. Fyodor Dostoevsky, Letter to Madame Ch. D. Altrschevsky, 9 April 1876, Letters (1914), tr. Ethel Colburn Mayne, excerpted in Miriam Allot (ed.), *Novelists on the Novel*, New York, Columbia University Press, 1959, p. 127.

84. Howard Nemerov, *Journal of the Fictive Life*, New Brunswick, NJ, Rutgers University Press, 1965, p. 39.

85. "Consumer journalism" comes from Leonard Downie, Jr., *The New Muckrakers*, New York, Mentor Books, 1978, p. 239. The other labels come from Tom Wolfe, "The New Journalism" in Tom Wolfe, *The New Journalism* (with an anthology edited by Tom Wolfe and E. W. Johnson), New York, Harper & Row, 1973, pp. 24, 42, 52.

86. Norman Mailer, *The Armies of the Night: History as a Novel, The Novel as History,* New York, New American Library, 1968, p. 281.

87. Kai T. Erikson, *Everything in its Path: Destruction of Community in the Buffalo Creek Flood,* New York, Simon and Schuster, Touchstone Book, 1976, pp. 186, 193–94.

88. Angus Fletcher, "Foreword" in Angus Fletcher (ed.), *The Literature of Fact: Selected Papers from the English Institute,* New York, Columbia University Press, 1976, p. x.

89. Sederbergs, "Transmitting," 184.

90. *Ibid.,* 182, 185.

91. Joan Didion, *Slouching Toward Bethlehem,* New York, Simon and Schuster, Touchstone Book, 1979, p. xiv.

92. Hayden White, "The Fictions of Factual Presentation" in Fletcher, *op. cit.,* p. 31.

93. This section relies on my "Ideology, Perspective, and Praxis," *Human Studies* 4 (1981), 167–86.

94. John Hewitt and James Hall, "The Quasi-Theory of Communication and the Management of Dissent," *Social Problems* 18 (Summer, 1970), 17–27.

95. Cf. Elizabeth and Tom Burns, "Introduction" in Elizabeth and Tom Burns (eds.), *Sociology of Literature and Drama: Selected Readings,* Harmondsworth, Middlesex, England, Penguin, 1973, p. 14.

96. Italo Calvino, *The Uses of Literature: Essays,* New York, Harcourt Brace Jovanovich, tr. Patrick Creagh, 1986, p. 14.

97. Foucault, *op. cit.,* pp. 40, 91, 297.

98. Stanley Fish, *Is There a Text in This Class? The Authority of Interpretative Communities,* Cambridge, Harvard University Press, 1980, pp. 14, 16.

99. Fuchs, "The Social Organization...," 126.

100. Jameson, *The Ideologies of Theory,* Vol. 1, pp. 18, 69.

101. Smith, "Narrative Versions...," pp. 229, 228, 222.

102. Hayden White, "The Value of Narrativity in the Representation of Reality," in Mitchell, *op. cit.,* pp. 4, 23.

103. Brown, *Society as Text,* pp. 114, 134, 143, 148.

104. Clifford, "Introduction," pp. 2, 10, 13, 26.

105. Jacques Derrida, "The Law of Genre" in Mitchell, *op. cit.,* pp. 60, 52.

106. Paul DiMaggio, "Classification in Art," *American Sociological Review* 52 (August, 1987), 441.

107. Victor Turner, "Social Dramas and Stories about Them" in Mitchell, *op. cit.*, pp. 155–56, 157.

108. Arthur L. Stinchcombe, *Constructing Social Theory*, Chicago, University of Chicago Press, 1987, pp. 38, 40.

109. Norman K. Denzin, "Postmodern Social Theory," *Sociological Theory* 4 (Fall, 1986), 202.

110. Foucault, *op. cit.*, p. 320.

111. Jeffrey L. Sammons, *Literary Sociology and Practical Criticism: An Inquiry*, Bloomington, Indiana University Press, 1977, pp. xi, xii.

112. Elaine Showalter, "Women's Time, Women's Space: Writing the History of Feminist Criticism," *Tulsa Studies in Women's Literature* 3 (Spring/Fall, 1984), 41.

113. Celeste M. Schenck, "Feminism and Deconstruction: Re-Constructing the Elegy," *Tulsa Studies in Women's Literature* 5 (Spring, 1985), 23.

114. Foucault, *op. cit.*, p. 300.

Chapter Eleven

1. Saul Bellow, *Dangling Man*, New York, Avon, 1975, p. 102. Subsequent references in the text are to this edition.

2. John Barth, *Sabbatical: A Romance*, New York, Putnam's, 1982. Subsequent references in the text are to this edition.

3. Among the best sources on the fictive is André de Muralt, *The Idea of Phenomenology: Husserlian Exemplarism*, Evanston, IL, Northwestern University Press, tr. Gary L. Breckon, 1974; see pp. 54–58, in particular.

4. Alfred Schutz, *Collected Papers I: The Problem of Social Reality*, The Hague, Nijhoff, ed. Maurice Natanson, 1973, p. 253.

5. Henry James, *Roderick Hudson*, Boston, Houghton Mifflin, 1977, p. 383.

6. Charles Dickens, *Hard Times*, New York, Signet, 1961, p. 122.

7. *Ibid.*, p. 184.

8. Wallace Stevens, *The Necessary Angel: Essays on Reality and the Imagination*, New York, Vintage, 1951, p. 75.

9. Mircea Eliade, *Myths, Dreams and Realities: The Encounter between Contemporary Faiths and Archaic Realities*, New York, Harper Colophon, 1975, p. 45.

10. Ursula K. Le Guin, "It Was a Dark and Stormy Night; or, Why Are We Huddling about the Campfire?" in W. J. T. Mitchell (ed.), *On Narrative*, Chicago, University of Chicago Press, 1981, p. 195.

❦ Bibliography

Asterisks indicate novels in the sample discussed in Chapter Four.

Adisenshiah, Malcolm S., "Functionalities of Literacy." Pp. 65–78 in Leon Bataille (ed.), *A Turning Point for Literacy: Adult Education for Development, The Spirit and Declaration of Persepolis*. Proceedings of the International Symposium for Literacy, Persepolis, Iran. New York: Pergamon Press, 1976.

Adler, Bill, *Inside Publishing*. Indianapolis: Bobbs-Merrill, 1982.

Adorno, Theodor W., "Lyric Poetry and Society." *Telos* 20 (Summer, 1974): 56–71.

Allen, James Sloan, *The Romance of Commerce and Culture: Capitalism, Modernism, and the Chicago-Aspen Crusade for Cultural Reform*. Chicago: University of Chicago Press, 1983.

Allott, Miriam (ed.), *Novelists on the Novel*. New York: Columbia University Press, 1959.

Alter, Robert, "History and Imagination in the Nineteenth-Century Novel." *The Georgia Review* 29 (Spring, 1975): 42–60.

*Alther, Lisa, *Other Women*. New York: Knopf, 1984.

*Amis, Kingsley, *Lucky Jim*. New York: Viking, 1958 (orig. 1953).

————, *I Want It Now*. New York: Harcourt, Brace, 1969.

Anderson, N., "Author Becomes Producer," *Las Vegas Sun*, September 24, 1982.

Anderson, Patrick, "King of the 'Techno-Thriller." *The New York Times Magazine* (May 1, 1988): 54–55, 83–85.

Anderson, Charles B. (ed.), *Bookselling in America and the World: Some Observations & Recollections*. New York: Quadrangle, 1975.

*Anderson, Sherwood, *Winesburg, Ohio: A Group of Tales of Ohio Small-Town Life*. New York: Signet, 1956 (orig. 1919).

André, Rae, *Homemakers: The Forgotten Workers*, Chicago, University of Chicago Press, 1981.

Anthony, Carolyn T., "John Wiley at 175." *Publishers Weekly* 222, No. 13 (September 24, 1982): 42–46.

————, "Are Reviewers Fair to Trade Paperbacks?" *Publishers Weekly* 222, No. 16 (October 15, 1982): 29–36.

Appelbaum, Judith, and Nancy Evans, *How to Get Happily Published*. New York: Harper & Row, 1978.

Aronowitz, Stanley, *Science as Power: Discourse and Ideology in Modern Society*. Minneapolis: University of Minnesota Press, 1988.

Ashby, Anna Lou, "Harper & Bros." Pp. 151–56 in Madeleine B. Stern (ed.), *Publishers for Mass Entertainment in Nineteenth Century America*. Boston: G. K. Hall, 1980.

*Atherton, Gertrude, *Black Oxen*. New York: Boni and Liverright, 1923.

*Atwood, Margaret, *The Handmaid's Tale*. New York: Fawcett Crest, 1986.

*Auchincloss, Louis, *The Rector of Justin*. Boston: Houghton Mifflin, 1964.

————, *The Embezzler*. Boston: Houghton Mifflin, 1966.

Auerbach, Nina, *Communities of Women: An Idea in Fiction*. Cambridge: Harvard University Press, 1978.

*Austen, Jane, *Pride and Prejudice*. New York: Washington Square Press, 1971 (orig. 1813).

————, *Emma*. New York: Bantam, 1958 (orig. 1814).

————, *Northanger Abbey*. New York: Dell, 1967 (orig. 1818).

————, *Persuasion*. New York: Airmont, 1966 (orig. 1818).

Bailey, Herbert S., Jr., *The Art and Science of Book Publishing*. New York: Harper & Row, 1970.

Baker, John F., "The New Look at Houghton Mifflin." *Publishers Weekly* 223, No. 1 (January 7, 1983): 26–32.

Baker, Sheridan, *The Practical Stylist*. New York: Crowell, Second Ed., 1969.

*Barnes, Julian, *Flaubert's Parrot*. New York: McGraw-Hill, 1985.

Barry, Elaine, "Frost as a Literary Critic." Pp. 3–53 in Elaine Barry (ed.), *Robert Frost on Writing*. New Brunswick: Rutgers University Press, 1973.

*Barth, John, *Giles Goat-Boy*. New York: Fawcett, 1967.

————, *The Sot-Weed Factor*. New York: Bantam, Second Ed., 1969.

————, *Lost in the Funhouse: Fiction for Print, Tape, Live Voice*. New York: Bantam, 1969.

————, *Sabbatical: A Romance*. New York: Putnam's, 1982.

*Barthelme, Donald, *The Dead Father*. New York: Farrar, Straus and Giroux, 1975.

Barthes, Roland. *S/Z*. New York: Hill and Wang. tr. Richard Miller, 1974.

————, *The Pleasures of the Text*. New York: Hill and Wang, tr. Richard Miller, 1975.

————, *Image-Music-Text*. New York: Hill and Wang, tr. Stephen Heath, 1977.

Bartimus, Ted, "Best-Selling Author Lives a Tale of Romance," *Pensacola News Journal*, August 16, 1981.

*Basso, Hamilton, *The View from Pompey's Head*. Garden City, NY: Doubleday, 1954.

Bataille, Leon (ed.), *A Turning Point for Literacy: Adult Education for Development, The Spirit and Declaration of Persepolis*. Proceeding of the International Symposium for Literacy, Persepolis, Iran, September, 1975. New York: Pergamon Press, 1976.

Bauman, Richard, "Verbal Art as Performance." *American Anthropologist* 77 (June, 1975): 290–311.

Bauman, Richard, *Story, Performance, and Event: Contextual Studies of Oral Narrative*. Cambridge: Cambridge University Press, 1986.

Baym, Nina, "The Madwoman and her Languages: Why I Don't Do Feminist Literary Theory." *Tulsa Studies in Women's Literature* 3 (Spring/Fall, 1984): 45–59.

Becker, Howard S., *Art Worlds*. Berkeley and San Francisco: University of California Press, 1982.

Bell, Michael Davitt, *The Development of American Romance: The Sacrifice of Relation*. Chicago: University of Chicago Press, 1980.

Bellah, Robert N., Richard Madsen, William M. Sullivan, Ann Swidler, and Steven M. Tipton, *Habits of the Heart: Individualism and Commitment in American Life*, New York, Perennial Library, 1986.

Bellamy, Joe David (ed.), *The New Fiction: Interviews with Innovative American Writers*, Urbana, University of Illinois Press, 1974, p. 189.

————, "Researchers Link Manic–Depressive Illness and Artistic Creativity," *The Chronicle of Higher Education* XXXV (June 21, 1989), A6.

*Bellow, Saul, *Dangling Man*. New York: Avon, 1975 (orig. 1944).

————, *The Victim*. New York: Avon, 1975 (orig. 1947).

————, "Distractions of a Fiction Writer." Pp. 13-31 in Granville Hicks (ed.),

The Living Novel: A Symposium. New York: Collier, 1962.

————, **Herzog.* New York: Fawcett, 1965.

————, **Mr. Sammler's Planet.* New York: Fawcett, 1971.

————, **Henderson the Rain King.* New York: Penguin, 1976.

————, **Humboldt's Gift.* New York: Avon, 1976.

Benda, Julien, "The Treason of the Intellectuals." Pp. 217–32 in George B. de Huszar (ed.), *The Intellectuals: A Controversial Protrait.* Glencoe, IL: Free Press of Glencoe, 1960 (reprinted from *The Treason of the Intellectuals,* New York, Morrow, tr. Richard Aldington, 1928).

Bender, Dean, "How They Choose the Book of the Month." *The Pensacola Journal.* September 2, 1981, 4D.

Benet, Mary Kathleen, *Writers in Love.* New York: Macmillan, 1977.

Benjamin, Walter, *Illuminations.* New York: Harcourt, Brace and World, tr. Hannah Arendt, 1968.

Berger, Morroe, *Real and Imagined Worlds: The Novel and Social Science.* Cambridge: Harvard University Press, 1977.

Berger, Peter L., *Invitation to Sociology: A Humanistic Perspective.* New York: Anchor, 1963.

Berger, Peter L. and Thomas Luckmann, *The Social Construction of Reality.* Garden City, NY: Anchor Books, 1967.

Berger, Peter, and Stanley Pullberg, "Reification and the Sociological Critique of Consciousness," *History and Theory* IV (1965), 207.

Bergonzi, Bernard, *The Situation of the Novel.* Pittsburgh: University of Pittsburg Press, 1972.

————, "H. G. Wells (1866–1946)." Pp. 3–14 in George A. Panichas (ed.), *The Politics of Twentieth-Century Novelists.* New York: Crowell, 1974.

Bessie, Simon Michael, "Small Publishing—Is It Beautiful?" Pp. 106–15 in Bill Henderson (ed.), *The Art of Literary Publishing: Editors on their Craft.* Yonkers, NY: Pushcart Book Press, 1980.

Beyard-Taylor, Karen C. and Howard J. Sullivan, "Adolescent Reading Preferences for Type of Theme and Sex of Character." *Reading Research Quarterly* XVI, No. 1 (1980): 104–20.

Black, Max, *Models and Metaphors: Essays in Logic and Language.* Ithaca, NY: Cornell University Press, 1962.

Bleich, David, "Gender Interests in Reading and Language." Pp. 234–66 in Elizabeth A. Flynn and Patrocinio C. Schweickart (eds.), *Gender and Reading: Essays on Readers, Texts, and Contexts*. Baltimore: Johns Hopkins University Press, 1986.

Bloom, Harold, *Kabbalah and Criticism*. New York: Seabury Press, 1975.

———, *A Map of Misreading*. New York: Oxford University Press, 1975.

———, *The Breaking of the Vessels*. Chicago: University of Chicago Press, 1982.

Bonny, Harold V., *Reading: An Historical and Psychological Study*. Gravesend, England: Alex J. Philip, 1939.

Boone, Joseph Allen, *Tradition Counter Tradition: Love and the Form of Fiction*. Chicago: University of Chicago Press, 1987.

Booth, Wayne C., *The Rhetoric of Fiction*. Chicago: University of Chicago Press, 1961.

———, *A Rhetoric of Irony*. Chicago: University of Chicago Press, 1975.

———, *Critical Understanding: The Powers and Limits of Pluralism*. Chicago: University of Chicago Press, 1979.

Borges, Jorge Luis, "Libraries, Books, and Reading." Pp. 3–5 in Robert Karlin (ed.), *Reading for All: Proceedings of the Fourth International Reading Association World Congress on Reading*. Newark, DE: International Reading Association, 1973.

Bormuth, John R., "Reading Literacy: Its Definition and Assessments." Pp. 61–100 in John B. Carroll and Jeanne S. Chall (eds.), *Toward a Literate Society: The Report of the Committee on Reading of the National Academy of Education*. New York: McGraw-Hill, 1975.

Boudon, Raymond, *The Crisis in Sociology: Problems of Sociological Epistemology*. New York: Columbia University Press, tr. Howard H. Davis, 1980.

Bourdieu, Pierre, *Distinction: A Social Critique of the Judgement of Taste*, Cambridge: Harvard University Press, tr. Richard Nice, 1984.

Boyers, Robert, "The Old-Fashioned Critic That Never Was" (Review of Robert Alter's *The Pleasures of Reading*), *The New York Times Book Review* (June 25, 1989), 22.

Bradbury, Malcolm, *The Social Context of Modern English Literature*. New York: Schocken, 1971.

Braine, John, *Writing a Novel*. New York: Coward, McCann & Geohegan, 1974.

*Brautigan, Richard, *The Abortion: An Historical Romance 1966*. New York: Pocket Books, 1972.

———, *Trout Fishing in America*. New York: Laurel, 1972.

*Brontë, Charlotte, *Jane Eyre*. New York: Modern Library, 1950 (orig. 1848).

*Brookner, Anita, *Hotel du Lac*. New York: Pantheon Books, 1982.

———,* *Providence*. New York: Pantheon Books, 1982.

Brooks, Jeffrey, "The Kopeck Novels of Early Twentieth Century Russia." *Journal of Popular Culture* 13 (Summer, 1979): 85–97.

Brooks, Van Wyck (ed.), *Writers at Work: The Paris Review Interviews*, Second Series. New York: Viking, 1965.

Brown, John Oliver, "Literary Agents" in Jean Spealman Kujoth, (compiler), *Book Publishing: Inside Views*. Metuchen, NJ: Scarecrow, 1971 (orig. Daedalus 92 (Winter, 1963), pp. 247–52.

Brown, Richard Harvey, *Society as Text: Essays on Rhetoric, Reason, and Reality*. Chicago: University of Chicago Press, 1987.

———, *A Poetic for Sociology: Toward a Logic of Discovery for the Human Sciences*, New York, Cambridge University Press, 1978.

*Brown, Rita Mae, *Rubyfruit Jungle*. New York: Bantam, 1977.

Bruford, Walter H., "Literary Criticism and Sociology." *Yearbook of Comparative Criticism* V (1973): 3–20 (ed. Joseph P. Strelka).

*Buck, Pearl S., *The Good Earth*. New York: John Day Co., 1965 (orig. 1931).

*Burdick, Eugene and Harvey Wheeler, *Fail-Safe*. New York: Dell, 1963.

*Burgess, Anthony, *The Long Day Wanes: A Malayan Trilogy*. New York: Ballantine, 1966.

Burnett, Hallie and Ivy, *Fiction Writer's Handbook*. New York: Harper & Row, 1975.

Burns, Elizabeth, and Tom Burns, "Introduction" in Elizabeth and Tom Burns (eds.), *Sociology of Literature and Drama: Selected Readings*, Harmondsworth, Middlesex, England, Penguin, 1973, pp. 9–30.

*Burroughs, William, Jr., *Speed*. New York: Olympia Press, 1970.

Calder, Jenni, *Women and Marriage in Victorian Fiction*, New York, Oxford University Press, 1976, p. 171.

Caldwell, Erskine, *Writing in America*, New York, Phaedra, 1957.

*Caldwell, Taylor, *This Side of Innocence*. New York: Scribner's, 1946.

———, *Dear and Glorious Physician*. Garden City, NY: Doubleday, 1959.

Calvino, Italo, *The Uses of Literature: Essays*. New York: Harcourt Brace Jovanovich, tr. Patrick Creagh, 1986.

Camus, Albert, *The Plague*. New York: Modern Library, 1948.

Canfield, Cass, "An Introductory Review of Harper Highlights." Pp. 147–50 in Madeleine B. Stern (ed.), *Publishers for Mass Entertainment in Nineteenth Century America*. Boston: G. K. Hall, 1980.

Capote, Truman, *In Cold Blood*. New York: Signet, 1971.

Carroll, John B., and Jeanne S. Chall (eds.), *Toward a Literate Society: The Report of the Committee on Reading of the National Academy of Education*. New York: McGraw-Hill, 1975.

Cartland, Barbara, *I Search for Rainbows*. New York: Bantam, 1977.

――――, *The Passion and the Flower* and *Love, Lords and Lady-Birds*. New York: Dutton, 1978.

――――, *Love in the Clouds* and *Imperial Splendour*. New York: Dutton, 1979.

*Cather, Willa, *The Professor's House*. New York: Vintage, 1973 (orig. 1925).

――――, *Shadows on the Rocks*. New York: Knopf, 1931.

Caute, David, "Commitment without Empathy: A Writer's Notes on Politics, Theatre and the Novel." *TriQuarterly* 30 (Spring, 1974); 51–70.

Cawelti, John, "The Concept of Formula in the Study of Popular Literature." Pp. 115–123 in Sherman Paul (ed.), *Criticism and Culture: Papers of the Midwest Modern Language Association* No. 2. Iowa City: Midwest Modern Language Association, 1972.

Cervantes, Miguel de, *Don Quixote of La Mancha*. New York: New American Library, tr. Walter Starkie, 1964 (orig. Part I, 1605; Part II, 1615).

*Charyn, Jerome, *Darlin' Bill: A Love Story of the Wild West*. New York: Arbor House, 1980.

Chase, Francis S., "Demands on the Readers in the Next Decade." Pp. 4–16 in Martha L. King, Bernice D. Ellinger, and Willavene Wolf (eds.), *Critical Reading*. New York: J.B. Lippincott, 1967 (orig. in Francis S. Chase, *Controversial Issues in Reading and Promising Solutions*, Supplementary Educational Monographs, No. 91, University of Chicago Press, 1961, pp. 7–18).

Chase, Richard, "Introduction." Pp. 9–21 in Thomas Wolfe, *You Can't Go Home Again*. New York: Dell, 1960.

――――, *The American Novel and Its Traditions*, Baltimore, Johns Hopkins University Press, 1957, p. 11.

*Cheever, John, *The Wapshot Chronicle*. New York: Perennial Library, 1973 (orig. 1957).

———, *The Wapshot Scandal*. New York: Perennial Library, 1973 (orig. 1964).

———, *Falconer*. New York: Knopf, 1977.

———, *Bullet Park*. New York: Ballantine, 1978.

*Cheuse, Allen, *The Grandmothers' Club*. Salt Lake City: Peregrine Smith Books, 1986.

Chodorow, Nancy, *The Reproduction of Mothering: Psychoanalysis and the Sociology of Gender*, Berkeley and Los Angeles, University of California Press, 1978.

*Cholmondeley, Mary, *Red Pottage*. New York: Harper, 1900.

*Chopin, Kate, *The Awakening*. New York: Avon, 1972 (orig. 1899).

*Churchill, Winston, *Mr. Crewe's Career*. New York: Macmillian, 1908.

Claunchy, Michael T., "Literate and Illiterate; Hearing and Seeing: England 1066–1307." Pp. 14–45 in Harvey J. Graff (ed.), *Literacy and Social Development in the West: A Reader*. Cambridge: Cambridge University Press, 1981 (orig. Michael T. Claunchy, *From Memory to Written Word: England, 1066–1307*. Cambridge: Harvard University Press, 1979).

Clifford, James, "Introduction: Partial Truths." Pp. 1–26 in James Clifford and George E. Marcus (eds.), *Writing Culture: The Poetics and Politics of Ethnography*. Berkeley and Los Angeles: University of California Press, 1986.

Cobb, Jonathan, and Richard Sennett, *The Hidden Injuries of Class*. New York: Vintage, 1973.

Cohen, Edward H., *Ebenezer Cooke: The Sot-Weed Canon*. Athens: University of Georgia Press, 1975.

Collins, Randall, *The Credential Society: An Historical Sociology of Education and Stratification*. New York: Academic Press, 1979.

Commins, Dorothy, *What Is An Editor? Saxe Commins at Work*. Chicago: University of Chicago Press, 1978.

Connerton, Paul, "Introduction." Pp. 11–39 in Paul Connerton (ed.), *Critical Sociology: Selected Readings*. New York: Penguin, 1976.

*Conrad, Joseph, *An Outcast of the Islands*. New York: Pyramid, 1960 (orig. 1897).

———, *Nostromo: A Tale of the Sea Board*. New York: New American Library, 1960 (orig. 1904).

Conroy, Pat, *The Prince of Tides*. Boston: Houghton Mifflin, 1986.

Corradi, Juan E., "Textures: Approaching Society, Ideology, Literature." *Ideologies & Literature* 1 (February–April, 1977): 5–21.

Coser, Lewis A. *Men of Ideas: A Sociologist's View*. New York: Free Press, 1970.

————, *Sociology Through Literature*. Englewood Cliffs, NJ: Prentice-Hall, 2nd Ed., 1972.

Coughlin, Ellen K., "Report Blames Racism and a Sagging U.S. Economy for Stagnation in Progress of Black Americans." *The Chronicle of Higher Education* (August 2, 1989): A4–A5, A7.

Coulter, Jeff, "Transparency of Mind: The Availability of Subjective Phenomena." *Philosophy of the Social Sciences* 7 (December, 1977): 321–50.

Cowan, Ruth Schwartz, *More Work for Mother: The Ironies of Household Technology from the Open Hearth to the Microwave*, New York, Basic, 1983.

Cowley, Malcom, "Sociological Habit Patterns in Linguistic Transmogrification." *The Reporter* 15 (September 20, 1956): 41–43.

*Cozzens, James Gould, *By Love Possessed*. New York: Harcourt, Brace, 1957.

Craig, George, "Reading: Who Is Doing What to Whom?" Pp. 15–36 in Gabriel Josipovici (ed.), *The Modern English Novel: The Reader, the Writer, and the Work*. London: Open Books, 1976.

*Crane, Stephen, *The Red Badge of Courage: An Episode of the American Civil War*. New York: Norton, ed. Henry Binder, 1982 (orig. 1895).

*Cronin, A. J., *The Keys of the Kingdom*. Boston: Little, Brown, 1941.

————, *The Judas Tree*. New York: Bantam, 1963.

Daiches, David, *The Novel and the Modern World*. Chicago: University of Chicago Press, Revised Edition, 1965.

Daigh, Ralph, *Maybe You Should Write a Book*. Englewood Clifs, NJ: Prentice-Hall, 1977.

*Dailey, Janet, *The Homeplace*. New York: Harlequin Books, 1976.

————, *Lord of the High Lonesome*. New York: Harlequin Books, 1980.

Dale, Edgar, "The Critical Reader." Pp. 25–34 in Martha L. King, Bernice D. Ellinger, and Willavene Wolf (eds.), *Critical Reading*. New York and Philadelphia: J. B. Lippincott, 1967 (orig. *The News Letter* XXX, No. 4 (January, 1965): 1–4).

Dardis, Tom, *Some Time in the Sun*. New York: Scribner's, 1976.

Dataller, Roger, *The Plain Man and the Novel*. Port Washington, NY: Kennikat, 1970 (orig. 1940).

Davis, Kenneth C., *Two-Bit Culture: The Paperbacking of America*. Boston: Houghton Mifflin, 1984.

Davis, Lennard J., "A Social History of Fact and Fiction: Authorial Disavowal in the Early English Novel." Pp. 120–148 in Edward W. Said (ed.), *Literature and Society*. Baltimore: Johns Hopkins University Press, 1986.

————, *Factual Fictions: The Origins of the English Novel*. New York: Columbia University Press, 1985.

Deer, Irving, and Harriet A. Deer, "Introduction." Pp. 1–20 in Irving Deer and Harriet A. Deer (eds.), *The Popular Arts: A Critical Reader*. New York: Scribner's, 1967.

Defoe, Daniel, *Moll Flanders*. New York: Pocket Books, 1952 (orig. 1722).

DeJong, Mary G., "Lines from a Partly Published Drama: The Romance of Frances Sargent Osgood and Edgar Allen Poe." Pp. 31–58 in Shirley Marchalonis (ed.), *Patrons and Protegees: Gender, Friendship, and Writing in Nineteenth-Century America*. New Brunswick, NJ: Rutgers University Press, 1988.

Delacorte, Albert, "Modern Romances." Pp. 54–70 in Aron M. Mathieu (ed.), *The Creative Writer*. Cincinnati: Writer's Digest, Second Revised Edition, 1972.

*DeLillo, Don, *White Noise*. New York: Penguin, 1986.

de Muralt, André, *The Idea of Phenomenology: Husserlian Exemplarism*. Evanston, IL: Northwestern University Press, tr. Garry L. Breckon, 1974.

*Dennis, Patrick, *Auntie Mame: An Irreverent Escapade*. New York: Vanguard, 1955.

Denzin, Norman K., "Postmodern Social Theory." *Sociological Theory* 4 (Fall, 1986): 194–204.

Derrida, Jacques, "The Law of Genre." Pp. 51–77 in W. J. T. Mitchell (ed.), *On Narrative*. Chicago: University of Chicago Press, 1981.

Desan, Phillippe, Priscilla Parkhurst Ferguson, and Wendy Griswold (eds.), *Literature and Social Practice*, Chicago, University of Chicago Press, 1989.

DeVault, Marjorie L., "Novel Readings: The Social Organization of Interpretation." *American Journal of Sociology* 95 (January, 1990): 887–921.

Devoe, Alan, "Literary Discipline." Pp. 271–75 in Trentwell Mason White, *How to Write for a Living*. New York: Reynal & Hitchcock, 1937.

Diamond, S. J., "Book Club Selling Methods Debated." *Las Vegas Review-Journal*, May 23, 1982, 10C.

*Dickens, Charles, *David Copperfield*. New York: Modern Library, 1950 (orig. 1849–50).

———, *Bleak House*. New York: New American Library, 1964 (orig. 1853)

———, *Hard Times*. New York: Signet, 1961 (orig. 1854).

———, *Great Expectations*. New York: Holt Rinehart Winston, 1966 (orig. 1860–61).

———, *Our Mutual Friend*. New York: Signet, 1964 (orig. 1864–65).

Didion, Joan, *Slouching Toward Bethlehem*. New York: Touchstone Book, Simon and Schuster, 1979.

Dillard, Annie, "Write Till You Drop." *The New York Times Book Review* (May 28, 1989): 1, 23.

DiMaggio, Paul, "Classification in Art." *American Sociological Review* 52 (August, 1987): 440–55.

DiMaggio, Paul, Michael Useem, and Paula Brown, *Audience Studies of the Performing Arts and Museums: A Critical Review*. Washington, DC: National Endowment for the Arts, Research Development Report No. 9, November, 1978.

*Doctorow, E. L. *Ragtime*. New York: Bantam, 1976.

*Dos Passos, John, *One Man's Initiation: 1917*. Ithaca, NY: Cornell University Press, 1970 (orig. 1920).

———, *The 42nd Parallel*. Volume I in *U.S.A.* New York: Modern Library, 1937.

———, *Nineteen-Nineteen*. Volume II in *U.S.A.* New York: Modern Library, 1937.

———, *The Big Money*. Volume III in *U.S.A.* New York: Modern Library, 1937.

Douglas, Ann, *The Feminization of American Culture*. New York: Avon Books, 1978.

*Douglas, Lloyd C. *Magnificent Obsession*. Boston: Houghton Mifflin, 1957 (orig. 1929).

Downie, Leonard, Jr., *The New Muckrakers*. New York: Mentor Books, New American Library, 1978.

*Doyle, Arthur Conan, *The Hound of the Baskervilles: A Sherlock Holmes Mystery*. New York: Buccaneer Books, 1977 (orig. 1902).

*Drabble, Margaret, *Thank You All Very Much*. New York: Signet, 1969 (orig. The Millstone).

——, *The Garrick Year.* New York: Popular Library, 1977.

——, *The Ice Age.* New York: Knopf, 1977.

——, *The Needle's Eye.* New York: Popular Library, 1977.

——, *The Realms of Gold.* New York: Popular Library, 1977.

——, *A Summer Bird-Cage.* New York: Popular Library, 1977.

*Dreiser, Theodore, *Sister Carrie.* Indianapolis: Bobbs-Merrill, 1970 (orig. 1900).

*Drury, Allen, *Advise and Consent.* New York: Pocket Books, 1961.

Dubin, Steven C., *Bureaucratizing the Muse: Public Funds and the Cultural Worker.* Chicago: University of Chicago Press, 1987.

Dubois, Jacques, and Pascal Durand, "Literary Field and Classes of Texts." Pp. 137–53 in Phillippe Desan, Priscilla Parkhurst Ferguson, and Wendy Griswold (eds.), *Literature and Social Practice.* Chicago: University of Chicago Press, 1989, tr. Priscilla Parkhurst Ferguson.

Duncan, Hugh Dalziel, *Language and Literature in Society: A Sociological Essay on Theory and Method in the Interpretation of Linguistic Symbols with a Bibliographic Guide to the Sociology of Literature.* New York: Bedminster, 1961.

*Dunne, Dominick, *People Like Us.* New York: Crown Publishers, 1988.

*Durrell, Lawrence. *Balthazar.* New York: Dutton, 1961.

——, *Clea.* New York: Dutton, 1961.

——, *Justine.* New York: Dutton, 1961.

——, *Mountolive.* New York: Dutton, 1961.

Eagleton, Terry, *Marxism and Literary Criticism.* Berkeley and Los Angeles: University of California Press, 1976.

Edwards, Thomas R., "Sad Young Men." (A Review of Paul Auster's *Moon Palace,* Dennis Cooper's *Closer,* and Barry Hannah's *Boomerang.*) *The New York Review of Books* XXXVI, No. 13 (August 17, 1989): 52–53.

Eisenstein, Elizabeth L., "Some Conjectures about the Impact of Printing on Western Society and Thought: A Preliminary Report." Pp. 53–68 in Harvey J. Graff (ed.), *Literacy and Social Development in the West: A Reader.* Cambridge: Cambridge University Press, 1981 (orig. *Journal of Modern History* 40 (1968), 7–29).

Eliade, Mircea, *Myths, Dreams, and Realities: The Encounter between Contemporary Faiths and Archaic Realities.* New York: Harper Colophon, 1975.

*Eliot, George, *Adam Bede*. New York: Signet, n.d. (orig. 1859).

——, *Felix Holt, The Radical*. New York: Oxford University Press, 1988 (orig. 1866)

——, *The Mill on the Floss*. New York: Signet, n.d. (orig. 1860).

——, *Silas Marner*. New York: Lancer Books, 1968 (orig. 1861).

——, *Middlemarch: A Study of Provincial Life*. New York: Norton, 1977 (orig. 1871–72).

Eliot, T. S., *Notes toward the Definition of Culture*. New York: Harcourt, Brace, 1949.

——, "Religion and Literature." Pp. 21–30 in G. B. Tennyson and Edward E. Ericson, Jr. (eds.), *Religion and Modern Literature: Essays in Theory and Criticism*. Grand Rapids: William B. Eerdmans Publishing Company, 1975.

Elliott, Robert C., *The Literary Persona*. Chicago: University of Chicago Press, 1982.

Ellis, John M., *The Theory of Literary Criticism: A Logical Analysis*. Berkeley and Los Angeles: University of California Press, 1977.

*Ellison, Ralph, *Invisible Man*. New York: Vintage, 1972 (orig. 1952).

——, "Society, Morality, and the Novel." Pp. 65–97 in Granville Hicks (ed.), *The Living Novel: A Symposium*. New York: Collier, 1962.

Ellman, Mary, *Thinking about Women*. New York: Harcourt Brace Jovanovich, 1968.

*Erdrich, Louise, *Love Medicine*. New York: Bantam, 1987.

Erikson, Kai T., *Everything in its Path: Destruction of Community in the Buffalo Creek Flood*. New York: Simon and Schuster, Touchstone Book, 1976.

Ermarth, Elizabeth, "Fictional Consensus and Female Casualties." Pp. 1–18 in Carolyn G. Heilbrun and Margaret R. Higonnet (eds.), *The Representation of Women in Fiction: Selected Papers from the English Institute, 1981*. Baltimore: Johns Hopkins University Press, 1983.

Escarpit, Robert, *The Book Revolution*. London: George C. Harrap & Company, 1966.

——, *Sociology of Literature*. Painesville, OH: Lake Erie College Studies, tr. Ernest Pick, 1965.

Evory, Ann (ed.), *Contemporary Authors*. Detroit: Gale Research Company, 1960.

*Exley, Frederick, *A Fan's Notes: A Fictional Memoir*. New York: Pocket Books, 1977.

Faranda, Lisa Porter, "A Social Necessity: The Friendship of Sherwood Bonner and Henry Wadsworth Longfellow." Pp. 184–211 in Shirley Marchalonis (ed.), *Patrons and Protegees: Gender, Friendship, and Writing in Nineteenth-Century America*. New Brunswick, NJ: Rutgers University Press, 1988.

Farrar, John, "Securing and Selling the Manuscript." Pp. 28–53 in Chandler B. Grannis (ed.), *What Happens in Book Publishing*. New York: Columbia University Press, Second Edition, 1967.

————, "Letter to an Unpublished Writer." Pp. 71–77 in Bill Henderson (ed.), *The Art of Literary Publishing: Editors on their Craft*. Yonkers, NY: Pushcart Book Press, 1980.

Fastian, Felix (aka Peter L. Berger), *The Enclaves*. Garden City, NY: Doubleday, 1965.

*Faulkner, William, *The Sound and the Fury*. New York: Vintage, 1954 (orig. 1929).

————, *As I Lay Dying*. New York: Vintage, 1957 (orig. 1930).

————, *Light in August*. New York: Modern Library, 1950 (orig. 1932).

————, *The Unvanquished*. New York: Vintage, 1966 (orig. 1938).

————, *The Hamlet*. New York: Vintage, 1956 (orig. 1940).

————, *The Reivers: A Reminiscence*. New York: New American Library, 1969 (orig. 1962).

*Ferber, Edna, *Showboat*. New York: The Book League of America, 1926.

————, *Giant*. Chicago: Sears Readers Club, 1952.

*Fern, Fanny (Sara Payson Willis), *Ruth Hall and Other Writings*. New Brunswick, NJ: Rutgers University Press, 1986 (ed. Joyce W. Warren).

Fetterly, Judith, "Reading about Reading: 'A Jury of her Peers,' 'The Murders in the Rue Morgue,' and 'The Yellow Wallpaper.'" Pp. 147–64 in Elizabeth A. Flynn and Patrocinio P. Schweickart (eds.), *Gender and Reading: Essays on Readers, Texts, and Contexts*. Baltimore: Johns Hopkins University Press, 1986.

Fiedler, Leslie A., *Waiting for the End*. New York: Stein and Day, 1964.

————, "Giving the Devil his Due." *Journal of Popular Culture* 12 (Fall, 1979): 197–207.

Fielding, Henry, *Joseph Andrews*. New York: Modern Library, 1939 (orig. 1742).

——, *The History of Tom Jones: A Foundling*. New York: Modern Library, 1950 (orig. 1749).

Figurel, J. Allen (ed.), *Reading in a Changing Society: Conference Proceedings, International Reading Association*, Volume 4, 1959. New York: International Reading Association and Scholastic Magazines, 1959.

Firchow, Peter (ed.), *The Writer's Place: Interviews on the Literary Situation in Contemporary Britain*. Minneapolis: University of Minnesota Press, 1974.

Fischer, John, "Myths about Publishing." Pp. 63–71 in Jean Spealman Kujoth (compiler), *Book Publishing: Inside Views*. Metuchen, NJ: Scarecrow, 1971 (orig. *Harper's Magazine*, July 1963).

Fish, Stanley, *Is There a Text in This Class? The Authority of Interpretive Communities*. Cambridge: Harvard University Press, 1980.

*Fleming, Ian, *Goldfinger*. New York: Macmillian, 1959.

Fletcher, Angus (ed.), *The Literature of Fact: Selected Papers from the English Institute*. New York: Columbia University Press, 1976.

Flynn, Elizabeth A., "Gender and Reading." Pp. 267–288 in Elizabeth A. Flynn and Patrocinio P. Schweickart (eds.), *Gender and Reading: Essays on Readers, Texts, and Contexts*. Baltimore: Johns Hopkins University Press, 1986.

*Ford, Ford Madox, *The Good Soldier: A Tale of Passion*. New York: Vintage, 1955 (orig. 1915).

*Forster, E. M., *Where Angels Fear to Tread*. New York: Vintage, 1958 (orig. 1905).

——, **A Room with a View*. New York: Vintage, 1961 (orig., 1908).

——, **Howards End*. New York: Vintage, 1954 (orig. 1910).

——, **A Passage to India*. New York: Harcourt, Brace & World, 1952 (orig. 1924).

——, *Aspects of the Novel*. New York: Harcourt Brace Jovanovich, 1955.

Forster, Peter, and Celia Kenneford, "Sociological Theory and the Sociology of Literature." *British Journal of Sociology* 24 (September, 1973): 355–64.

Foucault, Michel, *The Order of Things: An Archaeology of the Human Sciences*. New York: Vintage, [no translator cited], 1973.

Fowler, H. W., *A Dictionary of Modern English Usage*. New York: Oxford University Press, Second Edition, rev. Sir Ernest Gowers, 1965.

Fowler, Roger, *Literature as Social Discourse: The Practice of Linguistic Criticism*. Bloomington: Indiana University Press, 1981.

*Fowles, John, *The French Lieutenant's Woman*. New York: Bantam, 1978.

*Fox, Paula, *A Servant's Tale*. New York: Penguin, 1986.

Freud, Sigmund, *Civilization and its Discontents*. New York: Norton, tr. and ed. James Strachey, 1962.

Frisch, Max, *I'm Not Stiller*. New York: Vintage, 1958.

———, *Homo Faber*. New York: Harcourt Brace Jovanovich, tr. Michael Bullock, 1971.

Frost, Robert, *Robert Frost on Writing*. New Brunswick, NJ: Rutgers University Press, ed. Elaine Barry, 1973.

Fryckstedt, Monica Correa, "Defining the Domestic Genre: English Women Novelists of the 1850s." *Tulsa Studies in Women's Literature* 6 (Spring, 1987): 9–25.

Frye, Northrop, *The Well-Tempered Critic*. Bloomington: Indiana University Press, 1963.

———, *The Secular Scripture: A Study of the Structure of Romance*. Cambridge: Harvard University Press, 1976, pp. 24–28.

———, *The Educated Imagination*. Bloomington: Indiana University Press, 1964.

———, *The Stubborn Structure: Essays on Criticism and Society*. Ithaca, NY: Cornell University Press, 1970.

Fuchs, Stephan, "The Social Organization of Scientific Knowledge." *Sociological Theory* 4 (Fall, 1986): 126–42.

Fuchs, Stephan and Jonathan H. Turner, "What Makes a Science 'Mature'?: Patterns of Organziational Control in Scientific Production." *Sociological Theory* 4 (Fall, 1986): 143–50.

Fulton, Len, and Ellen Ferber, "Piecework." Pp. 163–78 in Bill Henderson (ed.), *The Art of Literary Publishing: Editors on their Craft*. Yonkers, NY: Pushcart Book Press, 1980.

Furbank, P. N., "The Twentieth-Century Best-Seller." Pp. 297–312 in Irving Deer and Harriet A. Deer (eds.), *The Popular Arts in America: A Critical Reader*. New York: Scribner's, 1967.

Fussell, Paul, *The Great War and Modern Memory*. New York: Oxford University Press, 1975.

Gabel, Joseph, *False Consciousness: An Essay on Reification*. New York, Harper Torchbooks, trs. Margaret A. Thompson and Kenneth A. Thompson, 1978.

Gadd, David, *The Loving Friends: A Portrait of Bloomsbury*. New York: Harcourt Brace Jovanovich, 1974.

Galassi, Jonathan, "The Double Agent: The Role of the Literary Editor in the Commercial Publishing House." Pp. 78–87 in Bill Henderson (ed.), *The Art of Literary Publishing: Editors on their Craft*. Yonkers, NY: Pushcart Book Press, 1980.

*Galsworthy, John, *One More River*. New York: Scribner's, 1933.

*Gann, Ernest K. *The High and the Mighty*. New York: William Sloane Associates, 1953.

Gans, Herbert J., "*Love Story:* A Romance of Upward Mobility." *Social Policy* 2 (May–June, 1971): 34–36.

Gardner, John, *On Moral Fiction*. New York: Basic, 1978.

*Gaskell, Elizabeth, *Wives and Daughters*. New York: Penguin, 1986 (orig. 1864–86).

Gass, William H., *Fiction and the Figure of Life*. New York: Vintage, 1972.

Gavin, Marian, *Writing Short Stories for Pleasure and Profit*. Boston: The Writer, 1973.

Gedin, Per, *Literature in the Marketplace*. London: Faber, 1977 (tr. George Bisset).

Geertz, Clifford, "Found in Translation: On the Social History of the Moral Imagination." *The Georgia Review* 31 (Winter, 1977): 788–810.

Gide, André, *The Counterfeiters* with Journal of "The Counterfeiters." New York: Modern Library, tr. Dorothy Bussy, 1955.

———, *The Immoralist*. New York: Vintage, tr. Richard Howard, 1970.

Gilman, Richard, *The Confusion of Realms*. New York: Vintage, 1970.

Giovannoni, Jean Owen, "8 Steps to Professional Writing." Pp. 31–36 in Aron M. Mathieu (ed.), *The Creative Writer*. Cincinnati: Writer's Digest, Second Revised Edition, 1972.

*Glasgow, Ellen, *Vein of Iron*. New York: Harcourt, Brace, 1935.

Godwin, Gail, "Keeping Track." Pp. 75–85 in Lyn Lifshin (ed.), *Ariadne's Thread: A Collection of Contemporary Women's Journals*. New York: Harper & Row, 1982.

Goffman, Erving, *The Presentation of Self in Everyday Life.* New York: Anchor Books, 1959.

———, *Asylums: Essays on the Social Situation of Mental Patients and Other Inmates.* New York: Anchor Books, 1961.

———, *Encounters.* Indianapolis: Bobbs-Merril, 1961.

———, *Behavior in Public Places: Notes on the Social Organization of Gatherings.* New York: Free Press, 1963.

———, *Stigma: Notes on the Management of Spoiled Identity.* Englewood Cliffs, NJ: Prentice-Hall, 1963.

———, *Interaction Ritual: Essays on Face-to-Face Behavior.* New York: Anchor Books, 1967.

———, *Strategic Interaction.* Philadelphia: University of Pennsylvania Press, 1969.

———, *Relations in Public: Microstudies of the Public Order.* New York: Harper Colophon Books, 1971.

———, *Frame Analysis: An Essay on the Organization of Experience.* New York: Harper Colophon Books, 1974.

———, *Forms of Talk.* Philadelphia: University of Pennsylvania Press, 1980.

Garner, Jack, "Author Is Slower, But Better with His Novels." *Pensacola News Journal,* August 20, 1981.

Gold, Herbert, "The Mystery of Personality in the Novel." Pp. 97–109 in Granville Hicks (ed.), *The Living Novel: A Symposium.* New York: Collier, 1962.

Goldberg, Phillip A., "Are Women Prejudiced Against Women?" *Trans-Action* 5 (1968): 28–30.

Golden, Joanne M. and John T. Guthrie, "Convergence and Divergence in Reader Response to Literature." *Reading Research Quarterly* XXI (Fall, 1986): 408–21.

Goldfarb, Jeffrey C., *On Cultural Freedom: An Exploration of Public Life in Poland and America.* Chicago: University of Chicago Press, 1982.

Goldmann, Lucien, *Cultural Creation in Modern Society.* Oxford: Basil Blackwell, tr. Bart Grahl, 1977.

Goodman, Nelson, *Ways of Worldmaking.* Indianapolis: Hackett, 1978.

Goody, Jack (ed.), *Literacy in Traditional Societies.* Cambridge: Cambridge University Press, 1968.

Goody, Jack, and Ian Watt, "The Consequences of Literacy." *Comparative Studies in Society and History* 5 (Fall, 1963): 304–45.

*Gordimer, Nadine, *Burger's Daughter*. New York: Viking, 1979.

Graff, Gerald, *Literature Against Itself: Literary Ideas in Modern Society*. Chicago: University of Chicago Press, 1979.

Graff, Gerald and William E. Cain, "Peace Plan for the Canon Wars." *National Forum* LXIX (Summer, 1989): 7–9.

Graff, Harvey J., "Literacy, Jobs, and Industrialization: The Nineteenth Century." Pp. 232–260 in Harvey J. Graff (ed.), *Literacy and Social Development in the West: A Reader*. Cambridge: Cambridge University Press, 1981 (orig. *The Literacy Myth: Literacy and Social Structure in the Nineteenth-Century City*. New York: Academic Press, 1979, Pp. 195–233).

Grannis, Chandler B., "Introduction: General View of a Diverse Industry." Pp. 3–23 in Chandler B. Grannis (ed.), *What Happens in Book Publishing*. New York: Columbia University Press, Second Edition, 1967.

———, "More Than Merchants: Seventy-Five Years of the ABA." Pp. 65–108 in Charles B. Anderson (ed.), *Bookselling in America and the World: Some Observations & Recollections*. New York: Quadrangle, 1975.

*Grau, Shirley Ann, *The House on Coliseum Street*. New York: Knopf, 1966.

———, *The Wind Shifting West*. New York: Knopf, 1973.

Gray, William S., and Ruth Munroe, *The Reading Interests and Habits of Adults: A Preliminary Report*. New York: Macmillan, 1930.

Green, Bryan S., *Literary Methods and Sociological Theory*. Chicago: University of Chicago Press, 1988.

*Green, Henry, *Living, Loving*, and *Party Going*. New York: Penguin, 1978 (orig. 1929, 1945, and 1948).

Green, Martin, *Transatlantic Patterns: Cultural Comparisons of England with America*. New York: Basic, 1977.

*Greene, Graham, *The Heart of the Matter*. New York: Viking, 1948.

———, *The Power and the Glory*. New York: Viking, 1970 (orig. 1940 as *The Labyrinthine Ways* in the United States).

*Grey, Zane, *The Lone Star Ranger*. New York: Black's Readers Service Company, 1943 (orig. 1915).

Griswold, Wendy, "The Fabrication of Meaning: Literary Interpretation in the United States, Great Britian, and the West Indies." *American Journal of Sociology* 92 (March, 1987): 1077–1117.

————, *Renaissance Revivals: City Comedy and Revenge Tragedy in the London Theatre, 1576–1980.* Chicago: University of Chicago Press, 1986.

Gross, John, *The Rise and Fall of the Man of Letters: A Study of the Idiosyncratic and the Humane in Modern Literature.* New York: Macmillan, 1969.

*Grumbach, Doris, *The Ladies.* New York: E. P. Dutton, 1984.

Guerard, Albert J., "Notes on the Rhetoric of Anti-Realist Fiction." *TriQuarterly* 30 (Spring, 1974): 3–50.

————, *The Triumph of the Novel: Dickens, Dostoevsky, Faulkner.* Chicago: University of Chicago Press, 1976.

Gurko, Leo, *Heroes, Highbrows, and the Popular Mind.* New York: Charter Books, 1962 (orig. 1953).

Habegger, Alfred, *Gender, Fantasy, and Realism in American Literature.* New York: Columbia University Press, 1982.

*Hailey, Arthur, *Hotel.* Garden City, NY: Doubleday, 1965.

Hall, James B., and Barry Ulanov (eds.), *Modern Culture and the Arts.* New York: McGraw-Hill, Second Edition, 1972.

Hall, John, *The Sociology of Literature.* New York: Longman, 1979.

Hall, Radclyffe, *The Well of Loneliness.* New York: Avon Books, 1981.

Hampden, John (ed.), *The Book World.* London: Thomas Nelson, 1935.

Handler, David, "Former Jockey Pens 21st Novel." *Las Vegas Review-Journal,* May 23, 1982, 10J.

*Hardwick, Elizabeth, *Sleepless Nights.* New York: Random House, 1979.

*Hardy, Thomas, *The Return of the Native.* New York: Scholastic Book Services, 1962 (orig. 1878).

————, **The Mayor of Casterbridge.* New York: Washington Square, 1956 (orig. 1886).

————, **Jude the Obscure.* New York: Penguin, 1978 (orig. 1896).

Harris, Mark, "Easy Does it Not." Pp. 110–22 in Granville Hicks (ed.), *The Living Novel: A Symposium.* New York: Collier, 1962.

Hart, James D., *The Popular Book: A History of America's Literary Taste.* New York: Oxford University Press, 1950.

Hartman, Geoffrey, "The Aesthetics of Complicity." *The Georgia Review* 28 (Fall, 1974): 384–88.

Hatt, Frank, *The Reading Process: A Framework for Analysis and Description*. London and Hamden, CN: Clive Bingley and Linnet Books, 1976.

Hauser, Arnold, *The Sociology of Art*. Chicago: University of Chicago Press, tr. Kenneth J. Northcott, 1982.

*Hawkes, John, *The Blood Oranges*. New York: New Directions, 1971.

———, *Death, Sleep & the Traveler*. New York: New Directions, 1974.

Hawthorne, Nathaniel, "The Custom House: Introductory to "The Scarlet Letter." Pp. 1–46 in Nathaniel Hawthorne, *The Scarlet Letter*. New York: Pocket Books, 1952 (orig. 1850).

———, *The Scarlet Letter*. New York: Pocket Books, 1952 (orig. 1850).

Heath, Stephen, *The Nouveau Roman: A Study in the Practice of Writing*. Philadelphia: Temple University Press, 1972.

*Heller, Joseph, *Catch-22*. New York: Dell, 1978.

*Hemingway, Ernest, *A Farewell to Arms*. New York: Scribner's 1975 (orig. 1929).

———, *The Sun Also Rises*. New York: Modern Library, 1930 (orig. 1926).

———, *To Have and Have Not*. New York: Permabooks, Doubleday, 1953 (orig. 1937).

———, *For Whom the Bell Tolls*. New York: Scribner's, 1940.

———, *Islands in the Stream*. New York: Bantam, 1972 (orig. 1970).

Henderson, Bill (ed.), *The Art of Literary Publishing: Editors on their Craft*. Yonkers, NY: Pushcart Book Press, 1980.

*Hersey, John, *A Bell for Adano*. Garden City, NY: Sun Dial Press, 1945.

Hesse, Hermann, *Reflections*. New York: Farrar, Straus and Giroux, tr. Ralph Manheim, 1974.

———, *Demian*. New York: Bantam, 1970, p. 97.

———, *Magister Ludi*. New York: Bantam, 1970 (later *The Glass Bead Game*).

———, *My Belief: Essays on Life and Art*. New York: Farrar, Straus and Giroux, tr. Denver Lindley, 1975.

Hewitt, John P. and James Hall, "The Quasi-Theory of Communication and the Management of Dissent." *Social Problems* 18 (Summer, 1970): 17–27.

Hicks, Granville, "Afterword: The Enemies of the Novel." Pp. 207–19 in Granville Hicks (ed.), *The Living Novel: A Symposium*. New York: Collier's, 1962.

Hills, Philip (ed.), *The Future of the Printed Word: The Impact and the Implications of the New Communications Technology.* Westport, CT: Greenwood, 1980.

*Hilton, James, *Good-Bye, Mr. Chips.* Boston: Little, Brown, 1934.

Hirsch, E. D., Jr. *The Aims of Interpretation.* Chicago: University of Chicago Press, 1976.

Hochschild, Arlie, *Second Shift.* New York: Viking Press, 1989.

Hoffman, Frederick J., "Aldous Huxley and the Novel of Ideas." Pp. 189–200 in William Van O'Connor (ed.), *Forms of Modern Fiction.* Bloomington: Indiana University Press, 1961.

*Holt, Victoria, *The Devil on Horseback.* Garden City: NY: Doubleday, 1977.

———, *The Spring of the Tiger.* Garden City, NY: Doubleday, 1979.

Howe, Irving, *The Critical Point: On Literature and Culture.* New York: Delta Books, 1975.

Howe, Susan and Charles Ruas, "New Directions: An Interview with James Laughlin." Pp. 13–48 in Bill Henderson (ed.), *The Art of Literary Publishing: Editors on their Craft.* Yonkers, NY: Pushcart Book Press, 1980.

*Howells, William Dean, *The Rise of Silas Lapham.*Boston: Houghton Mifflin, 1928 (orig. 1885).

———, *A Hazard of New Fortunes.* New York: Dutton, 1952 (orig. 1890).

Hunter, Carman St. John, and David Harman, *Adult Illiteracy in the United States: A Report to the Ford Foundation.* New York: McGraw-Hill, 1979.

*Hurston, Zora Neale, *Their Eyes Were Watching God.* Urbana: University of Illinois Press, 1978 (orig. 1937).

Husserl, Edmund, *Cartesian Meditations: An Introduction to Phenomenology.* The Hague: Nijhoff, tr. Dorian Cairns, 1970.

———, *Experience and Judgment: Investigations in a Genealogy of Logic.* Evanston: Northwestern University Press, rev. and ed. Ludwig Landgrebe, tr. James S. Churchill and Karl Ameriks, 1973.

*Hyman, Mac, *No Time for Sergeants.* New York: Random House, 1954.

Hyman, Stanley Edgar, *The Tangled Bank: Darwin, Marx, Frazer and Freud as Imaginative Writers.* New York: Atheneum, 1962.

*Ibanez, Vicenta Biasco, *The Four Horsemen of the Apocalypse.* New York: A. L. Burt Company, tr. Charlotte Brewster Jordan, 1918.

Ingalls, Rachel, *Mrs. Caliban.* Ipswich, MA: Gambit, 1983.

*Irving, John, *The 158-Pound Marriage*. New York: Pocket Books, 1978.

———, *The World According to Garp*. New York: Dutton, 1978.

———, *The Hotel New Hampshire*. New York: Dutton, 1981.

Iser, Wolfgang, *The Implied Reader: Patterns of Communication in Prose Fiction from Bunyan to Beckett*. Baltimore: Johns Hopkins University Press, 1974.

———, *The Act of Reading: A Theory of Aesthetic Response*. Baltimore: Johns Hopkins University Press, 1978.

Jackson, Holbrook, *The Printing of Books*. Freeport, NY: Books for Libraries Press, 1970 (orig. 1939).

———, *The Reading of Books*. New York: Scribner's, 1947.

*Jackson, Shirley, *Hangman*. New York: Ace Publishing, 1951.

*James, Henry, *Roderick Hudson*. Boston: Houghton Mifflin, 1977 (orig. 1875).

———, *The American*. New York: New American Library, 1963 (orig. 1877).

———, *The Portrait of a Lady*. New York: Modern Library, 1951 (orig. 1881).

———, *The Princess Casamassima*. New York: Crowell, 1976 (orig. 1886).

———, *The Tragic Muse*. New York: Crowell, 1975 (orig. 1890).

———, *What Maisie Knew*. New York: Anchor, 1954, (orig. 1897).

———, *The Ambassadors*. New York: Washington Square, 1963 (orig. 1903).

———, *The Art of the Novel: Critical Prefaces*. New York: Scribner's, 1934 (orig. 1909).

Jameson, Frederic, *The Ideologies of Theory: Essays 1971–1986*, Vol. 1, *Situations of Theory*. Minneapolis: University of Minnesota Press, 1988.

———, *The Ideologies of Theory: Essays 1971–1986*, Vol. 2, *Syntax of History*. Minneapolis: University of Minnesota Press, 1988.

———, "Introduction." Pp. vii–xxiv in Henri Arvon, *Marxist Asthetics*. Ithaca, NY: Cornell University Press, tr. Helen R. Lane, 1973.

*Jarrell, Randall, *Pictures from an Institution: A Comedy*. New York: Avon, 1980 (orig. 1954).

Jenkinson, Marion D., "Reading and Diversity." Pp. 6–8 in Robert Karlin (ed.), *Reading for All: Proceedings of the Fourth International Reading Association World Congress on Reading*. Newark, DE: International Reading Association, 1973.

Johnson, Barbara, *The Critical Difference: Essays in the Contemporary Rhetoric of Reading*. Baltimore: John Hopkins University Press, 1985.

*Johnson, Diane, *The Shadows Knows*. New York: Vintage, 1982 (orig. 1974).

——, *Terrorists and Novelists*. New York: Knopf, 1982.

*Johnson, Pamela Hansford, *Winter Quarters*. New York: Macmillan, 1944.

——, *The Survival of the Fittest*. Chicago: University of Chicago Press, 1983 (orig. 1968).

*Jolley, Elizabeth, *Foxybaby*. New York: Penguin Books, 1986.

*Jones, James, *From Here to Eternity*. New York: Scribner's, 1951.

Josipovici, Gabriel, "Introduction." Pp. 1–14 in Gabriel Josipovici (ed.), *The Modern English Novel: The Reader, the Writer and the Work*. London: Open Books, 1976.

Joyce, James, *A Portrait of the Artist as a Young Man*. New York: Penguin, 1976.

Karanikas, Alexander, *Tillers of a Myth: Southern Agrarians as Social and Literary Critics*. Madison: University of Wisconsin Press, 1969.

Kaplan, Abraham, "The Aesthetics of the Popular Arts." Pp. 315–42 in Irving Deer and Harriet A. Deer (eds.), *The Popular Arts: A Critical Reader*. New York: Scribner's, 1967.

Keller, Evelyn Fox, *Reflections on Gender and Science*. New Haven: Yale University Press, 1985.

Kempton, Kenneth Payson, "Are Editors People?" Pp. 243–53 in Trentwell Mason White, *How to Write for a Living*. New York: Reynal & Hitchcock, 1937.

*Kennedy, William, *Ironweed*. New York: Viking Press, 1983.

Kermode, Frank, "Introduction." Pp. ix–xviii in George Plimpton (ed.), *Writers at Work: The Paris Interviews*, Sixth Series. New York: Viking Press, 1984.

*Kerouac, Jack, *Lonesome Traveler*. New York: Ballantine, 1973 (orig. 1960).

*Kesey, Ken, *Sometimes a Great Notion*. New York: Bantam, 1965.

*Keyes, Frances Parkinson, *Dinner at Antoine's*. New York: Julian Messner, 1948.

Kierkegaard, Søren, *The Diary of Søren Kierkegaard*. New York: Philosophical Library, ed. Peter P. Rhode, 1960.

*Kingston, Maxine Hong, *The Woman Warrior: Memoirs of a Girlhood among Ghosts*. New York: Knopf, 1977.

*Kipling, Rudyard, *Kim*. New York: Modern Library, 1928 (orig. 1900).

Klapp, Orrin, *Models of Social Order: An Introduction to Sociological Theory*. Palo Alto, CA: National Press Books, 1973.

Koontz, Dean R., *How to Write Best-Selling Fiction*. Cincinnati: Writer's Digest Books, 1981.

*Kosinski, Jerzy, *The Painted Bird*. Boston: Houghton Mifflin, 1976.

————, *Blind Date. New York: Bantam, 1978.

Kraft, Eric, "At Last, a Boy to Toy With." (Review of *Second Fiddle* by Mary Wesley.) *The New York Times Book Review* (July 30, 1989), 8.

Kramer, Judith R., "The Social Role of the Literary Critic." Pp. 437–54 in Milton C. Albrecht, James H. Barnett, and Mason Griff (eds.), *The Sociology of Art and Literature*. New York: Praeger, 1970.

*Krantz, Judith, *Scruples*. New York: Warner Books, 1979.

Kujoth, Jean Spealman (compiler), *Book Publishing: Inside Views*. Metuchen, NJ: Scarecrow Press, 1971.

Kunitz, Stanley J. (ed.), *American Authors 1600–1900*. New York: H. W. Wilson Company, 1938.

————, (ed.), *British Authors of the Nineteenth Century*. New York: H. W. Wilson Company, 1936.

Kwant, Remy C., *Phenomenology of Expression*. Pittsburg: Duquesne University Press, 1969, p. 57.

Lacy, Dan, "The Economics of Publishing, or Adam Smith and Literature." Pp. 30–51 in Jean Spealman Kujoth (compiler), *Book Publishing: Inside Views*. Metuchen, NJ: Scarecrow, 1971 (orig. Daedalus 92 (Winter, 1963), 42–62).

————, "The Economics of Publishing, or Adam Smith and Literature." Pp. 407–425 in Milton C. Albrecht, James H. Barnett, and Mason Griff (eds.), *The Sociology of Art and Literature: A Reader*. New York: Praeger, 1970.

Landgrebe, Ludwig, "The World as a Phenomenological Problem." *Philosophy and Phenomenological Research* 1 (September, 1940): 38–58.

Lang, Kurt, "Mass, Class, and the Reviewer." Pp. 455–68 in Milton C. Albrecht, James H. Barnett, and Mason Griff (eds.), *The Sociology of Art and Literature*. New York: Praeger, 1970.

Langland, Elizabeth, *Society in the Novel*. Chapel Hill: University of North Carolina Press, 1984.

Lass, Abraham H. (ed.), *Plot Guides to 100 American and British Novels*. Boston: The Writer, 1966.

Laurenson, Diana T. and Alan Swingewood, *The Sociology of Literature*. New York: Schocken Books, 1972.

Laurenson, Diana T., "The Writer and Society." Part Two of Diana T. Laurenson and Alan Swingewood, *The Sociology of Literature*. New York: Schocken Books, 1972.

Lawall, Sarah, *Critics of Consciousness*. Cambridge: Harvard University Press, 1968.

*Lawrence, D. H., *Women in Love*. New York: Bantam, 1969 (orig. 1920).

———, *Lady Chatterly's Lover*. New York: Grove Press, 1962 (orig. 1929).

———, *Selected Literary Criticism*. New York: Viking Press, ed. Anthony Beal, 1966.

*LeCarré, John, *Tinker, Tailor, Soldier, Spy*. New York: Bantam, 1975.

Lee, Charles, *The Hidden Public: The Story of the Book-of-the-Month Club*. New York: Doubleday, 1958.

*Lee, Harper, *To Kill a Mockingbird*. Philadelphia: Lippincott, 1960.

Le Guin, Ursula K., "It Was a Dark and Stormy Night; or, Why Are We Huddling about the Campfire?" Pp. 187–95 in W. J. T. Mitchell (ed.), *On Narrative*. Chicago: University of Chicago Press, 1981.

Leithauser, Brad, "Microscopy." (Review of *The Mezzanine* by Nicholson Baker.) *The New York Review of Books* (August 17, 1989), 15.

Lentricchia, Frank, *After the New Criticism*. Chicago: University of Chicago Press, 1980.

Leonard, John, "Dedication—For Henry Robbins (1927–1979)." Pp. vii–viii in Bill Henderson (ed.), *The Art of Literary Publishing: Editors on their Craft*. Yonkers, NY: Pushcast Book Press, 1980.

Lepenies, Wolf, *Between Literature and Science: The Rise of Sociology*. New York: Cambridge University Press, tr. R. J. Hollingdale, 1988.

*Lessing, Doris, *The Four-Gated City*. New York: New American Library, 1976 (orig. 1969).

———, *A Small Personal Voice: Essays, Reviews, Interviews*. New York: Vintage Books, 1975.

Levine, George, *The Realistic Imagination: English Fiction from Frankenstein to Lady Chatterly*. Chicago: University of Chicago Press, 1981.

Lewis, Freeman, "Mass Market Paperbacks." Pp. 379–88 in Chandler B. Grannis (ed.), *What Happens in Publishing*. New York: Columbia University Press, Second Edition, 1967.

Lewis, M. M., *The Importance of Illiteracy*. London: George C. Harrap & Company, 1953.

Lewis, C. S., "Christianity and Literature." Pp. 46–54 in G. B. Tennyson and Edward E. Ericson, Jr. (eds.), *Religion and Modern Literature: Essays in Theory and Criticism*. Grand Rapids: William B. Eerdmans Publishing Company, 1975.

*Lewis, Sinclair, *Main Street: The Story of Carol Kennicott*. New York: Harcourt, Brace and Howe, 1920.

————, *Babbitt*. New York: Grosset & Dunlap, 1922.

————, *Arrowsmith*. New York: P. F. Collier & Son Company, 1925.

Levin, Harry, "Literature as an Institution." Pp. 56–70 in Elizabeth and Tom Burns (eds.), *Sociology of Literature and Drama: Selected Readings*. Harmondsworth, Middlesex, England: Penguin, 1973.

Line, Maurice B., "Some Questions Concerning the Unprinted Word." Pp. 27–35 in Philip Hills (ed.), *The Future of the Printed Word: The Impact and the Implications of the New Communications Technology*. Westport, CT: Greenwood Press, 1980.

Link, Henry C., and Harry Arthur Hopf, *People and Books: A Study of Reading and Book-Buying Habits*. New York: Book Industry Committee, Book Manufacturers' Institute, 1946.

Lockridge, Kenneth A., "Literacy in Early America 1650–1800." Pp. 183–200 in Harvey J. Graff (ed.), *Literacy and Social Development in the West: A Reader*. Cambridge: Cambridge University Press, 1981.

Lofland, John. "Early Goffman: Style, Structure, Substance, Soul." Pp. 24–51 in Jason Ditton (ed.), *The View from Goffman*. London: Macmillan, 1980.

*London, Jack, *The Valley of the Moon*. Santa Barbara: Peregrine Smith, Inc., 1975 (orig. 1913).

Long, Elizabeth, *The American Dream and the Popular Novel*. Boston: Routledge & Kegan Paul, 1985.

*Loos, Anita, *Gentlemen Prefer Blondes: The Illuminating Diary of a Professional Lady*. New York: Boni & Liveright, 1925.

L.A. Times/Washington Post News Service, "Textbook Company Succeeds with San Diego's Sea World." *Las Vegas Review-Journal*, May 23, 1982, 2J.

Lubbock, Percy, *The Craft of Fiction*. New York: Viking, 1957.

Lukacs, Georg, *Soul and Form*. Cambridge, MA: MIT Press, tr. Anna Bostock, 1978.

————, *History and Class Consciousness: Studies in Marxist Dialectics*. Cambridge, MA: MIT Press, tr. Rodney Livingstone, 1972.

*Lurie, Alison, *The War between the Tates*. New York: Warner Books, 1975.

Lyon, Bill, "Expatriate Writer Frank Yerby Is Grousing Even Though his 30th Best-Seller Is Coming Up." *People Magazine* 15 (March 30, 1981): 99+.

Macpherson, C. B., *The Political Theory of Possessive Individualism: Hobbes to Locke*. London: Oxford University Press, 1962.

Magliola, Robert R., *Phenomenology and Literature: An Introduction*. West Lafayette, IN: Purdue University Press, 1977.

*Mailer, Norman, *The Naked and the Dead*. New York: Signet, 1971 (orig. 1948).

————, *An American Dream*. New York: Dell, 1966.

————, *Why Are We in Vietnam?* New York: Berkley Publishing Corporation, 1967.

————, *The Armies of the Night: History as a Novel, The Novel as History*. New York: New American Library, 1968.

————, *The Prisoner of Sex*. New York: Signet, 1971.

————, "Preface." Pp. xvii–xxi in Hallie and White Burnett, *Fiction Writer's Handbook*. New York: Harper & Row, 1975.

Mainiero, Lisa (ed.), *American Women Writers*. New York: Frederick Ungar, 1979.

*Malamud, Bernard, *A New Life*. New York: Dell, 1963.

————, *The Fixer*. New York: Farrar, Straus and Giroux, 1966.

Malraux, André, *Man's Fate*. New York: Vintage, tr. Haakon M. Chevalier, 1961.

————, *The Temptation of the West*. New York: Jubilee Books, tr. Robert Hollander, 1974.

Mann, Peter H., *Author-Publisher Relationships in Scholarly Publishing*. London: The British Library Research and Development Department, 1978.

Manning, Peter K., "Goffman's Framing Order: Style as Structure." Pp. 252–84 in Jason Ditton (ed.), *The View from Goffman*. London: Macmillan, 1980.

Marchalonis, Shirley (ed.), *Patrons and Protegées: Gender, Friendship, and Writing in Nineteenth-Century America*. New Brunswick, NJ: Rutgers University Press, 1988.

Marcus, Jane, "Still Practice, A/Wrested Alphabet: Toward a Feminist Aesthetic." *Tulsa Studies in Women's Literature* 3 (Spring/Fall, 1984): 79–97.

Marks, Joseph, "Subsidiary Rights and Permissions." Pp. 230–41 in Chandler B. Grannis (ed.), *What Happens in Publishing.* New York: Columbia University Press, Second Edition, 1967.

*Marquand, John P., *The Late George Apley: A Novel in the Form of a Memoir.* New York: Modern Library, 1940 (orig. 1936).

———, *Point of No Return.* Boston: Little, Brown, 1949.

Martin, Wallace, *Recent Theories of Narrative.* Ithaca, NY: Cornell University Press, 1986.

Marx, Karl, *Capital*, Vol. 1. New York: International Publishers, tr. Samuel Morse and Edward Aveling, 1967, p. 75.

Mazlish, Bruce, *A New Science: The Breakdown of Connections and the Birth of Sociology.* New York: Oxford University Press, 1989.

Masuzawa, Tomoko, "The Sacred Difference: On Durkheim's Last Quest." *Representations* 23 (Summer, 1988): 25–50.

*Maugham, W. Somerset, *Of Human Bondage.* New York: Doubleday, 1936 (orig. 1915).

———, *The Summing Up.* New York: Doubleday, Doran & Company, 1938.

———, *The Razor's Edge.* New York: International Collectors Library, 1944.

McCaffery, Larry and Linda Gregory, *Alive and Writing: Interviews with American Authors of the 1980s.* Urbana: University of Illinois Press, 1987.

*McCarthy, Mary, *The Group.* New York: Signet, 1972.

———, *Ideas and the Novel.* New York: Harcourt Brace Jovanovich, 1980.

*McCullers, Carson, *The Heart Is a Lonely Hunter.* Boston: Houghton Mifflin, 1940.

———, *The Member of the Wedding.* New York: Bantam, 1958.

McKee, John B., *Literary Irony and the Literary Audience: Studies in the Victimization of the Reader in Augustan Fiction.* Amsterdam: Dodopi, N.V., 1974.

McKeon, Zahava Karl, *Novels and Arguments: Inventing Rhetorical Criticism.* Chicago: University of Chicago Press, 1982.

McLuhan, Marshall, *The Gutenberg Galaxy: The Making of Typographic Man.* New York: Signet, 1969 (orig. 1962).

Meadows, A. J., "The Future of the Printed Word: Economic and Social Factors." Pp. 149–61 in Philip Hills (ed.), *The Future of the Printed Word: The Impact and the Implications of the New Communication Technology.* Westport, CT: Greenwood, 1980.

*Melville, Herman, *Billy Budd.* New York: Scholastic Book Services, 1968 (orig. 1924).

———, *Moby Dick.* New York: Modern Library, n.d. (orig. 1851).

*Meredith, George, *The Ordeal of Richard Feverel: A History of a Father and Son.* New York: Macmillan, 1926 (orig. 1859).

———, *The Egoist: A Comedy in Narrative.* New York: Modern Library, 1951 (orig. 1879).

Merleau-Ponty, Maurice, *In Praise of Philosophy.* Evanston: Northwestern University Press, trs. John Wild and James M. Edie, 1963, p. 55.

*Metalious, Grace, *Peyton Place.* New York: Dell, 1957.

Meyers, Jeffrey, *Married to Genius.* New York: Barnes & Noble, 1977.

Michener, James, "A Writer's Public Image." Pp. 192–201 in Jean Spealman Kujoth (compiler), *Book Publishing: Inside Views.* Metuchen, NJ: Scarecrow 1971 (orig. *Esquire Magazine* 64 [December, 1965], 150).

*Miller, Henry, *Tropic of Cancer.* New York: Ballantine, 1973 (orig. 1934).

———, *Tropic of Capricorn.* New York: Ballantine, 1974 (orig. 1939).

Miller, James E. Jr., *World, Self, Reality: The Rhetoric of Imagination.* New York: Dodd, Mead & Company, 1974, p. 7.

Mills, C. Wright, "The Cultural Apparatus." Pp. 405–22 in Irving Louis Horowitz (ed.), *Power, Politics and People: The Collected Essays of C. Wright Mills.* New York: Oxford University Press, 1967.

———, *The Sociological Imagination.* New York: Oxford University Press, 1959.

Miner, Madonne N., "Guaranteed to Please: Twentieth-Century Women's Bestsellers." Pp. 187–211 in Elizabeth A. Flynn and Patrocinio P. Schweickart (eds.), *Gender and Reading: Essays on Readers, Texts, and Context.* Baltimore: Johns Hopkins University Press, 1986.

*Mitchell, Margaret, *Gone with the Wind.* New York: Macmillian, 1964 (orig. 1936).

Moers, Ellen, *Literary Women.* Garden City, NY: Anchor Books, 1977.

Monaghan, Peter, "Anthropologist Who Sparked Dispute by Criticizing Margaret Mead's Research on Samoan Life Finds New Backing for His

Claims, Some Still Skeptical." *The Chronicle of Higher Education* (August 2, 1989): A4–A6.

*Morris, Wright, *Cause for Wonder*. Lincoln: University of Nebraska Press, 1978 (orig. 1963).

———, *War Games*. Lincoln: University of Nebraska Press, 1978 (orig. 1972).

———, *The Territory Ahead*. Lincoln: University of Nebraska Press, 1978.

*Morrison, Toni, *Beloved*. New York: Knopf, 1988.

Morse, Grace, "Author-Agent-Publisher." Pp. 259–67 in Trentwell Mason White (ed.), *How to Write for a Living*. New York: Reynal & Hitchcock, 1937.

Moser, Howard Frank, "Far from Kennebunkport." (Review of *Monkey Bay* by Elaine Ford.) *The New York Times Book Review* (August 6, 1989), 9.

*Mortimer, Penelope, *The Pumpkin Eater*. New York: Dell, Laurel Books, 1986 (orig. 1962).

Muir, Edwin, *The Structure of the Novel*. New York: Harcourt, Brace, 1929.

Mumby, Frank Arthur, *Publishing and Bookselling: A History from Earliest Times to the Present Day*. London: Jonathan Cape, Fourth Edition, 1956 (orig. 1930).

*Murdoch, Iris, *An Accidental Man*. New York: Warner, 1973.

———, *The Good Apprentice*. New York: Viking, 1986.

Murphy, Lawrence Park, "Beadle & Co." Pp. 35–50 in Madeleine B. Stern (ed.), *Publishers for Mass Entertainment in Nineteenth Century America*. Boston: G. K. Hall, 1980.

Murray, Michele, *The Writer and Her Work*. New York: Norton, 1980.

Myoshi, Masao, *The Divided Self: A Perspective on the Literature of the Victorians*. New York: New York University Press, 1969.

*Nabokov, Vladimir, *Invitation to a Beheading*. Greenwich, CT: Fawcett, tr. Dmitri Nabokov with Vladimir Nabokov, 1960.

———, *Lolita*. New York: Berkeley, 1966.

Natanson, Maurice, *Edmund Husserl: Philosopher of Infinite Tasks*. Evanston: Northwest University Press, 1973.

National Committee on Reading, "Report of the Committee on Reading, National Academy of Education." Pp. 3–57 in John B. Carroll and Jeanne S. Chall (eds.), *Toward a Literate Society: The Report of the Commit-

tee on Reading of the National Academy of Education. New York: McGraw-Hill, 1975.

Nell, Victor, *Lost in a Book: The Psychology of Reading for Pleasure*. New Haven: Yale University Press, 1988.

———, "The Psychology of Reading for Pleasure: Needs and Gratifications." *Reading and Research Quarterly* XXIII, No. 1 (Winter, 1988): 6–50.

Nemerov, Howard, *Journal of the Fictive Life*. New Brunswick, NJ: Rutgers University Press, 1965.

Nisbet, Robert, *Sociology as an Art Form*. New York: Oxford University Press, 1976.

Noble, Trevor, "Sociology and Literature." *British Journal of Sociology* 27 (June, 1976): 211–24.

*Norris, Frank, *McTeague*. New York: Signet, 1964 (orig. 1899).

———, **The Octopus: A Story of California*. New York: Bantam, 1977 (orig. 1901).

———, **The Pit: A Story of Chicago*. Columbus, OH: Merrill, 1970 (orig. 1903).

Nye, Russell, *The Unembarrassed Muse: The Popular Arts in America*. New York: Dial, 1970.

Nyerere, Julius, "Preface." Pp. vii–viii in Leon Bataille (ed.), *A Turning Point for Literacy: Adult Education for Development, The Spirit and Declaration of Persepolis*. Proceedings of the International Symposium for Literacy; Persepolis, Iran, September, 1975. New York: Pergamon, 1976.

*Oates, Joyce Carol, *Expensive People*. New York: Fawcett, 1968.

———, **Them*. Greenwich, CT: Fawcett, 1969.

———, **Do With Me What You Will*. New York: Vanguard, 1973.

———, *(Woman) Writer: Occasions and Opportunities*. New York: Dutton, 1989.

*O'Connor, Edwin, *The Last Hurrah*. Boston: Little, Brown, 1956.

*O'Connor, Flannery, *The Violent Bear It Away*. New York: Noonday, 1974.

———, "Novelist and Believer." Pp. 68–75 in G. B. Tennyson and Edward E. Ericson, Jr. (eds.), *Religion and Modern Literature: Essays in Theory and Criticism*. Grand Rapids: William B. Eerdmans Publishing Company, 1975.

Ogden, Annagret S., *The Great American Housewife: From Helpmate to Wage Earner, 1776–1986*. Westport, CT: Greenwood, 1986.

*O'Hara, John, *A Rage to Live*. New York: Random House, 1949.

———, *My Turn*. New York: Random House, 1966.

Owen, Jean Z., *Professional Fiction Writing: A Practical Guide to Modern Techniques*. Boston: The Writer, 1974.

Parrinder, Patrick, *Authors and Authority: A Study of English Literary Criticism and its Relation to Culture, 1750–1900*. Boston: Routledge & Kegan Paul, 1977.

Parrington, Vernon Louis, *Main Currents in American Thought*. New York: Harcourt, Brace, 1930.

Patterson, Harry O., "Reading Improvement Programs in General Motors." Pp. 31–7 in Dorothy M. Dietrich and Virginia H. Mathews (eds.), *Reading and Revolution: The Role of Reading in Today's Society*. Newark, DE: International Reading Association, 1970.

———, "The Essential Ingredients of an Adult Reading Improvement Program in Industry." Pp. 213–15 in J. Allen Figurel (ed.), *Reading in a Changing Society*. Conference Proceedings, International Reading Association, Volume 4. New York: International Reading Association and Scholastic Magazines, 1959.

Peck, Robert Newton, *Secrets of Successful Fiction*. Cincinnati: Writer's Digest Books, 1980.

*Percy, Walker, *Lancelot*. New York: Avon, 1978.

———, *The Last Gentleman*. New York: Avon, 1978.

———, *The Moviegoer*. New York: Avon, 1980.

———, *Love in the Ruins*. New York: Avon, 1978.

Perkins, Maxwell, "Publishing Thomas Wolfe." Pp. 244–53 in Bill Henderson (ed.), *The Art of Literary Publishing: Editors on their Craft*. Yonkers, NY: Pushcart Press Books, 1980.

Peterson, Carla L., *The Determined Reader: Gender and Culture in the Novel from Napoleon to Victoria*. New Brunswick, NJ: Rutgers University Press, 1987.

Peterson, Richard, ed., *The Production of Culture*. Beverly Hills: Sage, 1976.

Phelan, James, *Worlds from Words: A Theory of Language in Fiction*. Chicago: University of Chicago Press, 1981.

*Phillips, Jayne Anne. *Machine Dreams*. New York: Dutton/Seymour Lawrence, 1984.

Piehl, Kathy, "E. L. Doctorow and Random House: The Ragtime Rhythm of Cash." *Journal of Popular Culture* 13 (Spring, 1980): 404–11.

Pivcevic, Edo, *Husserl and Phenomenology.* London: Hutchinson and Company, 1970.

Plante, David, "In the Heart of Literary London." *The New York Times Magazine* (September 11, 1988): 42–43, 80, 82, 84, 86.

*Plath, Sylvia, *The Bell Jar.* New York: Bantam: 1972 (orig. 1966).

——, *Letters Home: Correspondence 1950–1963.* New York: Harper & Row, 1975.

Plimpton, George (ed.), *Writers at Work: The Paris Interviews,* Sixth Series. New York: Viking Press, 1984.

Plotnik, Arthur, "Book Editors: A Special Breed." *Publishers Weekly* 222, No. 18 (October 29, 1982): 22–24.

Plotz, Judith A., "'Potatoes in a Cellar': Charlotte Brontë's *Villette* and the Feminized Imagination." *Journal of Women's Studies in Literature* 1 (Winter, 1979): 74–87.

Polanyi, Michael, and Harry Prosch, *Meaning.* Chicago: University of Chicago Press, 1975.

*Porter, Gene Stratton, *The Harvester.* New York: Grossett & Dunlap, 1916.

Powel, Harford, Jr., "The Author's Second Trade." Pp. 254–58 in Trentwell Mason White (ed.), *How to Write for a Living.* New York: Reynal & Hitchcock, 1937.

Price, Martin, "The Other Self: Thoughts about Character in the Novel." Pp. 260–79 in Elizabeth and Tom Burns (eds.), *Sociology of Literature and Drama: Selected Readings.* Harmondsworth, Middlesex, England: Penguin, 1973.

*Priestley, J. B., *Angel Pavement.* London: Heinemann, 1966 (orig. 1930).

——, "Publishing Stocks Soar 40% in 1982." *Publishers Weekly* 233, No. 3 (January 21, 1983), 26.

*Purdy, James, *Mourners Below.* New York: Penguin, 1982.

Purdy, Ken, "The Fruit of the Bittersweet." Pp. 266–73 in Aron M. Mathieu (ed.), *The Creative Writer.* Cincinnati: Writer's Digest, Second Revised Edition, 1972.

*Pym, Barbara, *A Glass of Blessings.* New York: Harper & Row, Perennial Library, 1981.

*Pynchon, Thomas, V. New York: Bantam, 1964.

———, *The Crying of Lot 49. Philadelphia: Lippincott, 1966.

———, *Gravity's Rainbow. New York: Bantam, 1974.

Queneau, Raymond, The Bark Tree. New York: New Directions, tr. Barbara Wright, 1971.

Radway, Janice, "The Book-of-the-Month Club and the General Reader: On the Uses of 'Serious' Fiction." Pp. 154–76 in Phillippe Desan, Priscilla Parkhurst Ferguson, and Wendy Griswold (eds.), Literature and Social Practice. Chicago: University of Chicago Press, 1989.

———, Reading the Romance: Women, Patriarchy, and Popular Literature. Chapel Hill: University of North Carolina Press, 1984.

———, "Phenomenology, Linguistics, and Popular Literature." Journal of Popular Culture 12 (Summer, 1978): 88–98.

Rahv, Philip, Literature and the Sixth Sense. Boston: Houghton Mifflin, 1969.

Raines, Howell, Whiskey Man. New York: Viking, 1977, p. 63.

Ramsey, Paul, "Literary Criticism and Sociology." Yearbook of Comparative Criticism V (1973): 21–29 (ed. Joseph P. Strelka).

*Rand, Ayn, Atlas Shrugged. New York: Random House, 1957.

———, The Romantic Manifesto: A Philosophy of Literature. New York: New American Library, Revised Edition, 1975.

Ransom, John Crowe, Beating the Bushes: Selected Essays, 1941–1970. New York: New Directions, 1972.

*Rawlings, Marjorie Kinnan, The Yearling. New York: Collier Books, 1986 (orig. 1938).

Raymond, Chris, "Researchers Link Manic-Depressive Illness and Creativity." The Chronicle of Higher Education (June 21, 1989): A4, A6.

Reed, Walter L., An Exemplary History of the Novel: The Quixotic Versus the Picaresque. Chicago: University of Chicago Press, 1981.

*Remarque, Erich Maria, All Quiet on the Western Front. Boston: Little, Brown, tr. A. W. Wheen, 1929.

Resnick, Lauren B., and Betty H. Robinson, "Motivational Aspects of the Literacy Problem." Pp. 257–77 in John B. Carroll and Jeanne S. Chall (eds.), Toward a Literate Society: The Report of the Committee on Reading of the National Academy of Education. New York: McGraw-Hill, 1975.

Reynolds, Paul R., "The Literary Agent—His Function, Life, and Power." Pp. 241–46 in Jean Spealman Kujoth (compiler), *Book Publishing: Inside Views*. Metuchen, NJ: Scarecrow, 1971 (orig. *Saturday Review* 49 (October 8, 1966), 113–14).

*Rhys, Jean, *Quartet*. New York: Vintage, 1974 (orig. 1928).

————, *Good Morning, Midnight*. New York: Vintage, 1974 (orig. 1939).

Ricoeur, Paul, *Fallible Man: Philosophy of the Will*. Chicago: Regnery, tr. Charles Kelbley, 1965.

————, *Interpretation Theory: Discourse and the Surplus of Meaning*. Fort Worth: Texas Christian University, 1976.

Rieser, Max, *Analysis of Poetic Thinking*. Detroit: Wayne State University press, tr. Herbert M. Schueller, 1969.

Rilke, Rainer Maria, *Letters to a Young Poet*. New York: Norton, tr. M. D. Herter Norton, 1962.

*Rinehart, Mary Roberts, *K*. Boston: Houghton Mifflin, 1915.

*Robbins, Harold, *Never Love a Stranger*. Anstey, Leicestershire, Great Britain: F. A. Thorpe, Ltd., 1982 (orig. 1958).

————, *The Carpetbaggers*. New York: Simon and Schuster, Trident Press Book, 1961.

*Robbins, Tom, *Still Life with Woodpecker*. New York: Bantam, 1980.

Roberts, Ruth, *The Moral Trollope*. Athens: Ohio University Press, 1971.

Robinson, Lillian S., "Treason Our Text: Feminist Challenges to the Literary Canon." *Tulsa Studies in Women's Literature* 2 (Spring, 1983): 83–98.

*Robinson, Marilynne, *Housekeeping*. New York: Bantam, 1982.

Rogers, Mary F., "Ideology, Perspective, and Praxis." *Human Studies: A Journal for Philosophy and the Social Sciences* 4 (1981): 167–86.

————, "Everyday Life As Text" in Randall Collins (ed.), *Sociological Theory*. San Francisco: Jossey-Bass, 1984, pp. 165–86.

————, "Literary Socialization and Literary Interaction: Novelists on Reading Novels." *Current Perspectives in Social Theory: A Research Annual* 6 (1985): 261–78.

————, "Taken for Grantedness." *Current Perspectives in Social Theory: A Research Annual* 2 (1981): 133–151.

*Roth, Philip, *Portnoy's Complaint*. New York: Bantam, 1970.

————, *My Life as a Man. New York: Bantam, 1975.

————, *The Ghost Writer. New York: Fawcett, 1979.

Rothstein, Mervyn, "Homegrown Fiction." *The New York Times Magazine* (Mary 15, 1988): 50, 98–99, 101, 108.

Rowe, Deborah Wells and Lawrence Rayford, "Activating Background Knowledge in Reading Comprehension Assessment." *Reading Research Quarterly* XXII (Summer, 1987): 160–176.

Ruas, Charles, *Conversations with American Writers.* New York: Alfred A. Knopf, 1985.

Rubin, Louis D., Jr., *The Teller in the Tale.* Seattle: University of Washington Press, 1967.

Rubins, Josh, "They All Want a Piece of the Legend." (Review of *Various Miracles* and *Swann* by Carol Shields.) *The New York Times Book Review* (August 6, 1989), 11.

Ruff, Ivan, "Can There Be A Sociology of Literature?" *British Journal of Sociology* 25 (September, 1974): 367–72.

Ryan, Desmond, "Sleeping His Way to the Middle." (Review of *Sacred Monster* by Donald E. Westlake.) *The New York Times Book Review* (July 30, 1989), 12.

Ryan, T. A., and Wiliam Furlong, "Literacy Programs in Industry, the Armed Forces, and Penal Institutions." Pp. 165–89 in John B. Carroll and Jeanne S. Chall (eds.), *Towards a Literate Society: Report of the Committee on Reading of the National Academy of Education.* New York: McGraw-Hill, 1975.

Ryan, William, *Blaming the Victim.* New York: Vintage, 1976.

*Salinger, J. D., *Catcher in the Rye.* New York: Bantam, 1964 (orig. 1951).

Sammons, Jeffrey L., *Literary Sociology and Practical Criticism: An Inquiry.* Bloomington: Indiana University Press, 1977.

————, "The Threat of Literary Sociology and What to Do about It." *Yearbook of Comparative Criticism* V (1973): 30–40 (ed. Joseph P. Strelka).

*Santayana, George, *The Last Puritan: A Memoir in the Form of a Novel.* New York: Scribner's, 1936.

————, *The Sense of Beauty: Being the Outline of Aesthetic Theory.* New York: Dover Publications, 1955 (orig. 1896).

*Saroyan, William, *The Human Comedy.* New York: Dell, Laurel Books, 1984 (orig. 1943).

*Sarton, May, *The Small Room.* New York: Norton, 1976 (orig. 1961).

———, *Mrs. Stevens Hears the Mermaids Singing. New York: Norton, 1975.

———, *The Magnificent Spinster. New York: W. W. Norton, 1985.

———, Journal of a Solitude. New York: Norton, 1977.

Sartre, Jean-Paul, Nausea. New York: New Directions, 1964.

———, The Age of Reason. New York: Vintage, 1973.

———, The Reprieve. New York: Vintage, 1973.

———, Troubled Sleep. New York: Vintage, 1973.

*Sayers, Dorothy L., Murder Must Advertise (a novel) and Hangman's Holiday (short stories). New York: Harcourt, Brace, 1933.

Schenck, Celeste M., "Feminism and Deconstruction: Re-Contructing the Elegy." Tulsa Studies in Women's Literature 5 (Spring, 1985): 13–27.

Schick, Frank L., The Paperbound Book in America. New York: Bowker, 1958.

Schofield, R. S., "The Measurement of Literacy in Pre-Industrial England." Pp. 311–25 in Jack Goody (ed.), Literacy in Traditional Societies. Cambridge: Cambridge University Press, 1968.

———, "Dimensions of Illiteracy in England 1750–1850." Pp. 201–13 in Harvey J. Graff (ed.), Literacy and Social Development in the West: A Reader. Cambridge: Cambridge University Press, 1981 (orig. Explorations in Economics History 10 (1973), 437–54).

Scholes, Robert, Fabulation and Metafiction. Urbana: University of Illinois Press, 1979.

Schorer, Mark, "Technique as Discovery." Pp. 9–29 in William Van O'Connor (ed.), Forms of Modern Fiction. Bloomington: Indiana University press, 1961.

Schucking, Levin L., The Sociology of Literary Taste. Chicago: University of Chicago Press, tr. Brian Battershaw, 1966 (orig. 1923).

Schutz, Alfred, The Phenomenology of the Social World. Evanston, IL: Northwestern University Press, tr. George Walsh and Frederick Lehnert, 1967.

———, Reflections on the Problem of Relevance. New Haven: Yale University Press, ed. and ann. Richard M. Zaner, 1970.

———, Collected Papers I: The Problem of Social Reality. The Hague: Nijhoff, ed. Maurice Natanson, 1973.

———, "Don Quixote and the Problem of Reality." Pp. 251–59 in Elizabeth and Tom Burns (eds.), Sociology of Literature and Drama: Selected Readings. Harmondsworth, Middlesex, England: Penguin, 1973.

————, *Collected Papers II: Studies in Social Theory*. The Hague: Nijhoff, ed. Arvid Brodersen, 1976.

Schutz, Alfred, and Thomas Luckmann, *The Structures of the Life-World*. Evanston: Northwestern University Press, tr. Richard M. Zaner and H. Tristram Engelhardt, Jr., 1973.

*Schwartz, Jane, *Caught*. New York: Ballantine, 1983.

Schweickart, Patrocinio P., "Reading Ourselves: Toward a Feminist Theory of Reading." Pp. 31–62 in Elizabeth A. Flynn and Patroncinio P. Schweickart (eds.), *Gender and Reading: Essays on Readers, Texts, and Contexts*. Baltimore: Johns Hopkins University Press, 1986.

Scott, Nathan A., Jr., "The Name and Nature of our Period-Style." Pp. 121–37 in G. B. Tennyson and Edward E. Ericson, Jr. (eds.), *Religion and Modern Literature: Essays in Theory and Criticism*. Grand Rapids: William B. Eerdmans Publishing Company, 1975.

Sederberg, Peter C. with Nancy B. Sederberg, "Transmitting the Nontransmissible: The Function of Literature in the Pursuit of Social Knowledge." *Philosophy and Phenomenological Research* 36 (December, 1975): 173–96.

*Segal, Erich, *Love Story*. New York: Signet, 1970.

Sennett, Richard, *The Frog Who Dared to Croak*. New York: Farrar, Straus & Giroux, 1982.

Sharon, Amiel T. "What Do Adults Read?" *Reading Research Quarterly* IX No. 2 (1973–1974): 148–69.

*Shaw, Irwin, *Rich Man, Poor Man*. New York: Dell, 1976.

*Sheldon, Charles Monroe, *In His Steps*. New York: Grosset & Dunlap, 1935.

Shelley, Dolores, "A Conversation with May Sarton." *Women & Literature* 7 (Spring, 1979): 33–41.

Shepard, Leslie, *The History of Street Literature: The Story of Broadside Ballads, Chapbooks, Proclamations, News-Sheets, Election Bills, Tracts, Pamphlets, Cocks, Catchpennies, and other Ephemera*. Detroit: Singing Tree Press, 1973.

Sherburn, George, "Introduction." Pp. v–xiv in Henry Fielding. *The History of Tom Jones: A Foundling*. New York: Modern Library, 1950.

Showalter, Elaine, *A Literature of Their Own*. Princeton: Princeton University Press, 1977.

————, "Women's Time, Women's Space: Writing the History of Feminist Criticism." *Tulsa Studies in Women's Literature* 3 (Spring/Fall, 1984): 29–43.

*Shulman, Max, *Rally Round the Flag, Boys!* Garden City, NY: Doubleday, 1957.

*Silber, Joan, *Household Words*. New York: Penguin, 1985.

Simmel, Georg, *On Women, Sexuality, and Love*. New Haven: Yale University Press, tr. Guy Oakes, 1984.

————, *On Individuality and Social Forms*, Chicago: University of Chicago Press, ed. Donald N. Levine, 1971, p. 180.

*Sinclair, Upton, *The Jungle*. New York: Airmont, 1965 (orig. 1906).

————, *The Cup of Fury*. New York: Hawthorn Books, 1956.

*Singer, Isaac Bashevis, *Shosha*. New York: Farrar, Straus and Giroux, 1978.

Slatoff, Walter, *With Respect to Readers: Dimensions of Literary Response*. Ithaca, NY: Cornell University Press, 1970.

Smith, Barbara Herrnstein, "Narrative Versions, Narrative Theories." Pp. 209–32 in W. J. T. Mitchel (ed.), *On Narrative*. Chicago: University of Chicago Press, 1981.

————, *On the Margins of Discourse: The Relation to Literature to Language*. Chicago: University of Chicago Press, 1978.

*Smith, Betty, *A Tree Grows In Brooklyn*. New York: Harper & Brothers, 1943.

Smith, G. Roysce, "The Future of Bookselling." Pp. 138–40 in Charles B. Anderson (ed.), *Bookselling in America and the World: Some Observations & Recollections*. New York: Quadrangle, 1975.

Smith, Jean Kennedy, and George Plimpton, "The Creative Uses of Disability, The Restorative Functions of Art," *The New York Times*, Section 2 (June 11, 1989), 6, 26.

*Smith, Lee, *Oral History*. New York: Ballantine, 1984.

*Smith, Mary-Ann Tirone , *The Book of Phoebe*. New York: Dell, Laurell Books, 1986.

Snow, C. P., *The Two Cultures: And a Second Look*. New York: Cambridge University Press, 1969.

Solotaroff, Ted, "Publishers, Booksellers, Readers, and Writers: Some Straws in a Whirlwind." Pp. 3–12 in Bill Henderson (ed.), *The Art of Literary Publishing: Editors on their Craft*. Yonkers, NY: Pushcart Book Press, 1980.

*Sontag, Susan, *The Benefactor*. New York: Dell, 1978 (orig. 1963).

————, *Against Interpretation and Other Essays*. New York: Delta Book, 1967.

————, *Death Kit*. New York: Dell, 1978 (orig. 1967).

————, *Styles of Radical Will*. New York: Delta Books, 1978.

*Spark, Muriel, *The Prime of Miss Jean Brodie*. New York: Dell, 1966.

——, *The Takeover*. New York: Viking, 1976.

Spender, Stephen, *The Making of a Poem*. New York: Norton, 1962.

——, *The Struggle of the Modern*. Berkeley and Los Angeles: University of California Press, 1965.

——, *Love-Hate Relations: English and American Sensibilities*. New York: Vintage, 1975.

*Spillane, Mickey, *I, the Jury*. New York: Signet, 1953 (orig. 1947).

Starkie, Walter, "Introduction." Pp. 15–35 in Miguel de Cervantes Saaverdra, *Don Quixote of La Mancha*. New York: New American Library, 1964.

Stedman, Lawrence C. and Carl F. Kaestle, "Literacy and Reading Performance in the United States, From 1880 to the Present." *Reading Research Quarterly* XXII (Winter, 1987): 8–46.

*Stegner, Wallace, *Crossing to Safety*. New York: Random House, 1987.

Stein, Gertrude, *Lectures in America*. New York: Vintage, 1975.

*Steinbeck, John, *Of Mice and Men*. New York: Viking, 1978 (orig. 1937).

——, *The Grapes of Wrath*. New York: Viking, 1967 (orig. 1939).

Stendhal, *The Red and the Black*. New York: Signet, 1970.

Stephens, H. Morse, "History." Pp. 23–94 in H. Morse Stephens, Agnes Repplier, Arthur T. Hadley, Brander Matthews, Bliss Perry, and Hamilton Wright Mabie, *Counsel Upon the Reading of Books*. Port Washington, NY: Kennikat, 1968 (orig. 1900).

Stern, Karl, *Love and Success: And Other Essays*. New York: Farrar, Straus, and Giroux, 1975.

Stern, Madeleine B., "Introduction." Pp. ix–xix in Madeleine B. Stern (ed.), *Publishers for Mass Entertainment in Nineteenth Century America*. Boston: G. K. Hall, 1980.

Stevens, Wallace, *The Necessary Angel: Essays on Reality and the Imagination*. New York: Vintage, 1951.

Stevick, Philip, "Metaphors for the Novel." *TriQuarterly* 30 (Spring, 1974): 127–38.

Stinchcombe, Arthur L., *Constructing Social Theories*. Chicago: University of Chicago Press, 1987 (orig. 1968).

*Stone, Irving, *Love Is Eternal: A Novel about Mary Todd and Abraham Lincoln*. Garden City, NY: Doubleday, 1954.

*Stowe, Harriet Beecher, Uncle Tom's Cabin. New York: New American Library, n.d. (orig. 1851–52).

Strasser, Susan, Never Done: A History of American Housework. New York: Pantheon, 1982.

Strauss, Anselm S., Qualitative Analysis for Social Scientists. New York: Cambridge University Press, 1987.

*Stribling, T. S., The Store. New York: Doubleday, Doran & Company, 1933.

Stubbs, Michael, Language and Literacy: The Sociolinguistics of Reading and Writing. Boston: Routledge & Kegan Paul, 1980.

Strunk, William, Jr., and E. B. White, The Elements of Style. New York: Macmillan, Third Edition, 1979.

*Styron, William, Set This House on Fire. New York: Signet, 1961.

Sundbye, Nita, "Text Explicitness and Inferential Questioning: Effects on Story Understanding and Recall." Reading Research Quarterly XXII (Winter, 1987): 82–98.

*Susann, Jacqueline, The Love Machine. New York: Bantam, 1970.

*Swados, Harvey, Celebration. New York: Simon and Schuster, 1974.

———, "The Image in the Mirror." Pp. 164–90 in Granville Hicks (ed.), The Living Novel: A Symposium. New York: Collier, 1962.

Swingewood, Alan, "Towards the Sociology of the Novel." Part Three in Diana T. Laureson and Alan Swingewood, The Sociology of Literature. New York: Schocken Books, 1972.

———, "Theory." Part One in Diana T. Laurenson and Alan Swingewood, The Sociology of Literature. New York: Schocken Books, 1972.

Swinnerton, Frank, Authors and the Book Trade. Freeport, NY: Books for Libraries Press, 1970 (orig. 1932).

———, "Authorship." Pp. 12–35 in John Hampden (ed.), The Book World. London: Thomas Nelson, 1935.

Szanto, George H. Narrative Consciousness: Structure and Perception in the Fiction of Kafka, Beckett, and Robbe-Grillet. Austin: University of Texas Press, 1972.

Tanner, Tony, "My Life in American Literature." TriQuarterly 30 (Spring, 1974): 83–108.

*Tarkington, Booth, The Plutocrat: A Novel. Garden City, NY: Doubleday, Page & Company, 1927.

Taubert, Sigfried, "World Bookselling: Some Historical Comments." Pp. 26–64 in Charles B. Anderson (ed.), *Bookselling in America and the World: Some Observations & Recollections.* New York: Quadrangle, 1975.

Tebbel, John, "Publishing Books to Sell by Mail." Pp. 399–419 in Chandler B. Grannis (ed.), *What Happens in Publishing.* New York: Columbia University Press, Second Edition, 1967.

————, "A Brief History of American Bookselling." Pp. 3–25 in Charles B. Anderson (ed.), *Bookselling in America and the World: Some Observations & Recollections.* New York: Quadrangle, 1975.

Tennyson, G. B., and Edward E. Ericson, Jr., "Introduction." Pp. 9–17 in G. B. Tennyson and Edward E. Ericson, Jr. (eds.), *Religion and Modern Literature: Essays in Theory and Criticism.* Grand Rapids: William B. Eerdmans Publishing Company, 1975.

Terhune, Albert Payson, "Why You Can't Write Dog Stories." Pp. 292–99 in Trentwell Mason White, *How to Write for a Living.* New York: Reynal & Hitchcock, 1937.

*Thackeray, William Makepeace, *The Memoirs of Barry Lyndon, Esq.* New York: Grosset & Dunlap, Tempo Books, 1975 (orig. 1844).

————, *The History of Pendennis: His Fortunes and Misfortunes; His Friends and His Greatest Enemy.* New York: Clarke, Given and Hooper, University Edition, n.d. (orig. 1848–50).

————, *Vanity Fair: A Novel without a Hero.* New York: Signet, 1962 (orig. 1848).

Thomas, Louise, "Book Publicity." Pp. 182–97 in Chandler B. Grannis (ed.), *What Happens in Book Publishing.* New York: Columbia University Press, Second Education, 1967.

Thompson, Hunter, *Hell's Angels: The Motor Cycle Gangs.* New York: Random House, 1967.

Toffler, Alvin, *The Culture Consumers: A Study of Art and Affluence in America.* New York: Vintage, 1973 (orig. 1964).

Tompkins, J. M. S., *The Popular Novel in England: 1770–1800.* Lincoln: University of Nebraska Press, 1961 (orig. 1932).

Tompkins, Jane, *Sensational Designs: The Cultural Work of American Fiction, 1790–1860.* New York: Oxford University Press, 1985.

Torsney, Cheryl B. "The Traditions of Gender: Constance Fenimore Woolson and Henry James." Pp. 161–183 in Shirley Marchalonis (ed.), *Patrons* and Protegees: Gender, Friendship, and Writing in Nineteenth-Century America. New Brunswick, NJ: Rutgers University Press, 1988.

Trickett, Rachel, "Vitality of Language in Nineteenth-Century Fiction." Pp. 37–53 in Gabriel Josipovici (ed.), The Modern English Novel: The Reader, the Writer, and the Work. London: Open Books, 1976.

Trilling, Lionel, The Liberal Imagination: Essays on Literature and Society. Garden City NY: Doubleday Anchor Books, 1950.

————, The Opposing Self: Nine Essays in Criticism. New York: Harcourt Brace Jovanovich, 1978 (orig. 1955).

————, Beyond Culture: Essays on Literature and Learning. New York: Viking Press, 1965.

————, Sincerity and Authenticity. Cambridge: Harvard University Press, 1972.

————, Speaking of Literature and Society. New York: Harcourt Brace Jovanovich, ed. Diana Trilling, 1980.

*Trollope, Anthony, Barchester Towers. New York: New American Library, 1963 (orig. 1857).

————, *Can You Forgive Her? New York: Oxford University Press, 1973 (orig. 1864–5).

————, *Phineas Finn. New York: Oxford University Press, 1973 (orig. 1869).

————, *The Eustace Diamonds. New York: Oxford University Press, 1973 (orig. 1873).

————, *Phineas Redux. New York: Oxford University Press, 1973 (orig. 1874).

————, *The Prime Minister. New York: Oxford University Press, 1973 (orig. 1876).

————, *The Duke's Children. New York: Oxford University Press, 1973 (orig. 1880).

————, *The Way We Live Now. Indianapolis: Bobbs-Merrill, 1974 (orig. 1875).

————, An Autobiography. Berkeley: University of California Press, 1978 (orig. 1883).

*Tryon, Thomas, Lady. Greenwich, CT: Fawcett Crest, 1975.

Tuchman, Gaye, with Nina Fortin, Edging Women Out: Victorian Novelists, Publishers, and Social Change. New Haven: Yale University Press, 1989.

Turgenev, Ivan, Fathers and Sons. New York: Signet. 1972.

Turner, Victor, "Social Dramas and Stories about Them." Pp. 137–64 in W. J. T. Mitchell (ed.), On Narrative. Chicago: University of Chicago Press, 1981.

*Twain, Mark, *Adventures of Huckleberry Finn*. Boston: Houghton Mifflin, 1958 (orig. 1884).

*Tyler, Anne, *The Accidental Tourist*. New York: Berkeley, 1986.

——, *Dinner at the Homesick Restaurant*. New York: Knopf, 1982.

Uhlan, Edward, *The Rogue of Publishers' Row: Confessions of a Publisher*. New York: Exposition Press, 1975 (orig. 1956).

UNESCO Secretariat for the International Symposium for Literacy, "Literacy in the World since the 1965 Teheran Conference: Shortcomings, Achievements, Tendencies." Pp. 3–33 in Leon Bataille (ed.), *A Turning Point for Literacy: Adult Education for Development, The Spirit and Declaration of Persepolis*. Proceedings of the International Symposium for Literacy; Persepolis, Iran, September, 1975. New York: Pergamon, 1976.

Unwin, Sir Stanley, *The Truth about Publishing*. London: George Allen & Unwin Ltd., Sixth Edition, 1950 (orig. 1926).

*Updike, John, *Couples*. New York: Fawcett, 1968.

——, *Marry Me: A Romance*. New York: Fawcett, 1976.

*Uris, Leon, *Exodus*. New York: Doubleday, 1958.

Van O'Connor, William, "The Novel in our Time." Pp. 1–8 William Van O'Connor (ed.), *Forms of Modern Fiction*. Bloomington: Indiana University Press, 1961.

Verne, E., "Literacy and Industralization—The Dispossession of Speech." Pp. 211–28 in Leon Bataille (ed.), *The Turning Point for Literacy: Adult Education for Development, The Spirit and Declaration of Persepolis*. Proceedings of the International Symposium for Literacy; Persepolis, Iran, September, 1975. New York: Pergamon, 1976.

Viala, Alain, "Prismatic Effects." Pp. 256–66 in Phillippe Desan, Priscilla Parkhurst Ferguson, and Wendy Griswold (eds.), *Literature and Social Practice*. Chicago: University of Chicago Press, tr. Paula Wissing, 1989.

*Vidal, Gore, *Burr*. New York: Bantan, 1974.

——, *Matters of Fact and Fiction: Essays, 1973–1976*. New York: Random House, 1977.

Vinson, James, and D. L. Kirkpatrick (eds.), *Great Writers of the English Language: Novelists and Prose Writers*. New York: St. Martin's, 1979.

*Vonnegut, Kurt, Jr., *God Bless You, Mr. Rosewater*. New York: Dell, 1970.

——, *Cat's Cradle*. New York: Dell, 1970.

————, *Slaughterhouse-Five. New York: Dell, 1971.

————, *Breakfast of Champions. New York: Dell, 1974.

————, *Player Piano. New York: Dell, 1974.

Walker, Scott (ed.), Buying Time: An Anthology Celebrating 20 Years of the Literary Program of the National Endowmen for the Arts. St. Paul: Graywolf
Press, 1985.

*Wallace, Irving, The Prize. New York: Signet, 1963.

————, *The Word. New York: Pocket Books, 1973.

Waples, Douglas, Research Memorandum on Social Aspects of Reading in the
Depression. New York: Arno Press, 1972 (orig. 1937).

Waples, Douglas, Bernard Berelson, and Franklyn R. Bradshaw, What Reading Does
to People: A Summary of Evidence on the Social Effects of Reading and a Statement
of Problems for Research. Chicago: University of Chicago Press, 1940.

Waples, Douglas, and Ralph W. Tyler, What People Want to Read About: A
Study of Group Interests and a Survey of Problems in Adult Reading. Chicago: University of Chicago Press, 1931.

Warren, Joyce W., The American Narcissus: Individualism and Women in Nineteenth-Century American Fiction. New Brunswick, NJ: Rutgers University
Press, 1984.

*Warren, Robert Penn, All the King's Men. New York: Bantam, 1959.

Watt, Ian, The Rise of the Novel: Studies in Defoe, Richardson, and Fielding. Berkeley and San Francisco: University of California Press, 1957.

————, "Robinson Crusoe as Myth." Pp. 226–50 in Elizabeth and Tom Burns
(eds.), Sociology of Literature and Drama: Selected Readings. Harmondsworth, Middlesex, England: Penguin, 1973.

*Waugh, Evelyn, Brideshead Revisited. Boston: Little, Brown, 1945.

Weber, Max, From Max Weber: Essays in Sociology. New York: Oxford University Press, trs. and eds. H. H. Gerth and C. Wright Mills, 1958.

Weber, Rose-Marie, "Adult Illiteracy in the United States." Pp. 147–64 in John
B. Carrol and Jeanne S. Chall (eds.), Toward a Literate Society: Report of
the Committee on Reading of the National Academy of Education. New York:
McGraw-Hill, 1975.

*Weldon, Fay, The Hearts and Lives of Men. New York: Dell Books, 1989.

*Wells, H. G., The Wealth of Mr. Waddy. Carbondale: Southern Illinois Universi-
ty Press, 1969.

Wells, Henry W., *The Realm of Literature*. Port Washington, NY: Kennikat, 1966 (orig. 1927).

*Welty, Eudora, *Losing Battles*. New York: Vintage, 1978 (orig. 1970).

*Werfel, Franz, *The Song of Bernadette*. New York: Viking, 1942.

*West, Morris L., *The Devil's Advocate*. New York: Dell, 1960.

——, *The Shoes of the Fisherman*. New York: Morrow, 1963.

*West, Nathaniel, *Miss Lonelyhearts* & *The Day of the Locust*. New York: New Directions, 1962 (orig. 1933 and 1939, respectively).

*West, Rebecca, *The Thinking Reed*. New York: Viking, 1936.

*Wharton, Edith, *The House of Mirth*. New York: Scribner's, 1973 (orig. 1905).

——, *The Writing of Fiction*. New York: Scribner's, 1925.

*Wheelis, Allen, *The Desert*. New York: Basic, 1970, p. 104.

White, Hayden, "The Fictions of Factual Presentation." Pp. 21–44 in Angus Fletcher (ed.), *The Literature of Fact: Selected Papers from the English Institute*. New York: Columbia University press, 1976.

——, "The Value of Narrativity in the Representation of Reality." Pp. 1–23 in W. J. T. Mitchell (ed.), *On Narrative*. Chicago: University of Chicago Press, 1981.

White, Trentwell Mason (ed.), *How to Write for a Living*. New York: Reynal & Hitchcock, 1937.

Whitehead, Alfred North, *Symbolism: Its Meaning and Effect*. New York: Putnam's, 1959.

Whyte, William H., Jr., "Literature in an Organization Society." Pp. 50–74 in Irving Deer and Harriet A. Deer (eds.), *The Popular Arts: A Critical Reader*. New York: Scribner's, 1967 (excerpted from *The Organization Man*, Chs. 19, 20).

*Wilder, Thornton, *The Bridge of San Luis Rey*. New York: Washington Square, 1959 (orig. 1955).

Williams, Raymond, *Marxism and Literature*. New York: Oxford University Press, 1977.

Williamson, Samuel T., "How to Write Like a Social Scientist." Pp. 196–202 in Norman Cousins (ed.), *Writing for Love or Money*. Freeport, NY: Books for Libraries Press, 1949.

*Wilson, Sloan, *The Man in the Gray Flannel Suit*. New York: Simon & Schuster, 1955.

*Wister, Owen, *The Virginian: A Horseman of the Plains*. New York: Harper & Row, Perennial Classic, 1965 (orig. 1902).

Wolf, Matt, "Barbara Cartland, at 86, Is Still a Whirlwind of Words," *Pensacola News Journal*, January 7, 1988, 5D.

*Wolfe, Thomas, *You Can't Go Home Again*. New York: Dell, 1960 (orig. 1934).

*Wolfe, Tom, *The Bonfire of the Vanities*. New York: Farrar, Straus, and Giroux, 1987.

———, "The New Journalism." Pp. 3–52 in Tom Wolfe, *The New Journalism* (With an Anthology edited by Tom Wolfe and E. W. Johnson). New York: Harper & Row, 1973.

———, *Mauve Gloves & Madmen, Clutter & Vine: And Other Stories, Sketches, and Essays*. New York: Bantam, 1977.

———, *The Electric Kool-Aid Acid Test*. New York: Bantam, 1969.

Wolff, Robert Paul, *Moneybags Must Be So Lucky: On the Literary Structure of Capital*. Amherst: University of Massachusetts Press, 1988.

*Wollstonecraft, Mary, *Mary: A Fiction*. New York: Schocken, 1977, p. 91.

*Woodford, Jack, *Sin and Such*. New York: Panurge Press, 1930.

———, *How to Write and Sell a Novel*. New York: Woodford Press, 1948 (revised edition of *Why Write a Novel?*, 1943).

*Woolf, Virginia, *Mrs. Dalloway*. New York: Harcourt Brace Jovanovich, 1925.

———, *To the Lighthouse*. New York: Harcourt Brace Jovanovich, 1927.

———, *The Years*. New York: Harcourt Brace and World, 1937.

———, *The Common Reader: First Series*. New York: Harcourt Brace Jovanovich, 1953.

———, *A Room of One's Own*. New York: Harcourt Brace Jovanovich, 1963.

———, *Three Guineas*. New York: Harcourt Brace Jovanovich, 1966.

———, *The Death of the Moth and Other Essays*. New York: Harcourt Brace Jovanovich, 1974.

———, *Moments of Being: Unpublished Autobiographical Writings*. New York: Harcourt Brace Jovanovich, ed. Jeanne Schulkind, 1976.

———, *Books and Portraits*. New York: Harcourt Brace Jovanovich, ed. Mary Lyon, 1977.

*Wouk, Herman, *The Caine Mutiny: A Novel of World War II*. New York: Doubleday, 1951.

———, *Marjorie Morningstar. New York: Doubleday, 1955.

Author X, "Counteragent." *Publishers Weekly* 196, No. 7 (August 8, 1969): 35–37.

*Yerby, Frank, *The Golden Hawk*. New York: Dial, 1948.

———, *Pride's Castle. New York: Dial, 1949.

Young, James N. *101 Plots Used and Abused*. Boston: The Writer, Revised Edition, 1946.

Zeraffa, Michael, "The Novel as Literary Form and as Social Institution." Pp. 35–55 in Elizabeth and Tom Burns (eds.), *Sociology of Literature and Drama: Selected Readings*. Harmondsworth, Middlesex, England: Penguin, 1973.

Zwerdling, Alex, *Virginia Woolf and the Real World*. Berkeley and Los Angeles: University of California Press, 1986.

❦ Proper Name Index

Abish, Walter, 154
Abortion, The (Brautigan), 47
Adam Bede (Eliot), 48, 132
Adorno, Theodor, 15
Advise and Consent (Drury), 57
Agee, James, 43
Alcott, Louisa May, 39, 42, 145, 159
Alger, Horatio, 41, 43
Alton Locke (Kingsley), 177
Amis, Kingsley, 41, 42, 60
Anderson, Sherwood, 42
Armies of the Night, The (Mailer), 190–91
Arnold, Matthew, 178
Aronowitz, Stanley, 187
Arrowsmith (Lewis), 57
As I Lay Dying (Faulkner), 55
Asimov, Isaac, 33
Atherton, Gertrude, 60
Auchincloss, Louis, 40, 41, 60; *The Embezzler*, 133
Austen, Jane, 35, 39, 46, 60, 68; *Emma*, 47, 123; *Mansfield Park*, 94; *Northanger Abbey*, 129

Baker, Nicholson, 166
Baldwin, James, 41, 172
Balzac, Honore de, 177
Bambara, Toni Cade, 38
Barchester Towers (Trollope), 132–33
Barth, John, 25, 32, 41, 42, 43, 60; *Giles Goat-Boy*, 58; *Sabbatical*, 206–08; *The Sot-Weed Factor*, 100, 207
Barthelme, Donald, 40, 42; *The Dead Father*, 85
Barthes, Roland, 94, 104
Basso, Hamilton, 154

Bauman, Richard, 200
Baym, Nina, 67
B. Dalton, 168
Beadle & Company, 159
Becker, Howard S., 19, 154, 156
Beckett, Samuel, 98, 119
Behn, Aphra, 145
Bell, Michael Davitt, 69
Bell, Vanessa, 36
Bellow, Saul, 42, 43, 49, 57, 60, 172; *Dangling Man*, 203–05; graduate education of, 41; *Henderson the Rain King*, 47; marriages of, 40
Benchley, Peter, 161
Benedict, Ruth, 177
Ben-Hur (Wallace), 159
Bennet, Arnold, 40, 43, 223n.3
Berger, Morroe, 182
Berger, Peter L., 177
Besant, Sir Walter, 30
Blackmore, R. D., 159
Bleich, David, 78
Blood Oranges, The (Hawkes), 58
Bloom, Harold, 177
Bonfire of the Vanities, The (Wolfe), 56
Bonny, Harold V., 81
Booker Prize, 62
Book of the Month Club (BOMC), 168–69
Boone, Joseph Allen, 65, 67, 78
Booth, Wayne C., 13, 94, 114
Boudon, Raymond, 19, 183, 185
Bourdieu, Pierre, 158, 183, 187
Boyle, Kay, 40, 43
Bradbury, Malcolm, 181
Bradbury, Ray, 142
Bradford, Barbara Taylor, 161
Brautigan, Richard, 47, 60
Breakfast of Champions (Vonnegut), 133

Brideshead (Waugh), 48
Bridge of San Luis Rey, The (Wilder), 57
Bronte, Charlotte, 26, 42; *Jane Eyre*, 48, 109, 143; *The Professor*, 132
Brookfield, Jane, 40
Brookner, Anita, 60
Brown, Charles Brockden, 69, 147
Brown, Paula, 77
Brown, Richard Harvey, 14, 182, 185, 199–200
Buck, Pearl, 41, 42, 57; *The Good Earth*, 57
Burgess, Anthony, 42, 60
Burnett, Hallie and Ivy, 32
Burroughs, Edgar Rice, 42, 43, 60
Burroughs, William, 41, 42, 43
Burroway, Janet, 37
Butler, Samuel, 40; *The Way of All Flesh*, 48

Caine Mutiny, The (Wouk), 57
Caldwell, Erskine, 31, 42, 43, 60
Calvino, Italo, 127, 144, 198
Camus, Albert, 169, 170
Capital (Marx), 182
Capote, Truman, 24, 40, 41, 43, 170, 172; *In Cold Blood*, 190
"Carter, Nick," 32
Cartland, Barbara, 32, 46, 60, 170
Cather, Willa, 40, 41, 42, 57; *The Professor's House*, 136–37, 142; *Shadows on the Rock*, 60
Cawelti, John C., 100–01
Cervantes, Miguel de, 54, 62; *Don Quixote*, 73, 134, 145
Chapman and Hall, 159
Chase, Richard, 69
Cheever, John, 40, 60
Cheston, Dorothy, 40
Cholmondeley, Mary, 60
Chopin, Kate, 40
Churchill, Winston, 110, 111
Clancy, Tom, 31–32, 34, 38, 41, 42, 63
Clemens, Samuel [pseud. Mark

Twain], 36, 41, 42, 43, 159, 171
"Clerical Scenes" (Eliot), 48
Clifford, James, 177, 183, 200
Colette, 25
Collins, Jackie, 170
Commins, Saxe, 154, 162
Compton-Burnett, Ivy, 98
Comte, Auguste, 176
Coniston (Churchill), 110
Conrad, Jessie, 40
Conrad, Joseph, 36, 49, 57, 60, 149; *The Secret Agent*, 48
Cooper, James Fenimore, 158
Corradi, Juan E., 108
Coser, Lewis, 14
Cowley, Malcolm, 188
Cozzens, James, 43, 169
Craft of Fiction, The (Lubbock), 151
Crane, Stephen, 25, 57, 150
Creative Artists Program Services, 172
Cronin, A. J., 60

Dailey, Janet, 29, 60
Daisy Miller (James), 94
Dangling Man (Bellow), 203–05
Darwin, Charles, 182
David Copperfield (Dickens), 8, 131, 132, 143
Davis, Kenneth C., 170
Davis, Lennard J., 178
Day of the Locust, The (West), 49
Dead Father, The (Barthelme), 85
Dear and Glorious Physician (Caldwell), 60
Deer Park (Mailer), 49
Defoe, Daniel, 43, 49, 154
Dell Publishing Company, 160
de Muralt, Andre, 16
Denizen, Norman K., 201
Derrida, Jacques, 280
DeVault, Marjorie L., 165–66
Devoe, Alan, 32
Dickens, Charles, 29, 40, 43, 60, 100, 108, 169; David Copperfield, 8,

131, 132, 143; *Hard Times*, 210; and publishers, 158
Dillard, Annie, 5
Dilthey, Wilhelm, 178
DiMaggio, Paul, 77, 90, 144, 151, 163, 200
Dinner at the Homesick Restaurant (Tyler), 56
Doctorow, E. L., 170
Don Quixote (Cervantes), 73, 134, 145
Dorrance and Company, 160
Dos Passos, John, 36, 41, 43, 58, 60, 172
Dostoevsky, Fyodor, 29, 189
Doubleday, 160
Douglas, Ann, 145, 149
Doyle, Arthur Conan, 41
Drabble, Margaret, 40, 60; *Realms of Gold*, 110
Dreiser, Theodore, 41, 43, 60, 150
Drury, Allen, *Advise and Consent*, 57
Dubin, Steven C., 155–56, 172
Dunne, Dominick, 60
Durkheim, Emile, 177, 178; *The Elementary Forms of Religious Life*, 182
Durrell, Lawrence, 23, 29, 40, 42, 43, 60; writing habits of, 10; writing speed, 222n.70

Eagleton, Terry, 25
Edinburgh Review, 163
Eliot, George, 25, 39, 60, 176, 177; *Adam Bede*, 48, 132; "Clerical Scenes," 48; *Middlemarch*, 71–72, 81; *The Mill on the Floss*, 8, 48, 143; and the realistic novel, 66, 150; self-experiences while writing, 28
Eliot, T. S., 177
Elliott, Robert C., 114
Ellis, John M., 94
Ellison, Ralph, 23, 36, 41, 42
Embezzler, The (Auchincloss), 133
Emerson, Ralph Waldo, 171
Emma (Austen), 47, 123
Erdrich, Louise, 56

Erikson, Kai T., 188, 191
Ermarth, Elizabeth, 150
Escarpit, Robert, 155
Eustace Diamonds, The (Trollope), 110
Everything in Its Path (Erikson), 110
Exley, Frederick, *A Fan's Notes*, 138–39, 142
Expensive People (Oates), 60, 91–94, 99, 102, 104, 117, 119, 123, 197
Exposition Press, 160

Fan's Notes, A (Exley), 138–39, 142
Faranda, Lisa Pater, 170
Farewell to Arms, A (Hemingway), 48, 60
Faulkner, William, 42, 43, 60, 108, 222n.70; *As I Lay Dying*, 55; and Saxe Commins, 162; *Pylon*, 49; *The Reivers*, 57; *The Sound and the Fury*, 55; *The Wild Palms*, 49
Ferber, Edna, 39, 43, 60
Fern, Fanny, 60, 145, 171
Fetterly, Judith, 77–78
Fielding, Henry, 62, 86, 145, 147; *Joseph Andrews*, 109, 110, 130, 132; *Tom Jones*, 109, 110, 130, 132
Fish, Stanley, 198–99
Fitzgerald, Edward, 168
Fitzgerald, F. Scott, 40, 43; *The Last Tycoon*, 49; *Save Me the Waltz*, 49; *Tender Is the Night*, 48, 49
Fitzgerald, Zelda, 40
Flaubert, Gustave, 177
Fleming, Ian, 40, 41, 42, 100, 223n.3
Flynn, Elizabeth A., 78
Follett, Ken, 30
Ford, Ford Madox, 119; *The Good Soldier*, 133
Forster, E. M., 26, 40, 41, 42, 60, 123; *A Room with a View*, 134–35
Fortin, Nina, 146, 149, 151, 165
Foucault, Michel, 189, 198, 201
Fowler, H. W., 188
Fowler, Roger, 183
Foxes of Harrow, The (Yerby), 30

Francis, Dick, 30, 63, 163
Frankenstein (Shelley), 14
Frazer, Sir James, 177, 182
Freeman, Derek, 157
Freud, Sigmund, 84, 177, 182
Frisch, Max, *Homo Faber*, 141, 42
Frost, Robert, 116
Frye, Northrop, 68
Fuchs, Stephan, 178, 199
Fuller, Margaret, 171

Galsworthy, John, 41, 57, 77
Gardner, Erle Stanley, 42, 43
Gardner, John, 23, 25, 41, 43
Gavin, Marian, 31
Gedin, Per, 155
George, Stefan, 178
Ghost and Flesh (Goyen), 27
Giles Goat-Boy (Barth), 58
Gilman, Charlotte Perkins, 66, 171
Gissing, George, 41, 43
Glaser, Barney, 18
Glasgow, Ellen, 57
Godwin, Gail, 28
Goffman, Erving, 107, 111, 114–15,
    149, 177, 183, 185; on framing,
    112, 143; *Strategic Interaction*, 197;
    on teams and teamwork, 124–25;
    writing style, 182, 185
Goldberg, Phillip, 166
Golden Bough, The (Frazer), 177
Goldfarb, Jeffrey C., 173
Goldmann, Lucien, 173
Good Earth, The (Buck), 57
Good Soldier, The (Ford), 133
Goody, Jack, 73
Gordimer, Nadine, 23, 28, 37, 38, 39,
    161–62; *The Late Bourgeois World*,
    165–66
Goyen, William, 27, 162, 170
Grant, Duncan, 36
Grapes of Wrath, The (Steinbeck), 57,
    94
Grass, Gunter, 169
Gravity's Rainbow (Pynchon), 98

Gray, William S., 75
Green, Bryan S., 182–83, 184, 185, 186
Green, Henry, 60
Greene, Graham, 57, 60, 100
Grey, Zane, 40, 41, 60, 159
Griswold, Wendy, 14, 94, 165, 166,
    184, 186; cultural-diamond
    model, 2
Guerard, Albert, 49, 108, 143
Guggenheim Fellowships, 172

Habegger, Alfred, 67, 146, 149, 150,
    171
Hackett, Alice Payne, 56
Hall, Radclyffe, 66
Hammett, Dashiell, 41, 42, 43
Hard Times (Dickens), 210
Hardy, Thomas, 36, 41, 42, 60; *Jude
    the Obscure*, 143; *Tess of the
    D'Urbervilles*, 10
Harper & Brothers, 158–59
Harper & Row, 160
Hart, James D., 77
Hauser, Arnold, 155
Hawkes, John, 40, 41, 42, 49, 60; *The
    Blood Oranges*, 58
Hawthorne, Nathaniel, 42, 60, 146,
    147, 158, 167; education, 41; mar-
    riages, 36, 40; as romance writer,
    69, 148; *The Scarlet Letter*, 99, 148
"Health Card" (Yerby), 30
Heller, Joseph, 40, 41, 42, 43, 172
Hell's Angels (Thompson), 190
Hemingway, Ernest, 24, 29, 36, 57,
    60, 63; education, 41; *A Farewell to
    Arms*, 48, 60; *For Whom the Bell
    Tolls*, 60; marriages, 40, 49; and
    Max Perkins, 162; *To Have and
    Have Not*, 60; writing habits, 10
Henderson the Rain King (Bellow), 47
Henry, O., 29
Hersey, John, 60
Hesse, Hermann, 84
Hicks, Granville, 98
High and the Mighty, The (Gann), 56

Hilton, James, 43, 49
History of Pendennis, The (Thackeray), 21–22, 109, 131, 132
Holroyd, Michael, 40
Holt, Victoria, 60
Homo Faber (Frisch), 141–42
Hopf, Harry Arthur, 75, 76
Houghton, William, 168
Howells, William Dean, 41, 43, 60, 149, 159, 165; and Charlotte Perkins Gilman, 171; The Rise of Silas Lapham, 142
Hughes, Ted, 40
Hurston, Zora Neale, 66
Husserl, Edmund, 105
Huxley, Aldous, 24, 41, 43, 142
Hyman, Stanley Edgar, 182

In Cold Blood (Capote), 190
Ingalls, Rachel, 60
Irving, John, 60; The World According to Garp, 140–41
Irving, Washington, 69
Iser, Wolfgang, 94, 103, 105, 177

Jakes, John, 159
James, Henry, 25, 60, 149, 151, 159, 165; Daisy Miller, 94; The Tragic Muse, 135–36, 142
Jameson, Frederic, 182, 184, 199
Jamison, Kay Redfield, 26
Jane Eyre (Bronte), 48, 109, 143
Jarrell, Randall, 175; Pictures from an Institution, 196
Jauss, Hans Robert, 94
Jaws (Benchley), 161
Johnson, Diane, 165
Johnson, Samuel, 163
Jolley, Elizabeth, 60
Joseph Andrews (Fielding), 109, 110, 130, 132
Joyce, James, 41, 42; A Portrait of the Artist As a Young Man, 54–55; Ulysses, 48

Joyce, Nora, 48
Jude the Obscure (Hardy), 143

Kafka, Franz, 119
Keller, Evelyn Fox, 14
Kennedy, William, 60
Kermode, Frank, 28
Kerouac, Jack, 40, 41, 42, 60
Kesey, Ken, One Flew Over the Cuckoo's Nest, 94
Key to Rebecca, The (Follett), 30
King, Stephen, 159
Kingsley, Charles, 177
Kingston, Maxine Hong, 60
Kipling, Rudyard, 40, 57, 60
Knopf, Alfred A., 160
Koestler, Arthur, 41, 43
Koontz, Dean R., 30, 32, 33, 163
Kosinski, Jerzy, 41, 48, 60, 172
Krantz, Judith, 161

Lamming, George, 165
L'Amour, Louis, 33, 100
Lang, Kurt, 163
Langland, Elizabeth, 184
Last Tycoon, The (Fitzgerald), 49
Laughlin, James, 160
Lawrence, D. H. 24, 40, 42, 43, 57, 60; Sons and Lovers, 48; Women in Love, 48
Lawrence, Frieda, 40
Leavis, F. R., 178
Lee, Harper, 60
Le Guin, Ursula, 163, 212
Leithauser, Brad, 166
Lepenies, Wolf, 178
Lessing, Doris, 27, 37
Levine, George, 147, 148
Lewis, Sinclair, 57; Arrowsmith, 57
Link, Henry C., 75, 76
Literary Guild, 168
Lofland, John, 182
Lolita (Nabokov), 58, 99
London, Jack, 60, 77

Long, Elizabeth, 14
Longmans, 159
Look Homeward, Angel (Wolfe), 153
Loos, Anita, 60
Lorna Doone (Blackmore), 159
Love Medicine (Erdrich), 56
Love Story (Segal), 102, 103–04
Lubbock, Percy, 151
Luce, Henry, 154
Lurie, Alison, 60

Macmillan Book Club, 168
Mailer, Norman, 40, 43, 47, 60, 170,
    172; *The Armies of the Night*,
    190–91; *Deer Park*, 49; *The Naked
    and the Dead*, 159
Malamud, Bernard, 23, 36, 40, 41, 42,
    60, 167
Malinowski, Bronislaw, 177
Mann, Thomas, 178
Mannheim, Karl, 177
Manning, Peter K., 182
Mansfield, Katherine, 25, 39, 40
Mansfield Park (Austen), 94
Mapplethorpe, Robert, 156
Marchalonis, Shirley, 171
Marquand, John, 43
Marx, Karl, 177, 182
Mason, Bobbie Ann, 41, 43
Masuzawa, Tomoko, 182
Maugham, Somerset, 41, 60, 100
Mazlish, Bruce, 176, 177
McCarthy, Mary, 40, 41, 42, 43, 133,
    172
McCullers, Carson, 39, 60
McGraw-Hill Publishing Company,
    160
McGuane, Thomas, 167
Mead, Margaret, 157, 177
Melville, Herman, 40, 42, 60, 146,
    147, 158; *Moby Dick*, 148, 167;
    Omoo, 131; as romance writer, 69,
    148; *Typee*, 131
Meredith, George, 48, 60, 159
Merleau-Ponty, Maurice, 9

Metalious, Grace, 48, 59, 60, 79
Meyers, Jeffrey, 40
Mezzanine, The (Baker), 166
Michener, James, 157, 168, 169
Mill, John Stuart, 178
Miller, Henry, 8, 25, 26
Mill on the Floss, The (Eliot), 8, 48, 143
Mills, C. Wright, 155, 156–57, 188
Milton, John, 68
Mitchell, Margaret, 60
Moby Dick (Melville), 148
Moers, Ellen, 25, 66, 145
Morley, Christopher, 41
Morris, Wright, 42, 60
Morrison, Toni, 170
Morrow, William, 160
Moviegoer, The (Percy), 137–38
Mr. Crewe's Career (Churchill), 110, 111
Munroe, Ruth, 75
Murdoch, Iris, 39, 41, 42
Murray, Michele, 37
Murry, John Middleton, 40

Nabokov, Vladimir, 40, 41, 42, 57,
    172; *Lolita*, 58, 99
Naked and the Dead, The (Mailer), 159
National Book Awards, 62
National Endowment for the Arts
    (NEA), 172
National Institute of Arts and Let-
    ters, 172
Naylor, Gloria, *The Women of Brew-
    ster Place*, 94
Nell, Victor, 77, 79, 80, 82, 100
Nemerov, Howard, 189
Nin, Anais, 41, 42, 171
Nisbet, Robert, 182
Nobel Prize, 57, 62
Norris, Frank, 40, 41, 43, 60, 150,
    223n.3
Northanger Abbey (Austen), 129

Oates, Joyce Carol, 23, 24, 28, 37, 38,
    60; *Do with Me What You Will*, 60;

Expensive People, 60, 91–94, 99, 102, 104, 117, 119, 123, 197; "madness," 27; on "text," 107; *them*, 60
O'Connor, Flannery, 41, 172
Of Time and the River (Wolfe), 153
O'Hara, John, 40, 43
Omoo (Melville), 131
One Flew Over the Cuckoo's Nest (Kesey), 94
O'Neill, Eugene, 154
Ordeal of Richard Feverel, The (Meredith), 48
Orlando (Woolf), 48
Orwell, George, 142
Osgood, Frances Sargent, 169

Painted Bird, The (Kosinski), 49
Percy, Walker, 40, 41, 60, 172; *The Moviegoer*, 137–38
Perkins, Maxwell, 153–54, 162
Peterson, Carla L., 143, 144
Peterson, Richard, 19
Peyton Place (Metalious), 48, 59, 79
Phineas Redux (Trollope), 110
Pictures from an Institution (Jarrell), 175–76, 196
Pilgrim's Progress, A (Bunyan), 10
Plath, Sylvia, 24, 28, 40
Player Piano (Vonnegut), 141, 142
Poe, Edgar Allen, 68, 147, 158, 169
Porter, Katherine Anne, 25, 38, 42, 43, 60, 172; childhood writing of, 23; domestic demands on, 37; vocation to write, 24
Portrait of the Artist As a Young Man, A (Joyce), 54–55
Powell, Anthony, 43
Princess Daisy (Krantz), 161
Professor, The (Bronte), 132
Professor's House, The (Cather), 136–37, 142
Pulitzer Prize, 56, 57
Purdy, Ken, 31
Putnam's, 160
Pym, Barbara, 60

Pylon (Faulkner), 49
Pynchon, Thomas, 41, 43, 58, 60; *Gravity's Rainbow*, 98

Radcliffe, Ann, 66
Radway, Janice A., 68, 78, 126, 169
Rahv, Phillip, 177
Rand, Ayn, 32, 60
Rawlings, Marjorie Kinnan, 39, 41, 43, 47, 60, 63
Realms of Gold (Drabble), 110
Reivers, The (Faulkner), 57
Rhys, Jean, 39, 60
Richards, I. A., 177
Richardson, Samuel, 62, 130–31
Rinehart, Mary Roberts, 39, 60, 77
Rise of Silas Lapham, The (Howells), 142
Robbe-Grille, Alain, 98, 119
Robbins, Harold, 60
Robbins, Tom, 157
Room of One's Own, A (Woolf), 35
Room with a View, A (Forster), 134–35
Roth, Phillip, 41, 42, 60, 172
Rushdie, Salman, 156
Ryan, Desmond, 166
Ryan, William, 81

Sabbatical (Barth), 206–08
Sackville-West, Vita, 48
Sacred Monster (Westlake), 166
Salinger, J. D., 41, 60, 169, 223n.3
Sammons, Jeffrey L., 108, 201
Sand, George, 25
Santayana, George, 5, 57, 60
Sapir, Edward, 177
Sarrasine (Balzac), 104
Sarton, May, 60, 167, 171
Save Me the Waltz (Fitzgerald), 49
Sayers, Dorothy, 41, 43, 60
Scarlet Letter, The (Hawthorne), 99, 148
Scholes, Robert, 145
Schutz, Alfred, 181; "cognitive style," 6; course-of-action types, 121; personal types, 121

Scott, Sarah, 66
Scott, Sir Walter, 68, 147
Secret Agent, The (Conrad), 48
Segal, Erich, *Love Story,* 102, 103–04
Sennett, Richard, 177
Serrano, Andres, 156
Set This House on Fire (Styron), 109
Shakespeare, William, 68
Sharon, Amiel T., 75, 76
Shaw, Charlotte, 40
Shaw, George Bernard, 43, 68
Sheldon, Sidney, 159
Showalter, Elaine, 148
Simmel, Georg, 6, 13, 151, 163, 178;
    on "aesthetic mastery," 45–46; on
    literature and masculinist values,
    63–64; on the novel, 63; "objec-
    tive" and "subjective" culture, 46;
    on "world," 7; writing style of,
    182, 184
Simon and Schuster, 160
Sinclair, Upton, 40, 60
Singer, Isaac Bashevis, 42, 57
Slapstick (Vonnegut), 167
Slaughterhouse Five (Vonnegut), 49
Smith, Barbara Herrnstein, 177, 186,
    199
Smollett, Tobias, 41, 62
Snow, C. P., 179
Sons and Lovers (Lawrence), 48
Sontag, Susan, 23, 60
Sot-Weed Factor, The (Barth), 100
Sound and the Fury, The (Faulkner), 55
Southworth, Mrs. Emma D. E. N.,
    171
Spark, Muriel, 60
Spencer, Herbert, 178
Spillane, Mickey, 60
Stafford, Jean, 42
Steele, Danielle, 159
Stein, Gertrude, 36, 40, 41, 47
Steinbeck, John, 40, 41, 42, 43, 57, 60;
    The Grapes of Wrath, 57, 94
Sterne, Laurence, 40, 41
Stevens, Wallace, 210
Store, The (Stribling), 57

Stowe, Harriet Beecher, 60, 145, 177;
    Uncle Tom's Cabin, 94
Strachey, Lytton, 36
Strategic Interaction (Goffman), 197
Strauss, Anselm S., 18
Stribling, T. S., 41, 60; *The Store,* 57
Styron, William, 40, 41; *Set This
    House on Fire,* 109
Susann, Jacqueline, 60, 170
Swingewood, Alan, 150

Talese, Gay, 190
Tarde, Gabriel, 178
Tarkington, Booth, 41, 60, 159
Tender Is the Night (Fitzgerald), 48, 49
Ternan, Ellen, 40
Tess of the D'Urbervilles (Hardy), 11
Thackeray, William Makepeace, 40,
    43, 60, 87, 148, 149, 151; female
    characters of, 150; *The History of
    Pendennis,* 21–22, 109, 131, 132
them (Oates), 60
Thompson, Hunter S., 100, 190
Three Guineas (Woolf), 35
Toklas, Alice B., 40
Tolstoy, Leo, 29; *War and Peace,* 73
Tom Jones (Fielding), 109, 110, 130, 132
Torsney, Cheryl B., 165
To the Lighthouse (Woolf), 26, 137, 142
Tragic Muse, The (James), 135–36, 142
Trilling, Lionel, 13
Trollope, Anthony, 25, 35, 60, 159;
    Barchester Towers, 132–33; *The
    Eustace Diamonds,* 110; *The Way
    We Live Now,* 51–53
Tuchman, Gaye, 14, 146, 149, 151, 165
Turner, Victor, 200
Twain, Mark. *See* Clemens, Samuel.
Tyler, Anne, 38, 56
Tyler, Ralph W., 81
Typee (Melville), 131

Ulysses (Joyce), 48
Uncle Tom's Cabin (Stowe), 94, 177

Unwin, Sir Stanley, 160
Updike, John, 36, 41, 60
Uris, Leon, 60
Useem, Michael, 77

Vantage Press, 160
Vidal, Gore, 23, 40, 98, 171
View from Pompey's Head, The (Basso), 154
Virginian, The (Wister), 77, 159
Vonnegut, Kurt, 23, 29, 41, 43, 60, 172; Breakfast of Champions, 133; Player Piano, 141, 142; Slapstick, 167; Slaughterhouse Five, 49

Waldenbooks, 168
Walker, Alice, 38
Wallace, Irving, 11, 57, 60
Wallace, Lew, 159
Waples, Douglas C., 76, 77, 81
War and Peace (Tolstoy), 73
Warhol, Andy, 170
Warren, Joyce W., 145
Warren, Robert Penn, 41, 42
Watt, Ian, 73
Waugh, Evelyn, 48, 60
Way of All Flesh, The (Butler), 48
Way We Live Now, The (Trollope), 51–53
Wealth of Mr. Waddy, The (Wells), 109
Webb, Beatrice, 178
Weber, Max, The Protestant Ethic and the Spirit of Capitalism, 177; on vocations, 22, 157; writing style of, 180, 182, 184
Weldon, Fay, 60
Wells, H. G., 40, 41, 42, 178; The Wealth of Mr. Waddy, 109
Wells, Henry W., 181
Welty, Eudora, 23, 39, 41, 58, 60, 172
Werfel, Franz, 60
West, Morris, 60
West, Nathanael, 40, 41, 42, 43, 60,

223n.3; The Day of the Locust, 49
West, Rebecca, 37, 40–41, 60, 171
Westlake, Donald E., 166
Wharton, Edith, 39
White, Hayden, 199
Whitman, Walt, 28, 171
Whittier, John Greenleaf, 171
Whyte, William H., Jr., 124
Wieland (Brown), 147
Wild Palms, The (Faulkner), 49
Wilde, Oscar, 40, 170
Wilder, Thornton, 41, 42; Bridge of San Luis Rey, 57
Wiley, Charles, 158
Williams, William Carlos, 24
Wilson, Sloan, 60
Wister, Owen, 41, 77, 159
Wodehouse, P. G., 77
Wolfe, Thomas, 56; Look Homeward, Angel, 153; and Maxwell Perkins, 153–54; Of Time and the River, 153; You Can't Go Home Again, 153
Wolfe, Tom, 8, 190
Wolff, Robert Paul, 182
Women in Love (Lawrence), 48
Women of Brewster Place, The (Naylor), 94
Woodford, Jack, 33, 60
Woolf, Leonard, 36, 39, 40, 248n.50
Woolf, Virginia, 29, 43, 47, 57, 60, 181; and Hogarth Press, 248n.50; "madness," 26, 27; marriage of, 39, 40; Orlando, 48; A Room of One's Own, 35; Three Guineas, 35; To the Lighthouse, 26, 48, 137, 142
Woolson, Constance Fenimore, 165
World According to Garp, The (Irving), 140–41
Wouk, Herman, 60, 169; The Caine Mutiny, 57
Wright, Richard, 41, 223n.3

Yerby, Frank, 29–30, 42, 60
You Can't Go Home Again (Wolfe), 153

❦ Subject Index

Action, 8. *See also* Social action
"Advances," 161, 162
Ambiguity (as a literary strategy),
  98, 116–17, 119
Artist (cultural notion of), 33, 34, 35,
  169, 170; literary, 46, 107, 133–34,
  144

Book clubs, 168–69
Book reviews, 163, 164, 165–68
Book-selling novels, 60; and consti-
  tutive demands on readers, 107,
  123, 124, 125; commercial defini-
  tions of, 159, 161; cultural defini-
  tion of, 61; and ideology, 193, 194;
  and propaganda, 195
Book clubs, 168–69
Book reviews, 163, 164, 165–68
Booksellers, 153, 168–69. See also
  Book clubs

Canon. *See* Literary canon
Canonical novels, 60, 123, 130,
  133–34; and constitutive demands
  on readers, 107; cultural definition of, 62; and ideology, 194; and
  male novelists, 64; and propaganda, 195
Chapter titles, 131, 132
Cognitive style, 6–7, 10, 11
Communication, 8, 9, 15; literary ideology of, 193–94; literary portrayals of, 84
Constitution, 8
Creative writers, advice books for,
  30–32; childhood reading of,
  23–24; cognitive styles of, 10, 33,

179; and facts, 177, 189; "madness" and, 24, 26–28; and solitude, 25–26; stereotypes of, 21, 26;
  and typification, 124, 180–81. *See
  also* Female novelists; Male novelists; Novelists
Cultural diamond, 2, 3, 166–67
Cultural freedom, 173

Debunking (defamiliarizing), 211;
  and the novel, 53–55, 61, 88, 111,
  194
Deconstructionism. *See* Poststructuralism
Dramatized author, 114, 115, 120

Editors, 153, 162, 170; female, 172
Emotions, literary portrayals of,
  84–86
Everyday life (world of), 7–8, 11, 53;
  and the fictive, 205–06, 207–08,
  209–10, 211; and world of literature, 49–50
Expression, 8, 9, 15, 89–90

Female novelists, 144, 145–46,
  164–66, 169, 171–72; domestic
  lives of, 36–39; financial support
  for, 172–73; and interpersonal networks ("contacts"), 170–71; and
  marriage, 39; and parenthood, 39;
  and the realistic novel, 64–67, 146,
  150
Fiction (as a cultural form), 178,
  189–92
Fictive, the, 202; in everyday life,

Fictive, *(continued)*
205–06, 207–08, 209–10, 211; and
literature, 206–07, 208–09, 211,
212; and science, 209, 211
Formulaic novels, 60, 123, 124, 161;
and constitutive demands on
readers, 107, 125–26; cultural definition of, 61; and ideology, 193,
194; and propaganda, 195
Framing, 112, 118, 143–44

Generalist readers, 97–101, 107.
122–23; cognitive style of, 115
Genre, 144, 151, 162–63, 167; as narrative constraint, 185, 186, 200;
and style, 186
Grounded theory, 18–19

"High" culture, 72, 133–34, 151, 165

Ideology, 118, 192–93, 194–95; and literature, 193–94; and propaganda,
195; and sociology, 195–96
Imagination, 8, 10, 47; and debunking, 211; social formation of, 48
Implied author, 114, 115, 120
Irony, 95, 118

Knowledge, social stock of, 13

Language, novelists' stances toward,
9–10, 54–55, 58–59, 61, 86–89, 179;
and poststructuralism, 198–99
Literacy, functions of, 73, 74–75; history of, 73–74; incidence of, 74, literary portrayals of, 72–73
Literary agents, 161–62
Literary canon, 63, 64, 158; masculine biases of, 65, 67, 144–51
Literary chroniclers, 46, 107
Literary criticism, 13, 16, 163–66, 167;

reader-response criticism, 94
Literary intellectuals, 47, 107, 133–34,
144
Literary interaction, 107, 108–09,
115–21, 125–26
Literary reporters, 47, 107
Literary socialization, 129–34
Literature, autobiographical dimension of, 8–9; and didacticism,
10–11; of fact, 190–92; and ideology, 193–94; and the marketplace,
21–22; and rhetoric, 196–97;
restorative functions of, 13; and
sociology, 176–82, 198, 202; world
of, 5, 6, 7, 8, 10, 15, 50, 95. *See also*
Fiction; Fictive; Novels
Love, literary portrayals of, 86–88

Male novelists, 36, 144, 169, 171, 172;
and canon making, 145–51;
domestic lives of, 38
Mass culture, 72, 193
Mediating institutions, 154–58, 187
Metatheory, 201

Natural attitude, 8
Novelists, artifices of, 108–11, 113,
117–20, 129, 130–33; bestselling,
29–30, 32, 63; as cultural types,
45–47; financial support for,
172–73; gay and lesbian, 40; and
imagination, 47–48, 49; lifestyles
of, 35–47; marriages of, 40; occupations of, 42–44, 170; and getting
published, 160; resources of,
111–13; schooling of, 41; and
social representation, 184–85; as
social types, 45; and *Verstehen* 111,
112, 180–81; and voice, 108; and
writing speed, 32, 222n.70. *See
also* Artist, literary; Creative writers; Dramatized author; Female
novelists; Implied author; Language, novelists' stances toward;

Novelists, *(continued)*
  Literary chroniclers; Literary
  intellectuals; Literary reporters;
  Male novelists
Novels, 15–16; autobiographical
  dimension of, 48–49; and debunking (defamiliarizing), 53–55, 61,
  88, 111, 194; history of, 176–78;
  horizons of, 99, 105; presuppositions of, 11; realistic, 65, 69, 148,
  149–51; relationship to sociology,
  179–82. *See also* Best-selling novels; Canonical novels; Formulaic
  novels; Subcultural novels

Paperback books, 159
Patronage, 155, 172
Persona, 114
Phenomenology, 17–18; Husserlian
  exemplarism, 16
Popular culture, 143, 145–46
Postmodernism, 107, 198–202. *See
  also* Poststructuralism
Poststructuralism, 5–6, 107, 198–202
Publishers, 148, 158–61, 162, 248n.50;
  fictional portrayals of, 21, 153–54

Rationality, literary, 179; sociological,
  179
Reader-response criticism, 94
Readers, aesthetic experiences of, 12;
  cognitive style of, 12; "common
  reader," 94–95; cultural types of,
  97–101; and imagination, 95,
  102–03, 109; and literary knowledge, 99–100; prepredicative and
  predicative experiences of, 103,
  122; self-experiences of, 11–12;
  social role of, 95–96; and the
  social stock of knowledge, 101–02,
  110–111; and typification, 121–22.
  See also Generalist readers; Reading; Specialist readers
Reading, 75–76; and the constitution

of meaning, 98–99, 104–05,
  109–10; and familiarization,
  103–05, 109; and freedom, 11, 12;
  functions of, 81–82; and gender,
  77–79, 80; as interaction, 107; literary portrayals of, 71–73, 134–43;
  as teamwork, 123–26; and typification, 103–04; as vicarious social
  action, 90. *See also* Generalist readers; Readers; Specialist readers
Realism, 200. *See also* Novels, realistic; Rhetoric of literary realism
Reification, 53
Representation, 198–99, 201
Rhetoric, 14; of literary realism, 148,
  149, 150, 178, 181; sociological,
  189
Romances, 68–69, 148; female-
  authored, 64–65, 171–72; and
  female readers, 68, 78–79, 80–81,
  100
Royalties, 161

Selfhood, literary portrayals of,
  82–84
Social action, 1, 2, 15, 88–89, 90; and
  ideology, 194–95
Social structure, 1, 15; and gender,
  44–45
Social stock of knowledge. *See*
  Knowledge, social stock of Sociologists, cognitive style of, 179; and
  language, 192, 201; and storytelling, 200, 201; and typification,
  180–81; and *Verstehen*, 180–81;
  writing styles of, 177, 182–89
Sociology as a cultural form, 177;
  history of, 176–78; and ideology,
  195–96; and literature, 176–82,
  198, 202; and the literature of fact,
  189, 191–92; and propaganda, 196;
  relationship to the novel, 179–82;
  and rhetoric, 189, 197–98. *See also*
  Sociology of literature
Sociology of literature, 13–15, 17

Sociology of science, 187–88; and sociology of knowledge, 188
Specialist readers, 97–101, 107, 126–27, 163
"Stars," 156–57
Storytelling, 9, 199; among sociologists, 200, 201
Strategic interaction, 116
Subcultural novels, 60, 62, 107, 123, 124, 125; and ideology, 193–94; and propaganda, 195

Texts, 101, 108, 112; poststructuralist concern with, 5, 107, 199, 201; as

scholarly product, 188
Trade books, 158, 160
"Two cultures," 179
Typification, 95, 103–04; and creative writing, 124, 180–81; and reading, 121–22

Verisimilitude, 130–31
Vocation, 22, 176; literary, 22–26, 33, 62, 157

Worlds (of experience), 5–6, 7
Writers. *See* Creative writers.